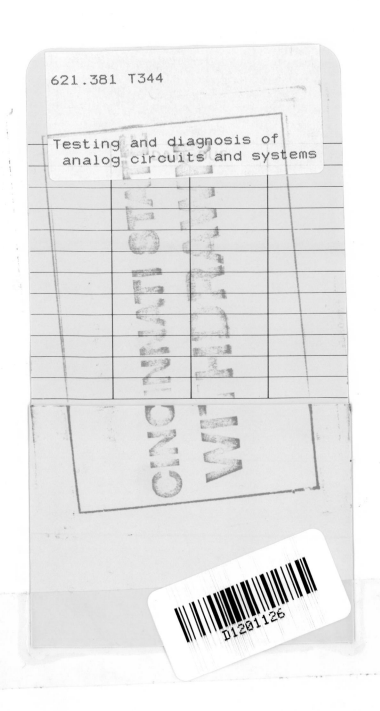

Testing and Diagnosis of Analog Circuits and Systems

Testing and Diagnosis of Analog Circuits and Systems

Edited by

Ruey-wen Liu

Department of Electrical and Computer Engineering
University of Notre Dame

VNR VAN NOSTRAND REINHOLD
——————————— New York

Library of Congress Catalog Card Number: 90-45217
ISBN 0-442-25932-8

Printed in the United States of America

Van Nostrand Reinhold
115 Fifth Avenue
New York, New York 10003

Chapman and Hall
2–6 Boundary Row
London, SE1 8HN, England

Thomas Nelson Australia
102 Dodds Street
South Melbourne 3205
Victoria, Australia

Nelson Canada
1120 Birchmount Road
Scarborough, Ontario M1K 5G4, Canada

16 15 14 13 12 11 10 9 8 7 6 5 4 3 2 1

Library of Congress Cataloging in Publication Data

Liu, Ruey-wen
    Testing and diagnosis of analog circuits and systems / Ruey-wen Liu.
      p.   cm.
Includes bibliographical references and index.
   ISBN 0-442-25932-8
   1. Analog electronic systems—Testing. I. Title
TK7870.L523   1991
621.381—dc20
                                           90-45217
                                             CIP

Contents

Preface

IS THE TOPIC ANALOG TESTING AND DIAGNOSIS TIMELY?

Yes, indeed it is.

Testing and Diagnosis is an important topic and fulfills a vital need for the electronic industry. *The testing and diagnosis of digital electronic circuits* has been successfully developed to the point that it can be automated. Unfortunately, its development for *analog electronic circuits* is still in its Stone Age. The engineer's intuition is still the most powerful tool used in the industry! There are two reasons for this. One is that there has been no pressing need from the industry. Analog circuits are usually small in size. Sometimes, the engineer's experience and intuition are sufficient to fulfill the need. The other reason is that there are no breakthrough results from academic research to provide the industry with critical ideas to develop tools. This is not because of a lack of effort. Both academic and industrial research groups have made major efforts to look into this problem. Unfortunately, the problem for analog circuits is fundamentally different from and much more difficult than its counterpart for digital circuits. These efforts have led to some important findings, but are still not at the point of being practically useful. However, these situations are now changing.

The current trend for the design of VLSI chips is to use analog/digital hybrid circuits, instead of digital circuits from the past. Therefore, even though the analog circuit may be small, the total circuit under testing is large. The engineer's intuition may no longer be sufficient. There is an urgent need for a more systematic approach to the problem of testing and diagnosis of analog or analog/digital hybrid electronic circuits.

Another trend toward a more systematic approach to the problem of testing and diagnosis of analog circuits is the recent *development of analog VLSI chips*. In neural networks, it is found that analog VLSI chips have advantages over digital VLSI chips in computational speed and adaptivity. In a recent extensive study by DARPA, it has been found that neural networks provide the only hope in sight for the successful development of intelligent machines. If this hope becomes a reality, the demand for analog VLSI chips would be tremendously high. The lack of testing and diagnosis technology would be a bottleneck problem for the manufacturing of analog VLSI chips. The urgency for the development of a viable analog testing and diagnosis technology is now, not then.

In the meantime, there have been some *breakthroughs at the frontiers of academic research*. The problem of *diagnosis of linear circuits* has been well developed in the past and well understood. But their application to modern circuits has been very limited because most modern devices are nonlinear, especially under faulty conditions. The extension of linear theory onto nonlinear ones is nontrivial because some nonlinear phenomena have to be dealt with. These were bottleneck problems. Recently, some efficient and reliable methods for nonlinear diagnosis have been developed. Two of them are reported in this book. Another frontier is in the area of analog/digital hybrid testing. Such technology does not exist at the present time, but will be needed in the near future. Recently, a mathematical foundation for the development of analog/digital hybrid testing has been formulated. These results can serve as a bridge to bring the academic research as close as it has ever been to the technology. The need for a viable technology for the analog testing and diagnosis from the industry is growing at this time. In the meantime, academic researchers have been reaching out and trying to touch the real world. I am very glad to see that this book is ready at this particular time.

WHO MAY BE INTERESTED IN THE TOPIC OF ANALOG TESTING AND DIAGNOSIS?

Testing and Diagnosis is an important engineering subject. It interacts with engineering processes in at least three different ways: manufacturing, maintenance, and research. Hence it is of immediate interest to electronic engineers. It also has appeal to academicians.

IC and VLSI Chip Manufacturing

A manufacturing process, such as the oxide thickness of an IC chip, is directly related to the circuit parameters to be manufactured. To make sure that a manufacturing process will reliably produce IC chips within a design specification, a design verification process is needed. This process usually involves simultaneously both modifications of the manufacturing process and testing and diagnosis of the chip. Hence, the technology to do so is clearly needed.

After a manufacturing process is set, it still cannot guarantee that every chip manufactured will be within design specifications. This is due to unavoidable manufacturing fluctuations. A testing process again is needed so that bad chips can be identified and rejected. Furthermore, in order to increase the yield of a manufacturing process, it is economically feasible to rewire those rejected faulty chips and change them from bad to good. This can be done by designing redundant components on a VLSI chip. If and when a faulty component is successfully identified (diagnosed), then a rewiring to its redundant good component will make the VLSI chip good. Hence, a viable diagnosis procedure is needed to enhance the yield of the manufacturing process.

The above gives two examples of why testing and diagnosis are important to the IC and VLSI chip manufacturing process.

Electron System Maintenance

During the past quarter century, the electronic engineering community has witnessed tremendous strides in the art of electronics design. On the other hand, maintenance of analog electronics has changed little since the days of vacuum tubes. As such, our ability to design complex electronic circuits is quickly outdistancing our ability to maintain them. In turn, the price reductions accomplished by modern electronic technology have been paralleled by the increasing maintenance and operational cost. Indeed, many industries are finding that the life cycle maintenance cost for their electronic equipment now exceeds their original capital investment. An urgent need for maintenance cost reduction is now at hand.

The maintenance cost is related to the per unit cost of testing and diagnosis of a faulty system and its recovery rate. The recovery rate is directly related to the technology used and inversely related to the complexity of the system under testing. Since modern electronic equipments become more and more complex, it can only be offset by better and better technology. Hence, it is of paramount importance to develop better testing and diagnosis technology with lower per unit cost. This is the only long-term solution to the ever-increasing maintenance cost.

Research

The topic of analog fault diagnosis does not fall into conventional topics of circuit theory such as analysis, synthesis, and sensitivity. As synthesis is an inverse problem of analysis, so fault diagnosis is an inverse problem of sensitivity. Hence, it is a new frontier for circuit theoretics. This area of research was very active in the 1970s, but slowed down because of the lack of pressing industrial need and the lack of breakthrough results beyond diagnosis of linear circuits. With the recent development in analog VLSI chips, it will not be surprising to see a renewed interest in analog fault diagnosis.

There is another uncharted area of research related to our topic: There is an urgent need for new design methods from the electronic industry so that the circuits so designed can be easily tested and diagnosed. Hence, the cost of doing it can be reduced. Few papers in the literature have addressed this problem.

ABOUT THIS BOOK

The material presented in this book is considered to be of value to all scientists and engineers concerned with testing and fault diagnosis of analog circuits and systems. It covers fundamental principles, bottleneck problems, and solutions, as well as many realistic illustrative examples. It is useful for the test engineers as well as maintenance engineers of electronic industry. It contains much fundamental information and hence could be useful as a reference book to academicians, or as a library reference.

This book is divided into two parts. The first seven chapters are concerned with fault diagnosis of analog electronic circuits, while the last three chapters are concerned with testing.

Analog Fault Diagnosis

The fundamental principle of fault diagnosis of linear analog electronic circuits is presented in the first two chapters. The background, the problem, and the important issues are discussed in Chapter 1. Several methods are presented and compared. The k-fault diagnosis approach may be the most efficient and effective approach. In Chapter 2, it is shown that this approach (named the linear method) is as powerful as nonlinear methods. A bottleneck problem for linear fault diagnosis is the existence of tolerance of linear parameters. In order to resolve this problem, some effective methods are presented in Chapters 1, 12, and 4. It is also shown in Chapter 2 that even if the testability condition is not satisfied, it still can be diagnosed up to an equivalence class.

In theory development, it is convenient to assume that all faults are possible and equally probable. In reality, it is not true. A testing engineer will decide a fault-set to be tested. This fault-set consists of a set of faults most likely to occur. How do we choose a set of testing points so that each fault in the fault-set can be diagnosed? Answers to this question are given in Chapters 3 and 6. The solution in Chapter 3 may be more easily applied because its criteria depend only on the graph of the circuit. Sometimes, the location of testing points can be found by inspection. In the application of these methods, note that the value of k in the k-fault approach used in Chapter 3 is the maximum number of parameters in a fault of the fault-set. It is also referred as the failure bond in Chapter 6.

The analog fault diagnosis of linear electronic circuits has reached its modern maturity. However, it is not very useful for modern electronic circuits because most modern electronic circuits are nonlinear. Overcoming many inherited difficulties of nonlinear circuits has been the bottleneck in the development of analog fault diagnosis. In Chapter 4, a unique approach is presented so that the linear theory can be extended to applicability to nonlinear electronic circuits with the same efficiency and effectiveness. This may be an important turning point in the history of analog fault diagnosis.

The method used for electronic circuits can be extended to general systems, and is presented in Chapters 5 and 6. The key to success is the abandonment of the conventional state equation and the adaptation of a component-connection model for the system description.

All the methods presented in the previous chapters are concerned with single-frequency testing. It is shown in Chapter 5 that, by using multiple-frequency testing, the number of test points can be reduced.

The problem and its theory presented in the previous chapters have been reformulated in Chapter 6 so that its results are closer to the needs of the industry. "Parameter" faults have been extended to "replaceable module" faults. Based on a searching approach self-testing algorithm, an analog automatic test program generator (AATPG) for both linear and nonlinear systems has been implemented.

Finally, an artificial intelligence approach to analog systems diagnosis is presented in Chapter 7. The issues of AI approach have been thoroughly discussed, and some efficient computing algorithms are presented. The authors were an integral part of a major Navy effort in analog fault diagnosis. Their research leads to a fully implemented research prototype diagnosis system.

Analog Testing

The testing of control systems is discussed in Chapter 8. The author is one of the leading scientists in this field with vast experience. An excellent overview of analog automatic testing is presented in this chapter.

Testing of analog integrated circuits is discussed in Chapter 9. This problem is still in its infancy. The author presents the problem, its difficulties, and its main issues very thoroughly. Finally, he provides a ray of hope.

Finally the testing of analog/digital hybrid systems is discussed in Chapter 10. This is a new frontier with little method available. This chapter presents a mathematical foundation, based on which useful algorithms could be formulated. Some illustrative examples are given.

A FINAL WORD

In summary, the materials selected in this book are balanced between theory and application. They represent the state-of-the-art analog testing and fault diagnosis. They also provide much useful fundamental information based on which further research as well as applications can be made.

The editor is indebted to Professor Sani K. Mitra for his initial suggestion and encouragement for this book, and to all authors for their devotion and patience. Finally, many thanks to Van Nostrand Reinhold for its publication of this book.

Special thanks go to David L. Standley of MIT for allowing a photograph of his integrated circuit to appear on the cover of this book. The analog circuit was designed by Mr. Standley from a proposal by Professor Berthold K. P. Horn at the Massachusetts Institute of Technology. Mr. Standley wishes to thank the National Science Foundation and the Defense Advanced Research Projects Agency for their support.

Contributors

Ray DeCarlo, School of Electrical Engineering, Purdue University, West Lafayette, Indiana.

Kenneth DeJong, Naval Center for Applied Research in Artificial Intelligence, Naval Research Laboratory, Washington, D.C.

Qiu Huang, Department of Electrical and Computer Engineering, University of Notre Dame, Notre Dame, Indiana.

Chen-Shang Lin, National Taiwan University, Taipei, Taiwan.

Ruey-wen Liu, Department of Electrical and Computer Engineering, University of Notre Dame, Notre Dame, Indiana.

T. Matsumoto, Department of Electrical Engineering, Waseda University, Tokyo, Japan.

Frank Pipitone, Naval Center for Applied Research in Artificial Intelligence, Naval Research Laboratory, Washington, D.C.

Lawrence Rapisarda, Department of Electrical Engineering, U.S. Military Academy, West Point, New York.

William Spears, Naval Center for Applied Research in Artificial Intelligence, Naval Research Laboratory, Washington, D.C.

Y. Togawa, Department of Information Systems, Science University of Tokyo, Chiba, Japan.

Lang Tong, Department of Electrical and Computer Engineering, University of Notre Dame, Notre Dame, Indiana.

Denis R. Towill, Dean, School of Engineering, Cardiff, Wales, United Kingdom.

V. Visvanathan, AT&T Bell Laboratories, Murray Hill, New Jersey.

Chin-Long Wey, Department of Electrical Engineering, Michigan State University, East Lansing, Michigan.

Mark Wicks, School of Electrical Engineering, Purdue University, West Lafayette, Indiana.

1

A Circuit Theoretic Approach to Analog Fault Diagnosis

RUEY-WEN LIU

BACKGROUND

During the past quarter century, the engineering community has been witness to tremendous strides in the art of electronics design. On the contrary, *analog* electronics maintenance has changed little since the days of the vacuum tube. As such, our ability to design a complex electronic circuit is quickly outdistancing our ability to maintain it. In turn, the price reductions which have accompanied modern electronics technology have been paralleled by increasing maintenance and operation costs. Indeed, many industries are finding that the life cycle maintenance costs for their electronic equipment now exceeds their original capitol investment.

Given the above, it is quickly becoming apparent that the electronics maintenance process, like the design process, must be automated. Unfortunately, the 50 years of progress in circuit theory, on which our electronics design automation has been predicted, does not exist in the maintenance area. As such, the past decade has witnessed the inauguration of a basic research program to lay the foundations for a theory of electronics maintenance and a parallel effort to develop operational electronic maintenance codes.

Thus far the greatest success has been achieved in the digital electronics area to the point that commercialized test programs are now readily available. On the other hand, analog testing is still in its infancy. This is not without reason.

For one, the analog fault diagnosis had a late start. The research and theory development of digital testing started in the mid-1960s when the large-scale computers were readily available. Not until a decade later did a commercialized test program first become available. On the other hand, it was not until the mid-1970s that the test technology community began to face up to the *analog* test problem. Indeed, even in a predominantly digital world, analog systems were not disappearing. On the other hand, analog systems were proving to be among the most unreliable and least readily testable of all electronic systems. The main reason is that the analog fault diagnosis has inherited certain difficult problems which are not shared by digital fault diagnosis. These will be explained later.

One can trace as far back as the early 1960s to find that circuit theorists had an interest in the analog fault diagnosis problem [1,2]. However, there was only sparse interest thereafter [3–9].

It was not until 1977 that a collection of papers [10] appeared, and a special issue followed [11]. In the meantime, the interest among circuit theorists suddenly became active [12–109]. An excellent review paper with extensive references for the pre-1979 period appeared in the special issue [12]. Other review papers appeared after 1983; see [55] and [56]. More recently, collections of paper reprints [57] and papers [58] have appeared.

In this chapter, the circuit-theoretic approach will be extensively discussed because it provides an understanding of the fundamental nature of analog fault problems and is probably the most promising approach at the present time (based on the author's prejudiced point of view?).

As a start, a simplified analog fault diagnosis problem is presented in the next section and some major issues are discussed in the third section. The Element-Value Solvability Problem is discussed in the fourth section. A Fault/Tolerance Compensation Model is presented next. The k-Fault Diagnosis Problem in the ideal case (sixth section) and the tolerance case (seventh section) follow. Several illustrative examples are given in the eighth section. Finally, a conclusion is given.

AN INTRODUCTION TO ANALOG FAULT DIAGNOSIS

Consider a simple system

$$Ax = u \tag{1-1}$$

$$y = Cx \tag{1-2}$$

where $A \in R^{n \times n}$ is nonsingular, $u \in R^n$ the input, $y \in R^m$ the output, $x \in R^n$ the internal variable, and C a selector matrix (each row of C has one and only one entry being 1 and the rest of them 0), which selects certain components of x for measurement. Therefore, m is the number of test points, and n the size of the system. In general, $m \ll n$.

Suppose that A is perturbed to $(A + \Delta A)$. With the same input u, x and y will be perturbed accordingly, i.e.,

$$(A + \Delta A)(x + \Delta x) = u \tag{1-3}$$

$$(y + \Delta y) = C(x + \Delta x) \tag{1-4}$$

We will now pose the first problem.

Problem 1   (Element-Value Solvability Problem)

Can we determine ΔA from the input/output measurements?

The answer to this problem is relatively simple. If all the internal variables can be measured, i.e., $m = n$, then one can determine $(A + \Delta A)$, and hence ΔA, with n independent inputs. The condition $m = n$ is also necessary if no additional information is known about ΔA.

Since the constraint $m \ll n$ is usually imposed upon us, we have to ask the next realistic question. Suppose that a perturbation $(y + \Delta y)$ is observed at the output and we want to locate which entries of A have been perturbed. In this case, it is quite realistic to assume that the number of perturbed entries of A is bounded, say by k, at an instant when a perturbation was observed at the output, and $k \ll n$. In other words, ΔA is a sparse matrix. Furthermore, we need only to determine the *location* of nonzero entries of A, not their values. We can now pose the second problem.

Problem 2   (k-Fault Diagnosis: The Ideal Case)

With the constraint $m \ll n$, and the assumption that ΔA is sparse, can we determine the *location* of nonzero entries of ΔA from the input/output measurements?

It turns out that if certain conditions are met, we can uniquely determine the nonzero rows of ΔA. (Fortunately, this information is enough for us to locate the faulty circuit elements.) This can be seen as follows.

Subtracting (1-1) and (1-2) from (1-3) and (1-4), one obtains

$$CA^{-1}\Delta A(x + \Delta x) = -\Delta y \tag{1-5}$$

or

$$CA^{-1}z = -\Delta y \tag{1-6}$$

where

$$z = \Delta A(x + \Delta x) \tag{1-7}$$

Note that since CA^{-1} is fat ($m < n$), the determination of ΔA from (1-5) is not possible. On the other hand, barring cancellations, it can be seen from (1-7) that a component of z is nonzero if and only if the corresponding row of ΔA is nonzero. Therefore, the problem is now reduced to one of locating the nonzero components of z from (1-6) when the matrix CA^{-1} is fat. A satisfactory solution to this problem can be found in [29] and [48], and it will be presented later.

In the final case, the problem of tolerance will be introduced. In practice, System (1-1) cannot be built precisely according to the specified A, i.e., the *nominal A*. Tolerance always is present so that an *actual* system is modeled by $(A + dA_t)$, where dA_t is within a certain tolerance range. In this case, the perturbation ΔA will have two components, namely,

$$\Delta A = dA_t + \Delta A_f \tag{1-8}$$

where dA_t is the deviation of actual A from nominal A due to the tolerance, and ΔA_f is due to some large deviation (fault) of some entries of A. In general, dA_t is not sparse when the value of each entry is "small," and ΔA_f is sparse and the values of nonzero entries are "large." Now, we can state the third problem.

Problem 3   (*k*-Fault Diagnosis: The Tolerance Case)

With the constraint $m \ll n$, and the assumption that dA_t is small and ΔA_f is sparse but nonzero entries are large, can we locate the nonzero entries of ΔA_f from the input/output measurements?

The above problem can be posed in two different kinds of setting.

1. *The Problem of Robustness.* We may design a testing program (for *k*-fault isolation) based on the ideal case, and the put the testing program into a simulation test to see if this program is robust under the tolerance case. It turns out that the design of a robust testing program is a very tough problem. This will be discussed in detail in a separate section.
2. *The Fault Decision Problem.* This tolerance problem can also be posed as one of estimation/detection problem. This can be seen as follows. Let

$$z_t = dA_t(x + \Delta x)$$
$$z_f = \Delta A_f(x + \Delta x)$$

Then Eq. (1-6) can be represented in Fig. 1–1. In this figure, z_t is generally small while the nonzero entries of z_f are generally large, but sparse. The problem is to *locate* the nonzero entries of z_f from Δy. This is a nonconventional estimation/detection problem. A successful approach to this problem will be presented in the section on the tolerance case for k-fault diagnosis.

IMPORTANT ISSUES OF ANALOG FAULT DIAGNOSIS

In this section, we will discuss two major issues of analog fault diagnosis problems and three important measures of the effectiveness of a testing program. The two major issues are the *problem of tolerance* and the *problem of modeling and simulation of faulty components:*

- *Tolerance.* Possibly the single greatest unknown in the design of an analog testing program is the effect of the tolerances of the "good" component on the performance of a testing program. *This tolerance problem has absolutely no counterpart in the digital testing problem.* The effect of these tolerances can completely dominate the performance of a testing program. In an analog circuit, unlike digital circuits, *the actual values of circuit parameters are unknown, and almost always deviate from the nominal values.* Therefore, any analog testing program has to face up to the problem of tolerance problem.
- *Modeling and Simulation of Faulty Components.* Unlike the digital testing, a complete modeling (and thus simulation) of faulty components is not available for the development of a testing problem. The modes of faulting are too many to encounter. For example, a faulty resistor may have an infinite number of possible resistances (outside of the tolerance). In fact, the fault model of a linear resistor can even be nonlinear. A faulty capacitor may have a model of parallel *RC*. A faulty operational amplifier may have a model of 22 transistors, 12 resistors, and a capacitor!

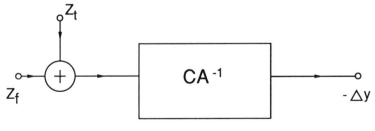

Figure 1–1

Even a good transistor may *behave like* a faulty one if its bias is switched due to a fault occurring elsewhere! In fact, in a nonlinear analog environment, we are still in the process of developing viable CAD models for nominal devices, let alone for faulty devices. As such, a thorough test of the performance of a testing progam is impossible. Because the modeling of faulty devices is usually not available to us, *each testing program has to be designed based solely on the nominal values of the circuit.*

Besides the two major problems mentioned above, there are three important measurements of the effectiveness of a testing program.

- *Test Points.* Due to the practical limitations, there are usually only a few nodes which are accessible for measurement and testing. Therefore, *a testing program is efficient if the number of required test points is small.*
- *Post-Fault Computation.* Since the post-fault computation is directly related to the per unit cost, *it is important to keep the post-fault computation time short and simple.*
- *Robustness.* A test program is robust if it is reliable even under the tolerance case. This issue has been raised many times, only because it is indeed the dominant issue at hand. We prefer the testing program *to be reliable even if the fault/tolerance ratio is small.*

THE ELEMENT-VALUE SOLVABILITY PROBLEM

The element-value solvability problem was initiated by Berkowitz [1] in 1962. This problem is presented in Fig. 1–2. The network N consists of RLC elements, possibly with dependent sources. There are m accessible terminals. The problem is to determine the circuit parameters, RLC, from the measurements at the accessible terminals.

It is easy to see that at the terminals one can at most measure the m-port input transfer function matrix $H(s)$, and this can be done, for example, by

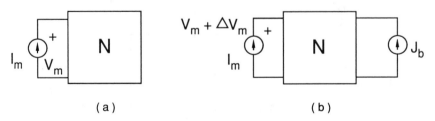

(a)   (b)

Figure 1–2

system identification methods. The transfer function matrix is a function M of frequency s and circuit parameter p, i.e.,

$$M(s,p) = H(s)$$

Hence, the problem is to solve for p from $H(s)$. In other words, it is equivalent to an m-port network synthesis problem when the graph and the element kind is prescribed.

In general, M is a nonlinear function of p. As a rule of thumb, when the number m of accessible nodes (test points) increases, M becomes "less nonlinear," and vice versa. This is an important trade-off problem. In this regard, there are two standard results to be quoted constantly as a measuring stick. The first one is given by Trick, Mayeda, and Sakla [15], who have shown that if *all* nodes are accessible, then M becomes linear and p can be uniquely determined.

On the other hand, for a one-port RC ladder, their element values can always be determined, regardless of the number of stages. This follows from a well-known RC synthesis theorem. This example shows that there exists a circuit type such that, regardless of how large the circuit is, the circuit parameters can be determined from only *two* accessible nodes. However, in this case M becomes "extremely nonlinear." To see this, a 4-stage RC ladder is studied [27]. The continued-fraction expansion method is used to determine the circuit values. A striking result has been found. When the significant digits used for the computation is eight, the answer comes out correctly. However, when it is reduced to seven, the answer becomes erroneous. In fact, some values of R and C become negative! This shows that the RC ladder is solvable in theory, but will yield erroneous conclusions even with the slightest computational error. Therefore, it becomes unreliable.

In between the above two extreme cases of the computation and test-point trade-off, the most elegant result is found by Navid and Willson [13]. First, their solvability condition is on the topology not on the element values. Therefore, it can be tested very easily. Second, the number of test points required is not too large, but roughly the square root of the number of branches. Finally, it is computationally tractable, although a set of nonlinear equations has to be solved. However, they can be applied only to a restricted class of circuits.

A necessary and sufficient condition on *local* diagnosability of *nonlinear* circuits is elegantly derived by Visvanathan and Sangiovanni-Vincentelli [38] and Saeks et al. [39]. This is an important contribution because it provides a theoretical limit. It will be most helpful to see if such a condition can be made robust in the presence of tolerance.

In summary, the advantage of the element-value solvability method is that it avoids the tolerance problem because *all* parameters are calculated and hence can be compared to their nominal values to see if they fall within the tolerance. As such, faulty elements can be located. The method also can be applied to the case when the number of faulty elements is large. The major difficulty with this method is that they have to solve, in general, a set of non-linear equations *every time they are tested.* The number of nonlinear equations to be solved is no less than the number of internal parameters, which in general is large. In order to make this method work, we need a computational procedure which is efficient and robust for a large number of nonlinear equations.

A FAULT/TOLERANCE COMPENSATION MODEL

In this section, a model is introduced which can be used effectively for fault diagnosis problems. This can be simply explained in Fig. 1–3.

Suppose that the actual admittance (Fig 1–3b) of a particular branch is deviated from its nominal admittance y (Fig. 1–3a) by Δy. The deviation may be caused by the tolerance (in which case Δy is small), or by a fault (in which case Δy is large). According to a circuit theory, the deviation can be compensated by a current source j which depends on the deviation Δy and its branch voltage. This is true whether Δy is linear or *nonlinear*. The value of j in general is a complex number (even when y is real) and it is "large" if the deviation is caused by a fault, and it is "small" if by a tolerance. Hence, the fault diagnosis problem becomes a detection problem which determines whether j is large or small.

The same is true for a three-terminal device as shown in Fig. 1–4. Here Y is a 2×2 admittance matrix. We need two current sources to compensate the deviations. If the device is a "good" transistor, Y is its linear model, and the compensators represent the errors caused by the linear approximation to the nonlinear transistor. If the device is a "faulty" operational amplifier, the com-

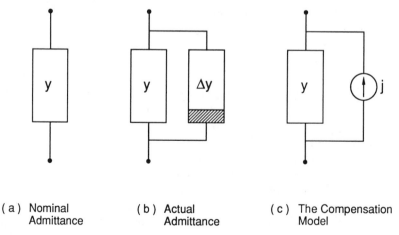

(a) Nominal   (b) Actual   (c) The Compensation
       Admittance   Admittance   Model

Figure 1–3 *A simple fault/tolerance compensation model. (a) Nominal admittance. (b) Actual admittance. (c) The compensation model.*

pensators may represent large deviations of the gain, or even the deviations caused by its internal transistors and capacitors. In fact, this model can be applied to any three-terminal device or any three-terminal subcircuit.

In general, an n-terminal device (chip) needs $(n - 1)$ current sources to compensate its deviations. When all actual devices are replaced by their compensation model, we have a Fault/Tolerance Compensation Model for the actual circuit. In this model, it consists only of the *nominal* (linear) circuit excited by actual excitations and by fault/tolerance compensators. Our problem is to locate the fault compensators.

Consider the circuit in Fig. 1–2a, with $(m + 1)$ accessible nodes and b branches. Its Fault/Tolerance Compensation Model is given in Fig. 1–2b, where J_b is the F/T compensator vector. When these two circuits are excited by the same I_m, and the responses V_m and $(V_m + \Delta V_m)$ are measured respectively, it is easy to show that

$$Z_{mb} J_b = -\Delta V_m \qquad (1\text{-}9)$$

where Z_{mb} is the branch-to-accessible node transfer function matrix, *depending only on the nominal circuit*.

Equation (1-9) was derived by Salka, El-Masry, and Trick [22] and by Biernacki and Bandler [36], based on linear perturbations. By use of the Fault/Tolerance Compensation Model, we have shown that Eq. (1-9) is also valid for linear nominal circuit with *nonlinear* perturbations. In fact, the perturbations can be from R to parallel RC, or from an operational amplifier to a complex circuit of (nonlinear) transistors and capacitors. Therefore, *the problem of modeling faulty devices can be avoided* as long as its nominal model is linear.

Finally, if the problem of tolerance is to be considered, the compensator J_b has two components:

$$J_b = J_{bF} + J_{bT} \qquad (1\text{-}10)$$

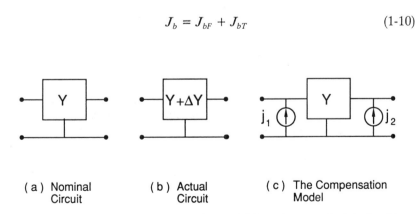

(a) Nominal   (b) Actual   (c) The Compensation
       Circuit   Circuit   Model

Figure 1–4   *A fault/tolerance compensation model for a three-terminal device. (a) Nominal circuit. (b) Actual circuit. (c) The compensation model.*

where J_{bF} is the fault compensator and J_{bT} is the tolerance compensator. J_{bF} is sparse but nonzero entries are large while J_{bT} is small but unknown to us. The problem becomes the determination of the nonzero entries of J_{bF} from Eqs. (1-9) and (1-10). This will be discussed in the next two sections.

k-FAULT DIAGNOSIS: THE IDEAL CASE

In this section, we assume that the number of accessible nodes m is much smaller than the total number of nodes n, i.e., $m \ll n$. We further assume that the number of faulty branches is bounded by k, which is much smaller than the total number of branches, i.e., $k \ll b$. First, let us consider the ideal case, i.e., $j_{bF} = 0$. In other words, we want to locate the nonzero entries of J_b from Eq. (1-9), where J_b is sparse.

A solution to this problem can be found in [48], which will be presented as follows: Equation (1-9) has the form

$$Bx = p \qquad (1\text{-}11)$$

where $x \in C^n, p \in C^m, B \in C^{m \times n}$, and $n > m$. Let

$$X_k = \{x \in C^n | \text{ number of nonzero components of } x \text{ not exceeding } k\}$$

be the set of vectors whose number of nonzero components is bounded by k. We want to investigate the uniqueness of the solution $x \in X_k$.

Definition.   The *global column rank* of B is said to be r if every combination of r columns of B is linearly independent, and some combination of $(r + 1)$ columns of B is linearly dependent.

Let Ω be the range of B. Then the following theorem is given in [98].

Theorem 1.   Let $p \in \Omega$. Then Eq. (1-11) has a unique solution $x \in X_k$ for almost all $p \in \Omega$ if and only if the global column rank of B is at least $k + 1$.

Note that for a fault diagnosis problem, the existence of a solution, i.e., $p \in \Omega$ is guaranteed. When Theorem 1 is satisfied, the solution of Eq. (1-11) can be obtained in the following way. Let the column vectors of B be denoted by

$$B = [b_1, b_2, \ldots, b_n]$$

Let the test matrices T_i be constructed in the following way:

$$T_i = [b_{i_1}, b_{i_2}, \ldots, b_{i_k}, p], \quad i = 1, 2, \ldots, s, \quad s = C(n, k)$$

for every combination of k columns of B. Then:

A. If

$$\text{Rank } T_i = k + 1, \quad i = 1, 2, \ldots, s \tag{1-12}$$

then there is *no* solution $x \in X_k$.

B. Otherwise, there is a *unique j* such that

$$\text{Rank } T_j = k \tag{1-13}$$

and

$$\text{Rank } T_i = k + 1, \quad i \neq j. \tag{1-14}$$

Furthermore, the unique solution $x \in X_k$ is given by

$$x = (B_j^T B_j)^{-1} B_j\, p \tag{1-15}$$

where $B_j = [b_{j_1}, b_{j_2}, \ldots, b_{j_k}]$ is obtained by deleting p from T_j.

As a consequence, the k-fault diagnosability depends on the global column rank of Z_{mb}. Let us now examine the issue of (1-1) post-fault computation and (1-2) the number of required test points.

1. *Post-Fault Computation.* The post-fault computation includes only Eqs. (1-12)–(1-15). It involves the test of the rank of $m \times (k + 1)$ matrices T_i, and an inversion of a $k \times k$ matrix $(B_i^T B_i)$. This is a very good feature since both m and k are small even when n is large. More importantly, *the size of these matrices does not depend on the complexity of the circuit.* The total post-fault computation can be implemented on a minicomputer or PC with computation time ranging from a fraction of a second to the order of a few seconds.

2. *Number of Required Test Points.* For k-fault diagnosis, it is necessary for the number of required test points $m \geq k + 1$. It is important to note that *it again depends mainly on k not on n, the complexity of the circuit.* Hence, the number of test points is small as long as k is small. Therefore, it is efficient.

As an example, assuming the optimal condition $m = k + 1$, for a single-fault diagnosis, we need only two test points, testing the rank of 2×2 matrices and an inverting a 1×1 matrix, regardless of how large n is.

Next, we will investigate how the optimal condition $m = k + 1$ can be achieved. This requires

$$\text{global column rank } Z_{mb} = m = k + 1 \tag{1-16}$$

The fulfillment of this condition depends on how the circuit is designed and more importantly how the test points are located. It turns out surprisingly that the global column rank of Z_{mb} depends mainly on the topology of the circuit, and less on its element values.

3. *Topological Conditions for* k-*Fault Diagnosibility.* First, it can be shown that if there is any internal loop (loops not incident with test nodes) consisting of r branches then the global column rank of Z_{mb} cannot be greater than $(r - 1)$. Therefore, we can diagnose at most $(r - 2)$ faults. Since most circuits have loops consisting of three branches, we can diagnose up to only one fault. This is a serious limitation. Alternatively, we can work on the node-fault diagnosis equation [48],

$$Z_{mn} J_n = - \Delta V_m \qquad (1\text{-}17)$$

where $J_n = AJ_b$ is the node compensator vector, $Z_{mb} = Z_{mn} A$, and A the incident matrix. Theorem 1 can now be applied to (1-15). In this case, a topological condition has been derived by Huang, Lin, and Liu [48]. First, construct a testing graph G_t from the given graph G by (1) deleting all branches which are incident between two accessible nodes and (2) connecting all accessible nodes, except the reference node, to a new node t.

Theorem 2.   Let the network be passive and G be connected. The following three statements are equivalent:

A.   The global column rank of Z_{mn} is k for almost all branch admittaces.
B.   The local connectivity[1] between the node t and any inaccessible node in G_t is k.
C.   There are at least k independent paths[1] in G_t from any inaccessible node to the node t.

A similar condition was given by Togawa and Matsumoto [71]. A more general topological condition is presented by Lin in this book [110]. These topological conditions are very useful: (1) They provide a very easy evaluation of the global column rank of a transfer function matrix, (2) they provide

---

[1]Here, the local connectivity of two nonadjacent nodes is the minimum number of nodes separating them, and two paths are independent if they do not have any common node, except at the terminal nodes.

a foundation for the design of diagnosable circuits, and (3) they provide the foundation for the design of locations of test points.

k-FAULT DIAGNOSIS: THE TOLERANCE CASE

The fault diagnosis equation for the tolerance case is obtained by (1-9) and (1-10):

$$Z_{mb}(J_{bF} + J_{bT}) = -\Delta V_m \tag{1-18}$$

which can be shown to have the form

$$(Z_{mb} + \Delta Z_{mb})J_{bT} = -\Delta V_m \tag{1-19}$$

where ΔZ_{mb} is caused by the tolerance. This can be viewed as the same problem as the ideal case except that the matrix Z_{mb} is now polluted by the noise ΔZ_{mb}. Therefore, we need robust computational methods for the testing procedures (1-12)–(1-15).

Singular Decomposition Method

When the procedure (1-12)–(1-15) is applied to (1-19), we need to determine the rank of A from $\tilde{A}$, where

$$\tilde{A} = A + \Delta A \tag{1-20}$$

where ΔA is unknown and whose elements are small. A well-known method for the test of the rank of such problem is the singular decomposition method [52]. The application of this method to the problem of analog fault diagnosis has been studied by Togawa, Matsumoto, and Arai [82].

Residual Number Method

Alternatively, the residual number method [53] can be used. Equation (1-20) has the form

$$\tilde{A} = A + V \tag{1-21}$$

where $A \in R^{m \times n}$ is corrupted by a noise metrix $V \in R^{m \times n}$. The problem is to determine the rank of A from the measured $\tilde{A}$. Assume that

$$E[V] = 0$$
$$E[V^T V] = m\sigma^2 I$$

where σ^2 is the variance of V and is preassigned. Let a_i denote the ith column vector of A, and A_i the remainder of A with a_i deleted. Then the n residual numbers of A is defined by

$$r_i = a_i^T(I - A_i A_i^+)a_i \qquad (1\text{-}22)$$

for $i = 1, 2, \ldots, n$, where A^+ is the pseudo-inverse of A_i [59]. It can be shown that if $m \geq n$ and

$$r_i(\bar{A}) > mn\sigma^2 \qquad (1\text{-}23)$$

for $i = 1, 2, \ldots, n$, then the rank of A is n.

A Nonlinear Estimation Approach

The fault diagnosis problem with tolerance can also be posed as a nonlinear estimation problem [77].

Let N be a circuit with n nodes. Denote

1. Y_0 as the *nominal* node admittance matrix,
2. $(Y_0 + Y_t)$ as the *actual nonfaulty* node admittance matrix, and
3. $(Y_0 + Y_t + Y_f)$ as the *actual faulty* node admittance matrix,

where Y_t is the deviation due to tolerance and Y_f is the deviation due to faults. In general, the entries of Y_t are small but not sparse, and the entries of Y_f are large but sparse if a limited number of faults are considered. Let

$$Z_0 = Y_0^{-1} \qquad (1\text{-}24)$$

$$Z = (Y_0 + Y_t + Y_f)^{-1} = Z_0 + \Delta Z \qquad (1\text{-}25)$$

Then,

$$\Delta Z = (Y_0 + Y_f + Y_T)^{-1} - Y_0^{-1}$$

$$= -Z_0 Y_f(Y_0 + Y_f)^{-1} - (Y_0 + Y_f)^{-1}Y_t(Y_0 + Y_f + Y_t)^{-1} \qquad (1\text{-}26)$$

The first term of Eq. (1-26) resulted only from faults, while the second term is due to both fault and tolerance effects and appears only when tolerance effects are present.

Note that Eq. (1-26) is nonlinear with respect to Y_f. Fortunately, this difficulty can be circumvented with some approximations along with some algebraic manipulations. The diagnosis equation is now derived in the following.

To start with, it is assumed that, with probability 1, the absolute value of every entry of Y_t is much smaller than the corresponding entry of Y_0 and $\| (Y_0 + Y_f)^{-1} Y_t \| < 1$. The notation $\| \cdot \|$ stands for the norm of the matrix, e.g., the Euclidean norm. It can then be shown that

$$\Delta Z = -Z_0 Y_f (Y_0 + Y_f)^{-1} - (Y_0 + Y_f)^{-1} Y_t (Y_0 + Y_f)^{-1} + (Y_0 + Y_f)^{-1} O(\|(Yt\,(Y_0 + Y_f)^{-1})\|^2)$$

As a first-order approximation, we have

$$\Delta Z = -Z_0 Y_f (Y_0 + Y_f)^{-1} - (Y_0 + YF)^{-1} Y_t (Y_0 + Y_f)^{-1} \qquad (1\text{-}27)$$

Now define

$$G = -Y_f (I + Z_0 Y_f)^{-1} \qquad (1\text{-}28)$$

Then

$$Y_f = -(I + GZ_0)^{-1} G \qquad (1\text{-}29)$$

and

$$(Y_0 + Y_f)^{-1} = Z_0 (I + GZ_0) \qquad (1\text{-}30)$$

Substituting Eq. (1-30) into Eq. (1-27) yields

$$\Delta Z = Z_0 G Z_0 - Z_0 (I + GZ_0) Y_t (I + Z_0 G) Z_0 \qquad (1\text{-}31)$$

In practice, the entire ΔZ is not available from measurements. Only a submatrix is available to us. Assume that the network N has input node set U and output node set M. Denote the transfer impedance matrix from U to M by Z_{mu} and $(Z_{mu} + \Delta Z_{mu})$, respectively, as in Eqs. (1-24) and (1-25). Note that ΔZ_{mu} is a submatrix of ΔZ. For this submatrix, Eq. (1-31) is reduced to

$$\Delta Z_{mu} = Z_{mn} G Z_{nu} - Z_{mn} (I + GZ_0) Y_t (I + Z_0 G) Z_{nu} \qquad (1\text{-}32)$$

This is the fault diagnosis equation, where Z_0, Z_{mn}, and Z_{nu} are known matrices which depend only on the nominal circuit values, the matrix Y_t is the tolerance matrix which is unknown to us, G is related to the matrix Y_f by Eq. (1-28) and is to be identified, and ΔZ_{mu} is a known matrix obtained from measurements.

The goal here is to locate the faults via estimating Y_f, taking into account the tolerance effect. Equation (1-32) is clearly an estimation problem. Namely, given the measurement ΔZ_{mu}, one is to estimate the parameter G

subject to the contaminating noise Y_t. Note that the tolerance effect Y_t comes into play multiplicatively with a quadratic function of G.

A Nonlinear Estimation Problem

The estimation problem of Eq. (1-32) can be rewritten in the following vector form:

$$V = X\theta + F(\theta)\eta \qquad (1\text{-}33)$$

where V is composed of all entries of ΔZ_{mu}, and θ consists of the entries of G. $F(\theta)$ is a matrix with an appropriate dimension and is a quadratic function of θ. The entries of η are linear functions of the corresponding entries of Y_t. The estimation problem of Eq. (1-33) is clearly a nonlinear one.

One of the most common methods to resolve this problem is the method of least squares. Of particular interest here is the linear least squares unbiased estimate (LLSUE). It is assumed here that the distribution of Y_t has zero mean. One can then show that $E\{\eta\} = 0$ and thus

$$E\{V\} = E\{X\theta\}$$

It can be shown straightforwardly that the LLSUE for θ is given by

$$\hat{\theta} = \left(X^T\Sigma^{-1}(\theta)X\right)^{-1}X^T\Sigma^{-1}(\theta)V \qquad (1\text{-}34)$$

Note that $\hat{\theta}$ is determined by a function of θ itself, namely, $\Sigma(\theta)$. To evaluate $\hat{\theta}$ with Eq. (1-34), $\Sigma(\theta)$ needs to be estimated.

In a standard estimation problem, it is usually required that the dimension of V should be greater than or equal to that of θ. This implies, with the assumption that $\Sigma(\theta)$ is positive definite, that the rank of X is greater than or equal to the dimension of θ. However, such is not necessarily the case in the fault diagnosis problem, as will be discussed in the next section. This involves the issue of identifiability. From Eq. (1-33), one can see that, given the distribution of the noise, η, the distribution of V depends on θ. Conceptually, if the rank of X is less than that of θ, different values of θ may yield the same distribution of V. This is simply because different values of θ may correspond to the same value of $X\theta$. Hence an observation V can give no discriminatory information between different values of θ corresponding to the same values of $X\theta$. The parameter θ in this case is referred to as "unidentifiable."

The key issue now is to convert the unidentifiable problem to an identifiable one. This can be accomplished with a key assumption that the matrix Y_f is sparse along with an important observation of the relation between Y_f and G.

The k-Fault Diagnosis Problem

Let k be the bound of the number of faults. By the definition of Y_f, its nonzero entries correspond to faulty elements. Assume that k is much smaller than n, the number of nodes. *Thus the matrix Y_f is sparse.* This property will enable us to convert the unidentifiable estimation problem to an identifiable one. In particular, it can be seen from Eq. (1-28) that

$$G = -Y_f(I + Z_0 Y_f)^{-1} = -(I + Y_f Z_0)^{-1} Y_f \qquad (1\text{-}35)$$

This equation leads to the following observation, which is a key to formulating the k-fault diagnosis as an identifiable estimation problem.

Observation. For each zero row of Y_f, there corresponds a zero row of G. Similarly, for each zero column of Y_f, there corresponds a zero column of G.

For the sake of illustration, let us consider the one-fault case. In this case all elements except one of Y_f are zero. From the above observation, the same is also true for G. The problem of diagnosis is to locate the position of the nonzero element of Y_f, and hence that of G. In other words, instead of locating the nonzero element of Y_f from Eq. (1-27), we can do the same for G from (1-31). Note that (1-27) is much more complicated than Eq. (1-31) because Y_f appears in an inverse function form.

Let us assume that the $(ij)th$ element of G, denoted by g_{ij}, is nonzero, and let its matrix be denoted by G_{ij}. Then, Eq. (1-32) becomes

$$\Delta Z_{mu} = Z_{mn} G_{ij} Z_{nu} - Z_{mn}(I + G_{ij} Z_0) Y_f (I + Z_0 G_{ij}) \qquad (1\text{-}36)$$

Since G_{ij} is a sparse matrix with the only element g_{ij} being nonzero, the above matrix equation (1-36) can be rearranged to a vector equation from (1-33), i.e.,

$$V = X_{ij} g_{ij} + F_{ij}(g_{ij})\eta \qquad (1\text{-}37)$$

where the vector V is composed of all the entries of ΔZ_{mu}, X_{ij} is an appropriate matrix, $F(g_{ij})$ is a matrix function of g_{ij}, and η is a noise vector composed by the entries of Y_t. The form of Eq. (1-37) is possible because the first term of Eq. (1-36) is linear with respect to g_{ij} and the second term is quadratic with respect to g_{ij} and linear with respect to Y_t.

We now can use Eq. (1-34) to estimate g_{ij}, i.e.,

$$g_{ij} = [X_{ij}^T \sigma_{ij}^{-1}(g_{ij}) X_{ij}]^{-1} X_{ij}^T \sigma_{ij}^{-1}(g_{ij}) V \qquad (1\text{-}38)$$

where

$$\sigma_{ij}(g_{ij}) = F_{ij}(sup\ g_{ij})\ Q F_{ij}^T(g_{ij}) \qquad (1\text{-}39)$$

and $Q = E[\eta\eta^T]$. It can be shown that the solution of Eq. (1-38) gives an optimal estimator of g_{ij}, i.e., unbiased and of minimum variance. Since Eq. (1-38) is non-linear, its explicit solution is hard to obtain. We have found that Eq. (1-38) can be easily solved by an iterative method. Note that Eq. (1-38) has the form

$$g_{ij} = h(g_{ij})$$

Let the initial guess be

$$g_{ij}^0 = [X_{ij}^T X_{ij}]^{-1} X_{ij}^T V \tag{1-40}$$

and let the next iterative steps be

$$g_{ij}^{k+1} = h(g_{ij}^k) \tag{1-41}$$

From our experience, a solution of (1-38) can be obtained in a few steps.

The same estimation process will be made for all elements of G. The element with the largest estimate determines the faulty one.

Examples and their simulation results will be shown in the next section. From our experience, this is a very powerful result. It can reliably handle a medium circuit (40 branches with 5% tolerance) with as little as five test points.

For the cases with $k > 1$, see [77].

ILLUSTRATIVE EXAMPLES

Example 1.   The purpose of this example is to illustrate the Fault Compensation Method given in two earlier sections.

Consider the nominal circuit in Fig. 1–5a. Suppose that the element g_5 is at fault so that $g_5 \rightarrow g_5 + \Delta g_5$. This fault causes a deviation Δv_1 and Δv_2 at the output, as shown in Fig. 1–5b. To compute the deviations Δv_1 and Δv_2, we can use the circuit in Fig. 1–5c, in with Δg_5 can be replaced by J_5. This is true even if Δg_5 is *nonlinear*. The transfer function between them can be obtained from the circuit in Fig. 1–5c which depends only on the *nominal* circuit values. This transfer function is given by

$$\begin{bmatrix} \Delta v_1 \\ \Delta v_2 \end{bmatrix} = \begin{bmatrix} z_{51} \\ z_{52} \end{bmatrix} J_5 \tag{1-42}$$

The important thing to notice here is that the vectors Δv and z_5 are *colinear*. This is the important fact diagnosis principles are based on.

If we repeat the same process for all elements, then we have

$$\Delta v = J_4 z_4 + J_5 z_5 + \cdots + J_{11} z_{11} = ZJ \tag{1-43}$$

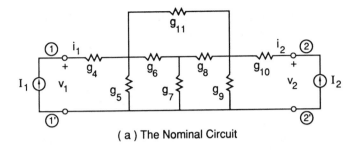

(a) The Nominal Circuit

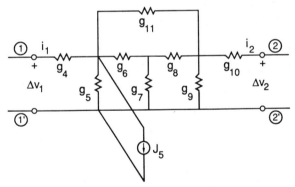

(b) Deviations (Δv_1, Δv_2) Caused by a Fault at g_5

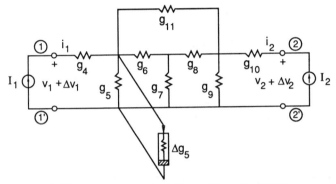

(c) The Equivalent Circuit for Computing Δv_1 and Δv_2

Figure 1–5   *Illustrative circuits for Example 1. (a) The nominal circuit. (b) Deviations (Δv_1, Δv_2) caused by fault at g_5. (c) The equivalent circuit for computing Δv_1 and Δv_2.*

which is (1-9). Note that if there is only one fault, then only one of the J's is nonzero and all other J's are zero. In this case, if g_i is at fault, then $\Delta \mathbf{v}$ is colinear with $\mathbf{z}_i$. Hence, the diagnosis procedure becomes one of finding which one of the vectors $\mathbf{z}_i$ is colinear with $\Delta \mathbf{v}$. This procedure guarantees to be successful if every pair of z_i is not colinear to each other, i.e., the global rank of Z is 2, as predicted by Theorem 1.

When $g_r = g_5 \cdots = g_{10} = 1\Omega$ and $g_{11} = 2\Omega$, we have

$$Z = \begin{bmatrix} 24 & 11 & 5 & 6 & 1 & 7 & 0 & 4 \\ 0 & 7 & 1 & 6 & 5 & 11 & 24 & -4 \end{bmatrix} \tag{1-44}$$

Its global rank is 2, and hence one fault can always be diagnosed correctly. For example, if $g_5 = \infty$, i.e., it is shorted, then

$$\Delta v = -\begin{bmatrix} 3/4 \\ 21/44 \end{bmatrix} = \frac{-3}{44}\begin{bmatrix} 11 \\ 7 \end{bmatrix} \tag{1-45}$$

which is colinear only with z_5, which correctly indicates that g_5 is at fault.

Example 2. Let us illustrate how Eq. (1-6) can be used for the purpose of diagnosis.

Consider the same circuit again, except that all current directions are added as shown in Fig. 1–6. Associate reference is used for the voltage references. In order to apply this method, we have to write Eqs. (1-1) and (1-2) in such a way that no rows of A has two or more g's. This is because the method can diagnose up to the *nonzero rows* of ΔA. Therefore, the Tableau Method will be used for the circuit equations. The Tableau equation is given at the top of page 21.

Note that all blank spaces are zeros. The first block equations are the KCL equations, the second ones are the KVL equations, the third ones are the element equations for the sources, and the fourth block equations are the

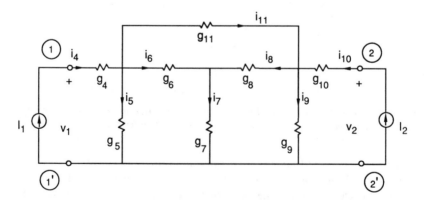

Figure 1–6 *Circuit for Example 2.*

$$
\begin{bmatrix}
-1 & 1 & 1 & 0 & 0 & 0 & 0 & 1 & & & & & & & & & & \\
0 & 0 & -1 & 1 & -1 & 0 & 0 & 0 & & & & & & & & & & \\
0 & 0 & 0 & 0 & 1 & 1 & -1 & -1 & & & & & & & & & & \\
& & & & & & & & -1 & 0 & 1 & 1 & 0 & 0 & 0 & 0 & 0 & 0 \\
& & & & & & & & 0 & 0 & 0 & -1 & 1 & 1 & 0 & 0 & 0 & 0 \\
& & & & & & & & 0 & 0 & 0 & 0 & 0 & -1 & -1 & 1 & 0 & 0 \\
& & & & & & & & 0 & 1 & 0 & 0 & 0 & 0 & 0 & -1 & -1 & 0 \\
& & & & & & & & 0 & 0 & 0 & 0 & -1 & 0 & 1 & 0 & 0 & 1 \\
1 & 0 & 0 & 0 & 0 & 0 & 0 & 0 & & & & & & & & & & \\
0 & 0 & 0 & 0 & 0 & 0 & 1 & 0 & & & & & & & & & & \\
-1 & & & & & & & & & & g_4 & 0 & 0 & 0 & 0 & 0 & 0 & 0 \\
& -1 & & & & & & & & & 0 & g_5 & 0 & 0 & 0 & 0 & 0 & 0 \\
& & -1 & & & & & & & & 0 & 0 & g_6 & 0 & 0 & 0 & 0 & 0 \\
& & & -1 & & & & & & & 0 & 0 & 0 & g_7 & 0 & 0 & 0 & 0 \\
& & & & -1 & & & & & & 0 & 0 & 0 & 0 & g_8 & 0 & 0 & 0 \\
& & & & & -1 & & & & & 0 & 0 & 0 & 0 & 0 & g_9 & 0 & 0 \\
& & & & & & -1 & & & & 0 & 0 & 0 & 0 & 0 & 0 & g_{10} & 0 \\
& & & & & & & -1 & & & 0 & 0 & 0 & 0 & 0 & 0 & 0 & g_{11}
\end{bmatrix}
\begin{bmatrix}
i_4 \\ i_5 \\ i_6 \\ i_7 \\ i_8 \\ i_9 \\ i_{10} \\ i_{11} \\ v_1 \\ v_2 \\ v_4 \\ v_5 \\ v_6 \\ v_7 \\ v_8 \\ v_9 \\ v_{10} \\ v_{11}
\end{bmatrix}
=
\begin{bmatrix}
I_1 \\ I_2 \\ \\ \\ \\ \\ \\ \\ \\ \\ \\ \\ \\ \\ \\ \\ \\
\end{bmatrix}
$$

$$
\begin{bmatrix}
 & & & & & & & & 1 & 0 & & & & & & & & \\
 & & & & & & & & 0 & 1 & & & & & & & &
\end{bmatrix} = C
$$

$$
y = \begin{bmatrix} v_1 \\ v_2 \end{bmatrix} = Cx
$$

element equations for resistors. Note that each g_i enters one and only one row. We want to show that Eq. (1-6),

$$
CA^{-1}J = -\Delta y
$$

is exactly the same as Eq. (1-43). This is because the entries of ΔA are zero for the first three blocks. Hence Eq. (1-7) becomes

$$
J = \begin{bmatrix} J_4 \\ J_5 \\ \cdot \\ \cdot \\ \cdot \\ J_{11} \end{bmatrix} = \begin{bmatrix} \Delta g_4 \\ & \Delta g_5 \\ & & \cdot \\ & & & \cdot \\ & & & & \cdot \\ & & & & & \Delta g_{11} \end{bmatrix} \begin{bmatrix} v_4 + \Delta v_4 \\ v_5 + \Delta v_5 \\ \cdot \\ \cdot \\ \cdot \\ v_{11} + \Delta v_{11} \end{bmatrix} \qquad (1\text{-}46)
$$

With this J, it can be shown that Eq. (1-6) is the same as (1-43).

Since these two methods lead to the same equation (1-43), the same diagnosis procedure can be followed afterwards. One may think that this method must be more complex than that of the Fault Compensation Method, since the inverse of a huge matrix A has to be evaluated. This may not be true. Although the dimension of A is large, A is sparse. Softwares for the inverse of a sparse matrix are readily available. In fact, many circuit simulation soft-wares prefer the Tableau equation approach. On the other hand, this approach is more general, and it is not limited to circuit equations. Furthermore, it can be easily extended to nonlinear circuits. (See Huang and Liu [112].)

Example 3. [60].   In this example, we will show how multiple frequencies testing can be used to aid the diagnosis procedure and how fault compensation methods can be used to do block faults.

Consider a 3-pole low-pass active filter as shown in Fig. 1–7a. We are to locate the single faults (resistors and capacitors) in this network by using the input and output terminals as the only accessible nodes. It can be easily shown that the global rank of Z_{mn} or Z_{mb} is one, and hence Theorem 1 cannot be immediately applied to solve the one-fault problem. We will show how to use multiple frequency and fault-logic equations to alleviate the problem.

Our algorithm is hierarchical, i.e., the fault is first isolated into a sub-network from a single test signal and then this faulty subnetwork is further diagnosed by the usage of multiple test frequencies. The algorithm will be described as follows.

Step A: The circuit is first reformulated into a block diagram as shown in Fig. 1–7b. The relationship between the transfer functions, denoted by A_i's and the R's and C's, is given as follows:

$$
\begin{aligned}
A_1 &= R_1 \\
A_2 &= 1/(SC_1) \\
A_3 &= 1/R_2 \\
A_4 &= 1/R_7 \\
A_5 &= -1/(G_3 + SC_2) \\
A_6 &= R_5/(R_4R_6SC_3)
\end{aligned}
\tag{1-47}
$$

I_i is the input, and V_i and V_0 are the outputs. The extra signal sources J_i, $i = 1, 2, \ldots, 6$, at the output of the blocks A_i is the *fault compensator* of the block A_i. The meaning of the fault compensator is given in Fig. 1–7c. Note that if A_i is changed to $(A_i + \Delta A_i)$, then $J_i = U_i \Delta A_i$, where U_i is the input to A_i. Assuming that $U_i \neq 0$, we have $J_i = 0$ if and only if $\Delta A_i = 0$. Our first step is to locate nonzero J_i's from V_i and V_0.

From Fig. 1–7b, it can be shown that

$$
\begin{bmatrix} \Delta V_i \\ \\ \Delta V_0 \end{bmatrix} = \begin{bmatrix} 1 & 1 & 0 & 0 & 0 & 0 \\ \\ 0 & A_3A_5A_6A_G & A_5A_6A_G & A_5A_6A_G & A_6A_gA_G \end{bmatrix} \begin{bmatrix} J_1 \\ J_2 \\ J_3 \\ J_4 \\ J_5 \\ J_6 \end{bmatrix}
\tag{1-48}
$$

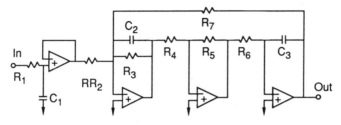

(a) The Nominal Circuit for Example 3

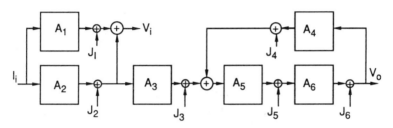

(b) Its Fault Compensate System Model

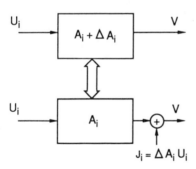

(c) Construction of Fault Compensate Model for System A_i

Figure 1–7 *Circuit for Example 3. (a) The nominal circuit. (b) Its fault compensate system model. (c) Construction of fault compensate model for system A_i.*

where $A_G = 1/(1 - A_4A_5A_6)$. This equation has the form of (1-11). Therefore, Theorem 1 can be applied. Since the last four column vectors are linearly dependent, we cannot distinguish among (J_3, J_4, J_5, J_6). Let the last four column vectors be grouped into one. Then the resulting matrix has three columns and whose global column rank is 2. Therefore, it is one-fault diagnosable, i.e., we may determine whether A_1, A_2, or one of (A_3, A_4, A_5, A_6) is at fault. In view of (1-47), by use of single signal testing, we can isolate the fault into three groups: R_1, C_1, and the rest. This is established in Table 1–1A.

Step B: The faulty subnetwork isolated by Step A can be further diagnosed by the usage of multiple test frequencies. First, observe that the only part that requires further diagnosis is the group of (A_3, A_4, A_5, A_6). It can be described by the transfer function of V_0/V_2, where V_0 is the output voltage of the circuit and V_2 is the output of A_2 and which can be calculated if A_2 is fault-free. This can be determined from Step A. The expression of V_0/V_2 is given by

$$\frac{V_0}{V_2} = \frac{B_4}{B_1 S + B_2 S^2 = B_3 S^3} \tag{1-49}$$

where S is the complex frequency, and

$$\begin{aligned}
B_1 &= 1/R_7 \\
B_2 &= (R_4 R_6 C_3)/(R_3 R_5) \\
B_3 &= (R_4 R_6 C_2 C_3)/R_5 \\
IB_4 &= 1/R_2
\end{aligned} \tag{1-50}$$

The relation between (V_0, V_2) and circuit parameters R's and C's is nonlinear. In order to avoid solving nonlinear equations, we propose to do the following. To save subscripts, denote V_0 by V and V_2 by W.

Assume that $B_i \rightarrow (B_i + \Delta B_i)$, $i = 1, 2, 3, 4$. Exciting the circuit by k different frequencies, the above equation becomes

$$\begin{bmatrix} S_1 V_1 & S_1^2 V_1 & S_1^3 V_1 & -W_1 \\ S_2 V_2 & S_2^2 V_2 & S_2^3 V_2 & -W_2 \\ \cdot & & & \cdot \\ \cdot & & & \cdot \\ \cdot & & & \cdot \\ S_k V_k & S_k^2 V_k & S_k^3 V_k & -W_k \end{bmatrix} \begin{bmatrix} \Delta B_1 \\ \Delta B_2 \\ \\ \Delta B_3 \\ \\ \Delta B_4 \end{bmatrix} = \begin{bmatrix} S_1 V_1 & S_1^2 V_1 & S_1^3 V_1 & -W_1 \\ S_2 V_2 & S_2^2 V_2 & S_2^3 V_2 & -W_2 \\ \cdot & & & \cdot \\ \cdot & & & \cdot \\ \cdot & & & \cdot \\ S_k V_k & S_k^2 V_k & S_k^2 V_k & -W_k \end{bmatrix} \begin{bmatrix} B_1 \\ B_2 \\ \\ B_3 \\ \\ B_4 \end{bmatrix} \tag{1-51}$$

We need to determine nonzero ΔB_i's from (1-51). Since the rhs is known, Eq. (1-51) has the form of (1-11). Therefore, Theorem 1 again can be applied. When the k different frequencies are properly chosen, the global column rank of the lhs matrix is 3. Therefore, we can uniquely determine two nonzero ΔB_i's. From these nonzero ΔB_i's, the faulty circuit parameters can be located from (1-50) by a logic argument. This can be presented formally as follows.

A set of *fault-logic equations* is constructed according to (1-50):

Table 1–1 Fault Patterns for Steps A and B

						Step A
A_1	A_2	A_3	A_4	A_5	A_6	Faulty Components
0	X	X	X	X	X	R_1
X	0	X	X	X	X	C_1
X	X	0	0	0	0	Others

				Step B
B_1	B_2	B_3	B_4	Faulty Components
0	X	X	X	R_7
X	0	X	X	R_3
X	X	0	X	C_2
X	X	X	0	R_2
X	0	0	X	R_4, R_5, R_6, C_3

$$
\begin{aligned}
F(B_1) &= F(R_7) \\
F(B_2) &= F(R_3)vF\,(R_4)vF\,(R_5)vF(R_6)vF(C_3) \\
F(B_3) &= F(C_2)vF\,(R_4)vF\,(R_5)vF(R_6)vF(C_3) \\
F(B_4) &= F(R_2)
\end{aligned}
\qquad (1\text{-}52)
$$

where V is the OR logic. The first fault-logic equation reads that ΔB_1 is nonzero if and only if ΔR_7 is nonzero. The second fault-logic equation reads that ΔB_2 is nonzero if and only if ΔR_3, ΔR_4, ΔR_5, ΔR_6, or ΔC_3 is nonzero. Similarly for the third and the fourth fault logic equations. We have assumed that no two faults will occur in such a way that their effects will cancel each other, which is rare in practice.

Finally, we need to solve the set of fault-logic equations (1-52). This can be done by use of a truth value table. The solution, together with the solution in Step A, is given in Table 1–1. An entry 0 means that $\Delta A_i, \neq 0$ in Table 1–1A and $\Delta B_i \neq 0$ in Table 1–1B. For example, the second row of Table 1–1A reads that if $\Delta A_2 \neq 0$, and $\Delta A_1 = \Delta A_3 = \Delta A_4 = \Delta A_5 = \Delta A_6 = 0$, then C_1 is faulty. The fifth row of Table 1–1B reads that if $\Delta B_2 \neq 0$, $\Delta B_3 \neq 0$, and $\Delta B_1 = \Delta B_4 = 0$, then a fault occurs among (R_4, R_5, R_6, C_5). The reason that the last group of circuit parameters cannot be further distinguished can be easily found from the circuit. They are related as a single product and, therefore, they cannot be further diagnosed unless additional test points are introduced.

This implementation has many interesting points:

1. The fault diagnosis decision is based on matching fault patterns (Table 1–1). It is like the fault dictionary approach for fault testing of digital systems. It is extremely simple from the user's point of view. Such a table is called a *fault directory.*

2. The post-fault computation is minimal. The only computation required is the calculation of residuals. Its complexity depends on the number of faults, not the size of the network.
3. The use of multiple frequency and fault-logic equation avoids a complex and nonrobust computation of solving a set of nonlinear equations.
4. Our computer simulation study shows that this method of implementation is very *robust*. It can accept tolerance up to 7% of the nominal value.
5. Note also that if only single frequency is used, this circuit is not even one-fault diagnosable. With multiple frequencies, the method becomes robust.

Example 4. In this example, fault diagnosis with tolerance will be considered. This example will illustrate the nonlinear estimation method.

A single transistor amplifier is considered. Its equivalent circuit is shown in Fig. 1–8. This circuit has been studied by Bandler et al. [47]. Excite the circuit at both node 1 and node 2 with four different frequencies: $\omega_1 = 0.0003$, $\omega_2 = 0.003$, $\omega_3 = 0.03$, and $\omega_4 = 0.3$. Suppose that the tolerance limit of each element is 5%. The actual values of the elements are assumed to have uniform distributions between 0% and 5%. Thirteen single fault cases were simulated. The magnitude of each fault ranges from 10% to 25%. The results are given in the Tableau equation.

In Table 1–2, every two rows of numbers between two lines present a single fault simulation. The first row gives the relative element values, i.e., the ratio between the actual element value used for simulation and its nominal value. For example, 0.9 represents 10% below its nominal value and 1.026 represents 2.6% above its nominal value. The second row gives the residual number for each element. Note that a residual number is defined by

$$\text{residual number} = \exp\left[-\text{ estimated value}\right]$$

Hence, if an estimated value is closed to 0, its residual number is closed to 1. Conversely, if the estimated value is large, its residual number is small. Hence, the smallest one indicates the faulty element. Take the first row as an example. In this case 10% fault is inserted at R_1 and 5% tolerance is randomly assigned to other elements. Using our method, the smallest residual in the second row is clearly pointed to R_1, and therefore the faulty element is successfully isolated.

In this circuit, there are 13 elements, two test points and four internal nodes. For the cases of 10–25% faults, with 5% tolerance, the faulty elements have been correctly isolated every time, as indicated in Table 1–2. Moreover, for each case, the total computing time (IBM 370) is only about 12 s! This demonstrates the powerfulness of the method.

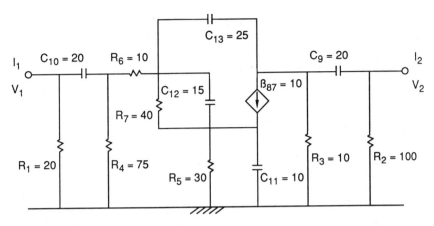

Figure 1–8 *Circuit for Example 4.*

CONCLUSION

Two main approaches to analog fault diagnosis have been presented. The element-value solvability problem and the k-fault diagnosis problem.

The element-value solvability problem is the same as the n-port synthesis problem except that the graph and the element type have been prescribed. Therefore, it is very much in the interest of circuit theorists. The major advantage of this approach is that the tough problem of tolerance is avoided. The difficulty of this approach is that its performance is limited by a trade-off between the large number of test points required and the complexity of post-fault computation.

The k-fault problem with the fault/tolerance compensation approach has shown that under the assumption that the number of faults is bounded by k, the fault diagnosis problem can be successfully carried out with only *a few test points* and *little post-fault computation.* For example, we have successfully solved a video amplifier circuit [23], which has eight transistors and 25 resistors and capacitors. In its equivalent circuit, there are 43 branches and 21 nodes. This is a typical medium size analog circuit. Of the 21 nodes, only five are accessible for use as test points. In order to test its robustness, every actual parameter is deviated from its nominal value with a tolerance uniformly distributed up to 5%. In every simulation case, we assigned a single fault to a parameter which is a multiplicity of 2, 0.5, or 0.1 of its nominal value. A total of 18 cases including transistor faults (two-element fault) have been tried and the fault branches are *correctly located every time*!

This method can also be extended to multi-frequency testing, and to hierarchical testing as shown in Example 3.

Table 1–2

	R_1	R_2	R_3	R_4	R_5	R_6	R_7	P_{87}	C_9	C_{10}	C_{11}	C_{12}	C_{13}
Relative value	0.9	1.026	0.984	1.003	1.024	1.044	0.972	1.049	1.001	0.962	1.015	0.967	1.044
Residual number	0.366	0.971	0.994	0.998	0.990	0.908	0.994	0.927	0.997	0.973	0.989	0.973	0.982
Relative value	0.987	0.9	0.960	0.987	1.038	0.987	0.970	0.966	0.970	0.988	0.987	0.968	1.020
Residual number	0.989	0.267	0.932	0.961	0.978	0.990	0.994	0.990	0.938	0.999	0.949	0.995	0.992
Relative value	1.007	1.009	0.9	0.971	1.027	1.019	1.015	1.003	1.023	0.994	1.003	1.036	1.013
Residual number	0.999	0.996	0.215	0.925	0.962	0.971	0.960	0.991	0.955	0.999	0.990	0.936	0.986
Relative value	1.003	0.952	1.047	0.85	1.004	0.994	1.040	0.960	1.020	0.963	0.968	1.039	0.978
Residual number	1.000	0.875	0.984	0.456	0.988	0.963	0.809	0.959	0.968	0.817	0.943	0.988	0.944
Relative value	0.950	0.995	1.019	1.005	0.85	0.969	1.028	0.966	1.038	1.016	1.040	1.026	1.029
Residual number	0.898	0.999	0.991	0.974	0.359	0.961	0.917	0.888	0.955	0.998	0.928	0.985	0.931
Relative value	1.027	1.034	1.031	1.032	1.028	0.85	0.999	1.018	1.029	1.022	0.992	0.951	1.027
Residual number	0.979	0.964	0.959	0.996	0.988	0.238	0.987	0.990	0.990	0.997	0.992	0.967	0.993
Relative value	0.961	0.973	1.012	0.960	1.017	1.027	0.8	0.994	1.010	1.040	0.958	1.036	0.999
Residual number	0.880	0.953	0.993	0.761	0.916	0.993	0.361	0.908	0.982	0.887	0.897	0.953	0.999
Relative value	1.016	0.993	0.953	1.011	1.020	0.959	0.992	0.8	1.045	0.963	0.983	1.032	0.978
Residual number	0.992	0.998	0.937	0.966	0.993	0.936	0.981	0.246	0.987	0.940	0.866	0.646	0.986
Relative value	1.033	1.016	1.042	0.954	0.964	0.979	1.019	0.999	0.8	1.038	0.996	1.030	0.971
Residual number	0.990	0.987	0.977	0.958	0.996	0.996	0.934	0.994	0.070	0.993	0.999	1.000	0.990
Relative value	0.962	1.009	1.012	1.034	0.962	0.964	0.960	1.048	10.42	0.75	0.964	0.985	0.954
Residual number	0.973	0.998	0.983	0.979	0.963	0.949	0.976	0.999	0.980	0.105	0.992	0.994	0.926
Relative value	0.982	1.031	1.033	1.028	1.005	1.040	1.024	0.980	0.962	0.974	0.75	0.987	1.046
Residual number	0.995	0.989	0.977	0.996	0.998	0.973	0.997	0.825	0.975	0.998	0.101	0.800	0.981
Relative value	1.042	0.955	0.990	1.036	0.963	0.984	0.956	0.952	1.006	0.993	1.049	0.75	0.967
Residual number	0.978	0.949	0.996	0.996	0.897	0.997	0.949	0.866	0.998	0.999	0.961	0.159	0.973
Relative value	1.033	1.008	0.990	0.981	0.972	1.033	1.042	1.046	0.970	0.952	0.997	0.951	0.75
Residual number	0.969	0.999	0.961	0.995	0.986	0.992	0.882	0.981	0.948	0.909	0.999	0.979	0.143

In recent years, activities have been emphasized on block diagnosis [51, 78, 97, 99, 101] and nonlinear circuits [76, 79, 81, 85, 89, 90, 92]. An efficient way to deal with nonlinear circuits is given in this book [112].

The fault diagnosis techniques have other applications. Since it has the capability of locating the faulty devices from available test points, it has the potential to be integrated with manufacture process to do CAM for IC chips. For another application, the single-frequency single-signal method can do *on line* fault diagnosis. Therefore, it provides an important link for the design of self-repairing systems.

I believe that the underline development for the analog fault diagnosis is very much completed, at least for medium size circuits. It is up to the industry to develop softwares to implement it.

REFERENCES

[1] R. S. Berkowitz, "Conditions for Network-Element-Value Solvability," *IRE Trans. Circuit Theory,* Vol. CT-9, pp. 19–24, 1962.

[2] S. D. Bedrosian, "On Element Value Solution of Single-Element-Kind Networks," Ph.D. Dissertation, University of Pennsylvania, Dec. 1961.

[3] S. Seshu and R. Waxman, "Fault Isolation in Conventional Linear Systems—A Feasibility Study," *IEEE Trans. Rel.,* Vol. R-15, pp. 11–16, May 1965.

[4] R. Saeks, S. P. Singh, and R. W. Liu, "Fault Isolation via Component Simulation," *IEEE Trans. Circuit Theory,* Vol. CT-19, pp. 634–640, Nov. 1972.

[5] G. C. Martens and J. D. Dyck, "Fault Identification in Electronic Circuits with the Aid of Bilinear Transformations," *IEEE Trans. Reliability,* Vol. R-21, pp. 99–104, May 1972.

[6] W. A. Plice, "Techniques for the Automatic Generation of Fault Isolation Tests for Analog Circuits," *IEEE 1975 ASSC,* pp. 127–130, 1975.

[7] G. C. Temes, "Efficient Methods of Fault Simulation," *Proc. of 20th Midwest Symp. on Circuits and Systems,* pp. 191–194, IEEE, NY, Aug. 1977.

[8] T. N. Trick and C. J. Alajajian, "Fault Analysis of Analog Circuits," *Proc. of 20th Midwest Symp. on Circuits and Systems,* Piscatataway NJ pp. 211–215.

[9] R. Liu and V. Visvanathan, "Diagnosability of Large-Scale Dynamical Systems," *Proc. of 20th Midwest Symposium on Circuits and Systems,* pp. 585–589, Lubbock, 1977.

[10] R. Saeks and S. R. Liberty (Ed.), *Rational Fault Analysis,* Marcel Dekker, New York, 1977.

[11] S. D. Bedrosian (Ed.), Special Issue on Automatic Analog Fault Diagnosis, *IEEE Trans. Circuit Syst.,* Vol. CAS-26, Jul. 1979.

[12] P. Duhamel and J. C. Rault, "Automatic Test Generation Techniques for Analog Circuits and Systems: A Review," *IEEE Trans. CAS,* Vol. CAS-26 pp. 411–440, 1979.

[13] N. Navid and A. N. Willson, "A Theory and an Algorithm for Analog Circuits Fault Diagnosis," *IEEE Trans. Circuits Syst.,* Vol. CAS-26, pp. 440–457, Jul. 1979.

[14] N. Sen and R. Saeks, "Fault Diagnosis for Linear Systems via Multifrequency

Measurements," *IEEE Trans. Circuits Syst.,* Vol. CAS-26, pp. 457–465, Jul. 1979.

[15] T. N. Trick, W. Mayeda, and A. A. Sakla, "Calculation of Parameter Values from Node Voltage Measurements," *IEEE Trans. Circuits Syst.,* Vol. Cas-26, pp. 466–475, Jul. 1979.

[16] R. W. Liu and V. Visvanathan, "Sequentially Linear Fault Diagnosis: Part I— Theory," *IEEE Trans. Circuits Syst.,* Vol. CAS-26, pp. 490–495, Jul. 1979.

[17] S. Freeman, "Optimum Fault Isolation by Statistical Inference," *IEEE Trans. Circuits Syst.,* Vol. CAS-26, pp. 505–512, Jul. 1979.

[18] J. Lee and S. D. Bedrosian, "Fault Isolation Algorithm for Analog Electronic Systems Using the Fuzzy Concept," *IEEE Trans. Circuits Syst.,* Vol. CAS-26, pp. 518–522, Jul. 1979.

[19] W. Hochwald and J. D. Bastian, "A DC Approach for Analog Fault Dictionary Determination," *IEEE Trans. Circuits Syst.,* Vol. CAS-26, pp. 523–528, Jul. 1979.

[20] C. S. Lin and R. Liu, "A Single-Fault Diagnosis Theory," *Proc. of Allerton Conf. on Communication, Control and Computing,* pp. 172–178, 1979.

[21] Z. F. Huang and G. M. Shen, "The Fault Diagnosis of Analog Network and System," *Proc. of 1980 National Symposium on Circuits and Systems,* Guang Zhou, Jan. 6–10, 1980.

[22] A. A. Sakla, E. I. El-Masry, and T. N. Trick, "A Sensitivity Algorithm for Fault Detection in Analog Circuits," *IEEE 1980 Int. Symposium on Circuits and Systems,* IEEE, New York, 1980, pp. 1075–1077.

[23] Z. F. Huang, "Applications of Generalized Incrementally Linear Functions to Fault Diagnosis of Analog Systems," Ph.D. Dissertation, University of Notre Dame, Notre Dame, IN, 1985.

[24] R. M. Biernacki and J. W. Bandler, "Fault Location of Analog Circuits," *IEEE 1980 Int. Symposium on Circuits and Systems,* IEEE, New York, 1980, pp. 1078–1081.

[25] R. M. Biernacki and J. W. Bandler, "Postproduction Parameter Identification of Analog Circuits," *IEEE 1980 Int. Symposium on Circuits and Systems,* IEEE, New York, 1980, pp. 1082–1086.

[26] R. Liu, C. S. Lin, A. Deng, and V. Raman, "System Diagnosis—A New System Problem," *Proc. National Electronics Conf.,* pp. 280–285, 1980.

[27] R. Saeks and R. Liu, *Proc. Workshop on Analog Automatic Test Program Generation,* University of Notre Dame, Notre Dame, IN, May 26–27, 1981.

[28] R. Saeks and R. Liu, "Fault Diagnosis in Electronic Circuits," *J. Soc. Instrum. Control Eng.,* Vol. 20, pp. 214–216, Tokyo, Japan, 1981.

[29] Z. F. Huang, C. S. Lin, and R. Liu, "Node-Fault Diagnosis and Design of Testability," *Tech. Report No. 811,* University of Notre Dame, Notre Dame, IN, July 27, 1981. Also, *20th IEEE Conference on Decision and Control,* pp. 1037–1042, IEEE, NY, 1981.

[30] Lin Xie-ting, "Fault Analysis of Nonlinear Analog Circuits," *Acta Electron. Sinica,* Vol. 9, No. 1, p. 70, 1981.

[31] C. S. Lin and R. Liu, "A Fault Directory Approach to Analog Fault Analysis— A Case Study," *Proc. 1980 IEEE Int. Symposium on Circuits and Systems,* pp. 239–242.

[32] R. DeCarlo and C. Gordon, "Tableau Approach to AC-Multifrequency Fault

Diagnosis," *Proc. 1981 IEEE Int. Symposium on CAS,* pp. 270–273, IEEE, NY, 1981.

[33] C. C. WU, A. Sangiovanni-Vercentelli, and R. Saeks, "A Differential-interpolative Approach to Analog Fault Simulation," *Proc. IEEE Int. Symposium on CAS,* IEEE, NY, 1981, pp. 266–269.

[34] Z. F. Huang and G. M. Shen, "Method of Fault Diagnosis in Linear Systems and Their Diagnosabilities," *Proc. 1981 IEEE Int. Symposium on Circuits and Systems,* 32, IEEE, New York, 1981, pp. 285–288.

[35] L. M. Roytman and M. N. S. Swamy, "Some Properties of Orthonomal Excitations of the Circuit and the Calculation of the Circuit Elements," *Proc. 1981 IEEE Int. Symposium on CAS,* IEEE, New York, 1981, pp. 292–294.

[36] R. M. Biernacki and J. W. Bandler, "Multiple-Fault Location of Analog Circuits," *IEEE Trans. Circuits Syst.,* Vol. CAS-28, pp. 361–366, May 1981.

[37] W. A. Plice, "The Model Adjusting Techniques for Analog Fault Detection and Location," *Technical Report,* Honeywell, Inc., System and Research Center, Minneapolis, MN, 1981.

[38] V. Visvanathan and A. Sangiovanni-Vincentelli, "Diagnosability of Nonlinear Circuits and Systems—Part I: The dc Case," *IEEE Trans. CAS,* pp. 1093–1102, 1981.

[39] R. Saeka, A. S. Vincentelli, and V. Visvanathan, "Diagnosability of Nonlinear Circuits and Systems—Part II: Dynamical Systems," *IEEE Trans. Circuits Syst.,* pp. 1103–1108, Nov. 1981.

[40] R. Saeks, "Criteria for Analog Fault Diagnosis," in *Proc. European Conf. Circuit Theory and Design,* The Hague, pp. 75–78, Aug. 1981.

[41] C. C. Wu, K. Nakazima, C. L. Wei, and R. Saek, "Analog Fault Diagnosis with Failure Bounds," *IEEE Trans. Circuits Syst.,* CAS-29, No. 5, pp. 277–284, 1982.

[42] Z. F. Huang, C. S. Lin, and R. Liu, "Topological Conditions on Multiple-Fault Testability of Analog Circuits," *1982 IEEE Int. Symposium on Circuits and Systems,* pp. 1152–1155 Rome, Italy, 1982.

[43] L. M. Roytman, E. Plotkin, and M. N. S. Swamy, "Multifrequency Method of Fault Diagnosis in Analogue Circuits," *Proc. 1982 IEEE Int. Symposium on Circuits and Systems,* pp. 1144–1147 Rome, Italy, 1982.

[44] J. A. Starzyk and J. W. Bandler, "Model Approach to Multi-Fault Location in Analog Circuits," *Proc. 1982 IEEE Int. Symposium on Circuits and Systems,* pp. 1136–1139 Rome, Italy, 1982.

[45] T. N. Trick and Y. Li, "Algorithms for the Location of Single and Multiple Fault in Analog Circuits with Inaccessible Nodes," *Proc. 1982 IEEE Int. Large Scale System Symposium,* Oct., pp. 491–494, IEEE, New York, 1982.

[46] P. M. Lin, "DC Fault Diagnosis Using Complimentary Pivot Theory," *Proc. 1982 IEEE Int. Symposium on CAS,* IEEE, New York, 1982, pp. 1132–1135.

[47] J. W. Bandler, R. M. Biernacki, A. E. Salama, and J. A. Starzyk, "Fault Isolation in Linear Analog Circuits Using the L_1 Norm," *Proc. 1982 IEEE Int. Symposium on CAS,* pp. 1140–1143 1982.

[48] Z. F. Huang, C. S. Lin, and R. Liu, "Node-Fault Diagnosis and A Design of Testability," *IEEE Trans. CAS,* Vol. CAS-30, No. 5 pp. 257–265, May 1983.

[49] C. S. Lin, Z. F. Huang, and R. Liu, "Topologic Conditions for Single-Branch-Fault," *IEEE Trans. CAS,* Vol. CAS-30, No. 6 pp. 376–381, 1983.

[50] Y. Togawa and T. Matsumoto, "On the Topological Testability Conjecture for Analog Fault Diagnosis Problem," *IEEE Trans. Circuits Syst.*, Vol. CAS-31, No. 2, pp. 147–158, 1984.

[51] C. S. Lin, "Reachability, Excitability, and Testability of Analog Networks," *Ph.D. Dissertation,* University of Notre Dame, IN, 1983.

[52] G. H. Golub and C. F. Van Loan, *Matrix Computations,* John Hopkins University Press, Baltimore 1989.

[53] L. C. Suen and R. Liu, "Determination of the Structure of Multivariable Stochastic Linear Systems," *IEEE Trans. Autom. Control,* Vol. AC-23, No. 3, pp. 458–464, 1978.

[54] L. C. Suen and R. Liu, "Numerical Rank Determination and Residual Numbers", *Technical Report No. EE-832,* University of Notre Dame, Jun. 1983.

[55] R. Liu, C. S. Lin, Z. F. Huang, and L. Z. Hu, "Analog Fault Diagnosis: A New Circuit Theory," *IEEE Int. Symp. Circuits Syst.*, pp. 931–939, 1983.

[56] J. W. Bandler and A. E. Salama, "Fault Diagnosis of Analog Circuits," *IEEE Proc.,* Vol. 73, No. 8. pp. 1279–1325, 1985.

[57] R. Liu (Ed.), *Selected Papers on Analog Fault Diagnosis,* IEEE, New York, 1987.

[58] R. Patton, P. Frank, and R. Clare (Ed.), *Fault Diagnosis in Dynamic Systems,* Prentice-Hall, Englewood Cliffs, NJ, 1989.

[59] C. R. Rao and S. K. Mitra, *Generalized Inverse of Matrices and Its Applications,* Wiley, New York, 1971.

[60] C. S. Lin, Z. F. Huang, and R. Liu, "Fault Diagnosis of Linear Analog Networks: A Theory and Its Implementation," *Proc. IEEE Int. Symp. Circuits Syst.,* pp. 1090–1093, 1983.

[61] S. Shinoda and I. Yamaguchi, "Parameter-Value Determinations of Linear Active Networks with Inaccessible Nodes," *Proc. IEEE Int. Symp. Circuits Syst.,* pp. 1114–1117, 1983. IEEE, NY

[62] J. A. Starzyk and J. W. Bandler, "Design of Tests for Parameters Evaluation within Remote Inaccessible Fault Subnetworks," *Proc. IEEE Int. Symp. Circuits Syst.,* pp. 1106–1109, 1983, IEEE, NY

[63] T. N. Trick and Y. Li, "A Sensitivity Based Algorithm for Fault Isolation in Analog Circuits," *Proc. IEEE Int. Symp. Circuits Syst.,* pp. 1098–1101, 1983, IEEE, NY

[64] C. L. Wey, D. Holder, and R. Saeks, "On the Implementation of Analog ATPG," *Proc. IEEE Int. Symp. Circuits Syst.,* pp. 1102–1105, 1983. IEEE, NY

[65] E. Flecha and R. DeCarlo, "Time Domain Tablean Approach to the Fault Diagnosis of Analog Nonlinear Circuits," *Proc. IEEE Int. Symp. Circuits Syst.,* pp. 1110–1113, 1983. IEEE, NY

[66] L. Rapisardo and R. DeCarlo, "Analog Multifrequency Fault Diagnosis," *IEEE Trans. Circuits Syst.*, Vol. CAS-30, No. 4, pp. 223–234, 1983.

[67] T. Ozawa, S. Shinoda, and M. Yamada, "An Equivalent-Circuit Transformation and Its Application to Network-Element-Value Calculation," *IEEE Trans. Circuits Syst.,* pp. 430–431, 1983. Vol. CAS-30, No. 7

[68] J. A. Starzyk and J. W. Bandler, "Multiport Approach to Multiple-Fault Location in Analog Cicuits," *IEEE Trans. Circuits Syst.,* pp. 762–765, 1983. Vol. CAS-30, No. 10

[69] E. Flecha and R. DeCarlo, "The Nonlinear Analog Fault Diagnosis Scheme of Wu, Nakajima, Wey and Saeks in the Tableau Context," *IEEE Trans. Circuits Syst.*, pp. 828–830, 1984. Vol. CAS-31, No. 9

[70] S. L. Hakimi and K. Nakajima, "On a Theory of t-Fault Diagnosable Analog Systems," *IEEE Trans. Circuits Syst.*, pp. 946–951, 1984. Vol. CAS-31, No. 11

[71] Y. Togawa and T. Matsumoto, "On the Topological Testability Conjecture for Analog Fault Diagnosis Problems," *IEEE Trans. Circuits Syst.*, pp. 147–158, 1984. Vol. CAS-31, No. 2

[72] A. E. Salama, J. A. Starzyk, and J. W. Bandler, "A Unified Decomposition Approach for Fault Location in Large Analog Circuits," *IEEE Trans. Circuits Syst.*, pp. 609–622, 1984. Vol. CAS-31, No. 7

[73] V. Visvanathan and Sangiovanni-Vincentelli, "A Computational Approach for the Diagnosability of Dynamical Circuits," *IEEE Trans. Computer-Aided Des.*, pp. 165–171, 1984. Vol. CAD-3, No. 3

[74] J. W. Bandler and A. E. Salama, "Recent Advances in Fault Location of Analog Networks," *Proc. of IEEE Int. Symp. Circuits Syst.*, pp. 660–663, 1984. IEEE, N.Y.

[75] T. Ozawa, "Topological Considerations in the Diagnosability of Analog Circuits," *Proc. of IEEE Int. Symp. Circuits Syst.*, pp. 664–667, 1984. IEEE, N.Y.

[76] D. Feng and S. D. Bedrosian, "Multiple-Fault Diagnosis of Analog Circuits and Its Applications to S-C Networks," *IEEE Int. Symp. Circuits Syst.*, pp. 693–696, 1984. IEEE, NY

[77] L. Hu, Z. F. Huang, Y. F. Huang, and R. Liu, "A Stochastic Model for Analog Fault Diagnosis with Tolerance," *IEEE Int. Symp. Circuits Syst.*, pp. 680–683, 1984. IEEE, NY

[78] C. L. Wey, "Design of Testability for Analog Fault Diagnosis," *Proc. of IEEE Int. Symp. Circuits Syst.*, pp. 555–558, 1985. IEEE NY

[79] F. M. El-Turky, "Identification of Device and Chip Faults in Analog Circuits," *Proc. of IEEE Int. Symp. Circuits Syst.*, pp. 563–566, 1985. IEEE, NY

[80] T. Ozawa, J. W. Bandler, and A. E. Salama, "Large Analog Networks, Diagnosability in Decomposition Approach for Fault Location," *IEEE Trans. Circuits Syst.*, pp. 415–416, 1985. Vol. CAS-32, No. 4

[81] C. S. Lin and R. Liu, "Identifiability of an Imbedding Unknown Subnetwork," *IEEE Trans. Circuits Syst.*, pp. 260–266, 1985. Vol. CAS-32, No. 3

[82] Y. Togawa, T. Matsumoto, and H. Arai, "Linear Algorithm for Branch Fault Diagnosis of Analog Circuits: T_F Equivalence-Class Approach," *IEEE Trans. Circuits Syst.*, pp. 992–1009, 1986. Vol. CAS-33, No. 10,

[83] G. Inculano, A. Liberatore, S. Manetti, and M. Marini, "Multifrequency Measurement of Testability with Application to Large Linear Analog Systems," *IEEE Trans. Circuits Syst.*, pp. 644–648, 1986. Vol. CAS-33, No. 6

[84] R. Liu, Q. Huang, C. S. Lin, H. Ammar, and Y. F. Huang, "Petri-Net Application to Functional Fault Diagnosis," *Proc. of IEEE Int. Symp. Circuits Syst.*, pp. 1323–1327, 1986. IEEE, NY

[85] M. Senzoku and S. Shinoda, "A Theory and An Algorithm for Fault Diagnosis of Directed Networks," *Proc. of IEEE Int. Symp. Circuits Syst.*, pp. 639–642, 1986. IEEE, NY.

[86] Z. F. Huang and R. Liu, "Analog Fault Diagnosis with Tolerance," *Proc. of IEEE Int. Symp. Circuits Syst.,* pp. 1332–1336, 1986, IEEE, NY.

[87] X. C. Gao, D. P. Leach and S. P. Shan, "Separability of Different Single Fault in Analog Circuits," *IEEE Int. Symp. Circuits Syst.,* pp. 1245–1248, 1986. IEEE, NY.

[88] C. C. Wu, "Coupling Table Construction Via Sensitivity Analysis for Self-Testing Analog Fault Diagnosis Systems," *IEEE Int. Symp. Circuits Syst.,* pp. 1249–1250, 1986. IEEE, NY

[89] Z. H. Lin and Q. Wu, "The Testability and Diagnosability of Analog Integrated Circuits," *IEEE Int. Symp. Circuits Syst.,* pp. 1251–1254, 1986. IEEE, NY

[90] C. L. Wey and F. Lombardi, "On a New Decision Process for the t-Diagnosis of an Analog System," *IEEE Int. Symp. Circuits Syst.,* pp. 1255–1256, 1986. IEEE, NY.

[91] D. Reisig and R. DeCarlo, "Multiple Fault Diagnosis for Analog Digital Circuits," *IEEE Int. Symp. Circuits Syst.,* pp. 1257–1260, 1986. IEEE, NY.

[92] B. L. Jiang and C. L. Wey, "Multiple Fault Analysis with Failure Bound for Analog Circuits," *IEEE Int. Symp. Circuits Syst.,* pp. 1261–1264, 1986. IEEE, NY

[93] L. S. Milor and V. Visvanathan, "Efficient Go/No-Go Testing of Analog Circuits," *IEEE Int. Symp. Circuits Syst.,* pp. 414–417, 1987. IEEE, NY.

[94] Q. Huang and R. Liu, "Fault Diagnosis of Piecewise-Linear Circuits," *IEEE Int. Symp. Circuits Syst.,* pp. 418–421, 1987. IEEE, NY.

[95] J. A. Starzyk and H. Pai, "Multifrequency Measurement of Testability in Analog Circuits," *IEEE Int. Symp. Circuits Syst.,* pp. 884–887, 1987. IEEE, NY.

[96] J. W. Bandler, W. Kellermann, and K. Madsen, "Nonlinear l_1-Optionization Algorithm for Design, Modeling and Diagnosis of Networks," *IEEE Trans. Circuits Syst.,* pp. 174–181, 1987. Vol. CAS-34, No. 2

[97] A. Sengupta, S. P. Durham, A. Sen, and S. Bandyophyay, "Measure of System Diagnosability in Presence of Intermittent and Permanent Faults," *IEEE Trans. Circuits Syst.,* pp. 1053–1058, 1987. Vol. CAS-34, No. 9

[98] M. E. Mokari-Bolhassan and S. M. Kang, "Analysis and Correction of VLSI Delay Measurement Errors Due to Transmission Lines Effects," *IEEE Trans. Circuits Syst.,* pp. 19–25, 1988. Vol. CAS-34, No. 1

[99] L. Fan and X. Luo, "Location of Faulty Subnetworks in Analog Network," *IEEE Int. Symp. Circuits Syst.,* pp. 929–932, 1988. IEEE, NY.

[100] F. A. Savaci and I. C. Goknar, "Fault Analysis and Parameter Identification in Linear Circuits in Terms of Topological Matrices," *IEEE Int. Symp. Circuits Syst.,* pp. 937–940, 1988. IEEE, NY.

[101] J. A. Starzyk and H. Dai, "Fault Diagnosis and Calibration of Large Analog Circuits," *IEEE Int. Symp. Circuits Syst.,* pp. 941–944, 1988. IEEE, NY.

[102] R. Zou, "Fault Analysis of Nonlinear Circuits from Node Voltage Measurements," *IEEE Int. Symp. Circuits Syst.,* pp. 1155–1158, 1988. IEEE, NY.

[103] J. A. Starzyk and H. Dai, "Sensitivity Based Testing of Nonlinear Circuits," *IEEE Int. Symp. Circuits Syst.,* pp. 1159–1162, 1988. IEEE, NY

[104] R. Zou and J. Huang, "Fault Location of Linear Nonreciprocal Circuit with Tolerance," *IEEE Int. Symp. Circuits Syst.,* pp. 1163–1166, 1988. IEEE, NY

[105] W. G. Luo and S. W. Zhang, "Multi-Fault Diagnosis of DC-Nonlinear Analog Circuits." *IEEE Int. Symp. Circuits Syst.,* pp. 1171–1174, 1988. IEEE, NY

[106] H. Yang and P. Qian, "A New Approach to Analog Fault Diagnosis and an Experimental Diagnostic System," *IEEE Int. Symp. Circuits Syst.,* pp. 1175–1178, 1988. IEEE, NY

[107] L. Tong, L. Zhang, and R. Liu, "A Necessary and Sufficient Condition for the Testability of Hybrid Circuits," *IEEE Int. Symp. Circuits Syst.,* pp. 845–848, 1989. IEEE, NY

[108] C. L. Wey, B. L. Jiang, and G. M. Wierzba, "Built-In Self-Test (BIST) Design of Large-Scale Analog Circuit Networks," *IEEE Int. Symp. Circuits Syst.,* pp. 2048–2951, 1989. IEEE, NY

[109] L. Chen and W. Yuan, "Multiple-Fault Diagnosis of Linear Active Multipart Networks," *IEEE Int. Symp. Circuits Syst.,* pp. 2036–2039, 1989. IEEE, NY.

[110] Chen-Shang Lin, "Topological Testability Conditions for Analog Fault Diagnosis," this book.

[111] T. Matsumoto and Y. Togawa, "Linear Method vs. Nonlinear Method," this book.

[112] Q. Huang and R. Liu, "Fault Diagnosis of Nonlinear Electronic Circuits," this book.

2

Linear Method vs. Nonlinear Method

T. MATSUMOTO
and
Y. TOGAWA

One of the main difficulties inherent to the fault diagnosis problem lies in the fact that the problem is *nonlinear even if* the system to be diagnosed is *linear.* This stems from the fact that the observables (measurements) depend on the system parameters in a *nonlinear* manner. It does not imply, however, that one has to solve complicated nonlinear equations in order to perform fault diagnosis. On the contrary, there are *linear* methods that are *as powerful as* any nonlinear method, which is rather surprising. The purpose of this chapter is to describe one such linear method together with *rigorous justifications.*

In reading this chapter, we would like to call the reader's attention to the following facts:

1. In order to deal with "exceptional" cases, one needs to consider *probability measure* in one way or another.
2. The probability measure should be over the set of system parameters rather than the set of measurements, and this complicates the rigorous treatment considerably.
3. The linear method given in this chapter *does not* require topological conditions assumed in other linear methods [2–6].

We will formulate the problem for general (abstract) systems and then specialize to electric circuits. This way, the reader can see how the probability measure is naturally involved in the problem.

Due to the restriction of the space allocated for this chapter, we will have to omit specific circuit examples. The interested reader is referred to [1]. Linear methods other than described in this chapter are given in [2–6]. The references, however, are far from exhaustive. There could be many works which should be referred to.

SETTING OF THE PROBLEM

Let $\mathfrak{S}$ be an abstract system with b parameters. The parameters take certain values called the *nominal* values if $\mathfrak{S}$ is not faulty. If $\mathfrak{S}$ is *faulty,* then some parameters are perturbed from the nominal values. Suppose that one has no means of observing the parameters directly, but one can observe certain observables which are functions of parameters. In the fault location problem, one is required, given a faulty system, to tell which parameters are perturbed. For more rigorous setting, we need some definitions (see Fig. 2–1):

$\mathbb{K}2$: $\mathbb{K}$ denotes either the set of real numbers $\mathbb{R}$, or the set of complex numbers $\mathbb{C}$.

$\mathbb{K}^b$: the b-dimensional vector space over $\mathbb{K}$ called *the parameter space*. A point in $\mathbb{K}^b$ is denoted by $\Delta \mathbf{g} = (\Delta g_1, \ldots, \Delta g_b)$.

$\mathbb{K}^m$: the m-dimensional vector space over $\mathbb{K}$ called *the observable space*. A point in $\mathbb{K}^m$ is denoted by $\Delta \mathbf{v_m} = (\Delta v_1, \ldots, \Delta v_m)$.

φ: a smooth function from $\mathbb{K}^b$ to $\mathbb{K}^m$: $\Delta \mathbf{v_m} = \varphi(\Delta \mathbf{g})$.

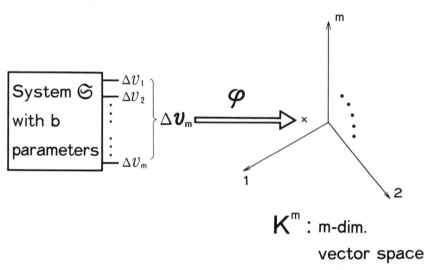

Figure 2–1   *A schematic description of fault diagnosis problems.*

$\mathfrak{F}$: a family of subsets of $\{1, 2, \ldots, b\}$. If $F \in \mathfrak{F}$, then F is of the form $\{j_1, \ldots, j_k\}$, $1 \leq j_1 < \cdots < j_k \leq b$.

$\mathbb{K}^F$: $\mathbb{K}^F \triangleq \{(\Delta g_1, \ldots, \Delta g_b) \mid \Delta g_k = 0 \text{ if } k \notin F\}$, where $F \in \mathfrak{F}$.

D_F: a subset D_F of $\mathbb{K}^b$ is assigned for each $F \in \mathfrak{F}$. D_F is the set of parameter values for which F is the faulty set. If $\Delta g = (\Delta g_1, \ldots, \Delta g_b) \in D_F$, then $\Delta g_j \neq 0$ iff $j \in F$. Note that D_F and $D_{F'}$ are disjoint if $F \neq F'$.

ED_F: $ED_F \triangleq \bigcup_{F' \subset F} D_{F'}$.

S_F: the image of $F \in \mathscr{F}$ under φ; S_F is the set of observed data when F is the faulty set:

$$S_F \triangleq \{\Delta \mathbf{v}_m = \varphi(\Delta g) \mid \Delta g \in D_F\}.$$

$\bigcup_{F \in \mathscr{F}} D_F$: the union of D_F's for all $F \in \mathscr{F}$.

S: $S \triangleq \bigcup_{F' \in \mathscr{F}} S_F$; S is the union of all S_F's for all $F \in \mathscr{F}$.

$S = \varphi(\bigcup_{F \in \mathscr{F}} D_F)$.

Main Example. Let $\mathcal{N}$ be a circuit with branches $b_1, \ldots, b_b$ and nodes $n_1, \ldots, n_n$. Suppose that the voltages of nodes $n_{j_1}, \ldots, n_{j_m}$ are accessible. Then

$$\varphi: (\Delta g_1, \ldots, \Delta g_b) \to (\Delta v_1, \ldots, \Delta v_m)$$

is given by

$$(g_1, \ldots, g_b) \to v_m = (A_i Y_b^T A_v^{-1})_{mn}^{-1} i$$

where $g_k = g_k^{nominal} + \Delta g_k$, $\Delta v_k = v_k - v_k^{nominal}$ $\mathbf{Y_b} = \text{diag}(g_1, \ldots, g_b)$ and g_k is the admittance of the kth branch. $\qquad\square$

When the system $\mathfrak{S}$ is not faulty, the parameter values take nominal values $\Delta \mathbf{g}^{nominal} = (\Delta g_1^{nominal}, \ldots, \Delta g_b^{nominal}) \in \mathbb{K}^b$. Without loss of any generality, we can suppose that $\Delta \mathbf{g}^{nominal} = (0, \ldots, 0) = \mathbf{0} \in \mathbb{K}^b$, and that $\varphi(\mathbf{0}) = \mathbf{0}$. Then if $\Delta \mathbf{v}_m = \varphi(\Delta \mathbf{g}) \neq \mathbf{0}$, it means some parameters, say $\Delta g_{j_1}, \ldots, \Delta g_{j_k}$, are faulty, and one is required to locate the *fault-set* $F = \{j_1, \ldots, j_k\} \in \mathscr{F}$. If $F \in \mathscr{F}$. If $F \in \mathscr{F}$ is the fault-set, then the parameter $\Delta \mathbf{g} = (\Delta g_1, \ldots, \Delta g_b)$ is in D_F, and $\Delta \mathbf{v}_m = \varphi(\Delta \mathbf{g}) \in S_F$. On the other hand, if the observed data $\Delta \mathbf{v}_m$ is in S_F, then F *might be* faulty. Moreover, if $\Delta \mathbf{v}_m \notin S_{F'}$, for all F' except $F' = F$, then F is assured to be the fault-set. Since all information is contained in S_F, *any* fault location algorithm has to check whether or not $\Delta \mathbf{v}_m \in \mathbb{K}^m$ belongs to S_F for a given $F \in \mathscr{F}$ and a $\Delta \mathbf{v}_m \in \mathbb{K}^m$. Notice that some characterization of S_F *in computable form* is necessary here. For instance, if we could find a function f_F for each $F \in \mathscr{F}$ such that the set S_F coincides with the zeros of f, then $\Delta \mathbf{v}_m \in S_F$ is easily checked by checking $f_F(\Delta \mathbf{v}_m) = 0$. In general, however, it is extremely difficult to find such an f_F if φ is nonlinear, even if the set D_F

is simple like a linear subspace. In the linear method one checks $\Delta v_m \in T_F$, where T_F is the *smallest linear subspace containing* S_F. Since T_F is linear, it is easier to check $\Delta v_m \in T_F$ than to check $\Delta v_m \in S_F$. However, if T_F is much larger than S_F (an extreme example is that T_F = the whole space $\mathbb{K}^m$), then essential information would be lost by replacing T_F with S_F. So we have to estimate how much information is lost by using T_F instead of S_F. It depends on the nature of the particular system $\mathbb{S}$ and the function φ. We will show that if $\mathbb{S}$ is a linear analog circuit driven by a *fixed* current source, and $\varphi(\Delta g)$ is the accessible node voltage, then the linear method works well: We will prove this by studying the geometry of the set S_F. The dimension of S_F turns out to equal to that of T_F. We will also show that the linear method is *as powerful as* the method of checking $\Delta v_m \in S_F$. For the sake of clarity, we summarize our usage of the "linear" vs. "nonlinear."

Nonlinear Method. Checks if

$$\Delta v_m \in S_F$$

Linear Method. Checks if

$$\Delta v_m \in T_F$$

where T_F is the smallest linear subspace containing S_F.

We will compare these methods in terms of the following three testability conditions:

1. Given an observed value $\Delta v_m \in S$, Δv_m is said to *determine the fault uniquely* if there exists unique $F \in \mathscr{F}$ such that $\Delta v_m \in S_F$.
2. F_1 and F_2 in $\mathscr{F}$ are said to be *independent* if their images S_{F_1} and S_{F_2} are disjoint.
3. $\mathscr{F}$ is said to be *testable* if each $\Delta v_m \in S$ determines the fault uniquely.

PROBABILITY

We start with several examples.

Example 1.   Let $\mathbb{K} = \mathbb{R}$, $b = 4$, $m = 3$, $F_1 = \{1, 2\}$, $F_2 = \{3, 4\}$, $D_{Fj} = \{\Delta g \in \mathbb{R}^4 | \Delta g_k \neq 0\, k \in F_j\}$, and let $\varphi: \mathbb{R}^4 \to \mathbb{R}^3$ be given by the linear map

$$\begin{bmatrix} \Delta v_1 \\ \Delta v_2 \\ \Delta v_3 \end{bmatrix} = \begin{bmatrix} 1 & 0 & 1 & 1 \\ 0 & 1 & 1 & 1 \\ 0 & 0 & 1 & -1 \end{bmatrix} \begin{bmatrix} \Delta g_1 \\ \Delta g_2 \\ \Delta g_3 \\ \Delta g_4 \end{bmatrix}$$

Notice that $S_{F_1} \cap S_{F_2} = \{ (\Delta v_1, \Delta v_2, \Delta v_3) \mid \Delta v_1 = \Delta v_2 \neq 0, \Delta v_3 = 0 \} \neq \phi$.
Suppose that F_1 is faulty. Then $\Delta g_1 \neq 0, \Delta g_2 \neq 0, \Delta g_3 = 0$, and $\Delta g_4 = 0$, and this implies $\Delta v_1 \neq 0, \Delta v_2 \neq 0$, and $\Delta v_3 = 0$. Therefore, $(\Delta v_1, \Delta v_2, \Delta v_3)$ can be in S_{F_2} only if $\Delta g_1 = \Delta g_2$. But if there is no particular mechanism to force Δg_1 and Δg_2 to be equal, the probability of $\Delta g_1 = \Delta g_2$ is zero. Hence for almost all faults with fault set F_1, the observed value does not hit S_{F_2}. Similarly, for almost all faults with fault set F_2, the observed value does not hit S_{F_1}. Therefore, from the probabilistic viewpoint, S_{F_1} is independent of S_{F_2}. The probability that $\Delta v_m \in S_{F_1} \cap S_{F_2}$ is zero.

Example 2. Let $\mathbb{K} = \mathbb{R}, b = 3, m = 2, F_1 = \{1\}, F_2 = \{2,3\}, D_{F_j} = \{\Delta g \mid \Delta g_k \neq 0 \text{ iff } k \in F_j\}$ $(j = 1, 2)$ and let $\varphi \colon \mathbb{R}^3 \to \mathbb{R}^2$ be defined by

$$
\begin{bmatrix} \Delta v_1 \\ \Delta v_2 \end{bmatrix} = \begin{bmatrix} 1 & 1 & 1 \\ 0 & 1 & -1 \end{bmatrix} \begin{bmatrix} \Delta g_1 \\ \Delta g_2 \\ \Delta g_3 \end{bmatrix}
$$

Notice that $S_{F_1} \subset S_{F_2}$. The probability that a faulty element value with fault set F_2 satisfies $\Delta g_2 = \Delta g_3$ is zero, if there is no particular constraint. Hence the probability that the observed value with fault set F_2 hits S_{F_1} is zero. Therefore, if an observed value is in S_{F_1}, then one can conclude that F_1 is a fault set even if there is a possibility (of zero probability) that F_2 is a fault set. In case F_2 is a fault set, the observed value hits $S_{F_2} \backslash S_{F_1}$ with probability 1. Therefore, one should use $S_{F_2} = S_{F_2} \backslash S_{F_1}$ instead of S_{F_2} for the test of F_2 being a fault set. $\square$

The above examples show that we need probability measure on the parameter space $\mathbb{K}^b$. In Example 1, we do not need to introduce any probability argument into the algorithm; the data do not hit the complicated set $S_{F_1} \cap S_{F_2}$ except for zero probability. On the other hand, we need to add a probabilistic argument to the algorithm in Example 2, and we have to modify the set S_F. Accordingly, the notion of testabilities should also be modified from a probabilistic view point.

PROBABILITY MEASURE

Let μ be the probability measure on $\mathfrak{D} = \cup_{F \in \mathcal{F}} D$, which gives the probability distribution of faulty element values. In principle, μ can be computed by considering a class $\mathcal{N}$ of large number of products of the same circuit and setting, for $X \subset \mathfrak{D}$

$$
\mu(X) \triangleq \frac{\{\# (N \in \mathcal{N} \mid \Delta g \in X\}}{\# \mathcal{N}}
$$

where # denotes the cardinality of a set. Therefore, $\mu(D_F)$ is the probability that F is the faulty set, while $\mu(ED_F)$ is the probability that F contains the faulty set. Though μ is computable in principle, it is required to test all element values $\Delta \mathbf{g}$ for large number of products. Therefore, it is practically impossible to compute numerical values of the measure, but we need only its existence and some of its properties, especially those concerning measure zero sets, which we will require as an assumption (see Assumption A below).

Measure zero sets of this probability measure are different from those of Lebesque measure. Recall that there is a natural measure on $\mathbb{K}^F$, the Lebesque measure denoted by m_F. Complicated measure theoretic results are not necessary here. One only needs to recall:

1. "Thin objects" such as lower dimensional subspaces are of Lebesque measure zero.
2. Any neighborhood of any point is of positive Lebesque measure. For instance, if $\mathbb{K}^F = \mathbb{R}^3$, then any plane, surface, line, and curve, and, of course, any point, is of Lebesque measure zero.

The μ-measure of these "thin objects" need not be zero, i.e., $m_F(X) = \mathbf{0}$ may not imply $\mu(X) = \mathbf{0}$.

Example 3.   Let $b = 3$, $\mathbb{K} = \mathbb{R}$, $\mathscr{F} = \{\{1\}, \{2\}, \{3\}, \{1, 2\}, \{2, 3\}, \{1, 3\}, \{1, 2, 3\}\}$ and $ED_F = \mathbb{K}^F$. Let $F = \{1, 2\}$ and $X = \mathbb{K}^{\{1\}}$. Then $m_F(X) = \mathbf{0}$, **but** $\mu(X) > 0$ if single branch faults with the first branch being faulty occur with positive probability. ☐

This example shows that "smaller" faults can cause thin objects with positive μ-measure. If $F' \subset F$, then $D_{F'} \subset \mathbb{K}^F$ is thin in $\mathbb{K}^F$, but $\mu(D_{F'})$ may be positive. Of course, there may be other kinds of thin objects with positive μ-measure. We will, however, assume that all thin objects with positive μ-measure are caused by "smaller" faults. We assume also that any neighborhood has a positive μ-measure.

Assumption A.

1. If $F \in \mathscr{F}$ and $X \subset \mathbb{K}^F$, then $m_F(X) = 0$ implies $\mu(X \cap D_F) = 0$.
2. If U is a neighborhood of $\mathbf{0}$ in ED_F, then $\mu(U \cup D_F) > 0$.

Note that $\mu(X)$ may be positive even if $m_F(X) = 0$. 2 is a weak assumption. It says that faults are not "discrete," e.g., Δg_k cannot always be 0 or 1. On the other hand, 1 is a very essential assumption which is not always satisfied. It depends on the set D_F. We will give examples in the next section.

Now suppose that

$$\Delta \mathbf{v_m} \in S_F \cup S_F$$

Then one cannot tell which is the fault set. Sometimes, however, the probability of F' being the fault set is zero provided that $\Delta v_m \in S_F$.

Definition

1. F' is *rare in F,* denoted by $F' < F$, if

$$\mu(\varphi^{-1}(SF') \cap D_F) = 0$$

2. $S_{F\mu} = S_F - \bigcup_{F' < F} S_{F'}.$

The meaning of this definition is clear from the following lemma.

Lemma 1. If F is the fault-set, then

$$\Delta v_m \in S_{F\mu}$$

with the probability 1:

$$\text{Prob}(\Delta v_m \in S_{F\mu} \mid \Delta g \in D_F) = 1$$

Proof.

$$\text{Prob}(\Delta v_m \notin S_{F\mu} \mid \Delta g \in D_F) = \frac{\mu(\varphi^{-1}(\bigcup_{F' < F} S_{F'}) \cap D_F)}{\mu(D_F)}$$

$$\leq \frac{\sum_{F' < F} \mu(\varphi^{-1}(S_{F'}) \cap D_F)}{\mu(D_F)}$$

$$= 0 \qquad \square$$

The lemma says that $S_{F\mu}$ contains the most important information in that Δv_m hits it almost surely if F is the fault-set, and Δv_m would not hit $S_{F\mu}$ if an F', $F' < F$, is the fault-set. Therefore, the fault location algorithm based on checking $\Delta v_m \in S_{F\mu}$ is the best one can do. We call this the *ideal method.*

Based upon the above arguments, one sees that the testability conditions should be modified to the following:

1. Given an observed value $\Delta v_m \in S$, Δv_m is said to *determine the fault uniquely* if there is unique $F \in \mathcal{F}$ such that $\Delta v_m \in S_{F\mu}$.
2. F_1 and F_2 are said to be *μ-independent* if $S_{F_1\mu}$ and $S_{F_2\mu}$ are disjoint.
3. $\mathcal{F}$ is said to be *testable* if μ-almost all Δv_m determine the fault uniquely.

Because the set $S_{F\mu}$ is more complicated that S_F, one would want to avoid the use of $S_{F\mu}$. At the first glance this seems to be possible if one starts the test of $\Delta \mathbf{v}_m \in S_F$ from the smallest F with respect to the relation $<$ ($S_{F\mu} = S_F$, since there is no $F' < F$), and proceeds to a larger F. When one checks $\Delta \mathbf{v}_m \in S_F$ for an F, one has already checked $\Delta \mathbf{v}_m \notin S_{F_1}$ for all smaller F', hence $\Delta \mathbf{v}_m \in S_F$ is equivalent to $\Delta \mathbf{v}_m \in S_{F\mu}$. However, this does not work because $<$ is *not* an order relation; hence "the smallest" and "the smaller" has no consistent meaning: There may be F and F' such that $F < F'$ and $F' < F$.

We will study the T_F method in a later section. This method is based on checking $\Delta \mathbf{v} \in T_F$, where T_F is the smallest linear subspace containing S_F. A geometric analysis of S_F and T_F shows that this is a good method and introduces an order relation in the family $\mathcal{F}$. This order relation makes it possible to avoid the use of $S_{F\mu}$ in the ideal method.

PERTURBATION OF PARAMETERS

In this section, we study the main examples more carefully. Recall that a parameter g_k corresponds to the admittance. The admittance may take

1. complex values,
2. real values, or
3. real values for some k and pure imaginary values for some k.

In the first and third cases, $\mathbb{K} = \mathbb{C}$, the set of complex numbers and in the second case $\mathbb{K} = \mathbb{R}$, the set of real numbers. In each case, let $\mathscr{D}_k$ be the set of all possible Δg_k's, i.e., the set of all possible perturbations of g_k and let

$$\mathscr{D} \triangleq \{\Delta g_k \in \mathbb{K}^b | \; \Delta g_k \in \mathscr{D}_k, k = 1, \ldots, b\}$$

Let

$$D \triangleq \{\Delta \mathbf{g} \in \mathscr{D} | \; \det (\mathbf{Y} + \Delta \mathbf{Y}) \neq 0\}$$

where $\mathbf{Y} + \Delta \mathbf{Y} = \mathbf{A}_i \{\mathbf{Y}_b + \Delta \mathbf{Y}_b\} \mathbf{A}_v^T$. The set D is obtained by removing the inessential values of $\Delta \mathbf{g}$ for which the node admittance matrix is singular. For a subset $F \in \mathcal{F}$, let

$$\mathscr{D}_F \triangleq \{\Delta \mathbf{g} \in \Delta | \; \Delta g_k \neq 0 \text{ iff } k \in F\}$$
$$D_F \triangleq \mathscr{D}_F \cap D$$

Now we will check whether Assumption A is satisfied for the cases 1, 2, and 3.

Case 1. $\mathbb{K} = \mathbb{C}$. Each Δg_k takes complex values without any constraint; therefore, $\mathscr{D}_k = \mathbb{C}$. Assumption A is satisfied in this setting.

Case 2. $\mathbb{K} = \mathbb{R}$. Each g_k takes only real values. There are neither capacitors nor inductors. Any fault is caused by parameter variations in the real numbers; stray capacitance and stray inductance are ignored. Some $g_k^{\text{nominal}} + \Delta g_k$ can take only nonnegative values and hence $\mathscr{D}_k$ is not necessarily the whole space $\mathbb{R}$ but an interval of $\mathbb{R}$. For instance, if the kth branch is a resistor with nominal value 1 (Ω), then $\mathscr{D}_k = \{\Delta g_k \in \mathbb{R} \mid -1 \le \Delta g_k\}$. Assumption A would not be satisfied if the probability that $\Delta g_k = -1$ ("open circuit") is positive; a single point $\{-1\} \in \mathscr{D}_k$ has a positive measure. The difficulty concerning the "open circuit" would be removed by extending the set $\mathscr{F}$. For instance, if Δg_1, Δg_2, Δg_3, Δg_4, and Δg_5 are nonzero where Δg_1 and Δg_4 correspond to "open circuit," and Δg_2 and Δg_3 to the usual "soft" fault, then the fault set is denoted by

$$F = \{ (1, O), (2, U), (3, U), (4, O) \}.$$

where O and U denote the "open fault" and the "usual soft" fault, respectively. The dimension of D_F is 2, though F is a 4-branch fault. One could extend the whole theory by considering all such F's by using affine subspaces and affine maps instead of the linear ones.

The difficulty in Case 3 is greater.

Case 3. $\mathbb{K} = \mathbb{C}$. Some branches are inductors or capacitors. Δg_k takes *pure imaginary values* on such a branch. Some branches are resistors, and Δg_k takes real values. Therefore,

$$\mathscr{D}_k = \mathbb{R} \text{ or } \mathscr{D}_k = \mathbf{j}\mathbb{R}$$

In this setting, Assumption A is definitely not satisfied, since both $\mathbb{R}$ and $\mathbf{j}\mathbb{R}$ are "thin objects" in $\mathbb{C}$ (1-dimensional set in the 2-dimensional space $\mathbb{C}$). Moreover, the dimension of S_F may be less than that of T_F; hence the linear method is not as powerful as the nonlinear method in this setting.

GEOMETRY OF S_F AND T_F

Let us consider the main example:

$$(\Delta g_1, \ldots, \Delta g_b) \rightarrow \Delta \mathbf{v}_m = (\mathbf{A}_i \mathbf{Y}_b^T \mathbf{A}_v^{-1})_{mn}^{-1}$$

Define

$$T_F \triangleq \{ -\mathbf{Z}_{mn} \mathbf{A}_i \mathbf{x} \mid \mathbf{x} \in \mathbb{K}^F \}$$

where $\mathbb{K}^F$ is defined by (4). We will prove that this set is the smallest linear subspace containing S_F. This set turns out to be the *tangent space* of S_F. Circuit theoretically, T_F is the space of all possible values of $\Delta\mathbf{v_m}$ when each of the faulty branches is replaced with a norator. The idea of the linear method is to replace the set S_F with the set T_F. We also need a linear analogy of the set $S_{F\mu}$.

Definition.   A set of branches F' is said to be *linearly rare in F,* denoted by $F' \lhd F$, if $\dim(T_F \cap T_{F'}) < \dim T_F$.

Notice that μ-measure is not used in the definition. Recall that the definition of "rare" is based on the μ-measure. Hence "linearly rare" and "rare" have no direct relationship. However, μ-measure zero sets are related to geometric measure zero set by Assumption A; "linearly rare" turns out to be a good substitution of the "rare."

Definition. $\hat{T}_F \triangleq T_F - \bigcup_{F' \lhd F} T_{F'}$.

The subset $\hat{T}_F$ is obtained by deleting "inessential" subsets from T_F. It turns out, under a mild technical condition, that S_F is a *neighborhood* of the origin in $\hat{T}_F$, even though S_F may not be a neighborhood in T_F.

Assumption B1.   The nominal value $\Delta g_k = 0$ belongs to the interior of the set $\mathcal{D}_k$ for each k.

Assumption B2.   At the nominal value $\Delta\mathbf{g} = \mathbf{0}$, every branch voltage is nonzero.

Theorem 1.   The set S_F is a neighborhood of $\mathbf{0}$ in $\hat{T}_F$.

The theorem says that S_F has the same dimension as that of T_F, and this implies that T_F is the smallest linear subspace containing S_F.

Proof of the theorem. Let

$$ES_F = \varphi_F(ED_F)$$

First we prove:

Proposition 1: The set ES_F is a neighborhood of $\mathbf{0}$ in T_F.

To prove this, we need:

Lemma 2.   Rank $\mathbf{D}\varphi_F(\mathbf{0}) = \dim T_F$, where $\mathbf{D}\varphi_F(\mathbf{0})$ denotes the derivative of $\varphi_F \triangleq \varphi|\mathbb{K}^F$ at $\mathbf{0}$.

Proof of Lemma 2. First observe that

$$
\begin{aligned}
\mathbf{\Delta v} &= -\mathbf{Z} \mathbf{A}_i (\mathbf{\Delta Y}_b \mathbf{A}_v^T (\mathbf{v} + \mathbf{\Delta v})) \\
\varphi_F(\mathbf{\Delta g}) &= -\mathbf{Z}_{mn} \mathbf{A}_i \mathbf{\Delta Y}_b (\mathbf{\Delta g}) \mathbf{A}_v^T (\mathbf{v} + \varphi(\mathbf{\Delta g}))
\end{aligned}
\tag{2-1}
$$

Differentiating (2-1), one has, for $\mathbf{x} \in \mathbb{K}^F$

$$
\begin{aligned}
\mathbf{D}\varphi_F(\mathbf{\Delta g})\mathbf{x} &= -\mathbf{Z}_{mn} \mathbf{A}_i \, (\mathbf{D}\mathbf{\Delta Y}_b(\mathbf{\Delta g}))\mathbf{x} \mathbf{A}_v^T (\mathbf{v} + \varphi(\mathbf{\Delta g})) \\
&= -\mathbf{Z}_{mn} \mathbf{A}_i \mathbf{\Delta Y}_b(\mathbf{\Delta g}) \mathbf{A}_v^T (\mathbf{v} + (\mathbf{D}\varphi \, (\mathbf{\Delta g}))\, \mathbf{x})
\end{aligned}
$$

At $\mathbf{\Delta g} = \mathbf{0}$, one has

$$
\mathbf{\Delta Y}_b(\mathbf{0}) = \mathbf{0}, \ \varphi(\mathbf{0}) = \mathbf{0}
$$
$$
(\mathbf{D}\mathbf{\Delta Y}_b \, (\mathbf{0}))\mathbf{x} = \mathrm{diag}(x_1, \ldots, x_b)
$$

Therefore,

$$
(\mathbf{D}\varphi_F \, (\mathbf{0}))\mathbf{x} = -\mathbf{Z}_{mn} \mathbf{A}_i \, \mathrm{diag}(x_1, \ldots, x_b) \mathbf{A}_v^T \mathbf{v}
$$

Assumption B2 implies that every element of $A_v^T \mathbf{v}$ is nonzero. Therefore,

$$
\begin{aligned}
\{\mathbf{D}\varphi_F \, (\mathbf{0})\mathbf{x} \mid \mathbf{x} \in \mathbb{K}^F\} &= \{-\mathbf{Z}_{mn} \mathbf{A}_i \, \mathrm{diag}(x_1, \ldots, x_b) \mathbf{A}_v^T \mathbf{v} \mid \mathbf{x} \in \mathbb{K}^F\} \\
&= \{-\mathbf{Z}_{mn} \mathbf{A}_i \, (x v_{b_1}, \ldots, x_b v_{b_b}) \mid \mathbf{x} \in \mathbb{K}^F\} \\
&= \{-\mathbf{Z}_{mn} \mathbf{A}_i \mathbf{x} \mid \mathbf{x} \in \mathbb{K}^F\} = T_F
\end{aligned}
$$

where $v_{b_1}, \ldots, v_{b_b}$ are the branch voltages. This implies the desired statement.

Remarks:

1. note that $\mathbf{D}\mathbf{\Delta Y}_b(\mathbf{\Delta g})$ is the derivative of the *matrix valued map* $\mathbf{\Delta Y}_b(\mathbf{\Delta g})$ with respect to $\mathbf{\Delta g}$. Therefore, $(\mathbf{D}\mathbf{\Delta Y}_b(\mathbf{\Delta g}))\mathbf{x}$ is a matrix.
2. it is clear from the above argument that T_F is the tangent space of S_F at $\mathbf{\Delta g} = \mathbf{0}$.

Let

$$
K_F \triangleq \mathrm{Ker} \ \mathbf{D}\varphi_F(\mathbf{0}) = \{\mathbf{x} \in \mathbb{K}^F \mid \mathbf{D}\varphi_F \, (\mathbf{0}) \, \mathbf{x} = \mathbf{0}\}
$$

Lemma 3: φ_F is locally C^1-equivalent to a projection, i.e.:

1. There is a (nonlinear) coordinate system $\mathbf{\Psi}$ on a neighborhood U of $\mathbf{0}$ in ED_F, i.e.,

    a. $\Psi\colon U \to T_F \times \mathbb{K}^F$ is C^1

    b. Ψ is invertible and the inverse is also C^1

2. With respect to this coordinate system φ_F is a projection: $T_F \times K_F \to T_F$, i.e., the following diagram commutes:

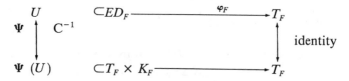

Proof. Let $\pi\colon \mathbb{K}^F \to K_F$ be the orthogonal projection and let $\Psi(x) \overset{\triangle}{=} (\varphi_F(x), \pi x)$ for $x \in \mathbb{K}^F$. Clearly, $\mathbf{D}\Psi(0)$ is an injection. Lemma 2 implies that

$$\dim T_F + \dim K_F$$
$$= \dim (\mathrm{Im}\, \mathbf{D}\varphi_F(0)) + \dim (\mathrm{Ker}\, \mathbf{D}\varphi_F(0)) = \dim \mathbb{K}^F$$

Therefore, $\dim (T_F \times K_F) = \dim \mathbb{K}^F$ and $\mathbf{D}\Psi(0)$ is an invertible linear map. The Inverse Function Theorem gives the result. $\square$

Proof of Proposition 1. Since $\varphi_F(U)$ is the image of the neighborhood $\varphi(U)$ under the projection map, and since ES_F contains $\varphi_F(U)$, one sees that the statement holds. $\square$

Proof of Theorem 1: For each $k \in F$, let $F_k \overset{\triangle}{=} F - \{k\}$. We decompose F into two disjoint subsets:

$$F_1 \overset{\triangle}{=} \{k \in F \mid F_k \lhd F\}$$
$$F_1 \overset{\triangle}{=} \{k \in F \mid F_k \ntriangleleft F\}$$

For $k \in F_1$, the set $\varphi_F(ED_{F_k})$ is contained in T_{F_k} with $\dim T_{F_k} > \dim T_F$ and T_{F_k} is disjoint from $\hat{T}_F$. This implies

$$
\begin{aligned}
S_F \cap \hat{T}_F &= \varphi_F(D_F) \cap \hat{T}_F \\
&= \varphi_F\left(HD_F - \bigcup_{k \in F_1} ED_{F_k}\right) \cap \hat{T}_F \\
&\supset \left(\varphi_F(HD_F) - \bigcup_{k \in F_1} \varphi_F(ED_{F_k})\right) \cap \hat{T}_F \\
&= \varphi_F(HD_F) \cap \hat{T}_F
\end{aligned}
$$

Therefore, it is sufficient to show that $\varphi_F(HD_F)$ is a neighborhood of 0 in T_F. To prove this, we suppose the contrary and deduce a contradiction. For each $k \in F_2$, $\dim T_F = \dim T_{F_k} = \mathrm{Rank}\, \mathbf{D}\varphi_{F_k}(0)$. Since $\mathrm{Rank}\, D\varphi_{F_k}(x)$ is continuous in x, one sees that there is a neighborhood U' of 0 in ED_F such that $U' \subset U$ and $U' \cap ED_{F_k} \subset W_k$ for each $k \in F_2$. By the above hypothesis, $\varphi_F (U' -$

$\bigcup_{k \in F_2} ED_{F_k}$), which is equal to $\varphi_F (U' \cap HD_F)$, is not a neighborhood of $\mathbf{0}$ in T_F. On the other hand, $\varphi_F(U')$ is a neighborhood of $\mathbf{0}$ in T_F since $\varphi_F(U')$ is the projected image of the neighborhood $\Psi(U')$ of $\mathbf{0}$ in $T_F \times K_F$. Therefore, there is at least one point $\mathbf{y}$ in $\varphi_F(U') - \bigcup_{k. F_2} ED_{F_k}$). Choose a point $\mathbf{x} \in U'$ such that $\varphi_F(\mathbf{x}) = \mathbf{y}$. Since φ_F is locally C^1-equivalent to the projection map, the set $\varphi_F^{-1}(\mathbf{y}) \cap U'$ is a submanifold ("surface") in U' and Ker $\mathbf{D}\varphi_F(\mathbf{x})$ it is tangent to it. Since

$$\varphi_F^{-1}(\mathbf{y}) \cap U' \subset \bigcup_{k \in F_2} ED_{F_k}$$

one has

$$\text{Ker } \mathbf{D}\varphi_F(\mathbf{x}) \subset \bigcup_{k \in F_2} \mathbb{K}^{F_k}$$

It is clear that if a linear subspace is contained in a union of linear space, then it is contained in one of these linear space. Hence, Ker $\mathbf{D}\varphi_F(\mathbf{x})$ is contained in $\mathbb{K}^{F_k}$. This implies that

$$\text{Ker } \mathbf{D}\varphi_F(\mathbf{x}) = \text{Ker } \mathbf{D}\varphi_{F_k}(\mathbf{x})$$

Now recall the well-known dimension formula:

$$\dim\big(\text{Dom } \mathbf{D}\varphi_F(\mathbf{x})\big) = \dim\big(\text{Im } \mathbf{D}\varphi_F(\mathbf{x})\big) + \dim\big(\text{Ker } \mathbf{D}\varphi_F(\mathbf{x})\big) \qquad (2\text{-}2)$$

$$\dim\big(\text{Dom } \mathbf{D}\varphi_{F_k}(\mathbf{x})\big) = \dim\big(\text{Im } \mathbf{D}\varphi_{F_k}(\mathbf{x})\big) + \dim\big(\text{Ker } \mathbf{D}\varphi_{F_k}(\mathbf{x})\big) \qquad (2\text{-}3)$$

But since

$$\dim\big(\text{Im } \mathbf{D}\varphi_{F_k}(\mathbf{x})\big) = \dim T_k = \dim\big(\text{Im } \mathbf{D}\varphi_F(\mathbf{x})\big)$$

and since

$$\text{Ker } \mathbf{D}\varphi_F(\mathbf{x}) = \text{Ker } \mathbf{D}\varphi_{F_k}(\mathbf{x})$$

one sees that the right-hand sides of (2-2) and (2-3) must coincide. On the other hand, the left-hand side of (2-3) is smaller than that of (2-2) by 1, a contradiction. $\square$

Now we study other examples. In general, T_F does not necessarily have the same dimension as that of S_F.

Example 4. Let $\mathbb{K} = \mathbb{R}$, $b = 2$, $m = 3$, $F = \{1\}$, $D_F = \mathbb{R}^{\{1\}} = \{(\Delta g_1, 0) \mid \Delta g_1 \in \mathbb{R}\}$. Suppose that $\varphi: \mathbb{R}^2 \to \mathbb{R}^3$ is defined by

$$\varphi: (\Delta g_1, \Delta g_2) \to (\Delta v_1, \Delta v_2, \Delta v_3)$$
$$\Delta v_1 = \Delta g_2 + \cos \Delta g_1$$
$$\Delta v_2 = \Delta g_2 + \sin \Delta g_1$$
$$\Delta v_3 = -\sin \Delta g_1$$

Let $\varphi_F = \varphi | D_F$. Then

$$\varphi_F: \mathbb{R} \to \mathbb{R}^3$$
$$s \to (\cos s, \sin s, -\sin s) \qquad (s \triangleq \Delta g_1)$$

The derivative of φ_F are

$$\left. \frac{d\varphi}{ds} \right|_{s=0} = (0, 1, -1)$$

$$\left. \frac{d^2\varphi}{ds^2} \right|_{s=0} = (-1, 0, 0)$$

$$\left. \frac{d^3\varphi}{ds^3} \right|_{s=0} = (0, -1, 1)$$

etc.

Since T_F is a linear subspace which contains S_F, T_F contains vectors $(0, 1, -1)$, $(-1, 0, 0)$, $(0, -1, 1)$, etc. Conversely, any linear subspace containing these vectors contains S_F by the Taylor expansion formula. Therefore, T_F is the linear subspace spanned by vectors $(0, 1, -1)$ and $(1, 0, 0)$:

$$T_F = \{(\Delta v_1, \Delta v_2, \Delta v_3) \in \mathbb{R}^3 \mid \Delta v_2 + \Delta v_3 = 0\}$$

In general, T_F contains the images of derivatives

$$\mathbf{D}\varphi_F(0), \mathbf{D}^2\varphi_F(0), \ldots, \mathbf{D}^n\varphi_F(0), \ldots$$

since $T_F \supset S_F = $ the image of the mapping φ_F. Note that the image of $\mathbf{D}^k\varphi_F(0)$ is spanned by the vectors

$$\left. \frac{\partial^k \varphi_F}{\partial \Delta g_{j_1} \Delta g_{j_2}, \ldots, \Delta g_{j_k}} \right|_{\Delta g = 0}, \quad j_1, \ldots, j_k \in F$$

Conversely, if L is the linear subspace spanned by the images of these derivatives, then L contains S_F (recall the Taylor expansion formula).

Example 5. Consider the circuit of the main example. Suppose, however, that the node currents of accessible branches can be varied freely. Then we can observe the matrix $(\mathbf{A}_i \mathbf{Y}_b \mathbf{A}_v^T)_{mn}^{-1}$ itself. Since an $m \times m$ matrix is identified with a point in $\mathbb{K}^{m^2}$, the dimension of the observable space is m^2 and

$$\varphi: \mathbb{K}^b \to \mathbb{K}^{m^2}$$

Furthermore,

$$
\begin{aligned}
\mathbf{D}\varphi(0)\mathbf{x} &= -\mathbf{Z}\mathbf{A}_i(\operatorname{diag} \mathbf{x})\mathbf{A}_v^T\mathbf{Z} \\
\mathbf{D}^2\varphi(0)\mathbf{x}_1\mathbf{x}_2 &= \mathbf{Z}\mathbf{A}_i(\operatorname{diag} \mathbf{x}_2)\mathbf{A}_v^T\mathbf{Z}\mathbf{A}_i(\operatorname{diag} \mathbf{x}_1)\mathbf{A}_v^T\mathbf{Z} \\
&+ \mathbf{Z}\mathbf{A}_i(\operatorname{diag} \mathbf{x}_1)\mathbf{A}_v^T\mathbf{Z}\mathbf{A}_i(\operatorname{diag} \mathbf{x}_2)\mathbf{A}_v^T\mathbf{Z}
\end{aligned}
$$

etc.

From these formula, one can conclude that $\dim S_F = \dim T_F$ for single branch fault, and that $\dim S_F$ can be *smaller* than $\dim T_F$ for two or more branch faults.

THE LINEAR METHOD IS AS POWERFUL AS THE NONLINEAR METHOD

In this section, we consider the main example and prove that the linear method is as powerful as the nonlinear one.

Definition. $q_F \triangleq \dim T_F$

The quantity q_F plays a key role in our algorithm. It should be noted that $\#F < F'$ (# denotes the cardinality) does not necessarily imply $q_F < q_{F'}$, as alluded to by the following example.

Example 6. Consider the circuit of Fig. 2–2. Let $F \triangleq \{1, 2\}$ and $F' \triangleq \{3, 4, 5\}$. Since

$$
\mathbf{A}_i = \begin{bmatrix} -1 & 1 & \cdot & \cdot & \cdot \\ 1 & \cdot & 1 & 1 & 1 \end{bmatrix}
$$

one sees that

$$
\{\mathbf{A}_i\mathbf{x} \mid \mathbf{x} \in \mathbb{R}^F\} = \begin{bmatrix} -x_1 + x_2 \\ x_1 \end{bmatrix} \;\Big|\; x_1, x_2 \in \mathbb{R}
$$

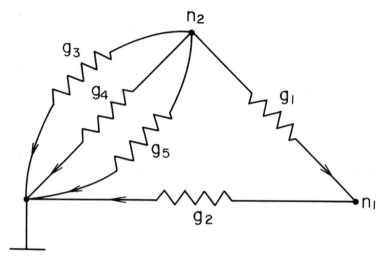

Figure 2–2   *An example where* $q_F = 2$ *while* $q_F = 1$.

$$\{A_i x \mid x \in \mathbb{R}^{F'}\} = \left\{ \begin{bmatrix} \\ x_3 + x_4 + x_5 \end{bmatrix} \middle| \; x_3, x_4, x_5 \in \mathbb{R} \right\}$$

If all nodes are accessible, then $q_F = 2$, while $q_F = 1$.   □

Recall that $\mathscr{F}$ is the family of all possible fault-sets of branches and define

$$\mathscr{F}^k \triangleq \{F \in \mathscr{F} \mid q_F = k\}$$

For each $\mathscr{F}$ define the equivalence relation

$$F \sim F', F, F' \in \mathscr{F}^k \; q \text{ iff }_{F \cup F'} = k$$

and decompose $\mathscr{F}^k$ according to the above equivalence class relation:

$$\mathscr{F}^k = \mathscr{F}^k_1 \cup \cdots \cup \mathscr{F}^k_{m_k}$$

Each $\mathscr{F}^k_j$ is called a T_F-equivalence class for $\mathscr{F}^k$.

Remark. Observe that

$$q_{F \cup F'} = k \text{ iff } T_F = T_F$$

i.e., F and F' belong to the same equivalence class if and only if their associated linear space T_F and T_F coincide. One of our main results (Theorem 2) tells us that, given the information Δv_m, there is no method of distinguishing F from F'. This, in turn, implies that there is no other decomposition of $\mathscr{F}$ finer than T_F-equivalence class decomposition. Therefore, the decomposition of $\mathscr{F}$ according to the T_F-equivalence class is the best one can do.

The Algorithm.
Step 1: Compute q_F for each $F \in \mathscr{F}$.
Step 2: Decompose $\mathscr{F}$ as

$$\mathscr{F} = \mathscr{F}^1 \cup \cdots \cup \mathscr{F}^p$$
$$p \triangleq \max_{F \in \mathscr{F}} q_F$$

and construct the T_F-equivalence class table:

q_F	T_F-equivalence class
0	$\mathscr{F}^0_1, \ldots, \mathscr{F}^0_{m_0}$
1	$\mathscr{F}^1_1, \ldots, \mathscr{F}^1_{m_1}$
2	$\mathscr{F}^2_1, \ldots, \mathscr{F}^1_{m_2}$
.	.
.	.
.	.
p	$\mathscr{F}^p_1, \ldots, \mathscr{F}^p_{m_p}$

Step 3: Set $k = 0$.
Step 4: For $j = 1, \ldots, m_k$, pick any $F \in \mathscr{F}^k_j$ and check if

$$\Delta v_m \in T_F \tag{*}$$

holds. If (*) holds, then, by definition, it holds for every $F' \in \mathscr{F}^k_j$. Let us denote this by

$$\Delta v_m \dashv \mathscr{F}^k_j \tag{**}$$

1. If (**) holds for some j, then there will be no other j' with $\Delta v_m \dashv \mathscr{F}^k_{j'}$: Conclude that at least one F in $\mathscr{F}^k_j$ is faulty. Terminate the algorithm.
1a. If this particular $\mathscr{F}^k_j$ is a singleton, i.e., $\mathscr{F}^k_j = \{F\}$, then conclude that F is faulty. Terminate the algorithm.
2. If

$$\Delta v_m \not\dashv \mathscr{F}^k_j$$

for any $j = 1, \ldots, m_k$, then go to Step 5.

Step 5: Set $k \to k+1$ and go to Step 4.

Remark. The algorithm terminates at the smallest k such that $\Delta v_m \not\in \mathscr{F}_j^k$ for some j. One does not have to check (*) for other sets.

Lemma 4. $\hat{T}_F \neq \hat{T}_{F'}$ iff $F \lhd F'$ and $F' \lhd F$, where $\hat{T}_F$ is defined by $\hat{T}_F \overset{\triangle}{=} T_F - \bigcup_{F \lhd F} T_{F'}$.

Proof. If $\hat{T}_F = \hat{T}_{F'}$ then $T_F = T_{F'}$; hence $F \lhd F'$ and $F' \lhd F$. Conversely, if $F \not\lhd F'$ and $F' \not\lhd F$, then $\dim T_F = \dim (T_F \cap T_{F'}) = \dim T_{F'}$, and therefore, $T_F = T_{F'}$, which implies $\hat{T}_F = \hat{T}_F{'}$ □

Corollary. $\hat{T}_F \neq \hat{T}_{F'}$ iff $\hat{T}_F \cap \hat{T}_{F'} = \phi$.

Lemma 5.   Let L be a linear subspace of T_F such that $\dim L < \dim T_F$. Then $m_F\big(\varphi_F^{-1}(L)\big) = 0$.

Proof. Let L^+ be the orthogonal complement of L in T_F and let $\tau: T_F \to L^+$ be the orthogonal projection. Then, $L = \operatorname{Ker} \tau$ and $\varphi_F^{-1}(L) = (\tau \circ \varphi_F)^{-1}(0)$ which is of Lebesque measure zero as the zero set of the polynomial map $\tau \circ \varphi_F$. □

The following says that if F' is linearly rare in F, then it is actually rare in F.

Proposition 2. $F' \lhd F$ implies $F' < F$.

Proof. If $F' \lhd F$, then $\dim (T_F \cap T_{F'}) < \dim T_F$. Lemma 5 implies $m_F(\varphi_F^{-1}(S_{F'})) = 0$. Since

$$\varphi_F^{-1}(S_{F'}) \cap D_F \subset \varphi_F^{-1}(S_{F'}) \subset \varphi_F^{-1}(T_{F'})$$

one has

$$m_F\left(\varphi_F^{-1}(S_{F'}) \cap D_F\right) = 0$$

Recall that we have assumed

$$m_F(X) = 0 \text{ implies } \mu(X \cap D_F) = 0$$

It implies

$$\mu(\varphi_F^{-1}(S_{F'}) \cap D_F) = 0$$

Hence, $F' < F$. □

Proposition 3. $T_F = T_{F'}$ implies $F < F'$ and $F' < F$

Proof. By Theorem 1, one can take a neighborhood of **0** in T_F such that

$$S_{F'} \supset \hat{T}_F \cap U$$

Then

$$T_F \cap S_{F'} \supset T_F \cap \hat{T}_F \cap U$$
$$= T_F \cap U - \bigcup_{F^* \lhd F} T_{F^*}$$

and therefore

$$\varphi_F^{-1}(S_{F'}) = \varphi_F^{-1}(T_F \cap S_{F'}) \supset \varphi_F^{-1}(T_F \cap U) - \bigcup_{F^* \lhd F} \varphi_F^{-1}(T_{F^*})$$

Note that $T_F \cap U$ is a neighborhood of **0** in T_F, and that $\varphi_F^{-1}(T_F \cap U)$ is a neighborhood of **0** in ED_F by the continuity of φ_F. Assumption A (ii) implies

$$\mu\left(\varphi_F^{-1}(T_F \cap U) \cap D_F\right) > 0$$

On the other hand, Lemma 4 implies

$$m_F\left(\varphi_F^{-1}(T_{F^*})\right) = 0 \quad \text{for } F^* \lhd F$$

It follows from Assumption A (i) that

$$\mu(\varphi_F^{-1}(T_F) \cap D) = 0$$

so that

$$\mu(\varphi_F^{-1}(S_F) \cap D_F)$$

$$\geq \mu\left(\varphi_F^{-1}(T_F \cap U) \cap D_F\right) - \Sigma_{F^* \lhd F} \, \mu\left(\varphi_F^{-1}(T_{F^*}) \cap D_F\right) > 0$$

Therefore, $F' \not< F$. Similarly, $F \not< F'$. $\square$

Corollary. $T_F = T_{F'}$ implies $S_{F\mu} \cap S_{F'\mu} \neq \phi$.

Proof. Suppose that $T_F = T_{F'}$ but $S_{F\mu} \cap S_{F'\mu} \neq \phi$. Since

$$S_{F\mu} = S_F - \bigcup_{F^* < F} S_{F^*}$$
$$S_{F'\mu} = S_{F'} - \bigcup_{F^* < F'} S_{F^*}$$

and since $S_F \cap S_{F'}$ is a neighborhood of **0** in $\hat{T}_F (= \hat{T}_{F'})$, one sees that

$$(\bigcup_{F^* < F} S_{F^*}) \ \cup \ (\bigcup_{F^* < F'} S_{F^*})$$

is a neighborhood of **0** in $\hat{T}_F$. Hence

$$(\bigcup_{F^* < F} T_{F^*}) \ \cup \ (\bigcup_{F^* < F'} T_{F^*}) \ = \ T_F$$

Since the finite union of lower-dimensional linear subspaces cannot be the whole space, $T_{F^*} \ = \ T_F (= T_{F'})$ for at least one F^* with $F^* < F$ or $F^* < F'$. By the Proposition 3, this is a contradiction. $\qquad\square$

Now observe that, given F and F', the following four cases are possible.

1. $T_{F'} \subsetneqq T_F$: In this case, $F' \lhd F$; hence $F' < F$.
2. $T_{F'} \ = \ T_F$: In this case, $S_{F_\mu} \cap S_{F'_\mu} \neq \phi$. The set F' is indistinguishable from F even by the ideal method unless $\Delta \mathbf{v}_m \not\in S_{F_\mu} \cap S_{F'_\mu}$.
3. $T_F \cap T_{F'} \subsetneqq T_F$ and $T_F \cap T_{F'} \subsetneqq T_{F'}$: In this case, $F \lhd F'$ and $F' \lhd F$ so that $F < F'$ and $F' < F$.
4. $T_F \subsetneqq T_{F'}$: In this case $F \lhd F'$; hence $F < F'$.

The T_F-equivalence class algorithm is an implementation of the above observation. Finally, note that in 1, 3, and 4 above, $S_{F_\mu} \cap S_{F'_\mu} \ = \ \phi$. This leads to our final goal.

Theorem 2.   The T_F-equivalence class algorithm is as powerful as the ideal method with probability 1 in the sense that $\hat{T}_F \ = \ T_{F'}$ iff $S_{F_\mu} \cap S_{F'_\mu} \neq \phi$.

As a corollary of Theorem 2, let us compare the ideal method and the T_F-equivalence class algorithm in terms of the testability conditions. The "linear" version of the testability conditions are as follows:

1. Given an observed value $\Delta \mathbf{v}_m \in S$, $\Delta \mathbf{v}_m$ is said to *linearly determine* the fault uniquely if there is unique $F \in \mathscr{F}$ such that $\Delta \mathbf{v}_m \in \hat{T}_F$.
2. F_1 and F_2 are said to be *linearly independent* if $\hat{T}_{F_1}$ and $\hat{T}_{F_2}$ are disjoint.
3. $\mathscr{F}$ is said to be *linearly testable* if μ-almost all $\Delta \mathbf{v}_m$ linearly determine the fault uniquely.

Corollary. F_1 and F_2 in $\mathscr{F}$ are μ-independent iff they are linearly independent. $\mathscr{F}$ is testable iff $\mathscr{F}$ is linearly testable.

Remark. There may be a $\Delta \mathbf{v}_m \in S$ which determines the fault uniquely but not linearly, as the following example shows:

Example 7. Consider a linear circuit which consists only of resistors: $\mathbb{K} = \mathbb{R}$. Suppose that the branch 1 and branch 2 are as in Fig 2–3. Then $F_1 = \{1\}$, $F_2 = \{2\}$, and $F_3 = \{1,2\}$ and all belong to the same T_F-equivalence class; hence they are not independent. However, if $\Delta v_1 < 1 \ (V)$, then both branch 1 and branch 2 must be faulty: The ideal method states that F_3 is the fault-set.

The above example depends on the fact that D_F is not $\mathbb{R}$ but an interval of $\mathbb{R}$. If $D_F = \mathbb{R}$, it would be more difficult to give an example. In case of $\mathbb{K} = \mathbb{C}$, we do not know any example.

We will close this chapter with a more realistic circuit example.

Example 8. Consider the notch filter of Fig. 2–4 where n_1, n_2 and n_3 are accessible while other nodes are inaccessible. The equivalent circuit for an operational amplifier is given by Fig. 2–5. An artificial branch c and an artificial node n_4 are introduced to represent an operational amplifier in terms of voltage controlled current sources. According to the notation of [7], the branch a with the symbol μ indicates that this is a controlled current source whose value is equal to $\mu(v_{n1} - v_{n2})$. Other symbols have similar meaning. This is only technical. One can allow controlled voltage sources if (φ) is modified in an appropriate manner. The current graph and the voltage graph of the cirucit are given by Fig. 2–6 and Fig. 2–7, respectively. We assume that faults in operational amps can come only from branches 9 and 10, which is a reasonable assumption if one looks at Fig. 2–5. Table 2–1 gives the T_F-equivalence class table *up to k = 2*, that is, up to cases where at most two branches can be simultaneously faulty. It was obtained via the singular value decomposition of matrices [8]. If we assume that at most two branches can be faulty simultaneously, then Table 1 is com-

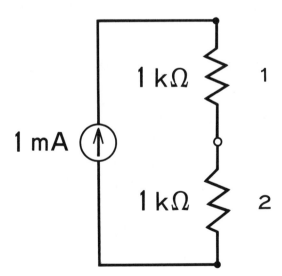

Figure 2–3 *An example where* $\Delta V_m \in S$ *determines a fault uniquely but not linearly.*

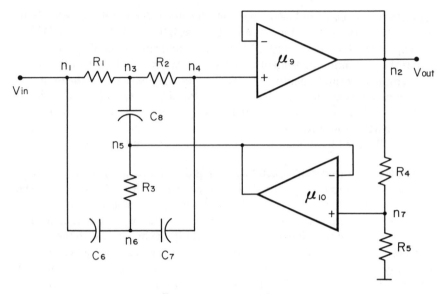

Figure 2–4   A notch filter.

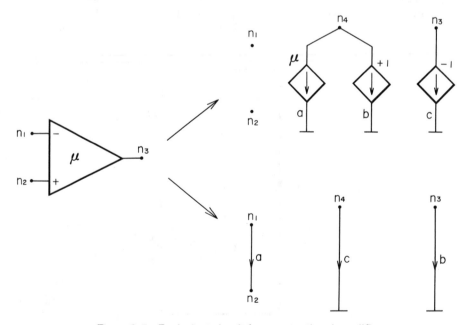

Figure 2–5   Equivalent circuit for an operational amplifier.

plete. It shows that the branches are nicely decomposed into 30 different equivalence classes out of $_1C_{10} + {}_2C_{10} = 55$ possible faulty sets. Observe that the 21 equivalence classes other than $\mathfrak{F}_4^1$, $\mathfrak{F}_3^2$, $\mathfrak{F}_9^2$, $\mathfrak{F}_{11}^2$, $\mathfrak{F}_{13}^2$ $\mathfrak{F}_{14}^2$, $\mathfrak{F}_{16}^2$, $\mathfrak{F}_{17}^2$, and $\mathfrak{F}_{18}^2$ are singleton and hence those 21 faulty sets can be identified *uniquely*. Let us explain in more detail.

Let the nominal values be

$$R_1 = 10\ M\Omega, \quad R_2 = 10\ M\Omega, \quad R_3 = 5M\Omega, \quad R_4 = 20\ K\Omega, \quad R_5 = 30\ K\Omega,$$
$$C_6 = 270\,pF, \quad C_7 = 270\,pF, \quad C_8 = 540pF, \quad m_9 = 10000, \quad \mu_{10} = 10000.$$

If one applies the current source of $1\mu A$ with frequency 1 KHz to node n_1, then the voltages at the accessible nodes are:

$$\mathbf{v_m} = \begin{bmatrix} 0.6239486D + 1 & -0.2216683D + 00 \\ 0.6204239D + 1 & 0.3657168D + 00 \\ 0.3722173D + 1 & 0.7204254D - 01 \end{bmatrix} \begin{matrix} n_1 \\ n_2 \\ n_3 \end{matrix}$$

Re   Im   node

where Re and Im denote the real part and imaginary part, respectively, D denotes that the computation was done with double precision, and the two digit number after D stands for the power of 10, for example,

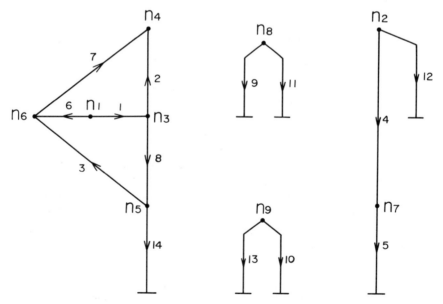

Figure 2–6   *Current graph of the circuit.*

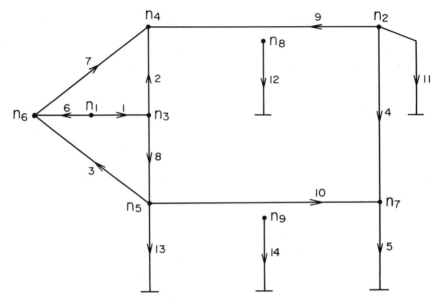

Figure 2–7 *Voltage graph of the circuit.*

$0.6239486D + 01 = 0.6239486 \times 10^{+1}$. Now if one perturbes C_7 from $270\,pF$ to $200\,pF$, then $\Delta\mathbf{v}_m$ is given by

$$\Delta\mathbf{v}_m = \begin{bmatrix} \text{Re} & \text{Im} & \text{node} \\ -0.6373902D - 02 & 0.4239953D - 01 & n_1 \\ -0.1568719D - 01 & 0.9048585D - 01 & n_2 \\ -0.8702616D - 02 & 0.5442337D - 01 & n_3 \end{bmatrix}$$

Table 2–2 gives necessary information for checking equation (*). The second column gives the singular values for $-\mathbf{Z}_{mn}\,\mathbf{A}_i \mid \mathbb{K}^F$ and the last column gives the vector $\mathbf{U}^*\,\Delta\mathbf{v}_m$, where $\mathbf{U}$ is a unitary matrix associated with the singular value decomposition and * denotes the adjoint. The method described in [1] says that $\Delta\mathbf{v}_m \in T_F$ *if and only if* the zero and nonzero patterns of the singular values coincide with those of $\mathbf{U}^*\Delta\mathbf{v}_m$. Since $\mathfrak{F}_6^1$ is the only one with this property[1], one concludes that C_7 is faulty. It is important to note that one *does not have to* check those equivalence classes with $q_F = 2$.

---

1. The last two components of $\mathbf{U}^*\,\Delta\mathbf{v}_m$ are of the order of 10^{-14} at most and, the corresponding singular values are zero, while with other equivalence classes, the last two components of $\mathbf{U}^*\,\Delta\mathbf{v}_m$ are of the order of at least 10^{-2}.

Table 2–1 T_F Equivalence Class Up to $k = Z$.

q_F		T_F-Equivalence Class
0		ϕ
1	$\mathfrak{F}_1^1$	(1)
	$\mathfrak{F}_2^1$	(2)
	$\mathfrak{F}_3^1$	(3)
	$\mathfrak{F}_4^1$	(4), (5), (10), (4,5), (4,10), (5,10)
	$\mathfrak{F}_5^1$	(6)
	$\mathfrak{F}_6^1$	(7)
	$\mathfrak{F}_7^1$	(8)
	$\mathfrak{F}_8^1$	(9)
2	$\mathfrak{F}_1^2$	(1,2)
	$\mathfrak{F}_2^2$	(1,3)
	$\mathfrak{F}_3^2$	(1,4), (1,5), (1,10)
	$\mathfrak{F}_4^2$	(1,6)
	$\mathfrak{F}_5^2$	(1,7)
	$\mathfrak{F}_6^2$	(1,8)
	$\mathfrak{F}_7^2$	(1,9)
	$\mathfrak{F}_8^2$	(2,3)
	$\mathfrak{F}_9^2$	(2,4), (2,5), (2,10)
	$\mathfrak{F}_{10}^2$	(2,6)
	$\mathfrak{F}_{11}^2$	(2,7), (2,9), (7,9)
	$\mathfrak{F}_{12}^2$	(2,8)
	$\mathfrak{F}_{13}^2$	(3,4), (3,5), (3,8) (3,10), (4,8), (5,8), (8,10)
	$\mathfrak{F}_{14}^2$	(3,6), (3,7), (6,7)
	$\mathfrak{F}_{15}^2$	(3,9)
	$\mathfrak{F}_{16}^2$	(4,6), (5,6), (6,10)
	$\mathfrak{F}_{17}^2$	(4,7), (5,7), (7,10)
	$\mathfrak{F}_{18}^2$	(4,9), (5,9), (9,10)
	$\mathfrak{F}_{19}^2$	(6,8)
	$\mathfrak{F}_{20}^2$	(6,9)
	$\mathfrak{F}_{21}^2$	(7,8)
	$\mathfrak{F}_{22}^2$	(8,9)

Table 2–2 Information Necessary to Check $\Delta V_m \in T_F$

T_F-Equivalence Class	Singular Values	$U*\Delta v_m$	
		Re	Im
$\mathfrak{F}_1^1$	0.9597865D + 07 0.0 0.0	$-0.67540330 - 02$ $-0.3916245D - 02$ $-0.2429079D - 03$	0.1089417D + 00 0.3171280D − 01 0.1935831D − 01
$\mathfrak{F}_2^1$	0.9671910D + 07 0.0 0.0	0.2687565D − 01 $-0.8991895D - 02$ 0.3338650D − 02	$-0.1059185D + 00$ 0.3040232D − 01 0.1877301D − 01
$\mathfrak{F}_3^1$	0.9602367D + 07 0.0 0.0	0.1859094D − 01 $-0.5847249D - 02$ $-0.4175542D - 02$	$-0.1076201D + 00$ 0.3135532D − 01 0.1863536D − 01
$\mathfrak{F}_4^1$	0.5193907D + 05 0.0 0.0	0.1776112D − 01 $-0.6853855D - 01$ 0.1316033D − 03	$-0.1081411D + 00$ 0.3538849D − 01 $-0.6795013D - 03$
$\mathfrak{F}_5^1$	0.4836803D + 06 0.0 0.0	0.7576517D − 01 $-0.1771372D - 01$ $-0.9499984D - 02$	0.1322636D − 03 0.72565660 − 01 0.4359986D − 01
$\mathfrak{F}_6^1$	0.1385763D + 07 0.0 0.0	0.1143578D + 00 0.4233809D − 16 0.1561251D − 15	0.1523334D − 01 $-0.3478988D - 14$ $-0.1826664D - 14$
$\mathfrak{F}_7^1$	0.7326204D + 06 0.0 0.0	$-0.1051717D + 00$ $-0.8013566D - 02$ 0.3192173D − 02	$-0.1656618D - 01$ 0.4112221D − 01 $-0.1444977D - 01$
$\mathfrak{F}_8^1$	0.3277274D-03 0.0 0.0	$-0.1885891D - 01$ $-0.2485785D - 02$ $-0.7825616D - 03$	0.1132912D + 00 0.9030951D − 02 0.5555300D − 02

Next suppose that R_1 ($10M\Omega \to 8M\Omega$) and C_7 ($270\,pF \to 200\,pF$) are perturbed. In this case,

$$\Delta \mathbf{v}_m = \begin{bmatrix} -0.3774938D + 00 & 0.7206432D - 01 \\ -0.3885029D + 00 & 0.8216249D - 01 \\ -0.2328623D + 00 & 0.4066110D - 01 \end{bmatrix} \begin{matrix} n_1 \\ n_2 \\ n_3 \end{matrix}$$

$$\begin{matrix} \text{Re} & \text{Im} & \text{node} \end{matrix}$$

Using the same method, one sees that there is no equivalence class for which equation (*) holds with $q_F = 1$ and one finds that

$$\Delta \mathbf{v}_m \longrightarrow | \ \mathfrak{F}_5^2$$

and concludes that R_1 and C_7 are faulty.

Finally let R_2 (10 MΩ → 9 MΩ) and C_7 (270 pF → 200 pF) be perturbed. Then

$$\Delta \mathbf{v}_m = \begin{bmatrix} -0.1733132D+00 & 0.2656931D-01 \\ -0.1867390D+00 & 0.9385537D-01 \\ -0.1104976D+00 & 0.5260487D-01 \end{bmatrix} \begin{matrix} n_1 \\ n_2 \\ n_3 \end{matrix}$$

$$\begin{matrix} \text{Re} & \text{Im} & \text{node} \end{matrix}$$

Table 2 shows the singular values of $-\mathbf{Z}_{mn} \mathbf{A}_i \, |\mathbb{K}^F$ and $\mathbf{U}^* \Delta \mathbf{v}_m$ with various F's. One finds that equation (*) holds for $F = \{2, 7\}$, $\{2, 9\}$ and $\{7, 9\}$, so that

$$\Delta \mathbf{v}_m \quad \boxed{} \quad \mathfrak{F}^2_{17}$$

Therefore, one concludes that one of the following pairs is faulty: (R_2, C_7), (R_2, μ_9), (C_7, μ_9)

REFERENCES

[1] Y. Togawa, T. Matsumoto, and H. Arai, "The T_F-equivalence Class Approach to Analog Fault Diagnosis Problems," *IEEE Trans. Circuits Syst.*, Vol. CAS-33, pp. 992–1009, 1986.

[2] R. M. Biernacki and J. W. Bandler, "Multiple-Fault Location in Analog Circuits," *IEEE Trans. Circuits Syst.*, Vol. CAS-28, pp. 361–366, 1981.

[3] Z. F. Huang, C. Lin, and R. W. Liu, "Node-Fault Diagnosis and a Design of Testability," *IEEE Trans. Circuits Syst.*, Vol. CAS-30, pp. 1098–1101, 1983.

[4] T. N. Trick and Y. Li, "A Sensitivity Based Algorithm for Fault Isolation in Analog Circuits," in *Proc 1983 ISCAS,* 1983, pp. 1098–1101.

[5] T. N. Trick, W. Mayeda, and A. Sakla, "Calculation of Parameter Values from Node Voltage Measurements," *IEEE Trans. Circuits Systs.*, Vol. CAS-31, pp. 147–158, 1984.

[6] T. Osawa, S. Shinoda, and M. Yamada, "An Equivalent-Circuit Transformation and Its Application to Network-Element-Value Calculation," *IEEE Trans. Circuit Syst.*, Vol. CAS-30, pp. 432–441, 1983.

3

Topological Testability Conditions for Analog Fault Diagnosis

CHEN-SHANG LIN

A circuit is said to be testable if the faulty components in the circuit can be located with a given set of test points, or accessible nodes. Analog fault diagnosis is the study of this testing problem in analog circuits. Analog fault diagnosis is considered more difficult than its counterpart in digital circuits because of the presence of soft faults in the analog circuit, which are caused by the deviation of component values. Much research has been devoted to the development of methods on analog fault diagnosis and significant progress has been made recently, most of which is described in this book. Among the numerous published methods for analog fault diagnosis, the linear method is particularly attractive. In the linear method, a single set of test signals, or excitation, is used to excite a linear circuit and the response is then used to locate the faults by a linear combination test with the impedance matrix of the nominal circuit. The advantages are (1) the number of test points required by the linear method is proportional to the number of faults which is usually small, and (2) there exist efficient and reliable algorithms for the linear combination test.

Furthermore, the testability conditions in the linear method for analog fault diagnosis can be shown to be topological: Namely, the conditions depend mainly on the interconnection and types of components but not on the component values. In other words, testability by the linear method is a topological property of a circuit. It is also interesting to note that another circuit property, reciprocity, depends only on the component types in the circuit and the stability property depends on the interconnections, the component types, and the component values. Thus the values of the components can then be arbitrarily varied without affecting the testability of the circuit. This feature is particularly useful during the circuit design process in which the component values are constantly adjusted to satisfy design goals.

From a practical viewpoint, the topological testability conditions allow us to determine whether a circuit is testable without any complex numerical computations. In fact, for small circuits, it is quite possible to verify the testability condition by inspection. Moreover, the topological conditions can also be employed to select the appropriate test points and to design circuits which satisfy testing requirements. Once the condition is satisfied, the circuit remains testable regardless of any change of component values in the subsequent design process.

In this chapter, the topological testability conditions derived from the linear method of analog fault diagnosis will be described, and the applications of these conditions will be discussed. In the next section, the basic theory of the topological testability conditions will be introduced. The fault diagnosis problem for the linear analog circuits will be formulated into a fault diagnosis equation; the topological cluster $\langle F_k \rangle$ will be introduced; then the topological testability conditions based on the clusters will be described, and the proofs will be outlined. In the second section, the topological conditions will be applied on the test point design and the design of testable circuits. Moreover, the modified conditions can be used to identify an imbedding device or subcircuit without directly accessing its terminals. Finally, the conclusion will be given.

THEORY

In this section, the fundamental theory on the topological conditions for analog circuit testability will be described.

Fault Diagnosis Equation

Consider a b-branch, $(n + 1)$-node, linear and time-invariant active circuit N. Out of the $n + 1$ nodes, $m + 1$ are accessible nodes, or terminals, for both excitation and measurement. Let one of the accessible nodes be the reference node, denoted by n_0. The following notation will be used for N in subsequent discussions:

$$v_n = \text{node voltage vector with respect to } n_0$$
$$v_m = \text{terminal voltage vector}$$
$$i_m = \text{terminal current vector}$$
$$v_b \ (i_b) = \text{branch voltage (current) vector}$$
$$Y_b = \text{branch admittance matrix}$$

By node analysis, it can be easily derived that

$$v_m = A_m^T (A_b Y_b A_b^T)^{-1} A_m i_m \tag{3-1}$$

where A_b is the incident matrix of N and $A_m^T = [I_m \mid 0]$. Here we assume that the inverse of $A_b Y_b A_b$ exists. This assumption is true for most practical cases.

The branch admittance matrix Y_b in general is not diagonal; however, for a nondiagonal Y_b, there always exists a diagonal Y_d such that

$$A_b Y_b A_b^T = A_I Y_d A_V^T \tag{3-2}$$

where A_I and A_V are the incident matrices of the current graph and voltage graph of N, respectively [1], and the diagonal entries of Y_d are those nonzero entries of Y_b. In Fig. 3–1, the current graph and the voltage graph associated with a circuit are shown. Note that the dependent source gm in Fig. 3–1, dependent on the voltage across Branch r2, assumes the connection of r2 in the voltage graph.

When the circuit N is faulty because some branches are at fault, N becomes $N + \Delta N$ in the way that Y_b is perturbed to $Y_b + \Delta Y_b$ and the graphs remain the same. In this faulty circuit, a circuit variable x is then perturbed to $x + \Delta x$.

Given N, the purpose of fault diagnosis is to locate the nonzero entries of ΔY_b from the information of v_m, i_m, Δv_m, and Δi_m. Here note that v_m can be obtained from i_m and N, the fault-free circuit. Without loss of generality, we may assume that

$$\Delta I_m = 0 \tag{3-3}$$

i.e., the same i_m is applied to the fault-free circuit N and the faulty $N + \Delta N$. When Δi_m is not zero, its value can also be measured and its contribution to Δv_m can then be computed. Then it can be shown that

$$\Delta v_m = Z_{md} j_d \tag{3-4}$$

where

$$Z_{md} = A_m^T (A_I Y_d A_V^T)^{-1} A_I$$

and

$$j_d = -\Delta Y_d A_V^T (v_n + \Delta v_n)$$

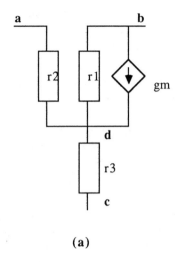

(a)

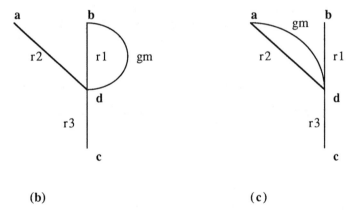

(b)   (c)

Figure 3–1   *A circuit and its associated graphs. (a) Circuit. (b) Current graph. (c) Voltage graph.*

Equation (3-4) is named the fault diagnosis equation [2], for the following reason. An entry of j_d in Eq. (3-4) is nonzero only if the corresponding branch is faulty. The converse is almost always true. In fact, the only exception is when there are two or more faults whose effects cancel each other out. Consequently, if the nonzero entries of j_d can be determined from Eq. (3-4), the faulty branches can be located. In other words, when a single excitation i_m is used, the faulty branches can be uniquely located if and only if the fault diagnosis equation can be solved uniquely.

$\langle F_k \rangle$-Testability

To solve the fault diagnosis equation, there are two problems to be reckoned with. First, since there are usually more branches than accessible nodes in a circuit, the solution of the equation cannot be unique. Fortunately, the number of faulty branches in a faulty circuit is small in most cases. Therefore, it is reasonable to preassume the maximum number of faults to be a small number so long as one is able to determine whether this number is exceeded. Under this assumption, only those solutions, j_d, of Eq. (3-4) whose nonzero entries do not exceed this number need to be considered. Then it is possible to uniquely solve the fault diagnosis equation but for an inherent property of Z_{md}. This leads to the second problem.

The second problem arises from the fact that there exist certain types of branch connection, such as parallel branches, within which the faults can never be distinguished with a single excitation. These types of connection can be identified from the current graph N_I of N. Let F be a forest of N_I; then an induced subgraph $\langle F \rangle$ of F in G is defined as the maximum subgraph of N_I such that F is a spanning forest in $\langle F \rangle$ [3]. It is easy to see that $\langle F' \rangle = \langle F'' \rangle$ does not imply $F' = F''$. However, in this case, the range spaces spanned by the column vectors of the incident matrix A_I of N_I, and thus those range spaces of Z_{md}, corresponding to F' and F'', cannot be distinguished. More specifically, it is possible to distinguish fault-sets $\langle F' \rangle$ and $\langle F'' \rangle$, if $\langle F' \rangle! = \langle F'' \rangle$, but not those on the spanning forests in the same $\langle F \rangle$. Consequently, it is natural to consider isolating faults into a topological cluster, or simply cluster, $\langle F \rangle$ which is an induced subgraph of a forest in N_I. When the spanning forest in a cluster consists of exactly k branches, the cluster is denoted by $\langle F_k \rangle$ and k is called the order of the cluster. For example, Fig. 3–2 shows all the $\langle F_1 \rangle$'s and $\langle F_2 \rangle$'s of the circuit in Fig. 3–1. Given a set of faulty branches B in N_I, it is always possible to find a unique $\langle F \rangle$ of minimum order which contains B. The goal of the fault diagnosis hence becomes to locate this minimum $\langle F \rangle$ containing the faulty B. Therefore, we have the following definition.

Definition 1. A circuit N is said to be $\langle F_k \rangle$-testable if when N is perturbed to $N + \Delta N$, by choosing one appropriate set of inputs i_m, one will be able to determine from the measurement on the accessible nodes:

1. Whether or not there exists a $\langle F_k \rangle$ in N_I of $N + \Delta N$ which contains all the faulty branches.
2. If affirmative, the minimum $\langle F \rangle$ containing these faulty branches can be uniquely determined.

When the decision of 1 in the above definition is negative, the minimum $\langle F \rangle$ containing the faulty B must have the order greater than the preassumed

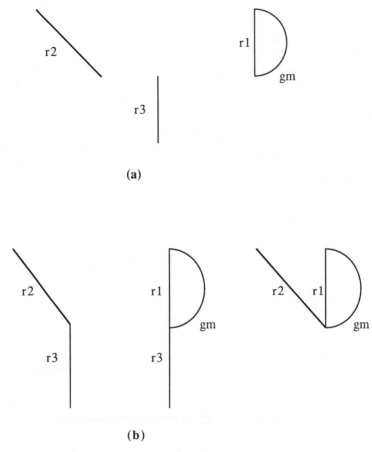

(a)

(b)

Figure 3–2 $\langle F_2 \rangle$'s of Figure 3–1. (a) $\langle F_1 \rangle$'s. (b) $\langle F_2 \rangle$'s.

k. In this case, additional accessible nodes will be needed to make the circuit testable.

Clearly $\langle F_k \rangle$-testability of a circuit depends on the linear independency of the column vectors of its Z_{md}. Define $\langle F_{k+1} \rangle$-rank condition of a circuit N as follows: for every $\langle F_{k+1} \rangle$ in N_1 of N, the space spanned by the corresponding column vectors of Z_{md} has dimension $k+1$. Then we have the following result.

Theorem 1.   A circuit N is $\langle F_k \rangle$-testable for almost all Δv_m if the above $\langle F_{k+1} \rangle$-rank condition is satisfied. Conversely, if only one set of inputs i_m is used, N being $\langle F_k \rangle$-testable also implies that $\langle F_{k+1} \rangle$-rank condition is satisfied.

Outline of Proof.

Sufficiency: Given N and the maximum order k, the following fault location algorithm can be shown to locate the faulty $\langle F \rangle$ if the $\langle F_{k+1} \rangle$-rank condition is satisfied.

1. Let $r = 1$.
2. For each $\langle F_r \rangle$ in N_I of N, check whether Δv_m is a linear combination of the column vectors of Z_{md} corresponding to this $\langle F_r \rangle$.
3. If affirmative for a certain $\langle F_r \rangle$, then this cluster is the minimum $\langle F \rangle$ containing all faulty branches. Otherwise, there is no $\langle F_r \rangle$ which contains all faulty branches. Increment r by one and go to 2 if the new r is no greater than k.
4. The indicator r is now equal to $k + 1$. There is no $\langle F_k \rangle$ in N_I, which contains all faulty branches.

It can be seen that 2, if affirmative, must have a unique solution because of the $\langle F_{k+1} \rangle$-rank condition.

Necessity: It is clear from the above discussion.   □

The dimension of the space spanned by the column vectors of Z_{md} corresponding to a $\langle F_k \rangle$ in N_I of N is the same as that corresponding to any spanning forest in this $\langle F_k \rangle$. Therefore, to verify $\langle F_{k+1} \rangle$-rank condition, one only has to check whether the column vectors of Z_{md} corresponding to a single spanning forest for each $\langle F_{k+1} \rangle$ are linearly independent. However, numerical computations are still involved in the verification process.

The topological conditions will then be investigated.

Topological Testability Conditions

Due to its conceptual simplicity, the topological condition for the circuits containing only uncoupled two-terminal components will first be discussed. The outline of the proof will also be given. Then the topological condition for the general linear circuit will be provided.

For the case that N contains only uncoupled two-terminal components, the current graph N_I and the voltage graph N_V are identical. Let Q be a given $(k + 1)$-forest F_{k+1} and Z_{mq} be the transfer impedance matrix from the soldering-iron-entry ports across branches in Q to the accessible nodes. Then we have the following theorem.

Theorem 2. Suppose that N contains only uncoupled two-terminal components. Then the matrix Z_{mq} has full column-rank only if, in N,

1. there exists a tree T containing Q, and
2. $(T\text{-}Q)$ is connected when all the accessible nodes are shorted together. The converse is true for almost all Y_b.

Outline of Proof.

Necessity: Without loss of generality, we may assume that Z_{mq} is a square matrix. Choose a tree T in N containing Q and label the branches in the following order: branches in Q, those in T-Q, and the rest. For simplicity, we denote $(k+1)$ by k'. Then Z_{mq} being full column rank is equivalent to the nonsingularity of the matrix W defined below:

$$W = \begin{bmatrix} A_b Y_b A_b{}^T & I_{k'} \\ \hline & 0 \\ \hline A_m^T & 0 \end{bmatrix}$$

where $I_{k'}$ is an identity matrix. Note that $A_m{}^T = [I_{k'} \mid 0]$ because of the labeling of the accessible nodes. Then the determinant of W can be expanded into

$$\det W = \det A_m * \text{SUM}\{\det(A')_j * \det(Y_b)_j * \det(A'')T_j\}$$

where the summation is over all $(n\text{-}k') \times (n\text{-}k')$ principle submatrices of Y_b according to the Binet–Cauchy formula [1], and A' is the submatrix of A_b with the first k' rows deleted and A'' is the submatrix of A_b with k' rows of accessible nodes deleted. The fact of Y_b being diagonal has been implicitly used in the above expansion.

It can be seen that W is nonsingular only if there exists a j such that each term in the above equation is nonzero. Since A_m and Y_b are nonsingular, we will examine the nonsingularity conditions of $(A')_j$ and $(A'')T_j$. The implication of $(A')_j$ being nonsingular is that the n-k' branches in $(Y_b)_j$ together with branches in Q form a tree in N. Moreover, the nonsingularity of $(A'')T_j$ implies that these same $(n\text{-}k')$ branches must be connected and loopless when all k' accessible nodes are shorted together.

Sufficiency: We want to show that when the two conditions are satisfied, the matrix W is nonsingular for almost all Y_b. Let T be the tree satisfying the two conditions. First note that W is nonsingular for the following particular Y_b: All branch admittances are zero except for those in $T-Q$ in which the branches have positive admittances. Then since $\det W$ is a polynomial of the diagonal entries in Y_b and is nonzero for the above chosen admittance values, the chances that W is nonsingular are small. Hence W is nonsingular for almost all Y_b [4], and Z_{mq} has full column rank for almost all Y_b.   ☐

From Theorem 2, it can be seen that $\langle F_k \rangle$-testability as a circuit property depends mainly on the interconnection of components but not on the parameters of components. Thus it is possible to determine the testability of a circuit by simply examining its graph without any numerical computation. For example, in the ladder circuit of three accessible nodes (a, b, c) as shown in

Fig. 3–3a, it can be seen that all $\langle F_1 \rangle$ single-component faults can be uniquely located. But this set of accessible nodes will fail to locate a $\langle F_2 \rangle$ fault.

When $k = 1$, the single-branch fault case, the above condition can be further simplified. Let N_t be the test graph of a given circuit N by connecting all accessible nodes to a new node n_t. In N_t, two paths are disjoint if they have no nodes in common except the end nodes.

Theorem 3. Let N be a circuit with uncoupled two-terminal components only. Then the following two statements are equivalent:

1. N satisfies $\langle F_1 \rangle$-rank condition for almost all Y_b.
2. There are at least three disjoint paths in N_t between n_t and any inaccessible node.

It is easy to see that (1) → (2) must be true; otherwise the $\langle F_1 \rangle$-faults cannot be distinguished. The proof of (2)→(1) is rather involved. The basic idea is to show that when (2) is satisfied, a tree satisfying the two conditions of Theorem 2 can always be constructed for each possible case. The detail of the proof can be found in [4].

The test graph N_t of the ladder circuit in Fig. 3–3a is shown in Fig. 3–3b. The $\langle F_1 \rangle$-testability of the circuit can be easily verified by the visual inspection.

The topological testability condition for a general circuit will be described in terms of both the associated current graph and voltage graph. Let Q be a given forest $\langle F_{k+1} \rangle$ in N_I of N and Z_{mq} be the transfer impedance matrix from the iron-entry ports across branches in Q to the accessible nodes.

Theorem 4. In a general linear circuit N, the transfer impedance matrix Z_{mq} has full column rank only if

1. in N_I of N, there exists a tree T containing Q, and
2. in N_v of N, the branches in $(T\text{-}Q)$ constitute a $(k + 2)$-forest and this forest is connected when all the accessible nodes are shorted together.

The converse is also true for almost all $Y_b(Y_d)$.

The proof of the above theorem follows an approach similar to Theorem 2 and is omitted here.

Related Works

In 1980, Biernacki and Bandler [5] and Sakla, El-Masry, and Trick [6] proposed independently the idea of setting up the algebraic linear fault diag-

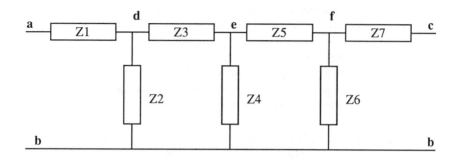

(a)

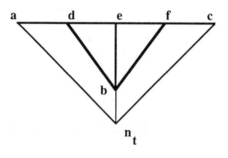

(b)

Figure 3–3   *A ladder circuit. (a) Circuit. (b) Test graph.*

nosis equation similar to Eq. (3-4) and locating the faulty components by the well-developed linear combination test vectors. Since then, many works [2, 4, 5–16] have been directed toward exploring this linear method. There are two major aspects to the research of the linear method: the topological aspect and the numerical aspect. The latter is concerned with the resolution of the method in the presence of component tolerance and is covered elsewhere in this book. In this subsection, the related works on the topological aspect of the linear method will be discussed.

Right after the proposal of linear method for analog fault diagnosis, re-searchers found that, in the ladder circuit as shown in Fig. 3–3, double branch faults in a three-branch loop cannot be located uniquely regardless of the excitation and the choice of accessible nodes [7]. The reason in fact is obvious because, by the well-known current-source shift property, any two of these three branches at fault will have an indistinguishable effect on any choice of accessible nodes. The topological difficulty clearly is the second problem described previously in this section. Various approaches have been employed to characterize this inherent dependency of Z_{md} column vectors, and then to reformulate the fault diagnosis equation based on the character-ization. Different formulations result in the topological testability conditions with various degrees of success.

The first success of dealing with the inherent dependency of Z_{md} column vectors is the node-fault diagnosis proposed by Huang, Lin, and Liu [10]. The basic concept of [10] is to transform the spurious current source j_d of each faulty branch into two grounded pseudocurrent sources j_n on two inci-dent nodes as shown in Fig. 3–4. Then the problem becomes finding the loca-tion of these pseudocurrent sources from the following equation:

$$\Delta v_m = Z_{mn} j_n \qquad (3\text{-}5)$$

where $Z_{mn} = A_m(A_I Y_d A_V^T)^{-1}$, and $j_n = A_I j_d$.

The above equation appears to be a simple rearrangement of the fault di-agnosis equation (3-4). However, by this rearrangement, the inherent depen-dency of Z_{md} can be removed and the column vectors of Z_{mn} can always be made linearly independent by the appropriate choice of accessible nodes. The problem is simplified and the topological condition for testability of the node-faults can be derived. The condition for circuits with uncoupled two-terminal components only is strikingly simple and worth restating in the fol-lowing. Construct a test graph N_t from the given circuit N by connecting all the accessible nodes except n_0 to a new node n_t. Then it was shown in [10] that the necessary and almost sufficient condition for k-node-fault testability is that there are at least $(k + 1)$ disjoint paths between n_t and any inaccessible node in N_t. Another proof of the above interesting result was given by Togawa, Matsumoto, and Arai [9]. Despite the elegance of the result, the simplicity of node-fault diagnosis nevertheless is achieved by sacrificing the full capability of the accessible nodes. It can be easily seen that a single branch fault will result in two node faults in the node-fault diagnosis; hence the node faults to be located may be twice as many as the actual branch faults. Consequently, the number of required accessible nodes in the node-fault diagnosis may be greater than that actually needed.

Inspired by the success of node-fault diagnosis, other formulations have also been proposed. A modified node-fault approach was investigated in [12] which also provided a testability condition based on Coates graph. In [15], a

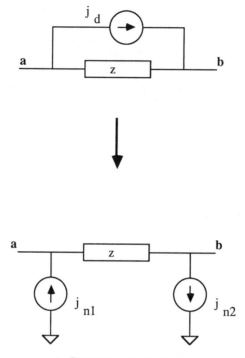

Figure 3–4 *Node faults.*

direct approach of Eq. (3-4) was taken, and some necessary but not sufficient topological conditions for testability were given. These formulations,
though useful in some practical cases, do not fully exploit the full capability
of the accessible nodes and the linear method.

The formulation presented in the previous subsection was proposed by
Huang, Lin, and Liu in 1982 [2], in which the k-rank branch set was used to
describe the $\langle F_k \rangle$-cluster. This formulation provides the genuine necessary
and sufficient topological testability condition for general circuits when a
single excitation is used. Similar formulation also appeared in [9], which,
however, employed a numerical approach, singular value decomposition, to
determine the linear dependency of Z_{md}.

APPLICATIONS

In this section, the applications of the theory and the topological testability
conditions discussed previously will be described.

Test Point Design for Diagnosis

The first task of diagnosing a given circuit is the selection of test points, or accessible nodes. With the topological conditions, the selection can be made by simply examining the associated current graph and voltage graph without any computation.

For the first example, consider the ladder circuit as shown in Fig. 3–3(a), which consists of uncoupled two-terminal components only. Let the original accessible nodes be (a, b, c). By inspecting the associated test graph N_t as shown in Fig. 3–3b, it can be easily seen that all single component faults, $\langle F_1 \rangle$, can be uniquely located. Moreover, by Theorem 2, it can be seen that double faults cannot be distinguished by these accessible nodes. Further investigation will reveal that only by accessing all the remaining inaccessible nodes (d, e, f), the faulty $\langle F_2 \rangle$ can be uniquely located. An engineer trade-off between the number of test points and the resolution of testing can then be made.

In the second example, consider the two-transistor amplifier with four accessible nodes (a, b, f, Ground) as shown in Fig. 3–5a. The linear equivalent circuit is shown in Fig. 3–5b and its associated current graph and voltage graph are shown in Figs. 3–5c and 5d, respectively. Since some physical devices, such as Q1, consist of three branches, such as (r8, r9, and gm1), which constitute an $\langle F_2 \rangle$, it makes more practical sense to consider the $\langle F_2 \rangle$ fault. From Theorem 4, it can be determined that the circuit is $\langle F_2 \rangle$-testable if node c can also be made accessible.

Design for Testability

The topological testability conditions also provide a convenient way to design circuits which satisfy diagnosis requirements. For example, the ladder circuit as shown in Fig. 3–3 has been shown to be not $\langle F_2 \rangle$-testable unless all nodes are accessible. The problem is the lack of incident branches of nodes $d, e,$ and f. Therefore, it can be seen that if an additional branch of the appropriate value can be connected between nodes d and f without deteriorating the circuit performance, then the circuit can be made $\langle F_2 \rangle$-testable by accessing node e in addition to the original accessible nodes (a, b, c). The topological condition, Theorem 2, renders the placement of the extra branch obvious.

Identification of Imbedding Subcircuits

A circuit may contain a sensitive and vulnerable device or subcircuit which one might desire to monitor or identify constantly without directly accessing the terminals. To identify such a device or a subcircuit, one must be

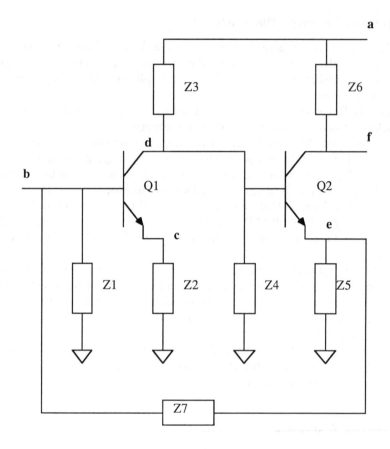

Figure 3–5   *(a) An amplifier.*

able to excite as well as determine the terminal voltages and currents. Denote the circuit deleted of the imbedding subcircuit as N'; let the set of ports of the imbedding subcircuit be denoted by Q, and the transfer impedance matrix of N' from Q to the accessible nodes by Z_{mq}. Our discussions in the previous section can be modified to solve these two parts of the identification problem.

An imbedding subcircuit is said to be reachable in a circuit if the terminal voltages and currents of the subcircuit can be determined from the accessible

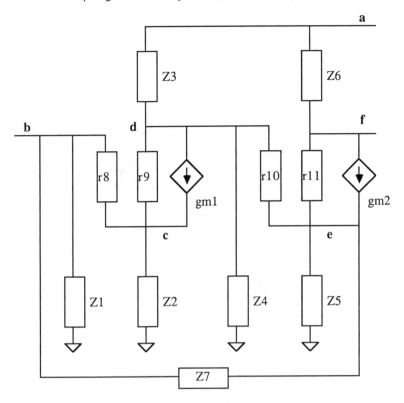

Figure 3–5   (Continued) *(b) Linear equivalent circuit.*

nodes. To solve the reachability problem, one may adopt the previous diagnosis theory by regarding the whole imbedding subcircuit as the deviation
from N', the remaining part of the original circuit. Then the problem becomes the diagnosis problem with known faulty branches Q and the equation
for determining the port currents j_q becomes

$$v_m = Z_{mq} j_q \tag{3-6}$$

If Z_{mq} has full column rank, j_q can be uniquely determined and thus the port
voltages v_q can be determined from j_q, i_m, and N'. The conditions for Z_{mq}

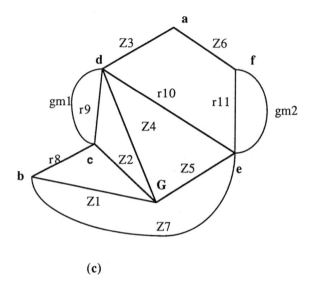

(c)

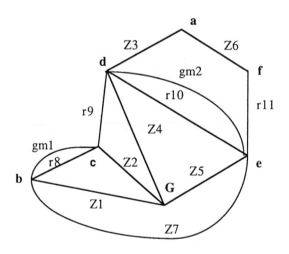

(d)

Figure 3–5   (Continued) *(c) Current graph. (d) Voltage graph.*

being full column rank are the same as those described in Theorems 2–4. Hence the topological conditions can be used to verify the reachability of the imbedding subcircuit without any computation.

Define the excitability as follows: The imbedding subcircuit is said to be excitable if its terminal voltages can be varied independently. It can be shown that, under some mild conditions of the imbedding subcircuit, the necessary and sufficient condition for excitability is Z_{qm} being full row rank, where Z_{qm} is the transfer impedance matrix of N' from the accessible nodes to Q [14]. Note that Z_{qm} being full row rank is equivalent to Z''_{mq} being full column rank where Z''_{mq} is the transfer matrix of the adjoint circuit N'' of N'. The adjoint circuit N'' is simply the circuit with Y_d of N' as the branch admittances, N'_V as the current graph, and N'_I as the voltage graph [17]. The topological conditions of the theory section can then be applied to N'' to verify the excitability.

As an example, consider the circuit with an imbedding device X to be identified as shown in Fig. 3–6a. The current graph (voltage graph) and the volt-

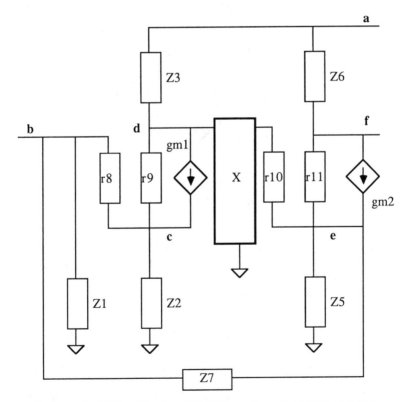

Figure 3–6   *(a) Identification of X. (b) Current graph. (c) Voltage graph.*

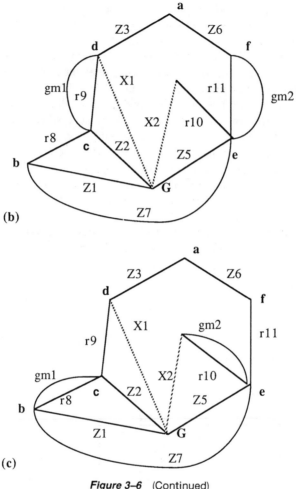

Figure 3–6   (Continued)

age graph (current graph) of N' (N'') are shown in Fig. 3–6b and 3–6c, respectively. Let the accessible nodes be (a, b, f, Ground). Then it can be shown from Theorem 4 that both Z_{mq} and Z''_{mq} have full column rank. Therefore, the imbedding device X is identifiable.

REFERENCES

[1] S. Seshu and M. B. Reed, *Linear Graph and Electrical Networks,* Addison-Wesley, Reading, MA, 1961.

[2] Z. F. Huang, C. Lin, and R. Liu, "Topological Conditions on Multiple-Fault Testability of Analog Circuits," in *Proc. 1982 ISCAS,* pp. 1152–1155.

[3] F. Harary, *Graph Theory,* Addison-Wesley, Reading, MA, 1972.

[4] C. Lin, Z. F. Huang, and R. Liu, "Topological Conditions for Single-Branch-Fault," *IEEE Trans. Circuits Syst.,* Vol. CAS-30, pp. 376–381, 1983.

[5] R. M. Biernacki and J. W. Bandler, "Fault Location of Analog Circuits," in *Proc. 1980 ISCAS,* pp. 1082–1086.

[6] A. A. Sakla, E. I. El-Masry, and T. N. Trick, "A Sensitivity Algorithm for Fault Detection in Analog Circuits," in *Proc. 1980 ISCAS,* pp. 1075–1077.

[7] T. N. Trick and Y. Li, "Algorithms for the Location of Single and Multiple Faults in Analog Circuits with Inaccessible Nodes," in *Proc. 1982 ISLSS,* pp. 491–494.

[8] Y. Togawa and T. Matsumoto, "On the Topological Testability Conjecture for Analog Fault Diagnosis Problems," *IEEE Trans. Circuits Syst.,* Vol. CAS-31, pp. 147–158, 1984.

[9] Y. Togawa, T. Matsumoto, and H. Arai, "The T_f-Equivalence Class Approach to Analog Fault Diagnosis Problems," *IEEE Trans. Circuits Syst.,* Vol. CAS-33, pp. 992–1009, 1986.

[10] Z. F. Huang, C. Lin, and R. Liu, "Node-Fault Diagnosis and Design of Testability," *IEEE Trans. Circuits Syst.,* Vol. CAS-30, pp. 257–265, 1983. Also, in *20th IEEE Conf. Decision and Control,* pp. 1037–1042, 1981.

[11] R. M. Biernacki and J. W. Bandler, "Multiple-Fault Location of Analog Circuits," *IEEE Trans. Circuits Syst.,* Vol. CAS-28, pp. 361–366, 1981.

[12] J. A. Starsky and J. W. Bandler, "Nodal Approach to Multiple-Fault in Analog Circuits," in *Proc. 1982 ISCAS,* pp. 1136–1139, 1982.

[13] C. Lin and R. Liu, "Fault Diagnosis of Linear Analog Networks-A Theory and Its Implementation," in *Proc. 1983 ISCAS,* pp. 1090–1093.

[14] C. Lin and R. Liu, "Identifiability of An Imbedding Unknown Subnetwork," *IEEE Trans. Circuits Syst.,* Vol. CAS-32, pp. 260–266, 1985.

[15] J. A. Starsky and J. W. Bandler, "Multiport Approach to Multiple-Fault Location in Analog Circuits," *IEEE Trans. Circuits Syst.,* Vol. CAS-30, pp. 762–765, 1983.

[16] A. E. Salama, R. M. Biernacki, and J. W. Bandler, "A Unified Decomposition Approach for Fault Location in Large Analog Circuits," *IEEE Trans. Circuits Syst.,* Vol. CSA-31, pp. 609–622, 1984.

[17] R. K. Brayton and R. Spence, *Sensitivity and Optimization,* Elsevier, New York, 1980.

4

Fault Diagnosis of Nonlinear Electronic Circuits

QIU HUANG
and
RUEY-WEN LIU

Testing and diagnosis are two important aspects in the design and maintenance of analog circuits. In testing, it is necessary to distinguish the faulty *circuits* from all good ones. In diagnosis, the goal is to distinguish faulty *circuit components* or elements from good ones. Usually, testing procedure precedes diagnosis procedures. In this chapter, we will only consider the diagnosis of *nonlinear* analog circuits.

Since the diagnosis problem is one which distinguishes bad ones from good ones, at the *subcircuit* level from possibly the same testing points, it is a much more challenging problem than the testing problem. Hence, it attracts much attention among academic researchers. The diagnosis problem of *linear* circuits is now well understood. However, the diagnosis problem of *nonlinear* circuits remains a frontier to be conquered. Many ideas have been proposed recently [1–11]. In this chapter, a method is presented which provides the best trade-off among reliability, efficiency, and post-fault computational complexity (a measure of cost per test).

There are two major issues which make the nonlinear fault diagnosis problem much more difficult than the linear ones. They are the *bias shifting of nonlinear devices* and the existence of *multiple solutions of nonlinear circuits,* which are discussed below.

1. Bias-Shifting of Nonlinear Devices. When a circuit element of a nonlinear circuit is at fault, it will influence the bias circuit (the DC circuit). Because every analog circuit is usually heavily feedback in nature, a deviation of one parameter may cause deviations of all voltages and currents of the bias circuit. Hence the bias of nonlinear devices will be shifted after a fault has occurred. This bias shift may make nonlinear devices "look-like faults," even though they are still normal. Therefore, from a circuit theoretic point of view, the number of faulty elements is "artificially" increased. This will make the circuit more difficult to diagnose. For example, it usually needs two test points to diagnose a one-element fault. If this one-element fault causes a bias shift of four other nonlinear devices, it would then require six test points because there are four elements look-like faults and one faulty element. Hence, the efficiency of the diagnosis procedure will be decreased.

This bias-shifting problem could be avoided if a "robust" bias circuit can be designed. We need a bias circuit which isolates each and every possible fault, that is, the bias point of every nonlinear device remains the same even when some element is at fault. Before such robust bias circuit is available to us, the fault diagnosis engineers will have to face up to the bias-shifting problem.

2. Existence of Multiple Solutions of Nonlinear Circuits. Unlike linear ones, a nonlinear circuit may admit multiple solutions. Only one of them is used under normal operation. When an element is at fault, it may trigger this normal solution to some other abnormal solution. Even when a circuit is normal but is at an abnormal solution, it will make all measurements look-like faulty. This phenomenon has caused many headaches to fault diagnosis engineers.

In this chapter, a new method will be presented. Every nonlinear device will be modeled by piecewise-linear characteristics. In doing so, some modeling error will be introduced. However, its advantages will outweigh the disadvantages. To begin with, it makes sense to model a nonlinear device by a piecewise-linear characteristic. For example, an operation amplifier will have a linear region, a saturation region, and a cut-off region from a circuit designer's point of view. Hence, it makes sense to model it by a piecewise-linear characteristic with three linear segments to represent the above three regions.

This method makes even more sense from the fault diagnosis point of view. It will be shown that the methods used for linear circuits can now also be used for nonlinear circuits. More importantly, the problem of bias shifting of nonlinear devices and the problem of existence of multiple solutions of nonlinear circuits will be circumvented. In short, all the advantages of linear circuit diagnosis are preserved and all the difficulties of nonlinear circuit diagnosis can be circumvented.

The proposed method is efficient because the number of test points need not be increased even with the presence of look-like faults due to bias shifting of nonlinear devices. Its post-fault computation is as simple as the linear ones, and hence its per unit cost is low. It is reliable because the method for linear circuits with tolerance can be extended to nonlinear ones. Finally, the topological conditions can also be used for the design of test points.

FAULT DIAGNOSIS OF LINEAR CIRCUITS

Let us first review the fault diagnosis of linear circuits.

The Ideal Case

A linear circuit with dependent and independent sources can be represented by a Tableau equation [12] of the following form:

Circuit Equation:

$$A x = b \tag{4-1}$$

Output Equation:

$$y = Cx \tag{4-2}$$

where $A \in R^{n \times n}$, $C \in R^{m \times n}$, $y \in R^m$, x and $b \in x^n$.

One example of writing the Tableau equation can be found in Example 2 of [13] in this book.

One important feature of Tableau equations is that each device parameter appears in one and only one row of A and no two device parameters appear in the same row.

When A is perturbed to $A + \Delta A$ due to a fault, x will be changed to $(x + \Delta x)$, i.e.,

$$(A + \Delta A)(x + \Delta x) = b \tag{4-3}$$

$$(y + \Delta y) = C(x + \Delta x) \tag{4-4}$$

Comparing (4-1) and (4-2) with (4-3) and (4-4), we have

$$\Delta y = -C(A + \Delta A)^{-1}\Delta A x \tag{4-5}$$

In a diagnosis problem, we need to solve for ΔA from Δy. Note that since $m < n$ in general, Eq. (4-5) may be indeterminate. Even if it is determinate, it is difficult to solve for ΔA because Eq. (4-5) is nonlinear. Numerical methods may be used to solve this equation, but as usual it may not converge to a solution or it may converge to a wrong solution. Moreover, if the fault is nonlinear, i.e., ΔA becomes a nonlinear operator instead of a matrix, the problem becomes impossible. We will show that with a key assumption on the nature of the fault, a change of objective of the diagnosis problem and a main feature of the Tableau equation, the diagnosis problem can be solved by a *linear* method.

In view of (4-3), Eq. (4-5) can be rewritten in the following form:

$$\Delta y = Mz \qquad (4\text{-}6)$$

where $z \in R^n$ is given by

$$z = \Delta A(x + \Delta x) \qquad (4\text{-}7)$$

and $M \in R^{m \times n}$ is defined by

$$M = -CA^{-1} \qquad (4\text{-}8)$$

which is a known matrix. Note that Eq. (4-6) is *linear,* and all the nonlinear part of (4-5) is lumped into (4-7). The advantages of doing this can be seen by the following proposition.

Proposition 1.

$$\Delta A_i = 0 \Leftrightarrow z_i = \Delta A_i(x + \Delta x) = 0, \quad \text{for almost all } (x + \Delta x) \text{ (4-9)}$$

where ΔA_i denotes the *ith* row of ΔA.

The proof of sufficiency is obvious. Intuitively, the proof of necessity is also clear. The only possibility that $z_i = 0$ but $\Delta A_i \neq 0$ is when the faults affect Δx in such a way that they cancel each other so that they are not observed at the testing points. This possibility is so small that it can be neglected in the practical situation.

We are now prepared to make the main argument.

Proposition 2.   Every nonzero component of z is associated uniquely with a faulty circuit parameter.

The above proposition is true only when each circuit parameter appears in one and only one row of A and no two circuit parameters appear in the same row of A. This is the main feature of Tableau equations. As such, each faulty circuit parameter will appear *uniquely* as a nonzero row of ΔA, and will be associated *uniquely* with a nonzero component of z by Proposition 1. Hence, Proposition 2 is proved.

The above arguments are made intuitively. It can also be made rigorous [14].

Because of Proposition 2, the *location* of faulty circuit parameters can be determined by the location of nonzero components of z. This can be done by solving the *linear* equation (4-6). This approach is henceforth called the *linear method.*

Note that in order to find the *values* of faulty circuit parameter, we still have to solve the nonlinear equation (4-7). However, the complexity of (4-7) will now be reduced because we need only to concern the part of the nonzero component of z in the nonzero rows of ΔA. In general, finding the location of a fault element is all we need to do in a diagnosis problem, and hence, we need only to concern the *linear* equation (4-6).

We have shown that if we are interested only in the *location* of a faulty element, not its value, and if Eq. (4-1) is a Tableau equation, then the fault diagnosis problem becomes one of finding the nonzero components of z, where z satisfies a *linear* equation (4-6), i.e.,

$$\Delta y = Mz$$

where $\Delta y \in R^m$ and $M \in R^{m \times n \to y}$ are known. Note that $n >> m$ in Tableau equation, where n is twice the number of branches, while m is the number of testing points. Hence the linear equation (4-6) is indeterminate and cannot be solved by conventional linear methods. A new method will have to be developed and it has to be consistent with the fault diagnosis problem.

Suppose that we consider only the case when the number of faulty elements is bounded by k. This is the k-fault diagnosis problem. This is reasonable from a practical point of view. Most digital testing programs are for the one-fault case because it is rare that many elements become faulty at the same time.

The k-fault diagnosis problem can now be formulated as follows. The linear equation (4-6) has the form

$$Bx = p \qquad (4-10)$$

where $x \in C^n$, $p \in C^m$, $B \in C^{m \times n}$, and $n > m$. Let

$$X_k = \{x \in C^n | \text{ number of nonzero components of } x \text{ not exceeding } k\}$$

be the set of vectors whose number of nonzero components is bounded by k. We want to investigate the uniqueness of the solution $x \in X_k$.

Definition. The *global column rank* of B is said to be r if every combination of r columns of B is linearly independent, and some combination of $(r + 1)$ columns of B is linearly dependent.

Let Ω be the range of B. Then the following theorem is given in [14].

Theorem 1. Let $p \in \Omega$. Then Eq. (4-10) has a unique solution $x \in X_k$ for almost all $p \in \Omega$ if and only if the global column rank of B is at least $k + 1$.

Note that for a fault diagnosis problem, the existence of a solution, i.e.,

$p \in \Omega$ is guaranteed. When Theorem 1 is satisfied, the solution of (4-10) can be obtained in the following way. Let the column vectors of B be denoted by

$$B = [b_1, b_2, \ldots, b_n]$$

Let the test matrices T_i be constructed in the following way:

$$T_i = [b_{i_1}, b_{i_2}, \ldots, b_{i_k}, p], \quad i = 1, 2, \ldots, s; \, s = C(n, k)$$

for every combination of k columns of B. Then:
  A. If

$$\text{Rank } T_i = k + 1, \quad i = 1, 2, \ldots, s \tag{4-11}$$

then there is *no* solution $x \in X_k$.
  B. Otherwise, there is a *unique j* such that

$$\text{Rank } T_j = k \tag{4-12}$$

and

$$\text{Rank } T_i = k + 1, \quad i \neq j. \tag{4-13}$$

Furthermore, the unique solution $x \in X_k$ is given by

$$x = (B_j^T B_j)^{-1} B_j \, p \tag{4-14}$$

where $B_j = [b_{j_1}, b_{j_2}, \ldots, b_{j_k}]$ is obtained by deleting p from T_j.
  As a consequence, the k-fault diagnosability depends on the global column rank of B.

Remark:

1.   The condition that the global rank of B being $k + 1$ is also called the k-fault testability condition. Based on this condition, a topological condition on k-fault testability of analog circuits can be derived [14].
2.   The minimum value of test points m for which the k-fault testability condition to be satisfied is $m = k + 1$. Therefore, it is possible to diagnose k-fault with $k + 1$ test points, *regardless of the complexity of the circuit, i.e., number of branches and number of nodes.*
3.   The matrices to be tested in (4-11)–(4-13) have a size of only $m \times (k + 1)$, regardless of how large the circuit is.

4. The testability condition depends on the normal circuit and can be tested before a normal fault occurs.
5. All the above are true not only for linear mapping ΔA, but also for *nonlinear operator* ΔA. It is due to this point that the linear method presented above is *powerful.*
6. If the testability condition is not satisfied, we may not, uniquely, locate the fault element, but we could find an equivalence class of fault elements [15].

The Tolerance Case

In actual circuits, the actual values are always different from the normal values of circuit elements. The difference is called the tolerance, which is not known to us. Let us model the k-fault diagnosis problem with tolerance.

In the tolerance case, we have three sets of equations to be considered:

1. Normal design equations:

$$Ax - b = 0 \qquad (4\text{-}15)$$

$$y = Cx \qquad (4\text{-}16)$$

2. Normal equations with tolerance:

$$(A + dA)(x + dx) - b = 0 \qquad (4\text{-}17)$$

$$y + dy = C(x + dx) \qquad (4\text{-}18)$$

where dA is the tolerance.
3. Faulty equations with tolerance:

$$(A + dA + \Delta A)(x + dx + \Delta x) - b = 0 \qquad (4\text{-}19)$$

$$y + dy + \Delta y = C(x + dx + \Delta x) \qquad (4\text{-}20)$$

By using (4-17) and (4-18), we can rewrite Eqs. (4-19) and (4-20) as

$$\Delta x = -(A + dA)^{-1}\Delta A(x + dx + \Delta x) \qquad (4\text{-}21)$$

$$\Delta y = C\Delta x \qquad (4\text{-}22)$$

With the assumption that

$$\|dA\| < \|A\|$$

we have, with approximation,

$$\Delta y = (M - dM)\Delta A(x + dx + \Delta x) \tag{4-23}$$

where $dM = M \times dA \times A^{-1}$ comes from the tolerance of components.

Due to Proposition 2, the problem of locating the fault elements is equivalent to the problem of locating the positions of nonzero rows of ΔA, in spite of the tolerance of elements. Therefore, a k-fault diagnosis problem, with tolerance, is again to find the solution z of the following equation:

$$\Delta y = Bz, \quad z \in X_k \tag{4-24}$$

where $B = M - dM$.

However, B is now not known due to unknown dM; we have to *estimate z* with given Δy. A nonlinear estimation method [16] has been proven to be working very well. Here, we present a simple way to solve Eq. (4-24). We define an *expected* testability condition as

$$E\{\text{Rank}[b_{i_1}, b_{i_2}, \ldots, b_{i_{k+1}}]\} = k + 1, \quad \forall 1 \le i_1 < i_2 < \cdots < i_{k+1} < i_n \tag{4-25}$$

where $E[\cdot]$ is the expected value. Note that if the *expected global column rank* of B is greater or equal to k then (4-25) is satisfied. Then the test conditions (4-11), (4-12), and (4-13) become:

A. If

$$E\{\text{Rank}[T_i]\} = k + 1, \quad \forall i = 1, 2, \ldots, C(n, k) \tag{4-26}$$

then the circuit has more than k number of faults.

B. Otherwise, there exists some j such that

$$E\{\text{Rank } T_j\} = k \tag{4-26}$$

In the following, we will present a method to determine such j for the case $k = 1$. The extension of this method to larger k is conceptually simple and hence omitted.

When $k = 1$,

$$T_i = [b_i, \Delta y], \quad i = 1, 2, \ldots, n \tag{4-27}$$

We want to test if

$$E\{\text{Rank } T_i\} = 1 \tag{4-28}$$

In order to do this, define an angle θ_i between the two vectors b_i and Δy. Since Rank $T_i = 1$ if and only if $\theta_i = n\pi$, it is reasonable to replace the test (4-28) by

$$|E\{\cos \theta_i\}| = 1 \tag{4-29}$$

Since $b_i = m_i - dm_i$, with approximation, it is easy to obtain

$$\cos \theta_i = \frac{\Delta y^T (m_i + dm_i)}{\|\Delta y\| \, \|m_i\|} \left(1 - \frac{m_i^T dm_i}{\|m_i\|^2} \right) \tag{4-30}$$

If dM satisfies a uniform distribution centered at its normal value, then

$$E[dm_i] = 0 \tag{4-31}$$

Hence,

$$E[\cos \theta_i] = \frac{\Delta y^T}{\|\Delta y\| \, \|m_i\|} \left(m_i - \frac{E(dm_i \, dm_i^T)}{\|m_i\|^2} m_i \right) \tag{4-32}$$

Note that the second term in bracket reflects the effect of tolerance. The criterion is to choose those i, for which $E[\cos \theta_i]$ is closest to 1.

FAULT DIAGNOSIS OF PWL CIRCUITS

In order to simplify the notation, we will restrict ourselves to the following type of PWL circuits. Let n_p be the number of PWL resistors, which consists of only 2-terminal element devices, and let the whole space R^{n_p} be divided into an N_p number of gridlike regions by a finite number of $(n_p - 1)$-dimensional hyperplanes. In each region, say $\Omega_j, j = 1, 2, \ldots, N_p$, the characteristic equation of each PWL resistor can be represented by an affine mapping. Then the system equation will become

$$A^{(j)}x - b^{(j)} = 0, \quad x \in \Omega_j \tag{4-33}$$

for $j = 1, 2, \ldots, n_p$, and the output equation

$$y = Cx \tag{4-34}$$

Again, $x, b \in R^n, y \in R^m, A \in R^{n \times n}$, and $C \in R^{m \times n}$. Note that (4-33) is written in the Tableau equation form. In this case n is twice the number of branches, of which n_p branches are piecewise-linear. Therefore, $n \gg n_p$. Note also $\Omega_j \subset R^n$. For an illustration of Tableau equations of PWL circuits, see Example 1.

Next, we want to model the perturbation in such a way that it can be non-linear. The n_p equation (4-33) can be viewed by a single equation as follows:

$$f(x) = 0, \quad x \in R^n \tag{4-35}$$

where

$$f(x) = A^{(j)}x - b^{(j)}, \quad x \in \Omega_j, \quad j = 1, 2, \ldots, n_p \tag{4-36}$$

Therefore, a perturbation of f can be written as

$$\tilde{f}(x) = f(x) + \phi(x) \tag{4-37}$$

where $\phi: R^n \to R^n$ is the (nonlinear) perturbation and $\tilde{f}(x)$ is the perturbed system. Note that $\phi(\cdot)$ is unknown and need not be piecewise-linear. The perturbed system equation then becomes

$$A^{(j)}x - b^{(j)} + \phi(x) = 0, \quad x \in \Omega_j \tag{4-38}$$

for $j = 1, 2, \ldots, n_p$. Since both the system equation (4-33) and its perturbed equation (4-38) are nonlinear, each of them may admit zero solution, one unique solution, or multiple solutions. For example, the system equation may have three solutions and its perturbed system may have five solutions which may not be in the same region as before.

Let $x \in \Omega_j$ be a solution of the normal circuit and $\hat{x} \in \Omega_k$ be one of the perturbed circuits. Then

$$A^{(j)}x - b^{(j)} = 0, \quad x \in \Omega_j \tag{4-39}$$

$$A^{(k)}\hat{x} - b^{(k)} + \phi(\hat{x}) = 0, \quad \hat{x} \in \Omega_k \tag{4-40}$$

Usually, the normal region Ω_j is known, but the perturbed region Ω_k is unknown and the determination of Ω_k is part of the diagnosis problem. Note that the system equation is written in such a way that each circuit element appears in one and only one row and no two circuit elements appear in the same row. Hence, *the ith circuit element is perturbed if and only if the ith component of $\phi(x)$ is nonzero*. Therefore, *the purpose of diagnosis is to identify the nonzero components of ϕ* from (4-39), (4-40), and the output equation (4-34).

This may be proceeded like the way we treat linear systems by combining (4-39) and (4-40) and putting it in terms of the normal circuit parameters. In doing so, we have

$$[A^{(j)} + \Delta A^{(j)}]\hat{x} - [b^{(j)} + \Delta b^{(j)}] = 0 \tag{4-41}$$

where

$$\Delta A^{(j)} \hat{x} = [A^{(k)} - A^{(j)}] \hat{x} + \phi(\hat{x}) \qquad (4\text{-}42)$$

$$\Delta b^{(j)} = b^{(k)} - b^{(j)} \qquad (4\text{-}43)$$

If we use Theorem 1 to determine the nonzero rows of $\Delta A^{(j)}$, we will not be able to locate the faulty elements, i.e., the nonzero components of $\phi(x)$. This can be seen from (4-42) that the nonzero rows of $\Delta A^{(j)}$ are no longer the same as the nonzero components of ϕ. This is because of the existence of nonzero rows of $[A^{(k)} - A^{(j)}]$. The latter creates a *look-like fault,* and they are caused by the shift of (operate) regions from Ω_j to Ω_k. This is a main source of difficulty when a *nonlinear* circuit is to be diagnosed. We will proceed to alleviate this difficulty.

If we combine (4-39), (4-40), and (4-34) in terms of parameters in Ω_k, we will have

$$\hat{y} - y^{(k)} = M^{(k)} \phi(\hat{x}), \hat{x} \in \Omega_k \qquad (4\text{-}44)$$

where

$$M^{(k)} = -C[A^{(k)}]^{-1} \qquad (4\text{-}45)$$

$$y^{(k)} = -M^{(k)} b^{(k)} \qquad (4\text{-}46)$$

If the faulty region Ω_k is identified, then $M^{(k)}$ and $y^{(k)}$ can be immediately computed from the *normal values* in Ω_k. As such, Theorem 1 can then be applied to (4-44) to locate the nonzero component of ϕ, and hence the faulty element.

The determination of the faulty region Ω_k is a very difficult problem. Fortunately, the total number of linear regions is finite and hence we can use a brute-force approach to deal with this problem as follows.

As the linear case in the previous section, let

$$Z_k = \{z \in C^n | \text{ number of nonzero components of } z \text{ not exceeding } k\} \quad (4\text{-}47)$$

Following (4-44), solve the *linear* problem

$$p^{(j)} = \hat{y}^{(j)} = M^{(j)} z, \quad z \in Z_k, \quad j = 1, 2, \ldots, n_p \qquad (4\text{-}48)$$

n_p times. Any solution of (4-48) is a candidate for solution of the diagnosis problem. Will the solution of (4-48) be unique? It may be interesting to see that the answer is affirmative.

Theorem 2.   Equation (4-48) has a unique solution $z \in Z_k$ for almost all $p^{(j)}$ if and only if the global column ranks of $M^{(j)}$ for $j = 1, 2, \ldots, n_p$ are at least $k + 1$.

When Theorem 2 is satisfied, the solution of (4-48) can be obtained in the following way: Let the column vectors of $M^{(j)}$ be denoted by

$$M^{(j)} = [m_1^{(j)}, m_2^{(j)}, \ldots, m_n^{(j)}]$$

Let the test matrices $T_i^{(j)}$ be constructed in the following way:

$$T_i^{(j)} = [m_{i_1}^{(j)}, m_{i_2}^{(j)}, \ldots, m_{i_k}^{(j)}, p^{(j)}], \quad i = 1, 2, \ldots, s, \quad s = C(n, k)$$

for every k columns of $M^{(j)}$, and for $j = 1, 2, \ldots, n_p$. Then:
A. If

$$\text{Rank } T_i^{(j)} = k + 1, \quad \forall i \text{ and } \forall j \tag{4-49}$$

then there is no solution $z \in Z_k$.
B. Otherwise, there is a *unique* $T_i^{(j)}$ such that

$$\text{Rank } T_i^{(j)} = k \tag{4-50}$$

and the rank for all other T's are $(k + 1)$. Furthermore, the unique solution $z \in Z_k$ of (4-48) is in Ω_j, and hence the faulty region is identified. Its solution can be obtained, for example, by (4-14).
Examples are given in the next section.
Let us evaluate this method:

1. *This method is efficient.* The optimal number of test points needed is the same as that for linear circuit, i.e., $(k + 1)$ test points for k-fault diagnosis.
2. *This method is robust.* In the tolerance case, all the methods applicable to linear circuits is also applicable to nonlinear circuits. They are equally as robust.
3. *The post-fault computation is low.* All the computation for $M^{(k)}$ and $y^{(k)}$ depends only on the *normal* values in Ω_k. Hence, they can be prefault computed. The post-fault computation involves the rank tests of T matrix, which has a size of $m \times (k + 1)$, *regardless of the complexity of the circuit.*

Here, m is the number of test points and k the number of faults under consideration. Both of them are much smaller than the complexity of the circuit.

Remarks:

1. *The problem of look-like faults has been alleviated.* By writing the fault equation in the faulty region instead of normal region, the problem of look-like faults disappears.
2. *The problem of multiple solutions disappeared.* It is not self-evident how the problem of multiple solutions disappeared. A close look at our method will see why. First, the test covers *all* regions, including those that have normal solutions. Secondly, the test is only on the particular fault solutions $x \in \Omega_k$ in a particular fault region which is measured by $\hat{y}$. With this faulty solution, the faulty element can already be isolated. Hence, other faulty solutions, which were not measured, were no longer needed for the purpose of diagnosis.
3. *This method accepts any nonlinear fault.* Although the normal model for the nonlinear circuit is by piecewise-linear circuit, no such assumption is made for the fault characteristic. Hence, it has wide applications.
4. *Design of testability.* For a linear circuit, according to the topology of the circuit, one can design the location of test points so that the circuits can be k-fault diagnosable. The same is true for nonlinear circuits. First, we will short a branch if any segment of its piecewise-linear characteristic is a short circuit, and, similarly, open a branch the same way. Then the same topological conditions for linear circuits can now be applied to the resulting graph of the nonlinear circuit for the design of the location of test points for k-fault diagnosis.
5. *Reduced Tableau equation.* The development of our method depends on the circuit equation being written in the Tableau equation form. Actually, we only need the property that every element appears in one and only one row of A and no two elements appear in the same row. Therefore, there is room for improvement. Is there a circuit equation which is smaller in size but still has the same property? One such answer is the reduced Tableau equation, which is given here:

$$A = \begin{bmatrix} K_1 & -K_v A_a^T \\ A_a & 0 \end{bmatrix}, \quad b = \begin{bmatrix} I_s \\ 0 \end{bmatrix} \qquad (4\text{-}51)$$

where K_I and K_v are $n_b \times n_b$ branch-impedance and conductance matrices, where n_b is the number of branches, I_s is the independent source vector, and A_a is the incidence matrix. An example is given in the next section.

EXAMPLES

In this section we give three examples to illustrate our method.

Example 1: Reduced Tabular Equation and Illustration of Diagnosis Procedure

In this example, the circuit in Fig. 4–1 consists of a transistor which will be modeled by small signal linear circuits as shown in Fig. 4–2, and a diode which will be modeled by a PWL resistor with two segments as shown in Fig. 4–3. The final circuit model is depicted as Fig. 4–4. Because of the diode, the whole space is divided into two regions, Ω_1 and Ω_2. The reduced Tabular equation (4-51) can be shown as following:

$$A^{(k)}x - b^{(k)} = 0, \quad x \in \Omega_k, \quad k = 1, 2$$

$$A^{(k)} = \begin{bmatrix}
1 & 0 & 0 & 0 & 0 & 0 & 0 & 0 & 0 & -g_0 & 0 & 0 \\
0 & 1 & 0 & 0 & 0 & 0 & 0 & 0 & -g_1 & g_1 & 0 & 0 \\
0 & 0 & 1 & 0 & 0 & 0 & 0 & 0 & -g_2 & 0 & g_2 & 0 \\
0 & 0 & 0 & 1 & 0 & 0 & 0 & 0 & -g_3 & 0 & 0 & g_3 \\
0 & 0 & 0 & 0 & 1 & 0 & 0 & 0 & 0 & 0 & 0 & -g_4 \\
-\beta & 0 & 0 & 0 & 0 & 1 & 0 & 0 & 0 & 0 & 0 & 0 \\
0 & 0 & 0 & 0 & 0 & 0 & 1 & 0 & 0 & 0 & -g^{(k)} & g^{(k)} \\
0 & 0 & 0 & 0 & 0 & 0 & 0 & 0 & 1 & 0 & 0 & 0 \\
0 & 1 & 1 & 1 & 0 & 0 & 0 & 1 & 0 & 0 & 0 & 0 \\
1 & -1 & 0 & 0 & 0 & 0 & 0 & 0 & 0 & 0 & 0 & 0 \\
0 & 0 & -1 & 0 & 0 & 1 & 1 & 0 & 0 & 0 & 0 & 0 \\
0 & 0 & 0 & -1 & 1 & 0 & -1 & 0 & 0 & 0 & 0 & 0
\end{bmatrix}$$

$$x = [i_0, i_1, i_2, i_3, i_4, i_5, i_6, i_7, e_1, e_2, e_3, e_4]^T$$

$$b^{(k)} = [0, 0, 0, 0, 0, 0, s^{(k)}, V_s, 0, 0, 0, 0]^T$$

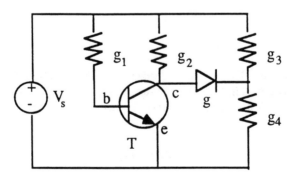

Figure 4–1   *Circuit of Example 1.*

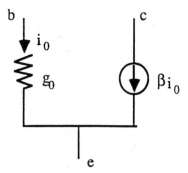

Figure 4–2 *A model of a transistor.*

Here, $x \in \Omega^{(1)}$, if $i_6 \geq 0$ and $x \in \Omega^{(2)}$ if $i_6 < 0$. Note that each element appears in one and only one row of $[A^{(k)}, b^{(k)}]$.

The testing nodes are assigned to be e_3 and e_4; then $M^{(1)}, y^{(1)}, M^{(2)}$, and $y^{(2)}$ can be calculated by (4-45) and (4-46) before the testing. Note that if a Tabular equation is used, the size of the matrix A would be 20×20. The reduced Tabular equation is only 12×12.

In region Ω_1:

$$A^{(1)}x - b^{(1)} = 0, \quad x \in \Omega_1$$

$$y = Cx$$

$$C = \begin{bmatrix} 0 & 0 & 0 & 0 & 0 & 0 & 0 & 0 & 0 & 0 & 1 & 0 \\ 0 & 0 & 0 & 0 & 0 & 0 & 0 & 0 & 0 & 0 & 0 & 1 \end{bmatrix}$$

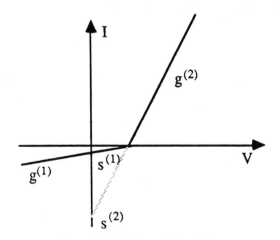

Figure 4–3 *V–I curve of a diode.*

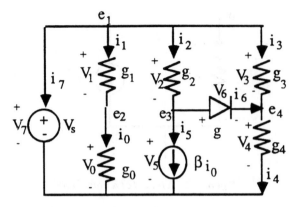

Figure 4–4   *Circuit model of Example 1.*

$$
A^{(1)} = \begin{bmatrix}
1 & 0 & 0 & 0 & 0 & 0 & 0 & 0 & 0 & -0.01 & 0 & 0 \\
0 & 1 & 0 & 0 & 0 & 0 & 0 & 0 & -0.001 & 0.001 & 0 & 0 \\
0 & 0 & 1 & 0 & 0 & 0 & 0 & 0 & -0.06 & 0 & 0.06 & 0 \\
0 & 0 & 0 & 1 & 0 & 0 & 0 & 0 & -0.005 & 0 & 0 & 0.005 \\
0 & 0 & 0 & 0 & 1 & 0 & 0 & 0 & 0 & 0 & 0 & -0.05 \\
-50 & 0 & 0 & 0 & 0 & 1 & 0 & 0 & 0 & 0 & 0 & 0 \\
0 & 0 & 0 & 0 & 0 & 0 & 1 & 0 & 0 & 0 & -0.0001 & 0.0001 \\
0 & 0 & 0 & 0 & 0 & 0 & 0 & 0 & 1 & 0 & 0 & 0 \\
0 & 1 & 1 & 1 & 0 & 0 & 0 & 1 & 0 & 0 & 0 & 0 \\
1 & -1 & 0 & 0 & 0 & 0 & 0 & 0 & 0 & 0 & 0 & 0 \\
0 & 0 & -1 & 0 & 0 & 1 & 1 & 0 & 0 & 0 & 0 & 0 \\
0 & 0 & 0 & -1 & 1 & 0 & -1 & 0 & 0 & 0 & 0 & 0
\end{bmatrix}
$$

$$
x = [i_0, i_1, i_2, i_3, i_4, i_5, i_6, i_7, e_1, e_2, e_3, e_4]^T
$$

$$
b^{(1)} = [0, 0, 0, 0, 0, 0, -0.0000325, 6, 0, 0, 0, 0]^T
$$

$$
M^{(1)} = -C\,[A^{(1)}]^{-1}
$$

$$
= \begin{bmatrix}
75.632 & 756.32 & -16.639 & -0.0302 & 0.0302 & 16.639 & 16.609 & -0.2422 & 0.0001 & 756.32 & -16.639 & -0.0302 \\
0.1373 & 1.3726 & -0.0302 & -18.149 & 18.149 & 0.0302 & -18.119 & -0.0912 & -0.0001 & 1.3726 & -0.0302 & -18.149
\end{bmatrix}
$$

$$
y^{(1)} = -M^{(1)}b^{(1)} = [1.4536,\ 0.5465]^T
$$

In region Ω_2:

$$
A^{(2)}x - b^{(2)} = 0,\ x \in \Omega_2
$$

$$
y = Cx
$$

$$
C = \begin{bmatrix}
0 & 0 & 0 & 0 & 0 & 0 & 0 & 0 & 0 & 0 & 1 & 0 \\
0 & 0 & 0 & 0 & 0 & 0 & 0 & 0 & 0 & 0 & 0 & 1
\end{bmatrix}
$$

$$A^{(2)} = \begin{bmatrix} 0 & 0 & 0 & 0 & 0 & 0 & 0 & 0 & 0 & -0.01 & 0 & 0 \\ 0 & 1 & 0 & 0 & 0 & 0 & 0 & 0 & -0.001 & 0.001 & 0 & 0 \\ 0 & 0 & 1 & 0 & 0 & 0 & 0 & 0 & -0.06 & 0 & 0.06 & 0 \\ 0 & 0 & 0 & 1 & 0 & 0 & 0 & 0 & -0.005 & 0 & 0 & 0.005 \\ 0 & 0 & 0 & 0 & 1 & 0 & 0 & 0 & 0 & 0 & 0 & -0.05 \\ -50 & 0 & 0 & 0 & 0 & 1 & 0 & 0 & 0 & 0 & 0 & 0 \\ 0 & 0 & 0 & 0 & 0 & 0 & 1 & 0 & 0 & 0 & -0.079 & 0.079 \\ 0 & 0 & 0 & 0 & 0 & 0 & 0 & 0 & 1 & 0 & 0 & 0 \\ 0 & 1 & 1 & 1 & 0 & 0 & 0 & 1 & 0 & 0 & 0 & 0 \\ 1 & -1 & 0 & 0 & 0 & 0 & 0 & 0 & 0 & 0 & 0 & 0 \\ 0 & 0 & -1 & 0 & 0 & 1 & 1 & 0 & 0 & 0 & 0 & 0 \\ 0 & 0 & 0 & -1 & 1 & 0 & -1 & 0 & 0 & 0 & 0 & 0 \end{bmatrix}$$

$$x = [i_0, i_1, i_2, i_3, i_4, i_5, i_6, i_7, e_1, e_2, e_3, e_4]^T$$

$$b^{(2)} = [0, 0, 0, 0, 0, 0, -0.0258, 6, 0, 0, 0, 0]^T$$

$$M^{(2)} = -C [A^{(2)}]^{-1}$$

$$= \begin{bmatrix} 49.144 & 491.44 & -10.812 & -6.387 & 6.387 & 10.82 & 4.424 & -0.1892 & 0.0001 & 491.44 & -10.812 & -6.3873 \\ 29.033 & 290.33 & -6.387 & -11.214 & 11.214 & 6.387 & -4.8266 & -0.149 & -0.0001 & 290.33 & -6.3873 & -11.214 \end{bmatrix}$$

$$y^{(2)} = -M^{(2)}b^{(2)} = [1.2493, 0.7693]^T$$

A normal solution x can be found *in the region* Ω_2, and

$$x = [i_0, i_1, i_2, i_3, i_4, i_5, i_6, i_7, e_1, e_2, e_3, e_4]^T$$

$$= [0.0055, 0.0055, 0.285, 0.0262, 0.0385, 0.2727, 0.0123, -0.3166, 6, 0.5455, 1.2493, 0.7693]^T$$

$$y = [e_3, e_4]^T = [1.2493, 0.7693]^T$$

When g_3 is faulty and its value changes from 0.005 to 0.02, $\phi(x)$ becomes

$$\phi(x) = \Delta A^{(2)}x - \Delta b^{(2)}$$

$$\Delta A^{(2)} = \begin{bmatrix} 0 & 0 & 0 & 0 & 0 & 0 & 0 & 0 & 0 & 0 & 0 & 0 \\ 0 & 0 & 0 & 0 & 0 & 0 & 0 & 0 & 0 & 0 & 0 & 0 \\ 0 & 0 & 0 & 0 & 0 & 0 & 0 & 0 & 0 & 0 & 0 & 0 \\ 0 & 0 & 0 & 0 & 0 & 0 & 0 & 0 & -0.015 & 0 & 0 & 0.015 \\ 0 & 0 & 0 & 0 & 0 & 0 & 0 & 0 & 0 & 0 & 0 & 0 \\ 0 & 0 & 0 & 0 & 0 & 0 & 0 & 0 & 0 & 0 & 0 & 0 \\ 0 & 0 & 0 & 0 & 0 & 0 & 0 & 0 & 0 & 0 & -0.0793 & 0.0793 \\ 0 & 0 & 0 & 0 & 0 & 0 & 0 & 0 & 0 & 0 & 0 & 0 \\ 0 & 0 & 0 & 0 & 0 & 0 & 0 & 0 & 0 & 0 & 0 & 0 \\ 0 & 0 & 0 & 0 & 0 & 0 & 0 & 0 & 0 & 0 & 0 & 0 \\ 0 & 0 & 0 & 0 & 0 & 0 & 0 & 0 & 0 & 0 & 0 & 0 \\ 0 & 0 & 0 & 0 & 0 & 0 & 0 & 0 & 0 & 0 & 0 & 0 \end{bmatrix}$$

$$x = [i_0, i_1, i_2, i_3, i_4, i_5, i_6, i_7, e_1, e_2, e_3, e_4]^T$$

$$\Delta b^{(2)} = [0, 0, 0, 0, 0, 0, -0.02577, 0, 0, 0, 0, 0]^T$$

There exist two nonzero rows in $\phi(x)$. The 4th row is nonzero as it should be because g_3 is faulty and it appears in the 4th row. However, the 7th row is also nonzero, which should not be because the diode g is not faulty. The reason why the 7th row is nonzero is that when g_3 is faulty, the solution region is changed from Ω_2 to Ω_1 and the nonlinear element g will shift its bias, and hence its slope from 0.079 to 0.0001 and its intersection point from -0.0258 to -0.0000325 (see Fig. 4–3), which causes the 7th row of both $\Delta A^{(2)}$ and $\Delta b^{(2)}$ to be nonzero. Therefore, the fault of g_3 makes the diode a look-like fault. This is one difficulty one has to deal with when a nonlinear circuit is to be diagnosed. In the following, we will use the method developed in this paper to test fault elements by only using two testing nodes, i.e., e_3 and e_4.

Note that a fault solution x_f is *in the region* Ω_1, and

$$x_f = [i_0, i_1, i_2, i_3, i_4, i_5, i_6, i_7, e_1, e_2, e_3, e_4]^T$$

$$= [0.0055, 0.0055, 0.2727, 0.0857, 0.0857, 0.2727, -0.0001, -0.3639, 6, 0.5455, 1.4555, 1.7135]^T$$

$$y_f = [e_3, e_4]^T = [1.4555, 1.7135]^T$$

By using the data $M^{(1)}$, $M^{(2)}$, $y^{(1)}$, and $y^{(2)}$ calculated before, the testing procedure follows from Theorem 2.

1. Testing in Ω_1, compute the following:

$$p^{(1)} = y - y^{(1)} = [0.0019, 1.1669]^T$$

$$T_1^{(1)} = \begin{bmatrix} 75.632 & 0.0019 \\ 0.1373 & 1.1669 \end{bmatrix}, \quad T_2^{(1)} = \begin{bmatrix} 756.32 & 0.0019 \\ 1.3726 & 1.1669 \end{bmatrix}, \quad T_3^{(1)} = \begin{bmatrix} -16.639 & 0.0019 \\ -0.0302 & 1.1669 \end{bmatrix}$$

$$T_4^{(1)} = \begin{bmatrix} -0.0302 & 0.0019 \\ -18.149 & 1.1669 \end{bmatrix}, \quad T_5^{(1)} = \begin{bmatrix} 0.0302 & 0.0019 \\ 18.149 & 1.1669 \end{bmatrix}, \quad T_6^{(1)} = \begin{bmatrix} 16.639 & 0.0019 \\ 0.0302 & 1.1669 \end{bmatrix}$$

$$T_7^{(1)} = \begin{bmatrix} 16.609 & 0.0019 \\ -18.119 & 1.1669 \end{bmatrix}, \quad T_8^{(1)} = \begin{bmatrix} -0.2422 & 0.0019 \\ -0.0912 & 1.1669 \end{bmatrix}, \quad T_9^{(1)} = \begin{bmatrix} 0.0001 & 0.0019 \\ -0.0001 & 1.1669 \end{bmatrix}$$

$$T_{10}^{(1)} = \begin{bmatrix} 756.32 & 0.0019 \\ 1.3726 & 1.1669 \end{bmatrix}, \quad T_{11}^{(1)} = \begin{bmatrix} -16.639 & 0.0019 \\ -0.0302 & 1.1669 \end{bmatrix}, \quad T_{12}^{(1)} = \begin{bmatrix} -0.0302 & 0.0019 \\ -18.149 & 1.1669 \end{bmatrix}$$

Clearly, Rank $T_i^{(1)} = 2$, for $i = 1,2,3,6,7,8,9,10,11,12$. But Rank $T_4^{(1)} =$ Rank $T_5^{(1)} = 1 \Rightarrow$ **there exist faults in Ω_1, i.e., g_3 and/or g_4 is faulty.**

The fault element g_3 cannot be uniquely located by the above computation because the testability condition of Theorem 2 is not satisfied. The testability condition requires the global column rank of both $M^{(1)}$ and $M^{(2)}$ to be 2. In this case, the 4th and 5th columns of $M^{(1)}$ and $M^{(2)}$ are identical and hence their global column rank is 1, less than 2.

Note that from this example, even though the testability condition is not satisfied, we can still locate a group of potential faulty elements in which g_3 is a member. In fact, such a group can always be found whether or not the testability is satisfied. For details, see [15], in which such a group is called the T_f-equivalent class.

The fulfillment of the testability condition depends on the choice of testing points. A quick way of checking the testability condition is by topological conditions [17], in which it is only required to check the graph of the circuit. In this case, it will be shown that the testability condition cannot be satisfied, even though all the nodes are used as testing points. Under this condition, we can only determine the faculty elements up to a T_f-equivalent class.

2. Testing in Ω_2, compute the following:

$$p^{(2)} = y - y^{(2)} = [0.2062, 0.9441]^T$$

$$T_1^{(2)} = \begin{bmatrix} 49.144 & 0.2062 \\ 29.033 & 0.9441 \end{bmatrix}, \quad T_2^{(2)} = \begin{bmatrix} 491.44 & 0.2062 \\ 290.33 & 0.9441 \end{bmatrix}, \quad T_3^{(2)} = \begin{bmatrix} -10.812 & 0.2062 \\ -6.387 & 0.9441 \end{bmatrix}$$

$$T_4^{(2)} = \begin{bmatrix} -6.387 & 0.2062 \\ -11.214 & 0.9441 \end{bmatrix}, \quad T_5^{(2)} = \begin{bmatrix} 6.387 & 0.2062 \\ 11.214 & 0.9441 \end{bmatrix}, \quad T_6^{(2)} = \begin{bmatrix} 10.820 & 0.2062 \\ 6.387 & 0.9441 \end{bmatrix}$$

$$T_7^{(2)} = \begin{bmatrix} 4.424 & 0.2062 \\ -4.827 & 0.9441 \end{bmatrix}, \quad T_8^{(2)} = \begin{bmatrix} -0.1892 & 0.2062 \\ -0.1490 & 1.9441 \end{bmatrix}, \quad T_9^{(2)} = \begin{bmatrix} 0.0001 & 0.2062 \\ -0.0001 & 0.9441 \end{bmatrix}$$

$$T_{10}^{(2)} = \begin{bmatrix} 491.44 & 0.2062 \\ 290.33 & 0.9441 \end{bmatrix}, \quad T_{11}^{(2)} = \begin{bmatrix} -10.812 & 0.2062 \\ -6.3873 & 0.9441 \end{bmatrix}, \quad T_{12}^{(2)} = \begin{bmatrix} -6.3873 & 0.2062 \\ -11.214 & 0.9441 \end{bmatrix}$$

Rank $T_i^{(2)} = 2$, $\forall i = 1, \ldots, 12. \Rightarrow$ **no fault in this region.**

Note that the post-fault computation is minimal. It involves only the computation of p and the rank test of matrices T. The size of T is only $m \times (k+1)$, where m is the number of test points and k the number of faults to be tested. These numbers are independent of the size of circuit and in general is much smaller than the size of the circuit. $\square$

In the following two examples, we will apply our method to a single fault diagnosis. For a single fault, a test matrix consists of only two column vectors. Instead of checking the rank of test matrices, an alternate method can be used. Denote θ the angle between those two column vectors. When $\theta = k\pi$, the rank of its associated matrix is equal to 1 which implies that a fault has been found. We define a residual number to be $\sin(\theta)$. Then the smaller the residual number, the closer θ is to $k\pi$, and hence the better possibility the element corresponding to this residual number is faulty. The alternate method is used because it gives a measure of "closeness" of a testing matrix whose rank degenerated to 1. Further, the computation of $\sin(\theta)$ is simpler than that of θ.

Example 2: Multiple Solutions and Nonlinear Fault

We will consider a circuit [18] in Fig. 4–5 which has multisolutions under normal condition. Each transistor is modeled by a controlled source in series with p–n junction diode as shown in Fig. 4–6a. The diode I–V characteristic is approximated by a continuous piecewise-linear function with two seg-

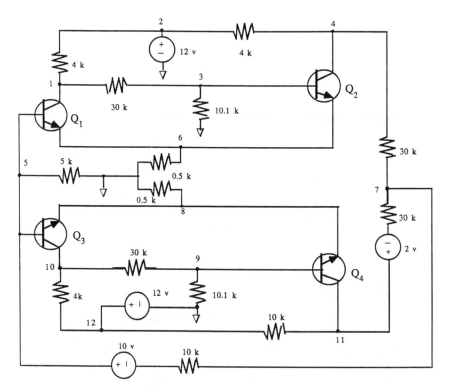

Figure 4–5 *Circuit of Example 2.*

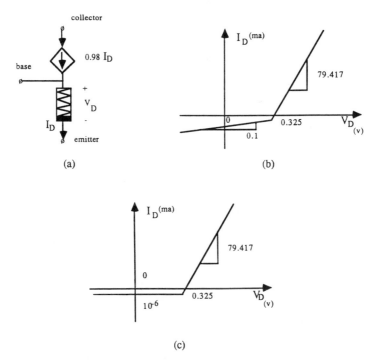

Figure 4–6 *The model of transistor in Example 2.*

ments as shown in Figs. 4–6b or c. Then the circuit model, corresponding to Fig. 4–5, is shown in Fig. 4–7. We will use (s_1,s_2,s_3,s_4) to denote the region in which the first PWL resistor is working in the s_1th segment, the second is working in the s_2th segment, and so on. This circuit has nine solutions under normal condition. When the fault is inserted into R_{14}, R_{16}, R_5, or R_4, the number of solutions will vary. In Table 4–1, the regions of solutions for each case are listed under the faulty condition specified in Table 4–2. For example, when R_4 is faulty, there will be four solutions one in each of the four regions given in the last column of Table 4–1. In the following, we will consider two cases: in Case 1, the characteristic curve of each PWL resistor has no zero admittance; in Case 2, the characteristic curve of the third PWL resistance has zero admittance.

Case 1. In this case, each diode has a characteristic given in Fig. 4–6b, where no segment has zero admittance. In order to determine a good set of test points, we need to use topological criterion given in [17]. Here, we will present a dirty but quick way of choosing testing points.

Observe the circuit N in Fig. 4–7. Pick all the nodes associated with series elements or parallel elements, after setting all dependent as well as indepen-

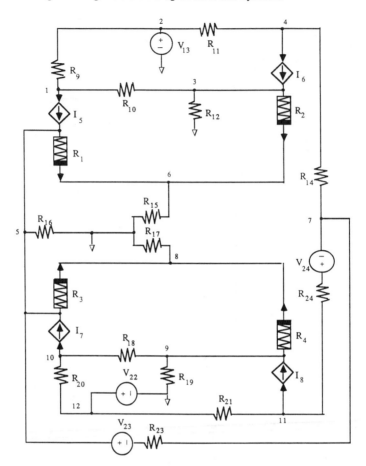

Figure 4–7   A large signal model of Example 2.

dent sources to zero. In this case, they are nodes $\{1,4,10,11\}$. Then construct $M^{(j)}$ for all 16 regions. In this case, the global column ranks of all of them are greater or equal to 2. According to Theorem 2, this circuit with the designated test points is 1-diagnosable.

Let us consider the case when R_{16} is changed from 5k to 5.001k, a mere 0.02% deviation. From Table 4–1, with this fault, we may have nine solutions, or nine stable operating points, each in one of the regions given in the third column. Therefore, the testing measurement can be any one of these nine solutions. Our method actually can pick out the faulty element wherever the measurement will be. For example, let the measurement be in the region (1,2,1,2). With this measurement, we complete the residual numbers of the pair of two columns in every test matrix $T_i^{(j)}$ for $i = 1,2, \ldots , 24$, where 24

Table 4–1   The Regions of Multisolutions in Example 2

No. of Solutions	Normal Case	R_{14} Fault Case	R_{16} Fault Case	R_5 Fault Case	R_4 Fault Case
1	(2,1,2,1)	(2,1,2,1)	(2,1,2,1)	(2,1,2,1)	(2,2,1,2)
2	(2,1,1,2)	(2,1,1,2)	(2,1,1,2)	(2,2,2,1)	(1,2,1,2)
3	(2,2,2,1)	(2,2,2,1)	(2,2,2,1)	(1,2,2,1)	(1,2,2,2)
4	(2,2,1,2)	(2,2,1,2)	(2,2,1,2)	(1,2,1,2)	(2,2,2,2)
5	(1,2,2,1)	(1,2,2,1)	(1,2,2,1)	(1,2,2,2)	
6	(1,2,1,2)	(1,2,1,2)	(1,2,1,2)	(2,2,2,2)	
7	(1,2,2,2)	(1,2,2,2)	(1,2,2,2)	(2,1,2,2)	
8	(2,2,2,2)	(2,2,2,2)	(2,2,2,2)		
9	(2,1,2,2)	(2,1,2,2)	(2,1,2,2)		

is the number of branch in the circuit. Then do the same for every region for all 16 regions. The smallest residual number indicates the faulty element.

All these residual numbers are tabulated in the Appendix. Note that all the residual numbers are in the order of 10^{-1}, except four numbers. The numbers in regions (1,2,1,1), (1,2,2,2), and (1,1,1,2) are on the order of 10^{-5}, while the one in (1,2,1,2) is on the order of 10^{-8}. Clearly, the last one indicates the faulty element. This element is found to be the 16th element and its operating point is in the region (1,2,1,2) as it should. This result is tabulated in the third row of Table 4–2. Other simulated results are also tabulated in Table 4–2. It can be seen that all diagnosed results are correct for different fault situations. For example, in the case of β_1, the fault is at the dependent source of the transistor β_1. Two of the seven possible solutions have been tested. The fault element and the region of operating point are correctly indicated in both cases. In the case of R_4, a nonlinear fault is simulated. Both slope and

Table 4–2   The Results of Fault Diagnosis in Case 1 of Example 2
(with Four Measurement Nodes: "1," "4," "10," "11")

Fault Case	Regions of Measurements	Smallest Residual No.	Diagnosed Fault Element	Diagnosed Operating Regions
R_{14}	(1,2,2,1)	2.3264E-8	R_{14}	(1,2,2,1)
(30k → 40k)	(2,1,2,2)	0.0	R_{14}	(2,1,2,2)
R_{16}	(1,2,1,2)	1.2355E-8	R_{16}	(1,2,1,2)
(5k → 5.001k)				
β_1	(1,2,2,2)	0.0	β_1	(1,2,2,2)
(0.98 → 0.8)	(2,1,2,2)	1.4428E-8	β_1	(2,1,2,2)
R_4	(1,2,1,2)	1.3433E-8	R_4	(1,2,1,1)
(0.325 → 0.725)		0.0	R_4	(1,2,1,2)
(0.1 → 1)				

Note that the smallest residual numbers indicate correct fault elements and operating regions.

breakpoint are deviated. Again the faulty element and its region of operating point are correctly indicated by the smallest residual number. However, one may also interpret that the region of operating point could be in either region $(1,2,1,1)$ or region $(1,2,1,2)$ if we consider $10^{-8} \approx 0$. This does not introduce any inconsistency because these two regions differ in the fourth number, which involves only R_4. When there is a nonlinear fault occurred in R_4, the operating region after the fault may no longer be the same as that before the fault. Hence, the residuals may indicate some ambiguity of the regions of operating points, but no ambiguity for the faulty element.

In summary, this case demonstrated the difficulty of diagnosis of nonlinear circuits when there are multiple solutions and nonlinear faults. It also demonstrated that our method can resolve all these difficulties efficiently.

Case 2.   In this case, all the circuit elements are the same as before, except the third diode, which has the characteristic given in Fig. 4–6c. If we use the same testing points $\{1,4,10,11\}$, we cannot diagnose the R_4 fault. This is indicated in the first and third rows of Table 4–3, for which two different operating points in regions $(1,2,1,2)$ and $(2,2,1,2)$ are used. The test will indicate that either R_4 or R_{17} is faulty. The reason is that, in both regions, the third diode is operated in the first segment and in this segment its admittance is zero, or R_3 is an open circuit. In this case, it can be seen from Fig. 4–7 that R_{17} and R_4 are in series and hence cannot be diagnosed. On the other hand, if we add one more test point at node 8, then it becomes diagnosable as is shown in the second and fourth rows of Table 4–3.

In summary, in the diagnosis of nonlinear circuits, beware of these nonlinear elements which have zero-admittance segments.

Table 4–3   The Results of Fault Diagnosis in Case 2 of Example 2 (R_4 Fault with Both Breakpoint Variation from 0.325 to 0.725 and Slope Variation from 0.1 to 1)

No. of Measurements	Regions of Measurements	Smallest Residual No.	Diagnosed Fault Elements	Diagnosed Operating Regions
Four nodes 1,4,10,11	$(1,2,1,2)$	1.0537E-8	R_4	$(1,2,1,1)$
		6.4524E-9	R_{17}	$(1,2,1,1)$
		0.0	R_4	$(1,2,1,2)$
		0.0	R_{17}	$(1,2,1,2)$
Five nodes 1,4,10,11,8	$(1,2,1,2)$	1.5805E-8	R_4	$(1,2,1,1)$
		0.0	R_4	$(1,2,1,2)$
Four nodes 1,4,10,11	$(2,2,1,2)$	1.3432E-8	R_4	$(2,2,1,1)$
		0.0	R_{17}	$(2,2,1,1)$
		5.2684E-9	R_4	$(2,2,1,2)$
		0.0	R_{17}	$(2,2,1,2)$
Five nodes 1,4,10,11,8	$(2,2,1,2)$	1.5805E-8	R_4	$(2,2,1,1)$
		0.0	R_4	$(2,2,1,2)$

Since this circuit exhibits all major issues of nonlinear circuit diagnosis, it can be used as a **benchmark circuit.**

Example 3: CMOS Operational Amplifier

The circuits used in this example are in typical two-stage CMOS operational amplifier as shown in Fig. 4–8. We use the circuit model shown in Fig. 4–9a to represent an MOS transistor, which consists of two current dependent sources, and one PWL resistor. For different channel MOS, the characteristic of PWL resistor will change, Fig. 4–9b represents a p-channel, and Fig. 4–9c an n-channel. The large signal circuit model of MOS operational amplifier is shown as in Fig. 4–10. The linear resistor is usually very large; we select linear resistor R_0 around 10^6. The parameters selected in these circuits are listed in Table 4–4. The normal circuits have been simulated. The gain of the circuit is around 1000, and the normal operating region of PWL resistors is in $(2,2,2,2,2,2,2,2)$.

We will use R_i in Fig. 4–10 to represent both resistors and dependent sources. For example, R_{21} represents the current dependent source in Q_2. This circuit has many more branches than nodes, and there are also many parallel elements, which makes the circuit extremely difficult to diagnose. But we still can obtain equivalent classes of fault elements [15]. In the large signal model of operational amplifier, as shown in Fig. 4–10, the dash line box outlines one MOS transistor; we can define that an MOS is fault when any one of the elements in the box is fault. Different faults have been inserted in R_1, R_5, R_{10}, R_{11}, and R_{33}. In Table 4–5, we not only use residual number to indicate the diagnosed fault elements, but also the diagnosed operating regions. For example, as shown in the second row, when the breakpoint of R_5 has changed

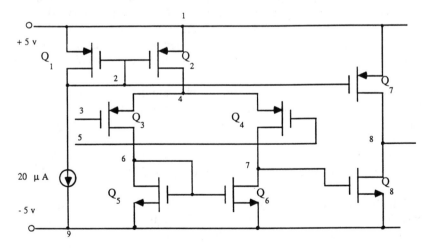

Figure 4–8 *CMOS operational amplifier.*

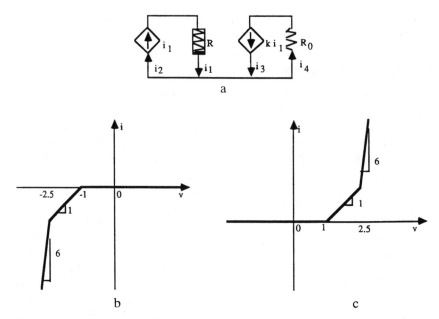

Figure 4–9 *(a) A model of MOS transistor. (b) p-Channel MOS characteristic of PWL resistor. (c) n-Channel MOS characteristic of PWL resistor.*

from 1 to 0.7, that is, the threshold voltage of MOS transistor Q_5 has changed, the region of operating point becomes (2,2,2,2,2,2,2,1), instead of normal operating region (2,2,2,2,2,2,2,2). The smallest residual number indicates correctly the diagnosed fault element, R_5, but ambiguously the operating regions (2,2,2,2,1,1,2,1), (2,2,2,2,2,2,2,1), and (2,2,2,2,3,3,2,1). Hence we have uniquely identified the fault element, by the measurements of four node voltages, "4," "6," "7," "8," even if we cannot uniquely identify its operating region.

Take the case of the R_{10} fault. Our test indicates its equivalence class $\{R_{21}, R_{24}, R_{27}, R_{10}\}$. This is no surprise because all these elements are in parallel and connecting node 4 and the ground, and they cannot be diagnosed by measuring node voltages.

Next, consider the case of R_{11}. Its equivalence class is $\{R_3, R_{25}, R_{11}\}$. The dependent current source R_{25} is parallel to R_{11}, and R_3 is the control branch of R_{25}.

Finally, consider the case of current dependent source R_{33}. Its equivalence class is $\{R_8, R_{23}, R_{33}, R_{15}, R_{16}, R_{17}\}$. The elements R_{16}, R_{17}, R_{15}, and R_{23} are parallel to R_{33}, connecting node 8 to the ground. The resistor R_8 is the control branch of R_{33}.

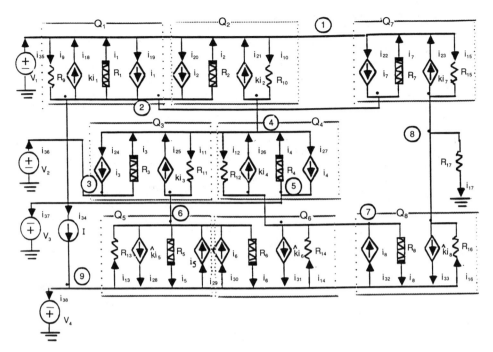

Figure 4–10 *A large signal model of CMOS operational amplifier in Example 3.*

Table 4–4 The Parameters in Circuits of Example 3

Element in Circuits	Characteristic of PWL Resistor R	$K\,(\times 10^{-6})$ in Dependent Source	Linear Resistor $R_0\,(\times 10^6)$
Q1	*p*-channel	−12.5	1.0
Q2	*p*-channel	−12.5	1.0
Q3	*p*-channel	−12.5	1.0
Q4	*p*-channel	−12.5	1.0
Q5	*n*-channel	−6.25	0.5
Q6	*n*-channel	−6.25	0.5
Q7	*p*-channel	−12.5	1.0
Q8	*n*-channel	−12.5	1.0

The load resistor, R_{17}, is 100 Ω, and independent sources I, V_1, V_2, V_3, and V_4 are 20 μA, 5 V, 1.0 V, 0.99 V, and 5 V, respectively.

Table 4–5 The Results of Fault Diagnosis in Example 3

Fault Case and No. of Measurements	Region of Measurement	Smallest Residual No.	Diagnosed Fault Elements	Diagnosed Operating Regions
R_1:	(2,2,2,2,2,2,2,2)	9.3143E-9	R_1	(1,1,2,2,2,2,1,2)
Slope: $1 \rightarrow 1.154$		9.8562E-9	R_1	(2,2,2,2,2,2,2,2)
Breakpoint: $-1 \rightarrow -1.2$		0.0	R_1	(3,3,2,2,2,2,3,2)
3 nodes: 2, 4, 8				
R_5:	(2,2,2,2,2,2,2,1)	0.0	R_5	(2,2,2,2,1,1,2,1)
Breakpoint: $1 \rightarrow 0.7$		0.0	R_5	(2,2,2,2,2,2,2,1)
4 nodes: 4, 6, 7, 8		0.0	R_5	(2,2,2,2,3,3,2,1)
R_{10}:	(2,2,2,2,2,2,2,2)	1.3432E-8	R_{21}	(2,2,2,2,2,2,2,2)
$1E+6 \rightarrow 0.5E+6$		1.1176E-8	R_{24}	(2,2,2,2,2,2,2,2)
4 nodes: 4, 6, 7, 8		1.3432E-8	R_{27}	(2,2,2,2,2,2,2,2)
		1.6238E-8	R_{10}	(2,2,2,2,2,2,2,2)
R_{11}	(2,2,3,3,2,2,2,1)	1.3432E-8	R_3	(2,2,3,3,2,2,2,1)
$1E+6 \rightarrow 1E+3$		0.0	R_3	(2,2,2,3,2,2,2,1)
4 nodes: 4, 6, 7, 8		1.8626E-8	R_3	(2,2,1,3,2,2,2,1)
		9.8562E-9	R_{25}	(2,2,3,3,2,2,2,1)
		0.0	R_{25}	(2,2,2,3,2,2,2,1)
		0.0	R_{25}	(2,2,1,3,2,2,2,1)
		0.0	R_{11}	(2,2,3,3,2,2,2,1)
		0.0	R_{11}	(2,2,2,3,2,2,2,1)
		1.2905E-8	R_{11}	(2,2,1,3,2,2,2,1)
R_{33}	(2,2,2,2,2,2,2,2)	7.4506E-9	R_8	(2,2,2,2,2,2,2,2)
$-12.5E-5 \rightarrow -12.5E-3$		0.0	R_{23}	(2,2,2,2,2,2,2,2)
4 nodes: 4, 6, 7, 8		0.0	R_{33}	(2,2,2,2,2,2,2,2)
		9.8562E-9	R_{15}	(2,2,2,2,2,2,2,2)
		0.0	R_{16}	(2,2,2,2,2,2,2,2)
		5.2684E-9	R_{17}	(2,2,2,2,2,2,2,2)

CONCLUSION

There are two major issues which make the nonlinear fault diagnosis problem much more difficult than the linear ones. One is the bias-shifting of nonlinear devices, the other is multiple-solutions of nonlinear circuits. In this chapter, we have presented a new method to circumvent these problems. In this method, all the advantages of linear circuit diagnosis are preserved. It is still efficient because the number of test points need not be increased. Its post fault computation is still as simple as the linear ones, and hence its per-unit cost is low. It is still reliable because the method for linear circuits with tolerance can be used. Finally, the topological conditions can still be used for the design of test points.

APPENDIX

In this appendix, the simulation result for the R_{16} fault case in Example 2 is presented. A 4-dimensional array X is used to denote the region. A vector with 24 components represents the residual number associated with each element in circuit. It is clear that all residual numbers are on the order 10^{-1}, except that numbers in regions $(1,2,1,1)$, $(1,2,2,2)$, and $(1,1,1,2)$ are in the order of 10^{-5}, while the one in $(1,2,1,2)$ is on the order of 10^{-8} which indicates the faulty element.

REFERENCES

[1] T. J. Rothenberg, "Identification in Parametric Models," *Econometrica*, Vol. 39, pp. 577–591, May 1971.

[2] K. C. Varghese, J. H. Williams, and D. R. Towill, "Simplified ATPG and Analog Fault Location Via a Clustering and Separability Technique," *IEEE Trans. Circuits Syst.*, Vol. CAS-26, pp. 496–505, 1979.

[3] W. Hochwald and J. D. Bastian, "A dc Approach for Analog Fault Dictionary Determination," *IEEE Trans. Circuits Syst.*, Vol. CAS-26, pp. 523–529, 1979.

[4] V. Visvanathan and A. Sangiovanni-Vincentelli, "Fault Diagnosis of Nonlinear Memoryless Systems," *Proc. IEEE Int. Symp. Circuits Syst.*, pp. 1087–1091, 1980.

[5] V. Visvanathan and A. Sangiovanni-Vincentelli, "Diagnosability of Nonlinear Circuits and Systems—Part I: the DC Case,"*IEEE Trans. Circuits Syst.*, Vol. CAS-28, pp. 1093–1102, 1981.

[6] P. M. Lin, "DC Fault Diagnosis using Complementary Pivot Theory," *Proc. IEEE Int. Symp. Circuits Syst.*, pp. 1132–1135, 1982.

[7] P. M. Lin and Y. S. Elcherif, "Analogue Circuits Fault Dictionary—New Approaches and Implementation," *Circuit Theory Appl.*, Vol. 13, pp. 149–172, 1985.

[8] D. C. Jiao, "Fault Diagnosis of Nonlinear Circuits and Systems via Volterra Series," *Proc. IEEE Int. Symp. Circuits Syst.*, pp. 1241–1244, 1985.

[9] Q. Huang and R. W. Liu, "Fault Diagnosis of Piecewise-Linear Circuits," *Proc. IEEE Int. Symp. Circuits Syst.*, pp. 418–421, 1987.

[10] W. G. Luo and S. W. Zhang, "Multi-Fault Diagnosis of DC-Nonlinear Analog Circuits," *Proc. IEEE Int. Symp. Circuits Syst.*, pp. 1171–1174, 1988.

[11] R. Zou, "Fault Analysis of Nonlinear Circuits from Node Voltage Measurements," *Proc. IEEE Int. Symp. Circuits Syst.*, pp. 1155–1158, 1988.

[12] G. O. Hachtel, R. K. Brayton, and F. G. Gustafson, "The Sparse Tableau Approach to Network Analysis and Design," *IEEE Trans. Circuit Theorem*, Vol. CT-18, pp. 101–113, 1971.

[13] R. Liu, "A Circuit Theoretic Approach to Analog Fault Diagnosis," this book.

[14] Z. F. Huang, C. S. Lin, and R. Liu, "Node-Fault Diagnosis and a Design of Testability," *IEEE Trans. CAS,* CAS-30, No. 5 pp. 257–265, May 1983.

[15] Y. Togawa, T. Matsumoto, and H. Arai, "The T_F-Equivalence Class Approach to Analog Fault Diagnosis Problems," *IEEE Trans. CAS,* CAS-33, No. 10. pp. 992–1009, Oct. 1986.

[16] Z. F. Huang and R. Liu, "Analog Fault Diagnosis with Tolerance," *IEEE Int. Symp. Circuits Syst.,* pp. 1332–1336, 1986.

[17] Chen-Shang Lin, "Topological Testability Conditions for Analog Fault Diagnosis," this book.

[18] Leon O. Chua and R. L. P. Ying, "Finding all Solutions of Piecewise-Linear Circuits," *Int. J. Circuit Theory Appl.,* Vol. 10, pp. 201–229, 1982.

5

Analog Multifrequency Fault Diagnosis with the Assumption of Limited Failures

RAY DECARLO,
LAWRENCE RAPISARDA,
and
MARK WICKS

This chapter deals with the problem of diagnosing a linearized time invariant circuit under the assumption that there are a limited number of failures/faults, n_f, whose number may equal or exceed the number of output test measurements, n_0 [1–3]. The problem is cast and its solution formulated in the context of a frequency domain tableau based on the component connection model (CCM) [4,5]. The basic thrust of the approach is to generalize the multifrequency diagnosis development and solution algorithm in [4] which focuses on the problem of complete fault diagnosis, i.e., $n_f = N$, where N is the total number of circuit parameters. The proper niche for the techniques explained here is after a nonlinear diagnosis of bias points and opens and shorts has taken place using, say, the methods of [6]. This is reasonable in view of the fact that approximately 65% of field failures are opens or shorts. Once open and short possibilities are eliminated and DC bias points determined, e.g., so as to determine a load line on a transistor equivalent circuit, it would be appropriate to diagnose the linearized circuit for those circuit elements or shop replaceable unit parameters which have drifted out of tolerance.

Implicit in the perspective of this chapter is the idea that the maximum number of potential simultaneous faults, n_f, is much much less than N. Intuitive justification comes about because parameter failures are often statistically independent. Even if they are not, the likelihood of more than a limited number of simultaneous failures has an extremely small probability of occurrence. In addition one would expect that the number of available test points, n_0, is also small and could be less than the assumed number of maximum failures, n_f. Hence throughout the chapter it is implicitly assumed that $n_0 \leq n_f$. This leads to a set of fault diagnosis equations which is nonlinear and requires multifrequency test measurements to obtain a solution. (This is in contrast to the developments of [7–10] where the assumption of $n_0 > n_f$ leads to linear diagnosis equations.) Fortunately, in contrast to a complete multifrequency diagnosis, there are fewer equations and unknowns leading to "simplified" calculations. From a design perspective the number of needed test points can be smaller; i.e., if one bounds the number of possible failures, then one can reduce the number of test point connectors needed for a diagnosis. To see this, realize that each one of the test points is a source of information. The amount of information needed to solve for the parameters is proportional to the dimension of the parameter space. The limited fault assumption forces the solution to lie in a lower dimensional subspace of the parameter space and thus will require fewer test points than a complete parameter diagnosis. Clearly it is preferable to have $n_f < n_0$. However, selection of n_0 is a trade-off between the cost of connectors for test point access and the complexity/overhead cost in having to implement a nonlinear solution scheme to solve for the faulty parameters.

The main objectives of the chapter are to adapt the multifrequency nonlinear fault diagnosis equations of [4] to the limited fault case, to state and prove various Jacobian based tests for diagnosability, and to develop two schemes for solving the equations to determine the faulty parameters. This will require some basic problem notations and a basic understanding of some simple diagnosability concepts. In order to motivate the notation and problem setting, the material of [4] is briefly reviewed in the next section and a motivational example detailed in the second section. The third section presents a rigorous development of the limited simultaneous failure fault diagnosis problem and various Jacobian tests for well posed diagnosability. The fourth section describes two solution algorithms and the fifth section presents two examples.

THE CCM AND THE FAULT DIAGNOSIS EQUATIONS OF [4]

The frequency domain CCM builds on the assumption that there are N components or subsystems or shop replaceable units. The ith such component is characterized by the transfer function (matrix) relationship

$$b_i(s) = Z_i(s, r_i) a_i(s) \tag{5-1}$$

where $a_i(s)$ is the Laplace transform of the *component input* (vector), $b_i(s)$ is the Laplace transform of the *component output* (vector), $Z_i(s, r_i)$ the *component transfer function* (matrix), and r_i a parameter (vector) pertinent to and characteristic of the component/subsystem. As a notational convenience one lumps all the component input (vectors) and component output (vectors) together to form *composite component input/output vectors* defined as

$$a(s) = \text{col}(a_1(s), \ldots, a_N(s)) \tag{5-2}$$

and

$$b(s) = \text{col}(b_1(s), \ldots, b_N(s)) \tag{5-3}$$

and the composite component transfer function

$$Z(s, r) = \text{block diag}(\ldots, Z_i(s, r_i), \ldots) \tag{5-4}$$

where $r = \text{col}(r_1, r_2, \ldots r_N)$. The composite component input and output vectors are related by

$$b(s) = Z(s, r)a(s) \tag{5-5}$$

The linear algebraic connection laws (e.g., KVL, KCL) have the form

$$a(s) = L_{11}b(s) + L_{12}u(s) \tag{5-6}$$

$$y(s) = L_{21}b(s) + L_{22}u(s) \tag{5-7}$$

where $u(s)$ and $y(s)$ are the circuit/system input and output vectors, respectively, and the L_{ij} are determined by the circuit or system topology (graph). Equations (5-5)–(5-7) constitute the CCM equations [5] and have a frequency domain (simulation) tableau formulation:

$$\begin{bmatrix} Z(s, r) & -I \\ -I & L_{11} \end{bmatrix} \begin{bmatrix} a(s) \\ b(s) \end{bmatrix} = \begin{bmatrix} 0 \\ -L_{12}u(s) \end{bmatrix} \tag{5-8a}$$

$$y(s, r) = L_{21}b(s) + L_{22}u(s) \tag{5-8b}$$

where $y(s, r)$ has the additional variable r to emphasize parameter dependence. This setup is equivalent in concept and form to frequency domain versions of [11,12].

Fault diagnosis, being the "inverse" of simulation, utilizes the tableau simulation equations to identify the parameter vector r given test inputs, $u(s_i)$, and test measurements, $y^m(s_i)$, at q different test input/frequency combinations. The vectors $u(s_i)$ and $y^m(s_i)$, $i = 1, \ldots, q$, are phasors and thus represent steady state operation. Under the assumption that L_{21} has full row rank (independent test measurements), it is possible to manipulate [4] the tableau simulation equation (5-8) [evaluated at the test measurements $(u(s_i), y^m(s_i))$, i $= 1, \ldots, q$] into the special form

$$[Z(s_i, r) \mid -V] \begin{bmatrix} L_{11} V\alpha_i + a_0(s_i) \\ \alpha_i \end{bmatrix} = b_0(s_i) \qquad (5\text{-}9)$$

for $i = 1, 2, \ldots, q$, where

1. q is the number of test input/frequency combinations,
2. $b_0(s_i) = L_{21}{}^{-R}[y^m_{s_i}(r) - L_{22}u(s_i)]$,
3. $y^m_{s_i}(r)$ is the test measurement at frequency s_i due to the parameter r,
4. $L_{21}{}^{-R}$ is any right inverse (Moore Penrose pseudoinverse) of L_{21},
5. $a_0(s_i) = L_{11}b_0(s_i) + L_{12}u(s_i)$,
6. V is a matrix whose columns span the null space of L_{21},
7. r is the unknown parameter vector, and
8. α_i is a vector of auxiliary unknowns which characterizes the ambiguity in the solution for r at any single frequency s_i.

The auxiliary variables α_i arise from a general solution of Eq. (5-8) for the unknown $b(s_i)$, i.e.,

$$b(s_i) = L_{21}^{-R}[y^m_{s_i}(r) - L_{22}u(s_i)] + V\alpha_i$$

This equation represents the first step in deriving (5-9): Making the identification $b_0(s_i) = L_{21}{}^{-R}[y^m_{s_i}(r) - L_{22}u(s_i)]$, a particular solution to (5-8b), leads to $b(s_i) = b_0(s_i) + V\alpha_i$, substituting this expression into (5-8a), combining the subequations into one equation, and making the association, $a_0(s_i) = L_{11}b_0(s_i)$ leads directly to (5-9).

These equations can be written compactly as follows: Let

$$f_i(r) \triangleq [Z(s_i, r) \mid -V] \qquad (5\text{-}10)$$

$$g_i(\alpha_i) \triangleq \begin{bmatrix} L_{11}V\alpha_i + a_0(s_i) \\ \alpha_i \end{bmatrix} \qquad (5\text{-}11)$$

$$\beta_i \triangleq b_0(s_i) \qquad (5\text{-}12)$$

$$x \triangleq \text{col}[\alpha_1, \alpha_2, \ldots, \alpha_q, r] \qquad (5\text{-}13)$$

The fault diagnosis equations (5-9) have the equivalent form

$$
F(x) = \begin{bmatrix} f_1(r)g_1(\alpha_1) - \beta_1 \\ \cdot \\ \cdot \\ \cdot \\ f_q(r)g_q(\alpha_q) - \beta_q \end{bmatrix} = \Theta \tag{5-14}
$$

where θ is the zero vector. Using a Newton–Raphson scheme modified to be globally convergent [1,4,13], one iteratively solves for the solution, say x^*, via

$$
J_F(x^k)[x^{k+1} - x^k] = -F(x^k) \tag{5-15}
$$

where x^k is the kth estimate of the solution to Eq. (5-14) and $J_F(\cdot)$ is the Jacobian of $F(\cdot)$ [4]. Because of the product structure of Eq. (5-14) and the sparsity inherent in Eq. (5-9), the Jacobian is sparse and has a well-defined structure. Specifically,

$$
J_F(x) = \begin{bmatrix} f_1(r)\dfrac{\partial g_1}{\partial \alpha_1}(\alpha_1) & 0 & \cdot & \cdot & \dfrac{\partial f_1}{\partial r}(r)g_1(\alpha_1) \\ 0 & f_2(r)\dfrac{\partial g_2}{\partial \alpha_2}(\alpha_2) & \cdot & \cdot & \dfrac{\partial f_2}{\partial r}(r)g_2(\alpha_2) \\ \vdots & 0 & \cdot & 0 & \vdots \\ 0 & \vdots & \cdot & f_q(r)\dfrac{\partial g_q}{\partial \alpha_q}(\alpha_q) & \dfrac{\partial f_q}{\partial r}(r)g_q(\alpha_q) \end{bmatrix} \tag{5-16}
$$

where

$$
f_i(r)\frac{\partial g_i}{\partial \alpha_i}(\alpha_i) = Z(s_i,r)L_{11}V - V \tag{5-17}
$$

and

$$
\frac{\partial f_i}{\partial r}(r)g_i(\alpha_i) = \begin{bmatrix} \cdots & \dfrac{\partial Z}{\partial r_j}(s_i,r)\left[L_{11}V\alpha_i + a_o(s_i)\right] & \cdots \end{bmatrix} \tag{5-18}
$$

Special solution techniques which exploit the "quadratic" structure of Eq. (5-14) can be found in [1,4].

A MOTIVATIONAL EXAMPLE

A set of diagnosability equations can be viewed as a mapping from the parameter space, R^N, to a measurement space. From a parameter identification perspective, the ability to diagnose a fault depends on (1) whether the mapping is invertible and (2) the facility with which one can numerically execute the inversion, i.e., compute the faulty parameters from the test measurements. Assuming that there are at most $n_f (<N)$ faults then the solution will lie in an n_f-dimensional subspace of R^N. To concretely illustrate these ideas, consider the three parameter circuit of Fig. 5–1. Assume that the nominal value of each parameter is one unit.

The component connection model for this circuit consists of the composite component equations (Eq. (5-5)).

$$\begin{bmatrix} b_1(s_i) \\ b_2(s_i) \\ b_3(s_i) \end{bmatrix} = \begin{bmatrix} R_1 & 0 & 0 \\ 0 & \dfrac{1}{C_2 s} & 0 \\ 0 & 0 & G_3 \end{bmatrix} \begin{bmatrix} a_1(s_i) \\ a_2(s_i) \\ a_3(s_i) \end{bmatrix} \tag{5-19}$$

and taking the current measurement $y^m = y^m(s_i, R_1, C_2, G_3)$ as the circuit output and $u(s_i) = 1 \angle 0°$ as the circuit input, the connection equations [Eq. (5-6) and (5-7)] are

$$\begin{bmatrix} a_1(s_i) \\ a_2(s_i) \\ a_3(s_i) \end{bmatrix} = \begin{bmatrix} 0 & -1 & 0 \\ 1 & 0 & -1 \\ 0 & 1 & 0 \end{bmatrix} \begin{bmatrix} b_1(s_i) \\ b_2(s_i) \\ b_3(s_i) \end{bmatrix} + \begin{bmatrix} 1 \\ 0 \\ 0 \end{bmatrix} u(s_i) \tag{5-20a}$$

$$y^m = \begin{bmatrix} 1 & 0 & 0 \end{bmatrix} \begin{bmatrix} b_1(s_i) \\ b_2(s_i) \\ b_3(s_i) \end{bmatrix} \tag{5-20b}$$

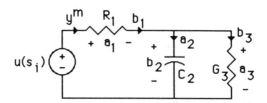

Figure 5–1 *A three-parameter circuit for motivational example.*

Manipulating the above equations into the usual transfer function [5], one obtains

$$y^m = y_{s_i}^m(R_1, C_2, G_3) = \frac{C_2 s_i + G_3}{R_1 C_2 s_i + R_1 G_3 + 1} \qquad (5\text{-}21)$$

where s_i is a user specified "test frequency." Suppose test frequencies are randomly chosen as $s_1 = 10$ and $s_2 = 1$. The resulting measurement set has the form

$$Y^M \triangleq \begin{bmatrix} y_{10}^m(R_1,C_2,G_3) \\ y_1^m(R_1,C_2,G_3) \end{bmatrix} = \begin{bmatrix} \dfrac{10C_2 + G_3}{10R_1C_2 + R_1G_3 + 1} \\ \dfrac{C_2 + G_3}{R_1C_2 + R_1G_3 + 1} \end{bmatrix} \qquad (5\text{-}22)$$

where Y^M represents a mapping from a 3-dimensional parameter space to a 2-dimensional measurement space. Define the set of possible measurements as

$$Y = \left\{ \begin{bmatrix} y_{10}^m(R_1,C_2,G_3) \\ y_1^m(R_1,C_2,G_3) \end{bmatrix} \middle| \begin{bmatrix} R_1 \\ C_2 \\ G_3 \end{bmatrix} \in R^3 \right\} \qquad (5\text{-}23)$$

Since the mapping from the set of possible faulty parameters, R_1, C_2, and G_3, (generically all of R^3) to the measurement set has image space of dimension two, two measurements are generally insufficient to invert the map and thus identify the particular values of R_1, C_2, and G_3, giving rise to the measurement.

On the other hand, if only one fault is possible, then the set of possible measurements, denoted as $\overline{Y} \in R^2$, is the union of three sets, $\overline{Y} = Y_1 \cup Y_2 \cup Y_3$, where

$$Y_1 = \left\{ \begin{bmatrix} y_{10}^m(R_1,1,1) \\ y_1^m(R_1,1,1) \end{bmatrix} \middle| R_1 \in R \right\} \qquad (5\text{-}24)$$

represents the nominal and possible failure measurements associated with R_1, and similarly for

$$Y_2 = \left\{ \begin{bmatrix} y_{10}^m(1,C_2,1) \\ y_1^m(1,C_2,1) \end{bmatrix} \middle| C_2 \in R \right\} \qquad (5\text{-}25)$$

and

$$Y_3 = \left\{ \begin{bmatrix} y_{10}^m(1,1,G_3) \\ y_1^m(1,1,G_3) \end{bmatrix} \middle| \; G_3 \in R \right\} \qquad (5\text{-}26)$$

Figure 5–2 sketches these measurement traces [Eqs. (5-24)–(5-26)] for the circuit of Fig. 5–1. Since the measurement for any single parameter failure must lie on one of these three traces, a fault is uniquely identifiable whenever the measurement point lies on only one trace. Note the point p, which lies on two traces. A measurement at this point is ambiguous. However, the set of such points is inconsequential since almost all points are unambiguous, i.e., the set of such ambiguous faults is an algebraic variety [14] of lower dimension than the traces.

To understand why each fault is identifiable if it lies on only one curve, note that each curve is a 1-dimensional manifold. Let $r = (R_1, C_2, G_3)^t \in R^3$

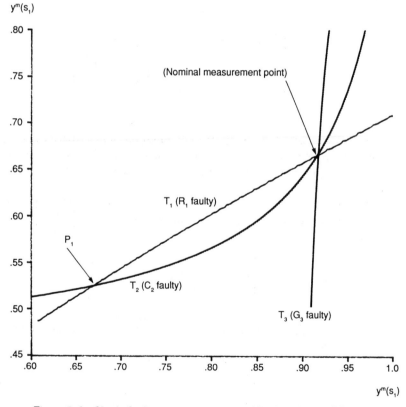

Figure 5–2 *Single fault measurement space for the circuit of Fig. 5–1.*

The subspace of R^3 giving rise to Y_1 is denoted as $P_1 = \{r|r=r_0+\varrho\,(1,0,0)^t\}$, where $r_0 = (1, 1,1)^t$ represents the nominal parameter vector and ϱ is an arbitrary variable which accounts for the deviations of R_1 from nominal. The space P_1 is a (1-dimensional) straight line. Hence, if a measurement lies on Y_1, one can solve for the parameter value whenever the tangent line at the fault in the measurement space has nonzero slope. Analogously, one can define fault spaces $P_2 = \{r|r=r_0+\varrho\,(0, 1, 0)^t\}$ and $P_3 = \{r|r=r_0+\varrho\,(0, 0, 1)^t\}$ and make a similar solvability statement. Unfortunately, one does not know the faulty parameter value beforehand and thus cannot execute this test. However, if the tangent slope is nonzero at r_0, the nominal parameter value, it is nonzero for almost all possible values of r. These ideas can be rigorously delineated using algebraic variety theory [14]. One then claims that, with probability 1, the slope is nonzero at the fault insuring well posedness of the diagnosability question.

Again from a diagnosis perspective one does not know a priori on which trace (Y_1, Y_2, or Y_3) the measurement lies. Hence one can only conclude that the fault lies in the subspace

$$P \triangleq P_1 \cup P_2 \cup P_3$$

In order to identify the fault from the measurement, it is necessary to be able to distinguish among the fault spaces, P_1, P_2, and P_3. Specifically one must at least be able to distinguish among the fault spaces in a neighborhood of the nominal parameter value r_0. This is possible whenever the slopes of the tangents to the measurement curves, at r_0, are different.

These notions of "solvability" and "distinguishability" can be explained in terms of the Jacobian of the measurement equations, 3.4, and alternately and much more practically in terms of the Jacobian of the fault diagnosis equations [Eq. (5-16)]. Such a development takes place in the next section. For future reference observe that the Jacobian of the measurement equation, (5-22), is

$$J_{Y^M}(r_0) = \begin{bmatrix} -\dfrac{(10C_2 + G_3)^2}{[d_{10}(r)]^2} & \dfrac{10}{d_{10}(r)} - \dfrac{10R_1(10C_2 + G_3)}{[d_{10}(r)]^2} & \dfrac{1}{d_{10}(r)} - \dfrac{R_1(10C_2 + G_3)}{[d_{10}(r)]^2} \\[4mm] -\dfrac{(C_2 + G_3)^2}{[d_1(r)]^2} & \dfrac{1}{d_1(r)} - \dfrac{R_1(C_2 + G_3)}{[d_1(r)]^2} & \dfrac{1}{d_1(r)} - \dfrac{R_1(C_2 + G_3)}{[d_1(r)]^2} \end{bmatrix}_{r = r_0}$$

$$= \begin{bmatrix} \dfrac{1}{144} & 0 \\[2mm] 0 & \dfrac{1}{9} \end{bmatrix} \begin{bmatrix} -121 & 10 & 1 \\ -4 & 1 & 1 \end{bmatrix} \tag{5-27}$$

where $d_{s_i}(r) = (s_i R_1 C_2 + R_1 G_3 + 1)$. The tableau fault diagnosis equations, (5-9), for the circuit of Fig. 5–1 has a Jacobian given by

$$
J_F(r_0) = \begin{bmatrix}
-1 & 0 & 0 & 0 & \vdots & -\dfrac{11}{12} & 0 & 0 \\
-1 & -.1 & 0 & 0 & \vdots & 0 & -\dfrac{1}{12} & 0 \\
1 & -1 & 0 & 0 & \vdots & 0 & 0 & \dfrac{1}{12} \\
0 & 0 & -1 & 0 & \vdots & -\dfrac{2}{3} & 0 & 0 \\
0 & 0 & -1 & -1 & \vdots & 0 & -\dfrac{1}{3} & 0 \\
0 & 0 & 1 & -1 & \vdots & 0 & 0 & \dfrac{1}{3}
\end{bmatrix}
\qquad (5\text{-}28)
$$

where in computing this Jacobian note that

$$
y_{s_i}^m(r_0) = \frac{s_i + 1}{s_i + 2}, \qquad V = \begin{bmatrix} 0 & 0 \\ 1 & 0 \\ 0 & 1 \end{bmatrix}
$$

$\alpha_i = (\alpha_{i1}, \alpha_{i2})^t$, $b_0(s_i) = \left(y_{s_i}^m(r_0), 0, 0 \right)^t$, $a_0(s_i) = \left(1, y_{s_i}^m(r_0), 0 \right)$, and the nominal values of the α_i are $\alpha_{10,\text{nom}} = (\frac{1}{12}, \frac{1}{12})^t$ and $\alpha_{1,\text{nom}} = (\frac{1}{3}, \frac{1}{3})^t$. This Jacobian will help illustrate the test for diagnosability developed in the next section.

As a final point, the reader should be aware that solving for the parameters using equations having a transfer function form as per Eq. (5-22) is numerically untenable [1, 4]. The sparsity and quadratic structure of Eq. (5-9) are far superior.

DIAGNOSABILITY FOR n_f FAULTS

The purpose of this section is to develop the notion of "n_f-fault diagnosability." Specifically, suppose the fault diagnosis equation, $F(x) = \theta$, Eq. (5-14), is not directly solvable for x. When is it possible to solve the fault diagnosis equations under the assumption that at most n_f parameters differ from nominal? This section rigorously answers the question.

Development of a test for diagnosability and an algorithm for identifying a fault requires some terminology and notation. Specifically, the *fault index*, denoted $<i_1, i_2, \ldots, i_{n_f}>$ is an n_f-tuple of positive integers satisfying $1 \le i_1$,

$i_2 < \ldots, i_{n_f} \leq N$. Assuming the parameters are numbered 1–N, each fault index represents a permissible combination of parameter failures. Let

$$\Omega(N, r_f) \triangleq \{<i_1, i_2, \ldots, i_{n_i}> \mid 1 \leq i_1 < i_2 < \cdots < i_{n_f} \leq N\} \tag{5-29}$$

denote the fault set, i.e., the set of all possible n_f-fault indices for a system of N parameters. Observe that there are $C_{N:n_f}$ elements (each denoted generically as γ) in $\Omega(N, n_f)$, where

$$C_{N:n_f} = \frac{N!}{(N - n_f)! n_f!} \tag{5-30}$$

is the number of combinations of N elements taken n_f at a time.

Associated with each fault index $\gamma \in \Omega(N, n_f)$ will be a *fault space*, P_γ, representing the space of all parameter values allowable for a specific fault index $\gamma = <i_1, i_2, \ldots, i_{n_f}> \in \Omega(N, n_f)$:

$$P_\gamma \triangleq \{r \mid r = r_0 + M_\gamma \varrho, \ \varrho \in R^{n_f}\} \tag{5-31}$$

where

$$M_\gamma \triangleq \left[e_{i_1} \mid e_{i_2} \mid \cdots \mid e_{i_{n_f}} \right] \tag{5-32}$$

is an N xn_f matrix whose column vectors, e_j, have zero entries excepting a 1 in the *j*th position. Denote $P = \cup_{\gamma \in \Omega(n,f_f)} P_\gamma$ as the entire fault space, i.e., the entire set of admissible parameter failures.

Strictly speaking, P_γ is not a linear space but rather a *flat* [15], also called an affine space—i.e., a translate of an n_f-dimensional linear subspace, say $\overline{P}_\gamma$, of R^N. The attribute of P_γ most pertinent to the following discussion is its dimension, which is simply the dimension of $\overline{P}_\gamma$ [15]. Since the distinction between a linear subspace and its translate is irrelevant to this discussion, we will continue to refer to P_γ as a fault space. For any specific system there might be additional constraints which limit the size and shape of the fault space in some way (e.g., some parameters can have positive values only). Such constraints will not be included in this discussion since they generally do not affect the dimension of P_γ.

These definitions are fundamental to the structure of the measurement space. To see this, define the measurement function

$$Y^M(r) = \begin{bmatrix} y_{s_1}^m(r) \\ y_{s_2}^m(r) \\ \vdots \\ y_{s_q}^m(r) \end{bmatrix} = \begin{bmatrix} L_{21} b(s_1, r) + L_{22} u(s_1) \\ L_{21} b(s_2, r) + L_{22} u(s_2) \\ \vdots \\ L_{21} b(s_q, r) + L_{22} u(s_q) \end{bmatrix} \tag{5-33}$$

where $b(s_i, r)$ satisfies Eq. (5-8a). $Y^M(r)$: $D \subset R^N \rightarrow R^{noq}$ defines a nonlinear map continuous in a neighborhood of r_0 with continuous Frechet derivative, $J_{yM}(r)$, in a neighborhood of r_0 provided that the same is true of $Z(s_i, r)$. This is reasonable in light of typical analog circuits, assuming s_i is chosen away from the transfer function critical values.

With reference to the motivational example of the previous section and Fig. 5-2 in particular, the fault space $Y = Y^M(P_{<1>} \cup P_{<2>} \cup P_{<3>}) = Y_1 \cup Y_2 \cup Y_3$. Observe that the set of ambiguous measurements is given by $Y^M(P)_{<1>} \cap Y^M(P)_{<2>}$, i.e., measurements at these points are insufficient to *distinguish* $<1>$ from $<2>$ or $<3>$. However, measurements at all other points are; indeed one can solve for the parameter value. Specifically, the fault represented by $\gamma \in \Omega(N, n_f)$ is *solvable* at r_0 if $Y_\gamma(\varrho) - Y^M(r_0) = 0$ has a locally unique solution at $\varrho = 0$, where

$$Y_\gamma(\varrho) = Y^M(r_0 + M_\gamma \varrho) \tag{5-34}$$

Solvability means that the restricted map $Y_\gamma(\varrho)$ is locally invertible at $\varrho = 0$: if a measurement is known to result from a specific fault γ, then it is possible to solve for the parameter vector. [Note that complete diagnosability is a special case wherein $n_f = N$ and $\Omega(N, n_f)$ contains a single fault index $\gamma = <1, 2, \ldots, N>$.] A sufficient condition for solvability is that the Jacobian, $J_{Y\gamma}(\varrho)$, be full rank (rank $= n_f$) at $\varrho = 0$. Using the chain rule on Eq. (5-34) establishes the following lemma.

Lemma 1.   The fault represented by the index $\gamma \in \Omega(N, n_f)$ is solvable at r_0 if

$$\text{Rank } [J_{Y^M}(r_0)M_\gamma] = n_f \tag{5-35}$$

To illustrate this lemma, refer again to the motivational example of the previous section. Let $\gamma_2 = <2>$, i.e., consider the measurement curve Y_2, and, referring to Eq. (5-27), observe that

$$\text{Rank } [J_{Y^M_D}(r_0)M_{\gamma_2}] = \text{Rank} \left[\begin{bmatrix} \frac{1}{144} & 0 \\ 0 & \frac{1}{9} \end{bmatrix} \begin{bmatrix} -121 & 10 & 1 \\ -4 & 1 & 1 \end{bmatrix} \begin{bmatrix} 0 \\ 1 \\ 0 \end{bmatrix} \right] = 1 = 1 n_f$$

A similar calculation holds for the other two faults $\gamma_1 = <1>$ and $\gamma_3 = <3>$.

Another notion, distinguishability among faults, underlies the diagnosability of a system. First let O be a neighborhood of r_0 on which $Y^M(r)$ is continuous and has continuous Frechet derivative, $J_{Y^M}(r)$, of full column rank. Since P_γ is a k-dimensional manifold, $k \leq n_0 q$, the set $Y^M(P_\gamma) \subset R^{noq}$ is a k-dimensional manifold [16]. Two faults $\gamma_i, \gamma_j \in \Omega(N, n_f)$ are *distinguishable* at r_0 if (i) each is solvable at r_0 and (ii) in a neighborhood of r_0, the dimension of $Y^M(P_{\gamma_i}) \cap Y^M(P_{\gamma_j})$ is strictly less than the dimension of $Y^M(P_{\gamma_i} \cup P_{\gamma_j})$. Thus distinguishable faults do not have everywhere coincident measurements in any neighborhood of r_0. This notation is similar to the k-Node-Fault testability concept in [7]. A test for distinguishability is given in Lemma 2.

Lemma 2. Let faults γ_i and γ_j satisfy condition (5-35). Then γ_i and γ_j are distinguishable if

$$\text{Rank} \left[J_{Y^M}(r_0) \left[M_{\gamma_i} \mid M_{\gamma_j} \right] \right] \ge n_f + 1 \tag{5-36}$$

A rigorous proof of this result can be found in [1, 3]. A sketch of the proof is as follows: First one shows that $\dim[Y^M(P_{\gamma_i} \cup P_{\gamma_j})] \ge n_f$ and then assumes γ_i and γ_j are not distinguishable; as such, the dimensions of the intersection and union of the manifolds, $Y^M(P_{\gamma_i})$ and $Y^M(P_{\gamma_j})$, coincide with n_f. It follows that Rank $[J_{YM}(r_0)[M_{\gamma_i} \mid M_{\gamma_j}]] = n_f$, implying that two nondistinguishable faults fail the test of (5-36).

To illustrate this concept, again with reference to the example of the previous section, let $\gamma_1 = \,<1>$ and $\gamma_3 = \,<3>$. Then

$$\text{Rank} \left[J_{Y^M}(r_0) \left[M_{\gamma_1} \vdots M_{\gamma_3} \right] \right] = \text{Rank} \left[\begin{bmatrix} \dfrac{1}{144} & 0 \\ 0 & \dfrac{1}{9} \end{bmatrix} \begin{bmatrix} -121 & 1 \\ -4 & 1 \end{bmatrix} \right] = 2 \ge n_f + 1$$

implying that the faults γ_1 and γ_3 are distinguishable

Definition 1. A circuit/system is n_f-fault diagnosable at r_0 if for all $\gamma_i, \gamma_j \in \Omega(N, n_f)$, $\gamma_i \ne \gamma_j$, γ_i and γ_j are distinguishable.

Theorem 1. A system/circuit is n_f-*fault diagnosable* at r_0 if every combination of $n_f + 1$ columns of $J_{YM}(r_0)$ is independent.

The proof is straightforward and can be found in [1, 3]. Briefly, however, since every $n_f + 1$ column of $J_{YM}(r_0)$ is linearly independent, every n_f-fault is solvable and every pair of faults satisfies the Jacobian test of Eq. (5-36).

The motivational example of the previous section simply illustrates this. In particular from Eq. (5-27)

$$
J_{Y^M}(r_0)M_{\gamma_2} = \begin{bmatrix} \dfrac{1}{144} & 0 \\ \\ 0 & \dfrac{1}{9} \end{bmatrix} \begin{bmatrix} -121 & 10 & 1 \\ \\ -4 & 1 & 1 \end{bmatrix}
$$

has every pair of columns linearly independent and thus the circuit is 1-fault diagnosable as intuitively expected by viewing the measurement curves in Fig. 5–2.

Although the n_f-fault diagnosability test in terms of the Jacobian matrix J_{Y^M} is usable, it is far more convenient to have a test in terms of J_F given in Eq. (5-16). This follows because J_F is sparse and its computation requires no matrix inversions whereas the computation of J_{Y^M} does. Furthermore, J_F is necessary for the solution algorithm. Hence the software developed for its computation is usable in both places.

To determine an n_f-fault diagnosability test in a neighborhood of the nominal point, consider that the Jacobian of Eq. (5-16) has the form

$$
J_F(x) = \left[\frac{\partial F}{\partial \alpha}(x) \;\middle|\; \frac{\partial F}{\partial r}(x) \right] \triangleq \left[J_\alpha(x) \;\middle|\; J_r(x) \right] \tag{5-37}
$$

where each term in $\frac{\partial F}{\partial \alpha}$, i.e., $\frac{\partial f_i}{\partial \alpha_j}$, is given by Eq. (5-17) and similarly each term in, $\frac{\partial F}{\partial r}$, i.e., $\frac{\partial f_i}{\partial r_j}$, is given by Eq. (5-18). Plugging these expressions into (5-37) produces the following factorization of $J_F(x_0)$:

$$
J_F(x_0) = \begin{bmatrix} Z(s_1,r)L_{11}-I & & & \\ & Z(s_2,r)L_{11}-I & & \\ & & \cdot & \\ & & & \cdot \\ & & & & \cdot \\ & & & & & Z(s_q,r)L_{11}-I \end{bmatrix} \begin{bmatrix} -V & & & B_1(r_0) \\ & -V & & B_2(r_0) \\ & & \cdot & \\ & & & \cdot \\ & & & \cdot \\ & & & -V\, B_q(r_0) \end{bmatrix} \tag{5-38}
$$

where

$$
B_i(r_0) = [I-Z(s_i,r)L_{11}]^{-1}\left[\frac{\partial Z}{\partial r_1}(s_i,r)\left[L_{11}V\alpha_i + a_0(s_i) \right] \middle| \cdots \middle| \frac{\partial Z}{\partial r_N}(s_i,r)\left[L_{11}V\alpha_i + a_0(s_i) \right] \right]_{x=x_0} \tag{5-39}
$$

Observe also that $J_{Y^M}(r_0)$ has the factorization:

$$J_{Y^M}(r_0) = \frac{\partial Y^M}{\partial r}(r_0) = \begin{bmatrix} L_{21} & & \\ & \cdot & \\ & & \cdot \\ & & \cdot \\ & & L_{21} \end{bmatrix} \begin{bmatrix} \frac{\partial b}{\partial r}(s_1, r_0) \\ \vdots \\ \frac{\partial b}{\partial r}(s_q, r_0) \end{bmatrix} \quad (5\text{-}40)$$

A commonality between (5-38) and (5-40) is

Lemma 3. $B_i(x_0) = (s_i, r_0)$

In order to prove this theorem, one must show equality between the jth entry of $\frac{\partial b}{\partial r}(s_i, r_0)$, i.e., $\frac{\partial b}{\partial r_j}(s_i, r_0)$, and the jth entry of $B_i(r_0)$ given in Eq. (5-39). The key is to differentiate the frequency domain tableau (Eq. 5-8a) with respect to r_j. Manipulating the resultant equations produces the expression

$$\frac{\partial b}{\partial r_j}(s_i, r_0) = [I - Z(s_i, r_0)L_{11}]^{-1} \frac{\partial Z}{\partial r_j}(s_i, r_0)a(s_i, r_0)$$

At the nominal solution point, $x_0 = \text{col}[\alpha_{10}, \ldots, \alpha_{q0}, r_0]$, $a(s_i, r_0) = L_{11}V\alpha_0 + a_0(s_i)$, establishing the necessary equality. Details can be found in [1, 3].

The main theorem and its proof require one more preliminary lemma.

Lemma 4.   The matrix product XY has full column rank if and only if $[\hat{V}^{\dagger}Y]$ has full column rank where the columns of $\hat{V}$ are a basis for the null space of X.

This well-known result from linear algebra (see, for example, [1, 7]) simply means that the column space of Y has a null intersection with the null space of X. It is now possible to state and prove the desired Jacobian test for n_f-diagnosability.

Theorem 2.   Let $J_\alpha(x_0)$ denote the matrix which consists of the first pq columns of $J_F(x_0)$; let $J_r(x_0)$ denote the matrix which consists of the last N columns of $J_F(x_0)$; and let $J_r^\eta(x_0) = J_r(x_0)M_\eta$ denote the matrix which consists of the $n_f + 1$ columns of $J_r(x_0)$ corresponding to the elements of the index $\eta \in \Omega(N, n_f + 1)$. A circuit/system is n_f-fault diagnosable at r_0 if the matrix $[J_\alpha(x_0) \, J_r^\eta(x_0)]$ has full column rank for every $\eta \in \Omega(N, n_f + 1)$.

Remark.   The space $\Omega(N, n_f + 1)$ is used as a notational convenience and should not be confused with the set of fault indicies $\Omega(N, n_f)$.

A synopsis of the proof is as follows. The factorization of (5-38) implies

$$
\left[J_\alpha(x_0) \mid J_r^n(x^0) \right] = \text{block-diag} \left[\ldots, I - Z(s_i,r)L_{11}, \ldots \right]
$$

$$
\times \begin{bmatrix} -V & & & \vdots & B_1(x_0)M_\eta \\ & \ddots & & \vdots & \vdots \\ & & -V & \vdots & B_q(x_0)M_\eta \end{bmatrix} \tag{5-41}
$$

where it is presumed that the s_i's are chosen so that $(I - Z(s_i,r)L_{11})$ is nonsingular for $i = 1, \ldots, q$. Since, at x_0, $B_i(x_0) = \partial b/\partial r\, (s_i,r_0)$ and since $(I - Z(s_i,r)L_{11})$ is nonsingular in a neighborhood of r_0, it follows that the right-hand side of (5-41) has full column rank for each $\eta \in \Omega(N, n_f + 1)$. Since $L_{21}V = [0]$, it follows by Lemma 4 that

$$
\begin{bmatrix} 0 & \vdots & J_{Y^M}(r_0)M_\eta \end{bmatrix}
$$

[in particular, $J_{Y^M}(r_0)M_\eta$] has rank $n_f + 1$ for each $\eta \in \Omega(N, n_f + 1)$ as was necessary to show.

It is easily verified that the Jacobian $J_F(x)$ given in Eq. (5-28) in the context of the motivational example satisfies the conditions of the theorem for single fault diagnosability as expected.

Another point which merits mention is the fact that n_f-fault diagnosability is a generic property for systems whose components are rational functions of their parameters.

Proposition 1.   Suppose $Z(s,r)$ is a rational function of r. If a set of n_f+1 columns of $J_{Y^M}(r_0)$ is independent, then the same set of columns of $J_{Y^M}(r)$ is independent for almost all $r \in R^N$.

The proof of this lemma is essentially the same as the proof of Theorem 4.5 in [4].

Theorem 3.   Suppose a system for which $Z(s,r)$ is a rational function of r is known to be n_f-fault diagnosable at r_0 via Theorem 1 (or equivalently Theorem 2). Then it is n_f-fault diagnosable for almost all $r \in R^N$.

The proof of this theorem follows from Theorem 1, which implies that every set of $n_f + 1$ columns of $J_{Y^M}(r_0)$ is independent. Using Proposition 1 and the fact that there are only a finite number of combinations of $n_f + 1$ columns, the result follows immediately.

As a final note to this section, observe that the following test for full diagnosability which appears as Theorem 4.2 in [4] follows as a corollary to Lemma 1 and the proof of Theorem 2.

Corollary 1. A circuit/system is N-diagnosable if $J_F(x_0)$ has full column rank.

This establishes the desired test for n_f-diagnosability and completes this section. We now turn to a discussion of two solution algorithms. For a discussion of generic diagnosability conditions in a Hilbert space context, see [18].

LIMITED FAULT ALGORITHM

Assuming the circuit/system is n_f-fault diagnosable, the problem is to develop an algorithm to identify the particular fault combination, γ, by identifying the parameter vector $r \in P_\gamma$ for some $\gamma \in \Omega(N, n_f)$. Given sufficient input–output measurements at several (q) frequencies and the stipulation, $r \in P_\gamma$ for some $\gamma \in \Omega(N, n_f)$, the problem is to identify $x = \text{col}(\alpha_1, \ldots, \alpha_q, r)$ from the information

$$F(x) = \theta; \ r \in P = \bigcup_{\gamma \in \Omega(N, n_f)} P_\gamma \tag{5-42}$$

There are two techniques given in this section.

The first approach to obtaining a solution is to reformulate (5-42) as a constrained minimization problem. In this vein, define an objective function

$$\phi(r, \gamma) = \|r - r_\gamma\|$$

where $r \in \text{IR}^N, r_\gamma \in P_\gamma$, and $\gamma \in \Omega(N, n_f)$. The second constraint in (5-42) is satisfied when $\phi(r, \gamma)$ is a minimum—i.e., zero. Hence, identifying the faulty parameter is equivalent to solving the constrained minimization problem:

$$\text{minimize}_{r \in \text{R}^n, \gamma \in \Omega(N, n_f)} \ \phi(r, \gamma) \tag{5-43a}$$

$$\text{subject to } F(x) = \theta \tag{5-43b}$$

An adaptation of the gradient projection method [19] provides the solution technique. The three steps are: (i) determine a feasible solution point x_{fe} of (5-43b) from an initial guess; (ii) minimize $\phi(r, \gamma)$ by "selectively" searching the various fault combinations of $\gamma \in \Omega(N, n_f)$; (iii) using the result of step (ii), return to step (i) until obtaining convergence.

Step (i) entails solving (5-43b) by the modified Newton–Raphson scheme described in [4]. This algorithm exploits the bilinear nature of the tableau formulation of the fault diagnosis equations. At each iteration of the Newton–Raphson scheme, one computes the Moore–Penrose pseudo (right) inverse of the Jacobian to produce a least square fit.

Step (ii) of the algorithm corrects the parameter estimate (feasible solution, x_{fe}) of step (i). This correction step utilizes the null space information of the Jacobian at x_{fe} to obtain an estimate $\hat{x}$ which lines up with a potential fault space P_γ. To accomplish the update add to x_{fe} a vector tangent (at x_{fe}) to the curve defined by the equality constraints. The direction of this tangent vector is the projection of the gradient of the objective function into the tangent space (hence the gradient projection method.) The updated r-vector is the value along the tangent projection for which the objective function is minimized. From this, one constructs an updated x, say $\hat{x}^{\,i}$. In order to analytically specify the procedure, let

$$ V(x_{fe}) = \begin{bmatrix} V_\alpha(x_{fe}) \\ V_r(x_{fe}) \end{bmatrix} \qquad (5\text{-}44) $$

be a matrix whose columns span $\text{Null}[J_F(x_{fe})]$. Let $\dim(\text{Null}[J_F(x_{fe})]) = m$. Hence the last N rows of $V(x_{fe})$ are given by the $N \times m$ matrix $V_r(x_{fe})$. The feasible solution $x_{fe} = \text{col}[\alpha_{fe}, r_{fe}]$. The correction procedure affects only r_{fe}. The corrected parameter vector, denoted r_t, must lie in the tangent space of the constraint equations (5-43b) at x_{fe}, i.e.,

$$ r_t = r_{fe} + V_r(x_{fe})\beta $$

for an appropriate vector $\beta \in \mathbf{IR}^m$. With reference to the minimization of Eq. (5-43a), step (ii) requires solving

$$ \min_{r_t, \gamma \in \Omega(N, n_f)} \phi(r_t, \gamma) = \min_{r_t, \gamma \in \Omega(N, n_f)} \|r_t - r_\gamma\| \qquad (5\text{-}45) $$

$$ = \min_{\beta \in \mathbf{R}^m} \|D_\gamma(r_{fe} + V_r(x_{fe})\beta - r_\gamma)\| $$

where D_γ is an identity matrix with rows $i_1, i_2, \dots, i_{nf}$ deleted and where $\gamma = \langle i_1, i_2, \dots, i_{nf} \rangle$. Introduction of the matrix D_γ restricts the minimization process to the fault index γ. Since $D_\gamma r_\gamma = D_\gamma r_0$, (5.4) reduces to

$$ \min_{\beta \in \mathbf{R}^m, \gamma \in \Omega(N, n_f)} \|A_\gamma \beta - B_\gamma\| \qquad (5\text{-}46) $$

where $A_\gamma = D_\gamma V_r(x_{fe})$ and $B_\gamma = D_\gamma(r_0 - r_{fe})$. Ideally one would search all $\gamma \in \Omega(N, n_f)$ until finding the minimum. Once the minimum is known, the new initial point (at the *j*th iteration) is $\hat{x}_j = x_{fe} + V(x_{fe})\beta$. See Fig. 5–3 for a pictorial illustration of the procedure.

Searching through the $C_{N:n_f}$ combinations of $\Omega(N, n_f)$ would not yield an efficient implementation of the scheme. As an alternative, one implements the following heuristic: (i) Eliminate from consideration all faults containing component *i* whenever the *i*th entry of r_{fe} is within a small tolerance of nominal, say 10%; (ii) eliminate all fault combinations which do not contain the *j*th component whenever the *j*th entry of r_{fe} has an unreasonable deviation from nominal, for example, has the largest deviation from nominal. Let $\Gamma \subset \Omega(N, n_f)$ be a set constructed according to the above rules, then step (ii) reduces to

$$\min_{\beta \in_{\mathbb{R}^m}, \gamma \in \Gamma} \|A_\gamma \beta - B_\gamma\| \tag{5-47}$$

The second algorithm builds around the *t*-fault diagnosability ideas of [20] applied to the multifrequency fault diagnosis equations [eq. (5-9) or (5-14)]. These ideas have been applied to a time domain CCM in [2,8,10]. The

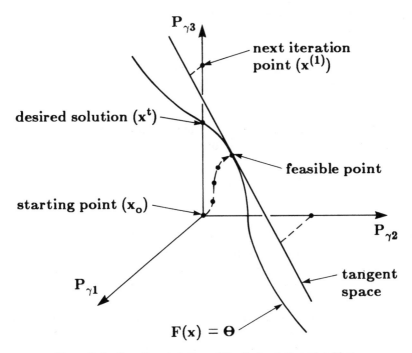

Figure 5–3 *Functional picture of the first solution algorithm.*

algorithm utilizes a partition of the circuit elements into two groups: Group 1 (denoted G1) contains components assumed to operate at nominal parameter values whereas group 2 (denoted G2) contains components under test by the G1 units. Given an initial partitioning for which the number of G2 units satisfies $n_f + 1 \leq \#\text{G2} \leq qn_0$ and a set of output measurements, one solves the equations (or at least finds the solution minimizing the Euclidean norm) under the assumption that the G1 devices have parameters fixed at nominal. This will provide parameter values for the G2 devices which are either at nominal or differ from nominal. Those devices whose parameters adequately differ from nominal are said to test faulty and those which are at nominal test healthy. Of course, if the G1 group contains a faulty device, a G2 device may test faulty even if it is healthy. At any rate this data is then fed into a decision algorithm which stores the data, interprets the data in light of any past data, determines a new partition based on the accumulated data, and repeats the process until identifying the faulty element. This requires that the algorithm sequentially insert verifiably healthy units into G1 until all G1 units are known to be fault free. Thus the resulting test is correct and a decision as to which units are faulty is easily made.

After choosing the G1 and G2 components, one must solve or at least find the solution minimizing the Euclidean norm of the diagnosis equations, $F(x) = 0$, under the condition that the parameter values of the G1 devices are always at nominal. If Δx is the error at each Newton–Raphson iteration, then the above conditions are met by solving

$$J_F(x) \begin{bmatrix} I & 0 \\ 0 & D_{G1} \end{bmatrix} \begin{bmatrix} \Delta\alpha \\ \Delta r \end{bmatrix} = -F(x) \qquad (5\text{-}48)$$

where D_{G1} is an identity matrix whose diagonal elements corresponding to G1 components are set to zero. The solution takes the form

$$\begin{bmatrix} \Delta\alpha \\ \Delta r \end{bmatrix} = - \left[J_F(x) \begin{bmatrix} I & 0 \\ 0 & D_{G1} \end{bmatrix} \right]^+ F(x) \qquad (5\text{-}49)$$

where superscript $+$ indicates the Moore–Penrose pseudoinverse [17]. This solution allows no changes in the G1 devices since the solution must be orthogonal to the null space of the product-matrix on the left of Eq. (5-48). In addition, (5-49) provides the least squares solution to the equations under this constraint.

The need for a least square solution exists because a given set of test measurements and a given (G1,G2) partition may preclude a solution consistent with the measurements. To see what is happening, suppose the actual fault, $\gamma^* \notin \Omega(N, n_f)$, lies in G2. Then the fault diagnosis equations will always have a solution which is consistent with the measurement data. On the other hand, if $\gamma^* \notin \Omega(N, n_f)$, then the fault diagnosis equations may not be solvable for a solution consistent with the measurement data; a minimization may be all that is possible.

For the sake of argument suppose the measurement space is R^{n_f+1}, i.e., $Y^M(r) \in R^{n_f+1}$. If γ^* is not in G2, then the partition (G1,G2) has an associated fault space P_{G2} with dimension $\geq n_f + 1$ and with measurement space $Y_{G2} = Y^M(P_{G2})$ which in general is an $(n_f + 1)$-dimensional subset of R^{n_f+1}. This space Y_{G2}, may or may not intersect the point $Y^M(r^*)$, where r^* is the actual parameter value giving rise to the measurement. In such cases one can only hope to minimize the solution. Minimization of the solution can proceed via Newton–Raphson provided that one uses the Moore–Penrose pseudoinverse for solving at each iteration since the minimization necessarily leads to a Jacobian rank reduction. It is suggested that a numerical implementation utilize a Newton–Raphson iteration until sensing a rank reduction and then switching to a canned minimization algorithm. A rank reduction occurs because the derivative of $F(x)$, i.e., the Jacobian, must be singular at a local minimum.

The decision algorithm utilized here represents so-called asymmetric invalidation [20]. Briefly asymmetric invalidation means that a G2 device which is in fact faulty always fails a test, i.e. looks faulty, even when G1 contains faulty components. This is consistent with the analog heuristic [8] which says that the probability of two analog faults cancelling each other is zero. Thus any G2 device which tests healthy is healthy and can be routed to G1 until obtaining a set of G1 devices which are all healthy. For a more thorough discussion of asymmetric invalidation and its more general counterpart symmetric invalidation see [2,20].

For this chapter only the single fault case is illustrated. Here there are some special properties. First, for single faults, G2 must contain at least two units. If any of the units in G2 test healthy, they are healthy; if some units test healthy and some test faulty, then no decision about the faulty units can be made. However, if all the G2 devices test faulty, then they all must be good. This follows because there is only one faulty device and that device must be in G1 for all the G2 devices to test faulty.

Example 2 of the next section illustrates these ideas.

LIMITED FAULT ALGORITHM EXAMPLES

The purpose of this section is to present two example problems which illustrate the theory and limited fault algorithms developed. The first example is based on the 12-parameter circuit of Fig. 5–4. The solution of this example includes the use of the diagnosability test of Theorem 2 and the application of the first solution algorithm to ten randomly selected fault combinations.

The second example is an adaptation of the second approach to the circuit of Fig. 5–5.

Example 1. Consider the circuit of Fig. 5–4. The circuit input and outputs are

$$u_1 = V_1, \quad y_1 = I_{c_1}, \quad y_2 = V_o \qquad (5\text{-}50)$$

The parameter definitions, nominal values, and component transfer functions appear in Table 5–1. The nonzero entries of the sparse set of connection matrices, L_{11}, L_{12}, L_{21}, and L_{22} appear in Table 5–2. The nonzero entries of L_{21}^{-R} and V, computed via IMSL[21] routines lginf and llsqf respectively, appear in Table 5–3.

For $q = 2$, $s_1 = j10$ and $s_2 = j0.6$ and $u(s_1) = u(s_2) = 1$, we computed the nominal α_i. With this information it is possible to compute the nominal Jacobian, $J_F(x_o)$, which indicates via Theorem 2 that the circuit is 3-fault diagnosable.

The next step in the example is to simulate several 3-faults (three parameters differ from nominal) and see if the solution algorithm works. Table 5–4 displays a set of 16 randomly selected fault indices and corresponding faulty parameter values. Each of these faults was simulated and the resulting measurement data applied to the algorithms.

Although the circuit is theoretically 3-fault diagnosable the results in Table 5–4 indicate that there are some practical problems associated with the determination of certain faults. For any given fault the most reliable indication of the theoretical capability to determine the fault is a test of the Jacobian evaluated at the fault, but this is impractical since it is impossible to anticipate all possible faults. Instead the diagnosability test is based on the rank of selected columns of the Jacobian, J_F, evaluated at the nominal point. Theoretically the results at the nominal point hold for almost all faults. Unfortunately, it is quite possible for a matrix which is theoretically full rank to

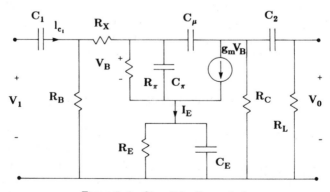

Figure 5–4   *Circuit for Example 1.*

Table 5-1 Component Information for Example 5.1

Parameter	Nominal Value	Definition	$Z_i(s, r_i)$
r_1	0.1	$1/C_1$	r_1/s
r_2	0.5	R_x	r_2
r_3	1.0	R_π	r_3
r_4	1.0	$1/C_\mu$	r_4/s
r_5	0.1	$1/C_2$	r_5/s
r_6	1.0	$1/R_B$	r_6
r_7	1.0	$1/R_E$	r_7
r_8	1.0	C_π	$r_8 s$
r_9	0.1	C_E	$r_9 s$
r_{10}	1.0	g_n	r_{10}
r_{11}	1.0	$1/R_C$	r_{11}
r_{12}	0.5	$1/R_L$	r_{12}

be less than full rank for a solution algorithm due to the finite word length of the computer.

A technique for circumventing this problem is to perform the diagnosis at several sets of test frequencies. Only those faults which are poorly conditioned at all test frequencies used would not be detectable. Suppose that the present example is repeated with the following test frequencies: $s_1 = j4$ and $s_2 = j.2$. The results of the diagnosis of the same 16 faults appear in Table 5-5.

Table 5-2 Nonzero Entries of the Connection Matrices for Example 5.1

L_{ij}	Row, Column	Value	Row, Column	Value	Row, Column	Value
L_{11}	1,6	1	1,7	1	1,9	1
	1,11	1	1,12	1	2,7	1
	2,9	1	2,11	1	2,12	1
	3,7	1	3,8	−1	3,9	1
	3,10	−1	4,10	1	4,11	1
	4,12	1	5,12	1	6,1	−1
	7,1	−1	7,2	−1	7,3	−1
	8,3	1	9,1	−1	9,2	−1
	9,3	−1	10,3	1	11,1	−1
	11,2	−1	11,4	−1	12,1	−1
	12,2	−1	12,4	−1	12,5	−1
L_{12}	6,1	1	7,1	1	9,1	1
	11,1	1	12,1	1		
L_{21}	1,1	−1	1,2	−1	1,4	−1
	1,5	−1	2,6	1	2,7	1
	2,9	1	2,11	1	2,12	1
L_{22}	1,1	1				

Table 5-3 Nonzero entries of the L_{21}^{-R} and V matrices for Example 5.1

Matrix	Row, Column	Value	Row Column	Value
L_{21}^{-R}	1,1	−0.25	2,1	−0.25
	4,1	−0.25	5,1	−0.25
	6,2	0.2	7,2	0.2
	9,2	0.2	11,2	0.2
	12,2	0.2		
V	1,1	0.866025	2,1	−0.288675
	2,2	−0.57735	2,3	−0.57735
	3,8	1	4,1	−0.288675
	4,2	0.788675	4,3	−0.211325
	5,1	−0.288675	5,2	−0.211325
	5,3	0.788675	6,4	0.861803
	6,5	−0.138197	6,6	−0.138197
	6,7	−0.138197	7,4	−0.138197
	7,5	0.861803	7,3	−0.138197
	7,7	−0.138197	8,9	1
	9,4	−0.138197	9,5	−0.138197
	9,6	−0.138197	9,7	0.861803
	10,10	1	11,4	−0.138197
	11,5	−0.138197	11,6	0.861803
	11,7	−0.138197	12,4	−0.447214
	12,5	−0.447214	12,6	−0.447214
	12,7	−0.447214		

Table 5-4 Fault List and Algorithm Performance Summary for $s_1 = j10$ and $s_2 = j.6$

Actual Fault Index	Faulty Parameter Values			Algorithm Fault Index
$\langle 6,7,10 \rangle$	$r_6 = 0.5$	$r_7 = 2.0$	$r_{10} = 2.0$	$\langle 6,7,10 \rangle$
$\langle 2,5,9 \rangle$	$r_2 = 1.0$	$r_5 = 0.05$	$r_9 = 0.2$	$\langle 2,9 \rangle$
$\langle 1,4,9 \rangle$	$r_1 = 0.2$	$r_4 = 0.5$	$r_9 = 0.2$	$\langle 1,4,9 \rangle$
$\langle 2,5,6 \rangle$	$r_2 = 0.3$	$r_5 = 0.07$	$r_6 = 1.4$	$\langle 2,6 \rangle$
$\langle 4,5,9 \rangle$	$r_4 = 2.0$	$r_5 = 0.05$	$r_9 = 0.2$	$\langle 4,5,9 \rangle$
$\langle 2,6,11 \rangle$	$r_2 = 1.0$	$r_6 = 0.5$	$r_{11} = 0.5$	$\langle 2,6,11 \rangle$
$\langle 2,6,12 \rangle$	$r_2 = 1.0$	$r_6 = 0.5$	$r_{12} = 0.25$	$\langle 2,6,12 \rangle$
$\langle 7,8,9 \rangle$	$r_7 = 0.5$	$r_8 = 2.0$	$r_9 = 0.2$	$\langle 7,8,9 \rangle$
$\langle 2,4,12 \rangle$	$r_2 = 0.25$	$r_4 = 0.5$	$r_{12} = 0.25$	$\langle 2,4,12 \rangle$
$\langle 5,6,8 \rangle$	$r_5 = 0.05$	$r_6 = 0.7$	$r_8 = 1.6$	$\langle 6,8 \rangle$
$\langle 2,8,10 \rangle$	$r_2 = 0.25$	$r_8 = 2.0$	$r_{10} = 2.0$	$\langle 2,8,10 \rangle$
$\langle 3,4,7 \rangle$	$r_3 = 0.5$	$r_4 = 2.0$	$r_7 = 2.0$	$\langle 3,4,7 \rangle$
$\langle 3,6,9 \rangle$	$r_3 = 2.0$	$r_6 = 0.5$	$r_9 = 0.2$	$\langle 3,6,9 \rangle$
$\langle 3,7,12 \rangle$	$r_3 = 2.0$	$r_7 = 2.0$	$r_{12} = 0.25$	$\langle 3,7,12 \rangle$
$\langle 2,4,5 \rangle$	$r_2 = 0.3$	$r_4 = 1.5$	$r_5 = 0.07$	$\langle 2,4 \rangle$
$\langle 5,7,12 \rangle$	$r_5 = 0.05$	$r_7 = 2.0$	$r_{12} = 1.0$	$\langle 7,11,12 \rangle$

Table 5–5   Fault List and Algorithm Performance Summary for $s_1 = j4$ and $s_2 = j.2$

Actual Fault Index	Faulty Parameter Values			Algorithm Fault Index
$\langle 6,7,10 \rangle$	$r_6 = 0.5$	$r_7 = 2.0$	$r_{10} = 2.0$	$\langle 6,7,10 \rangle$
$\langle 2,5,9 \rangle$	$r_2 = 1.0$	$r_5 = 0.05$	$r_9 = 0.2$	$\langle 2,5,9 \rangle$
$\langle 1,4,9 \rangle$	$r_1 = 0.2$	$r_4 = 0.5$	$r_9 = 0.2$	$\langle 1,4,9 \rangle$
$\langle 2,5,6 \rangle$	$r_2 = 0.3$	$r_5 = 0.07$	$r_6 = 1.4$	$\langle 2,5,6 \rangle$
$\langle 4,5,9 \rangle$	$r_4 = 2.0$	$r_5 = 0.05$	$r_9 = 0.2$	$\langle 4,5,9 \rangle$
$\langle 2,6,11 \rangle$	$r_2 = 1.0$	$r_6 = 0.5$	$r_{11} = 0.5$	$\langle 2,6,11 \rangle$
$\langle 2,6,12 \rangle$	$r_2 = 1.0$	$r_6 = 0.5$	$r_{12} = 0.25$	$\langle 2,6,12 \rangle$
$\langle 7,8,9 \rangle$	$r_7 = 0.5$	$r_8 = 2.0$	$r_9 = 0.2$	$\langle 5,7,9 \rangle$
$\langle 2,4,12 \rangle$	$r_2 = 0.25$	$r_4 = 0.5$	$r_{12} = 0.25$	$\langle 2,4,12 \rangle$
$\langle 5,6,8 \rangle$	$r_5 = 0.05$	$r_6 = 0.7$	$r_8 = 1.6$	$\langle 5,6,8 \rangle$
$\langle 2,8,10 \rangle$	$r_2 = 0.25$	$r_8 = 2.0$	$r_{10} = 2.0$	$\langle 2,3,10 \rangle$
$\langle 3,4,7 \rangle$	$r_3 = 0.5$	$r_4 = 2.0$	$r_7 = 2.0$	$\langle 3,4,7 \rangle$
$\langle 3,6,9 \rangle$	$r_3 = 2.0$	$r_6 = 0.5$	$r_9 = 0.2$	$\langle 3,6,9 \rangle$
$\langle 3,7,12 \rangle$	$r_3 = 2.0$	$r_7 = 2.0$	$r_{12} = 0.25$	$\langle 3,7,12 \rangle$
$\langle 2,4,5 \rangle$	$r_2 = 0.3$	$r_4 = 1.5$	$r_5 = 0.07$	$\langle 2,4,5 \rangle$
$\langle 5,7,12 \rangle$	$r_5 = 0.05$	$r_7 = 2.0$	$r_{12} = 1.0$	$\langle 5,7,11 \rangle$

A diagnosis based on the combination of the results of Tables 5–4 and 5–5 identifies ALL faulty components in the sixteen randomly selected fault combinations. In three cases a good component was identified as faulty but this would not result in an improperly repaired circuit.

Example 2.   To utilize the second solution method (single fault case only) of the diagnosis equations consider the circuit of Fig. 5–5. With the input taken as the voltage source and the input current as the only measurement, the CCM equations are easily obtained as

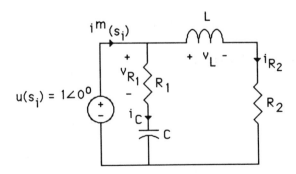

Figure 5–5   *Circuit for Example 2.*

$$
\begin{bmatrix} i_C(s) \\ v_L(s) \\ i_{R_1}(s) \\ v_{R_2}(s) \end{bmatrix} = \begin{bmatrix} \dfrac{r_1}{s} & 0 & 0 & 0 \\ 0 & \dfrac{r_2}{s} & 0 & 0 \\ 0 & 0 & r_3 & 0 \\ 0 & 0 & 0 & r_4 \end{bmatrix} \begin{bmatrix} v_C(s) \\ i_L(s) \\ v_{R_1}(s) \\ i_{R_2}(s) \end{bmatrix}
$$

where $r_1 = C^{-1}, r_2 = L^{-1}, r_3 = R_1^{-1}$, and $r_4 = R_2$; and the connection equations are

$$
\begin{bmatrix} i_C \\ v_L \\ v_{R_1} \\ i_{R_2} \end{bmatrix} = \begin{bmatrix} 0 & 0 & 1 & 0 \\ 0 & 0 & 0 & -1 \\ -1 & 0 & 0 & 0 \\ 0 & 1 & 0 & 0 \end{bmatrix} \begin{bmatrix} v_C \\ i_L \\ i_{R_1} \\ v_{R_2} \end{bmatrix} + \begin{bmatrix} 0 \\ 1 \\ 1 \\ 0 \end{bmatrix} [v_{in}]
$$

$$
[i^m] = [0 \ 1 \ 1 \ 0] \begin{bmatrix} v_C \\ i_L \\ i_{R_1} \\ v_{R_2} \end{bmatrix} + [0] [v_{in}]
$$

Assuming a single complex frequency measurement, the fault diagnosis equations take the form

$$
[Z(s_i,r) \ \vdots \ -V] \begin{bmatrix} a_0(s_1) + L_{11}V\alpha(s_1) \\ \alpha(s_1) \end{bmatrix} - b_0(s_1) = 0 \qquad (5\text{-}51)
$$

where $b_0(s_1) = L_{21}{}^{-R}Y^M(s_1)$ and $a_0(s_1) = L_{11}b_0(s_1) + L_{12}u(s_1)$. The Jacobian of this equation,

$$
J_F\big(\alpha(s_1),r\big) = [M(s_1) \ \vdots \ N(s_1)]
$$

is a complex matrix for which

$$
M(s_1) = [Z(s_1,r)L_{11}V - V] = \begin{bmatrix} -1 & -\dfrac{r_1}{s_1} & 0 \\ 0 & -1 & -\dfrac{r_2}{s_1} \\ -r_3 & 1 & 0 \\ 0 & r_4 & -1 \end{bmatrix}
$$

and

$$N(s_1) = \left[\ldots, \frac{\partial}{\partial r_j} Z(s_1, r)[a_0(s_1) + L_{11} V \alpha(s_1)], \ldots \right]$$

$$= \text{diag}[(a_{01} - \alpha_2)/s_1, (a_{02} - \alpha_3)/s_1, (a_{03} - \alpha_1), (a_{04} + \alpha_2)]$$

where a_{0j} and α_j denote the jth entries of $a_0(s_1)$ and $\alpha(s_1)$, respectively.

Since the Jacobian is complex, in order to use real arithmetic, one modifies $F(x) = 0$ to

$$\left[\begin{array}{c} \text{Re } [F(x)] \\ \text{Im } [F(x)] \end{array} \right] = 0$$

in which case the new Jacobian becomes

$$\left[\begin{array}{ccc} \text{Re}[M(s_1)] & -\text{Im}[M(s_1)] & \text{Re}[N(s_1)] \\ \text{Im}[M(s_1)] & \text{Re}[M(s_1)] & \text{Im}[N(s_1)] \end{array} \right]$$

with new solution vector $\hat{x} = \text{col}[\text{Re}(\alpha(s_1)), \text{Im}(\alpha(s_1)), r_1, r_2, r_3, r_4]$. Nominal values of the parameters are $C = 0.5$, $L = 0.5$, $R_1 = 0.5$, and $R_2 = 10$. In the first case studied, C was made faulty and measurement data generated was $[Y^M(2\pi) = .9416 \angle 56.87°]$. This data was used in the fault diagnosis equations [Eq. (5-51)] with the following results (Table 5-6):

In the case of test #1, a solution to the diagnosis equations did not exist, i.e., the actual measurements and the set of possible measurements over all possible values of components 3 and 4, had a null intersection. Thus the resultant solution was the one which minimized (in the Euclidean norm sense) the diagnosis equations. The computed minimum was $\sqrt{2.83}$. Recall that if both test faulty, it must result from a faulty unit in G1. Since there is only one fault, both must be good.

As a second test case (L_2 faulty), measurement data was taken as $Y^M(2\pi)$ $= 1.7668 \angle 30.5°$. Nominal parameter values as before. The test results are listed in Table 5-7. Other cases with R_1 faulty and R_2 faulty were run with similar successful results. This concludes the example.

Table 5–6

Test #	G1	G2	Test Results	Comments
1	1,2	3,4	$R_1 = 0.697, R_2 = 1.691$	Both test faulty, hence both good
2	3,4	1,2	$C = 0.165, L = 0.498$	C is faulty

Table 5–7

Test #	G1	G2	Test Results	Comments
1	1,2	3,4	$R_1 = 0.493, R_2 = 10.08$	Both test good, hence both are good
2	3,4	1,2	$C_1 = 0.5, L_2 = 0.15$	L_2 is faulty

CONCLUSIONS

This chapter has described the problem of fault diagnosis for the case where $n_f \geq n_0$. It has presented Jacobian tests for the diagnosability of a circuit/system under this assumption and explained two algorithms for the solution of the diagnosis equations. Each technique was illustrated with a simple example. For a 26-parameter video amplifier illustration see [1,4].

The major difficulty associated with solving the diagnosis equations with algorithm 1 under the limited fault assumption when $n_f \geq n_0$ is the need to avoid testing the enormous number of fault indices possible for large circuits/systems having multiple fault possibilities. Algorithm 1 avoids this problem by utilizing the information available at the surface defined by the equality constraints.

The second algorithm avoids the need to search over all possible fault combinations by using the self-testing ideas of [8,10,20] to sequentially reduce the fault possibilities by sequentially determining good components. These t-fault diagnosability ideas in conjunction with the multifrequency fault diagnosis equations appear to have simple implementation and good convergence properties. Further investigations especially for the multiple fault case would seem to be in order. The reader might note that the t-fault diagnosability ideas with a time domain formulation of the fault diagnosis equations for analog-digital circuits was successfully implementated as described in [2].

Other areas of continued research are in the areas of test point and test frequency selection and the problem of a global measure of diagnosability in the limited fault case. Some preliminary results on test point and test frequency selection can be found in [1].

REFERENCES

[1] L. Rapisarda, "Multifrequency Analog Fault Diagnosis for Linearized Circuits," Ph.D. dissertation, Purdue University, May 1983.
[2] D. Reisig and R. DeCarlo, "A Method of Analogue-Digital Fault Diagnosis," *Circuit Theory Appl.*, Vol. 15, pp. 1–22, 1987.
[3] R. DeCarlo and R. Rapisarda, "Fault Diagnosis under a Limited Fault Assumption and Limited Test Point Availability," Circuits, Systems, and Signal Processing, Vol 7, No 4, 1988.

[4] L. Rapisarda and R. DeCarlo, "Analog Multifrequency Fault Diagnosis," *IEEE Trans. Circuits Syst.*, Vol. CAS-30, No. 4, Apr. 1983.

[5] R. A. DeCarlo and R. Saeks, *Interconnected Dynamical Systems*, Marcel Dekker, New York, 1981.

[6] P. M. Lin and Y. S. Elcherif, "Analogue Circuits Fault Dictionary: New Approaches and Implementation," *Circuit Theory Appl.*, Vol. 13, pp. 149–172, 1985.

[7] Z. F. Huang, C. Lin, and R. Liu, "Node-Fault Diagnosis and Design of Testability," *Proc. 20th IEEE Conf. on Decision and Control, 1981*, Vol. 3, pp. 1037–1042.

[8] C.-C. Wu, K. Nakajima, C.-L. Wey, and R. Saeks, "Analog Fault Diagnosis with Failure Bounds," *IEEE Trans. Circuits Syst.*, Vol. CAS-29, pp. 277–284, May 1982.

[9] R. M. Biernacki and J. W. Bandler, "Multiple-Fault Location of Analog Circuits," *IEEE Trans. Circuits Syst.*, Vol. CAS-28, pp. 361–367, May 1981.

[10] C.-L. Wey, "Design of Testability for Analog Fault Diagnosis," *Proc. 1985 IEEE Int. Symp. on Circuits and Systems*, Kyoto, Japan, May 1985.

[11] R. Saeks, "Criteria for Analog Fault Diagnosis," *Proc. European Conf. Circuit Theory and Design*, The Hague, Netherlands Aug. 1981, pp. 75–78.

[12] G. D. Hachtel, R. K. Brayton, and F. G. Gustavson, "The Sparse Tableau Approach to Network Analysis and Design," *IEEE Trans. Circuit Theory*, Vol. CT-18, pp. 101–113, 1971.

[13] N. Navid and A. N. Willson, "A Theory and an Algorithm for Analog Circuit Fault Diagnosis," *IEEE Trans. Circuits Syst.*, Vol. CAS-26, pp. 440–457, Jul. 1979.

[14] Keith Kendig, *Elementary Algebraic Geometry*, Springer-Verlag, New York, 1977.

[15] S. R. Lay, *Convex Sets and Their Applications*, Wiley, New York, 1982.

[16] G. L. Nabor, *Topological Methods in Euclidean Spaces*, Cambridge University Press, Cambridge, 1980.

[17] Gilbert Strang, *Linear Algebra and Its Application*, Academic, New York, 1976.

[18] R. Saeks, A. Sangiovanni-Vincentelli, and V. Visvanathan, "Diagnosability of Nonlinear Circuits and Systems—Part II: Dynamical Systems," *IEEE Trans. Circuits and Systems*, Vol. CAS-28, pp. 1103–1108, 1981.

[19] D. G. Luenberger, *Introduction to Linear and Nonlinear Programming*, Addison-Wesley, Reading, MA, 1973.

[20] S. Louis Haakimi and Kaxuo Nakajima, "On a Theory of t-Fault Diagnosable Analog Systems," *IEEE Trans. Circuits Syst.*, Vol. CAS-31, No. 11, Nov. 1984.

[21] IMSL—International Mathematical and Statistical Libraries, IMSL Inc., Houston.

6

A Searching Approach Self-Testing Algorithm for Analog Fault Diagnosis

CHIN-LONG WEY

Given our experience with the digital test problem and the analog computer-aided design (CAD) problem, one might initially assume that the analog test problem could be resolved simply by integrating the tools and techniques of these two well-established fields. In fact, however, the analog problem is characterized by tolerance, modeling, and simulation problems which have no counterpart in the digital problem, while many of the concepts derived from the analog design problem are incompatible with the economics of the test environment.

Over the past decade, the circuits and systems community has undertaken a considerable research effort directed at the development of a viable analog fault diagnosis algorithm [1–21]. The various proposed algorithms for an analog automatic test program generator (AATPG) may naturally be divided into three categories characterized by the simulation occurrence, the test inputs allowed, and the fault hypotheses employed. These include [6,9]:

1. Pretest simulation techniques
2. Post-test simulation with multiple test vectors,
3. Post-test simulation with failure bounds.

To evaluate analog diagnosis algorithms, a set of criteria has been proposed [9]. The criteria are: computational requirements, number of test points and test vector employed, robustness to tolerance effects, availability of models, and the degree to which the algorithm is amenable to parallel processing. Based on the above criteria, the above three simulation techniques are compared and the post-test simulation with failure bounds seems to be the closest to the "ideal" algorithm [9].

Motivated by the above considerations, a self-test theory has been developed for analog circuit fault isolation [8,19–21] to reduce the complexity of the nonlinear fault diagnosis equations while still retaining computational simplicity. The salient features of the proposed self-test algorithm are that the algorithm:

1. works with both linear and nonlinear systems modelled in either the time or frequency domain;
2. can be used to locate multiple hard or soft faults;
3. is designed to locate failures in "replaceable modules" such as an IC chip, PC board, or subsystem rather than in discrete components.

Moreover, this is achieved at an acceptable computational cost and with minimal test point requirements.

Based on the proposed self-testing algorithm, an AATPG for both linear [19,20] and nonlinear [21] circuits has been implemented. The AATPG code is subdivided into off-line and on-line processes. The former is used by the test system designer to input nominal system specifications and to generate a database used by the on-line process. To implement the actual test, the field engineer invokes the on-line process inputting data describing the unit under test (UUT) and the source of the test data. The actual test can then be run in a fully automatic and/or an interactive mode.

In the following section, the simulation model known as the component connection model and the detailed implementation of the self-testing algorithm are discussed. Although it is reasonable to assume that at most two or three components have failed simultaneously in a given circuit containing several hundred components, we do not know which two or three. Therefore, some type of search is still required. Three decision algorithms are presented to search for the faulty components in the second section. The parallel processing algorithm and the associated parallel test system architecture are demonstrated in the third section. Design of testability is discussed in the fourth section, and, finally, the work is summarized in the fifth section.

AUTOMATIC TEST PROGRAM GENERATION

For the purpose of doing fault diagnosis, we work with an interconnection system model known as the component connection model (CCM) [22]. Assume the analog circuit or system under test consists of n components, k external test inputs, and m external test points. In the linear case, the unit under test (UUT) characterizes its components and/or subsystems together with an algebraic connection equation as follows:

$$b = Za \qquad (6\text{-}1)$$

and

$$a = L_{11}b + L_{12}u \qquad (6\text{-}2)$$

$$y = L_{21}b + L_{22}u \qquad (6\text{-}3)$$

where $a = \text{col}(a_i)$ and $b = \text{col}(b_i)$, $i = 1, 2, \ldots, n$, are the column vectors composed of the component input and output variables, respectively, while u is the vector of external test inputs applied to the system and y is the vector of system responses measured at the various test points. The L_{ij}'s are constant, generally sparse matrices, known as the connection matrices, whose dimensions conform to the given vector quantities.

For the linear case, the component equation (6-1) is modeled in the frequency domain, where $Z = \text{diag}(Z_i)$, $i = 1, 2, \ldots, n$, is a frequency domain composite component transfer matrix. Each of such $Z_i [-Z_i(s, r)]$ describes the ith component of the circuit or system; here $r = \text{col}(r_i)$ is the column vector of unknown component parameters and s is the complex frequency variable. Typically, the unknown component parameters take the form of resistances, capacitances, inductances, amplifier gains, etc. In particular, it is assumed that enough parameters are employed to completely characterize the performance of the device.

Example 1 [20].   Consider a linear circuit, a BJT small signal amplifier circuit with beta-independent bias, as shown in Fig. 6-1. With the appropriate test points the component and connection equations are generated as follows:

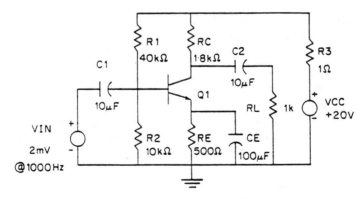

Figure 6–1   *A linear circuit.*

Connection equations:

$$\begin{bmatrix} IC1 \\ IR1 \\ VR2 \\ IRC \\ IBQ1 \\ VCEQ1 \\ VRE \\ VCE \\ VC2 \\ IRL \\ VR3 \\ \hline IC1 \\ IR1 \\ V45 \\ V13 \end{bmatrix} = \left[\begin{array}{ccccccccccc} 0 & 0 & 1 & 0 & 0 & 0 & 1 & 1 & 1 & 0 & 1 \\ 0 & 0 & 0 & 0 & 0 & -1 & 0 & 0 & -1 & 0 & -1 \\ -1 & 0 & 0 & 0 & 0 & 0 & 0 & 0 & 0 & 0 & 0 \\ 0 & 0 & 0 & 0 & 0 & 1 & 0 & 0 & 1 & 0 & 0 \\ 0 & 0 & 0 & 0 & 0 & -1 & 1 & 1 & 0 & 0 & 0 \\ 0 & 1 & 0 & -1 & 1 & 0 & 0 & 0 & 0 & 0 & 0 \\ -1 & 0 & 0 & 0 & -1 & 0 & 0 & 0 & 0 & 0 & 0 \\ -1 & 0 & 0 & 0 & -1 & 0 & 0 & 0 & 0 & 0 & 0 \\ -1 & 1 & 0 & -1 & 0 & 0 & 0 & 0 & 0 & -1 & 0 \\ 0 & 0 & 0 & 0 & 0 & 0 & 0 & 0 & 1 & 0 & 0 \\ -1 & 1 & 0 & 0 & 0 & 0 & 0 & 0 & 0 & 0 & 0 \\ \hline 0 & 0 & 1 & 0 & 0 & 0 & 1 & 1 & 1 & 0 & 1 \\ 0 & 0 & 0 & 0 & 0 & -1 & 0 & 0 & -1 & 0 & -1 \\ -1 & 0 & 0 & 0 & -1 & 0 & 0 & 0 & 0 & -1 & 0 \\ 0 & 1 & 0 & -1 & 0 & 0 & 0 & 0 & 0 & 0 & 0 \end{array}\right] \begin{bmatrix} VC1 \\ VR1 \\ IR2 \\ VRC \\ VBEQ1 \\ ICQ1 \\ IRE \\ ICE \\ IC2 \\ VRL \\ IR3 \end{bmatrix} + \begin{bmatrix} 0 & 0 \\ 0 & 0 \\ 1 & 0 \\ 0 & 0 \\ 0 & 0 \\ 0 & 0 \\ 1 & 0 \\ 1 & 0 \\ 1 & 0 \\ 0 & 0 \\ 1 & -1 \\ \hline 0 & 0 \\ 0 & 0 \\ 0 & 0 \\ 0 & 0 \end{bmatrix} \begin{bmatrix} VIN \\ VCC \end{bmatrix}$$

(6-4)

Component equations:

$$Z = \begin{bmatrix} Z_{C1} & 0 & 0 & 0 & 0 & 0 & 0 & 0 & 0 & 0 & 0 \\ 0 & Z_{R1} & 0 & 0 & 0 & 0 & 0 & 0 & 0 & 0 & 0 \\ 0 & 0 & Y_{R2} & 0 & 0 & 0 & 0 & 0 & 0 & 0 & 0 \\ 0 & 0 & 0 & Z_{RC} & 0 & 0 & 0 & 0 & 0 & 0 & 0 \\ 0 & 0 & 0 & 0 & Z_{h1} & Z_{h2} & 0 & 0 & 0 & 0 & 0 \\ 0 & 0 & 0 & 0 & Z_{h3} & Z_{h4} & 0 & 0 & 0 & 0 & 0 \\ 0 & 0 & 0 & 0 & 0 & 0 & Y_{RE} & 0 & 0 & 0 & 0 \\ 0 & 0 & 0 & 0 & 0 & 0 & 0 & Y_{CE} & 0 & 0 & 0 \\ 0 & 0 & 0 & 0 & 0 & 0 & 0 & 0 & Y_{C2} & 0 & 0 \\ 0 & 0 & 0 & 0 & 0 & 0 & 0 & 0 & 0 & Z_{RL} & 0 \\ 0 & 0 & 0 & 0 & 0 & 0 & 0 & 0 & 0 & 0 & Y_{R3} \end{bmatrix}$$

For the nonlinear case, a similar model is used with the component characteristics represented by a set of decoupled state models,

$$\begin{aligned} \dot{x}_i &= f_i(x_i, a_i), \\ b_i &= g_i(x_i, a_i), \end{aligned} \qquad x_i(0) = 0, \quad i = 1, 2, \ldots, n$$

where x_i is the state vector for component i. For notational purpose we stack the individual component equations together to form the composite component equations:

$$\begin{aligned} \dot{x} &= f(x, a), \\ b &= g(x, a), \end{aligned} \qquad x(0) = 0$$

(6-5)

Similar to the linear case, we append the connection equations (6-2) and (6-3) to these component equations to form the CCM for the nonlinear case.

The Self-Testing Algorithm

Conceptually, at each step of the test algorithm the components (individual chips, discrete components, or subsystems) are subdivided into two groups: the "Tester Group" (or Group 1) and the "Testee Group" (or Group 2). At each step one assumes that the Tester Group is composed of good components and one uses the known characteristics of those components together with the test data (test inputs and measured system responses at the external accessible test points), to determine if the remaining components in the Testee Group are good. In fact, the first group of components is testing the second, hence the "self-testing" algorithm. Of course, if all components in the Tester Group are actually good, then the resultant test outcome for each component in the Testee Group will be reliable. On the other hand, if any one of the testers is faulty, the test outcomes on the testee will be unreliable. Consequently, one repeats the process at the next step of the test algorithm with a different subdivision of components. Finally, after a number of such repetitions, the test outcomes obtained at the various steps are analyzed to determine the faulty component.

Of course, the number of components which may be tested at any step is dependent on the number of test points available, whereas the number of steps required is determined by the number of testee components and the bound on the maximum number of simultaneous failures. Therefore, this procedure yields a natural set of trade-offs between the number of test points, simultaneous failures, and steps required by the algorithm.

Pseudocircuit Generation

In order to represent the subdivision step in the self-testing algorithm, a superscript is assigned to denote the group designation, i.e., superscript 1 for Group 1 components, etc.

Linear Case

Equations (6-1)–(6-3) are partitioned as

$$b^1 = Z^1 a^1 \tag{6-6}$$

$$b^2 = Z^2 a^2 \tag{6-7}$$

and

$$a^1 = L_{11}^{11}b^1 + L_{11}^{12}b^2 + L_{12}^1u \tag{6-8}$$

$$a^2 = L_{11}^{21}b^1 = L_{11}^{22}b^2 + L_{12}^2u \tag{6-9}$$

$$y = L_{21}^1b^1 + L_{21}^2b^2 + L_{22}\,u \tag{6-10}$$

Since, in our application, the test responses y and the test inputs u are known, and the Group 1 components are assumed to be good, the remaining objective is to compute the Group 2 component input and output waveforms, a^2 and b^2. To this end we assume that L_{21}^2 admits a left inverse. Under this assumption, Eq. (6-9) becomes

$$b^2 = [L_{21}^2]^{-L}[-L_{21}^1b^1 - L_{22}u + y] \tag{6-11}$$

By making substitutions into Eq. (6-8) and (6-10), the "pseudocircuit" connection equations are

$$a^1 = K_{11}b^1 + K_{12}u^P \tag{6-12}$$

$$y^P = K_{21}b^1 + K_{22}u^P \tag{6-13}$$

where $u^P = \mathrm{col}(u,y)$ and $y^P = \mathrm{col}(a^2,b^2)$ are the column vectors of the external inputs and outputs of the pseudocircuit, while the connection matrices K_{ij}'s are defined as

$$K_{11} = [L_{11}^{11} - L_{11}^{12}[L_{21}^2]^{-L}L_{21}^1] \tag{6-14}$$

$$K_{12} = [L_{12}^1 - L_{11}^{12}[L_{21}^2]^{-L}L_{22} \mid L_{11}^{12}\,[L_{21}^2]^{-L}] \tag{6-15}$$

$$K_{21} = \left[\begin{array}{c} L_{11}^{21} - L_{11}^{22}[L_{21}^2]^{-L}L_{21}^1 \\ \hline - [L_{21}^2]^{-L}L_{21}^1 \end{array} \right] \tag{6-16}$$

$$K_{21} = \left[\begin{array}{c|c} L_{12}^2 - L_{11}^{22}[L_{21}^2]^{-L}L_{22} & L_{11}^{22}[L_{21}^2]^{-L} \\ \hline - [L_{21}^2]^{-L}L_{22} & [L_{21}^2]^{-L} \end{array} \right] \tag{6-17}$$

For each pseudocircuit, substituting (6-6) into (6-12) and (6-13), the input–output relation

$$y^P = Mu^P \tag{6-18}$$

is obtained, where

$$M = K_{21}Z^1[I - K_{11}Z^1]^{-1}K_{12} + K_{22} \qquad (6\text{-}19)$$

Upon the partitioning M to conform with the partitions of y^p and u^p, this then becomes

$$a^2 = M_{11}u + M_{12}y \qquad (6\text{-}20)$$

$$b^2 = M_{21}u + M_{22}y \qquad (6\text{-}21)$$

Note that since Eq. (6-19) is dependent only on the nominal values of the Tester Group components, the M_{ij}'s may be computed off-line and stored in a database to be retrieved at the time when a test is conducted. Furthermore, since only a single test vector is required, single-frequency testing can be employed. In this case, the M_{ij}'s need only be computed at a single frequency. The only on-line computation required for the fault diagnosis of a linear system is thus the matrix/vector multiplication indicated in Eq. (6-20) and (6-21) together with the computation of

$$\hat{b}^2 = Z^2 a^2 \qquad (6\text{-}22)$$

to determine which, if any, of the Testee Group components are faulty.

The test outcome (either "good" or "bad," for each Testee Group component) is obtained by comparing the b^2 and $\hat{b}^2$. If their ith elements are the same, or $b^2_i = \hat{b}^2_i$, then we say that the test outcome for the ith component in the Testee Group is good; otherwise, the component is "bad." In a more realistic environment, instead of requiring that b^2_i and $\hat{b}^2_i$ be equal, one may say that a component is "good" if b^2_i is sufficiently close to $\hat{b}^2_i$. In this way one may compensate for numerical errors and tolerances. Moreover, b^2_i and $\hat{b}^2_i$ are not necessarily scalars; they may be vectors, depending upon the component type with which one deals. For instance, a two-port component may require a twotuple vector to represent its input/output characteristics.

Example 2.   Consider the linear circuit of Fig. 6–1 and its connection matrix of Eq. (6-4). Based on the fact that a component subdivision is allowable if the corresponding matrix $[L^2_{21}]^{-L}$ exists, it is possible to generate 34 allowable component subdivisions, as illustrated in Table 6–1. The first component subdivision indicates that the Testee Group (Group 2) consists of components #1, #2, #3, and #9, and the remaining components are contained in the

Table 6–1   Allowable Component Subdivisions

Subdivision Number	Testee Group Components				Subdivision Number	Testee Group Components			
1	1	2	3	9	18	2	8	10	11
2	1	2	3	11	19	3	4	9	10
3	1	2	7	9	20	3	4	10	11
4	1	2	7	11	21	4	7	9	10
5	1	2	8	9	22	4	7	10	11
6	1	2	8	11	23	4	8	9	10
7	1	3	4	9	24	4	8	10	11
8	1	3	4	11	25	2	3	5	6
9	1	4	7	9	26	2	5	6	7
10	1	4	7	11	27	2	5	6	8
11	1	4	8	9	28	2	5	6	9
12	1	4	8	11	29	2	5	6	11
13	2	3	9	10	30	3	4	5	6
14	2	3	10	11	31	4	5	6	7
15	2	7	9	10	32	4	5	6	8
16	2	7	10	11	33	4	5	6	9
17	2	8	9	10	34	4	5	6	11

Tester Group. The K-matrix of this component subdivision, corresponding to Eq. (6-14)–(6-17), is generated as follows:

$$
\begin{bmatrix}
IRC \\ IBQ1 \\ VCEQ1 \\ VRE \\ VCE \\ IRL \\ VR3 \\ \hline \\ IC1 \\ IR1 \\ VR2 \\ VC2 \\ \hline \\ VC1 \\ VR1 \\ IR2 \\ IC2
\end{bmatrix}
=
\left[
\begin{array}{ccccccc|ccccc}
0 & 0 & 0 & 0 & 0 & 0 & -1 & 0 & 0 & 1 & 0 & 0 \\
0 & 0 & -1 & 1 & 1 & 0 & 0 & 0 & 0 & 0 & 0 & 0 \\
0 & 1 & 0 & 0 & 0 & 0 & 0 & 0 & 0 & 0 & 0 & 1 \\
0 & 0 & 0 & 0 & 0 & 1 & 0 & 0 & 0 & 0 & 1 & 0 \\
0 & 0 & 0 & 0 & 0 & 1 & 0 & 0 & 0 & 0 & 1 & 0 \\
0 & 0 & -1 & 0 & 0 & 0 & -1 & 0 & 0 & -1 & 0 & 0 \\
1 & 1 & 0 & 0 & 0 & 1 & 0 & -1 & 0 & 0 & 1 & 1 \\
\hline
0 & 0 & 0 & 0 & 0 & 0 & 0 & 0 & 1 & 0 & 0 & 0 \\
0 & 0 & 0 & 0 & 0 & 0 & 0 & 0 & 0 & 1 & 0 & 0 \\
0 & 1 & 0 & 0 & 0 & 1 & 0 & 0 & 0 & 0 & 1 & 0 \\
0 & 1 & 0 & 0 & 0 & 0 & 0 & 0 & 0 & 0 & 1 & 1 \\
\hline
0 & -1 & 0 & 0 & 0 & -1 & 0 & 0 & 0 & 0 & -1 & 0 \\
1 & 0 & 0 & 0 & 0 & 0 & 0 & 0 & 0 & 0 & 0 & 1 \\
0 & 0 & 1 & -1 & -1 & 0 & 0 & 0 & 1 & 1 & 0 & 0 \\
0 & 0 & -1 & 0 & 0 & 0 & -1 & 0 & 0 & -1 & 0 & 0
\end{array}
\right]
\begin{bmatrix}
VRC \\ VBEQ1 \\ ICQ1 \\ IRE \\ ICE \\ VRL \\ IR3 \\ \hline \\ u1 \\ u2 \\ y1 \\ y2 \\ y3 \\ y4
\end{bmatrix}
\tag{6-23}
$$

Given the above K-matrix, one can easily calculate the M-matrix of Eq. (6-19) and then further compute both b^2 and $\hat{b}^2$ from Eq. (6-20)–(6-22) to determine the status of the components in that pseudocircuit.

Nonlinear Case

Similar to the linear case, a pseudocircuit is generated in the form

$$\begin{aligned}
\dot{x}^1 &= f^1(x^1, a^1), \\
b^1 &= g^1(x^1, a^1),
\end{aligned} \qquad x^1(0) = 0 \qquad (6\text{-}24)$$

and

$$a^1 = K_{11}b^1 + K_{12}u^P \qquad (6\text{-}25)$$

$$y^P = K_{21}b^1 + K_{22}u^P \qquad (6\text{-}26)$$

where the notations have been defined as in the linear case.

Although these equations have the same form as a set of standard circuit equations, they do not correspond to a physical circuit and hence the term "pseudocircuit" equations. Since both parameters u and y are known in the test algorithm, these pseudocircuit equations can be solved via any standard circuit analysis code, such as SPICE [23]. Once the component variables in Testee Group, a^2 and b^2, are computed, we calculate

$$\begin{aligned}
\dot{x}^2 &= f^2(x^2, a^2), \\
\hat{b}^2 &= g^2(x^2, a^2),
\end{aligned} \qquad x^2(0) = 0 \qquad (6\text{-}27)$$

and compare b^2 and $\hat{b}^2$ to determine which, if any, of the Group 2 components are faulty.

Since we work with an algebraic representation of the system connectivity structure rather than a graph or a schematic diagram to facilitate the use of SPICE, we first develop a "controlled source equivalent circuit" for the algebraic equations. Indeed, this greatly simplifies the database generation process for our "pseudocircuits" which have no "obvious" physical realization.

The SPICE code is generated as follows. Since the internal input vector u and the external output vector y are known when the test is conducted, these known values can thus be modelled by independent sources. Consider Eq. (6-25) and suppose that the vectors b^1 and u^P in a pseudocircuit are

$$b^1 = \mathrm{col}[V_{b1}, I_{b2}, V_{b3}, I_{b4}, V_{b5}]$$

$$u^P = \mathrm{col}[V_{u1}, V_{u2}, I_{u3}, V_{u4}]$$

Suppose also the ith rows of K_{11} and K_{12} are respectively given by

$$P_i = [1 \quad 0 \quad -1 \quad 0 \quad 0] \quad \text{and} \quad Q_i = [1 \quad 0 \quad 0 \quad -1]$$

If the voltage measurement at the ith component of a^1, or a_i, is considered, then

$$V_{ai} = P_i b^1 + Q_i u^P = V_{b1} - V_{b3} + V_{u1} - V_{u4} \qquad (6\text{-}28)$$

Here V_{bi} may be implemented as a dependent voltage source controlled by the voltage measured across component b_1 and similarly for V_{b3}, V_{u1}, and V_{u4}. Physically, from Eq. (6-28), V_{ai} is the voltage measured across the serial connection of the above four dependent sources. Thus, Eq. (6-28) may be modelled as shown in Fig. 6–2.

Therefore, b^1 may be computed from the characteristics of the components, or Eq. (6-24), and the known vector value a^1, by simulating the circuit shown in Fig. 6–2. To implement this simulation, the box of Fig. 6–2 is replaced by the component employed. More specifically, if the component is a resistor, the resistor will be connected in series with those four dependent voltage sources, as illustrated in Fig. 6–3. If V_R is known, by Ohm's law, the current I_R can be calculated. In SPICE code, the current flow through a component is modeled by connecting a zero-valued voltage source in series with the component [23]. The current flow through the voltage source is then the current to be measured.

Similarly, for the current measurement of an element of a^1, Fig. 6–4 shows that the circuit can be modeled by connecting dependent current sources in parallel to produce the sum of the currents, a zero-valued voltage source in serial to represent the sum, and the type of component in serial to measure the voltage across the component.

For multiport components, the circuit is modeled in the similar way using multiple connection and component equations.

Given that the SPICE code for Eq. (6-25) has been generated, consider Eq. (6-26) with the partitioned matrices,

$$a^2 = K_{21}^1 b^1 + K_{22}^1 u^P \qquad (6\text{-}29)$$

$$b^2 = K^2_{21} b^1 + K^2_{22} u^P \qquad (6\text{-}30)$$

SPICE code for Eq. (6-30) is generated in a similar manner except that the box in Fig. 6–2 is replaced by a zero-valued voltage source if the element of

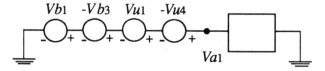

Figure 6–2 *Circuit modeling of Eq. (6-28).*

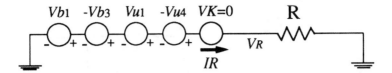

Figure 6-3 *Circuit modeling of Eq. (6-28) with a resistor.*

b^2 is a current measurement, or a resistor with resistance 1 Ω for a voltage measurement. The SPICE code for Eq. (6-29) can be generated in the same way, however, in this case we are interested in is the vector value b^2. Therefore, the box in Fig. 6–2 is determined by Eq. (6-27).

Example 3 [21]. Consider the nonlinear power supply circuit shown in Fig. 6–5. The connection matrix L and vectors a, b, u, and y are automatically generated in the form

$$a = \begin{bmatrix} IR1 \\ VC1 \\ ID1 \\ VC2 \\ IL1 \\ VC3 \\ VRL \end{bmatrix}, b = \begin{bmatrix} VR1 \\ IC1 \\ VD1 \\ IC2 \\ IL1 \\ IC3 \\ IRL \end{bmatrix} \qquad u = \begin{bmatrix} u1 \end{bmatrix} = \begin{bmatrix} VIN \end{bmatrix}$$

$$y = \begin{bmatrix} y1 \\ y2 \\ y3 \end{bmatrix} = \begin{bmatrix} ID1 \\ IL1 \\ VRL \end{bmatrix}$$

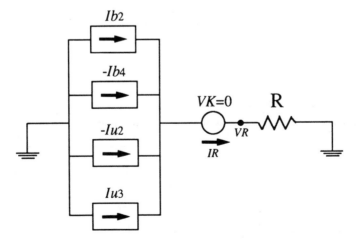

Figure 6-4 *Circuit modeling for current measurement.*

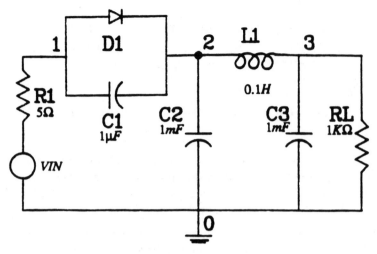

Figure 6–5   *A power supply circuit.*

$$L = \left[\begin{array}{c|c} L_{11} & L_{12} \\ \hline L_{21} & L_{22} \end{array}\right] = \left[\begin{array}{ccccccc|c} 0 & 0 & 0 & 1 & 0 & 1 & 1 & 0 \\ 0 & 0 & 1 & 0 & 0 & 0 & 0 & 0 \\ 0 & -1 & 0 & 1 & 0 & 1 & 1 & 0 \\ -1 & 0 & -1 & 0 & 0 & 0 & 0 & 1 \\ 0 & 0 & 0 & 0 & 0 & 1 & 1 & 0 \\ -1 & 0 & -1 & 0 & -1 & 0 & 0 & 1 \\ -1 & 0 & -1 & 0 & -1 & 0 & 0 & 1 \\ \hline 0 & -1 & 0 & 1 & 0 & 1 & 1 & 0 \\ 0 & 0 & 0 & 0 & 0 & 1 & 1 & 0 \\ -1 & 0 & -1 & 0 & -1 & 0 & 0 & 1 \end{array}\right]$$

Table 6–2   Component Subdivisions Table

Subdivision Number	Component Number			Subdivision Number	Component Number		
(1)	1	2	6	(7)	2	5	6
(2)	1	2	7	(8)	2	5	7
(3)	1	4	6	(9)	3	4	6
(4)	1	4	7	(10)	3	4	7
(5)	2	3	6	(11)	4	5	6
(6)	2	3	7	(12)	4	5	7

Similar to Example 2, it is possible to generate 12 component subdivisions, as listed in Table 6–2. If the first component subdivision is considered, i.e., components #3, #4, #5, and #7 and test components #1, #2, and #6, then the corresponding K-matrix is generated as follows:

$$
\begin{bmatrix}
\text{ID1} \\ \text{VC2} \\ \text{IL1} \\ \text{VRL} \\ \hdashline \text{IR1} \\ \text{VC1} \\ \text{VC3} \\ \hdashline \text{VR1} \\ \text{IC1} \\ \text{IC3}
\end{bmatrix}
=
\left[
\begin{array}{cccc:cccc}
0 & 0 & 0 & 0 & 0 & 1 & 0 & 0 \\
0 & 0 & 1 & 0 & 0 & 0 & 0 & 1 \\
0 & 0 & 0 & 0 & 0 & 0 & 1 & 0 \\
0 & 0 & 0 & 0 & 0 & 0 & 0 & 1 \\ \hline
0 & 1 & 0 & 0 & 0 & 0 & 1 & 0 \\
1 & 0 & 0 & 0 & 0 & 0 & 0 & 0 \\
0 & 0 & 0 & 0 & 0 & 0 & 0 & 0 \\ \hline
-1 & 0 & -1 & 0 & 1 & 0 & 0 & -1 \\
0 & 1 & 0 & 0 & 0 & -1 & 1 & 0 \\
0 & 0 & 0 & -1 & 0 & 0 & 1 & 0
\end{array}
\right]
\begin{bmatrix}
\text{VD1} \\ \text{IC2} \\ \text{VL1} \\ \text{IRL} \\ \hdashline u1 \\ y1 \\ y2 \\ y3
\end{bmatrix}
\quad (6\text{-}31)
$$

where $u1 = \text{VIN}$, $y1 = \text{ID1}$, $y2 = \text{IL1}$, and $y3 = \text{VRL}$.

Since the current measurement at the components L1 and D1 is required, the circuit of Fig. 6–5 with two zero-valued voltage sources, as shown in Fig. 6–6, is simulated. The SPICE code for simulating Eq. (6-31) is given below. The SPICE code consists of three parts: circuit, source, and pseudocircuit descriptions. The third part is the code that describes the controlled source equivalent circuit of the connection equation (6-31). In that equation, it is assumed that the measured data at the test points are known and used as the sources of the pseudocircuit. As shown in the listing, the first part is the code that describes the circuit of Fig. 6–6, while the second part describes four controlled sources that are simulated as the known measured data.

POWER SUPPLY CIRCUIT

VIN	4	0	SIN (0 10 60)	
.MODEL	DMOD1	D	IS = 1.0E-06	N = 0.97
VK21	1	5	0	
VK22	2	6	0	
R1	4	1	5	
C1	1	2	1U	
D1	5	2	DMOD1	
C2	2	0	1M	
L1	6	3	0.1	
C3	3	0	1M	
RL	3	0	1K	
·TRAN	10M	200M		

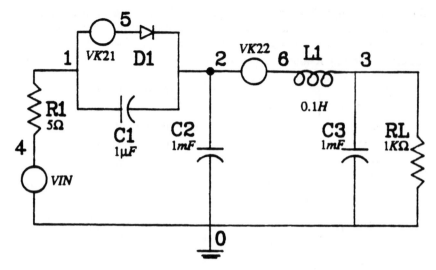

Figure 6–6 A power supply circuit with additional sources for SPICE simulation.

```
* Source Description
EE701      701        0        4        0     1
RR701      701        0        1
FF702        0      702      VK21       1
VK702      702        0        0
FF703        0      703      VK22       1
VK703      703        0        0
EE704      704        0        3        0     1
RR704      704        0        1
* Pseudocircuit Description
****         1
FF101        0      101      VK702      1
VK101      101      102        0
DD101      102        0      DMOD1
****         2
EE101      103        0      POLY(2)    106 0 704 0 0 1 1
VK102      103      104        0
CC101      104        0        1M
****         3
FF102        0      105      VK703      1
VK103      105      106        0
LL101      106        0        0.1
****         4
EE102      107        0      704        0     1
```

VK104	107	108	0	
RR101	108	0	1K	
****	1			
FF103	0	109	POLY (2)	VK102 VK703 0 1 1
VK105	109	110	0	
RR102	110	0	5	
****	2			
EE103	111	0	102	0 1
VK106	111	112	0	
CC102	112	0	1U	
****	3			
EE104	113	0	704	0 1
VK107	113	114	0	
CC103	114	0	1M	
****	1			
EE105	115	0	POLY(4)	102 0 106 0 701 0 704 0 0 -1 -1
RR108	115	0	1	
****	2			
FF104	0	116	POLY(3)	VK102 VK702 VK703 0 1 -1 1
VK109	116	0	0	
****	3			
FF105	0	117	POLY(2)	VK104 VK703 0-1 1
VK110	117	0	0	
·PRINT	TRAN	V(115), V(110)		
·PRINT	TRAN	I (VK109),I(VK106)		
·PRINT	TRAN	I(VK110),I(VK107)		
·END				

Software Implementation

The AATPG code for both the linear and nonlinear circuits consists of off-line and on-line processes. The former, corresponding to the test system design stage, is used by the test system designer to input nominal system specifications to generate a database which is used during the on-line process. To implement the actual test on a UUT (unit under test), the field engineer invokes the on-line process by inputting data describing the UUT, the assumed maximum number of simultaneous failures, the type of decision algorithm to be employed, and the resources of the test data. The actual test can then be run in a fully automatic mode, or interactively.

A circuit description and test objectives are initially given in the off-line process to generate the test program. Necessary changes may be implemented if the resultant test does not satisfy all requirements. On the other hand, if the design is satisfactory, the off-line process will then generate the test program and its associated test data for the use of the on-line process. In the test package, the greatest part of the required computation is carried out by the off-line process which computes the "pseudointernal test data." This "test data" is computed from the test measurements via a simple on-line matrix/vector multiplication for the linear case. To the contrary, in the non-linear case, a circuit simulator, SPICE, is used to compute the "pseudointernal test data" via an on-line simulation of an appropriate pseudo circuit.

In our implementation, the AATPG code resides in the host computer. When the on-line process is conducted, the ATE (automatic test equipment) receives the commands from the host computer instructing the ATE to perform the measurements. After the ATE completes, it transmits the test data to the host to identify the faulty component(s).

Both the off-line and the on-line processes have user-oriented interfaces to simplify the process of generating a new test program. The AATPG has been implemented on a VMS operating system VAX 11/780 in FORTRAN 77 and DCL (DEC Command Language). The input syntax is a free-format style; in other words, it does not require that data be entered in fixed column locations [24].

DECISION ALGORITHMS

Since the test results described in the preceding section are dependent on our assumption that the Group 1 components are not faulty, they are not immediately applicable. A decision algorithm is required to cope with this ambiguity so that the actual fault(s) can be precisely identified. Following the philosophy initiated by Preparata, Metze, and Chien, in their study of self-testing computer network [25–27], if one assumes a bound on the maximum number of simultaneous failures, it is possible to determine the actual fault(s) from an analysis of the test results obtained at the various steps of algorithm. To this end, we have formulated three decision algorithms [20,21,24], namely, an exact algorithm, a heuristic algorithm, and a Boolean algorithm. The exact algorithm is employed to locate a single fault, while the heuristic algorithm is used to identify the multiple faults. The Boolean algorithm is a formal decision algorithm that can be implemented for both single and multiple faults.

The Exact Algorithm

Consider an analog system which is known to contain at most one faulty component. Assume that m test points are available; in other words, the Testee Group, Group 2, consists of m components. Suppose that the test outcomes obtained from a given step of the algorithm indicate that all Group 2 components are good as indicated in the following table, where 0 (1) indicates the component is good (faulty) according to the results of that test step:

"2"		"1" a b c . . . k
0	x	
0	y	
.	.	
.	.	
0	z	

In this case, we claim that the Group 2 components are, in fact, good. Indeed, if a good component were actually faulty, then our test outcomes are incorrect, which could only happen if one of the Group 1 components was faulty. Therefore, the system would have two faulty components, contradicting our assumption to the effect that at most one component is faulty.

Now consider the case where the test outcomes from a given step of the test algorithm indicates that exactly one Group 2 component, say x, is faulty:

"2"		"1" a b c . . . k
1	x	
0	y	
.	.	
.	.	
0	z	

In this case, the same argument used above will guarantee that the components which test good—say, y through z—are, in fact, good. On the other hand, we have no information about x. It may be faulty or, alternatively, the test outcome may be due to a faulty Group 1 component.

Finally, consider the case where two or more Group 2 components test bad in a given step indicated in the following table:

"2"		"1" a b c . . . k
1	x	
1	y	
.	.	
.	.	
0	z	

Since, under our assumption of a single fault, it is impossible for two or more Group 2 components to be faulty, this test result implies that at least one of the group 1 components is bad. Since we have assumed that there is at most one faulty component, this implies that all of the Group 2 components are, in fact, good.

Table 6-3 summarizes all possible test outcomes obtained from one step of the test algorithm and the conclusions.

Consistent with the above arguments, at each step of the test algorithm, either all, or all but one, of the components in Group 2 are found to be good. Therefore, if one repeats the process several times, eventually arriving at a component subdivision in which only known good components are included in the Group 1, then the test outcome obtained at that step will be reliable. Thus, an accurate determination of the faulty component(s) in Group 2 at that step will be obtained and the process will terminate.

Algorithm 1 describes that the software implementation of the exact algorithm for the single failure analysis.

Algorithm 1 [20].   (Exact Algorithm for a Single Failure).

Step 0.   In the preprocess, a component subdivision table must be generated, and a weight, the number of components in Group 2, is assigned to each subdivision.

Step 1.   Retrieve the component subdivision table and the weight for each subdivision.

Step 2.   Choose a subdivision with the maximum weight, and delete it from table.

Step 3.   If the maximum weight is less than or equal to 1, then go to Step 6. Otherwise, derive the test outcome and determine the good components.

Step 4.   Reduce the weight of each subdivision by the good components it currently contains.

Table 6–3   Test Results for Single Fault

Test Results	Conclusions
(1 2 3 4 . . m)	
0 0 0 0 . . 0	all components in group "2" are good
1 0 0 0 . . 0	all components in group "2" except (possibly) component #1 are good
1 1 0 0 . . 0	all components in group "2" are good
1 1 1 0 . . 0	: :
: : : . . . :	: :
1 1 1 1 . . 1	all components in group "2" are good

Step 5. Record the undetermined component number, then go to Step 2 to repeat the process.

Step 6. (Case of the maximum weight equal to 1). Choose the first subdivision that contains an undetermined component and check if the component is good. Repeat this step until all undetermined components have been chosen.

Step 7. The actual faulty component is then determined.

THE HEURISTIC ALGORITHM

The problem of multiple faults location can be greatly simplified if one adopts an "analog heuristic" to the effect that two independent analog failures will never cancel [28]. Needless to say, this is an inherently analog heuristic since two binary failures have a fifty-fifty chance of cancelling one another. In the analog case, however, two independent failures are highly unlikely to cancel each other (as long as one works with reasonably small tolerances).

Recall from our discussion of the single fault case that whenever a test result indicates that a component is good, then it is, in fact, good. Although this is not rigorously true in the multiple fault case, it is true under the assumption of our heuristic. For instance, consider the test outcomes indicated in the following table in which x is found to be good:

	"2"	"1" $a\ b\ c\ .\ .\ .\ k$
0	x	
1	y	
·	·	
·	·	
0	z	

Now, if x is actually faulty, there must be a faulty Group 1 component whose effect is to cancel the error in x as observed during this step of the test algorithm. This is, however, forbidden by our heuristic and, thus, we conclude that x is actually good.

Interestingly, our heuristic can be carried a step further than that indicated above since, under our heuristic, a bad Group 1 component would always yield erroneous test results. An exception would, however, occur if some of the Group 1 components are totally decoupled from some of the Group 2 components. Therefore, if prior to our test we generate a coupling table (by simulation, or a sensitivity analysis) which indicates whether or not a faulty Group 1 component will affect the test results on a Group 2 component, our heuristic may be used to verify that certain group 1 components are good whenever a good Group 2 component is located. Consider the following table:

	"1"
"2"	$a\ b\ c\ \ldots\ k$
0 x	1 0 1 . . . 1
1 y	1 1 0 . . . 0
. .	. . . .
. .	. . . .
0 z	0 1 1 . . . 0

in which a "1" in the i–j position indicates that the test result for component i is affected by component j, while a "0" indicates that the component j does not affect the test result for component i. Now, since component x has been found to be good in this test, our heuristic implies that those Group 1 components which are coupled to x in this test are also good. Similarly, since z is good, the heuristic implies that b and c are also good. Thus, with a single test step, we have verified that x, z, a, b, c, and k are all good.

Since in any practical circuit the coupling table is composed mostly of 1's, it has been our experience that relatively few steps of the algorithm will yield a complete diagnosis. To implement the heuristic, however, one must assume that the maximum number of faulty components is strictly less than the number of Group 2 components. If not, the test results at each step may show that all Group 2 components are faulty, in which case no reliable test information is obtained. Moreover, the degree to which the number of Group 2 components exceeds the maximum number of faulty components determines the number of algorithm steps which will be required to fully diagnose a circuit.

Algorithm 2 [20].

Step 0. Retrieve the component subdivision table and input t (t is the number of simultaneous failures)

Step 1. Choose a subdivision and call subroutine to derive the test results (indicating a 0 for a good component and a 1 for a bad component.)

Step 2. Retrieve the coupling table corresponding to this subdivision.

Step 3. If the ith test result is 0, then all components with 1 in the ith row of the coupling table are good.

Step 4. Repeat Step 3 until all 0 test results have been processed.

Step 5. Repeat Steps 1–4 until the actual faulty components are determined.

The Boolean Algorithm

A Boolean expression is derived from each step of the test algorithm which includes all possible fault patterns associated with the test data. The actual fault(s) can then be located by "multiplying" the Boolean expressions associated with several steps of the algorithm or equivalently comparing the fault patterns obtained from each test step and excluding the impossible fault patterns.

Consider the case where Group 1 contains five components, namely, a b, c, d, and e, and Group 2 contains three components, x, y, and z. Suppose that the test results is as follows:

	"1"
"2"	$a\ b\ c\ d\ e$
0 x	
1 y	
0 z	

All possible faulty patterns for this test result can be expressed by a Boolean form as:

$$T1 = a + b + c + d + e + \bar{a}\ \bar{b}\ \bar{c}\ \bar{d}\ \bar{e}\ x\ y\ \bar{z}$$

(Here, the letter a indicates the component is bad, and its complement $\bar{a}$ means the component a is good.) The first five terms of $T1$ represent the case where one of the Group 1 components is faulty and, thus, the remaining components are unknown, or "don't care;" whereas the last term of $T1$ indicates that all Group 1 components are good and the test results for the Group 2 components are as shown.

To implement this symbolic Boolean expression, a simple "arraylike" data structure (a tabulated expression) is presented [20] as follows (where Ø denotes the "don't care" term):

a	b	c	d	e	x	y	z
1	Ø	Ø	Ø	Ø	Ø	Ø	Ø
Ø	1	Ø	Ø	Ø	Ø	Ø	Ø
Ø	Ø	1	Ø	Ø	Ø	Ø	Ø
Ø	Ø	Ø	1	Ø	Ø	Ø	Ø
Ø	Ø	Ø	Ø	1	Ø	Ø	Ø
0	0	0	0	0	0	1	0

The following rules are used to compute the production of any two Boolean expressions:

Rule 1: Let the Boolean set B = {0,1, Ø}; then
$x * x = x$, $x * Ø = Ø * x = x$, where $x = 0, 1$, or Ø, and
$0 * 1 = 1 * 0 =$ null (impossible pattern).
Rule 2: $(A + B + C) * (A + B + D) = A + B + CD.$

This effectively excludes all possible fault patterns which are not consistent with the test data. The above algorithm is termed a regular Boolean algorithm.

Unfortunately, the following problem may be encountered: "How fast are the impossible fault patterns excluded so that the actual faulty component(s) can be determined?" To accelerate the speed of convergence, one may specify the maximum number of simultaneous failures. Once this number has been specified, the number of impossible patterns will be reduced. For example, if a single failure is assumed, recall from the first term of $T1$, a, that the component a is bad and the remaining components are "don't care." If, at most, one faulty component is allowed, however, the remaining components would not be bad. Therefore, component a is the only bad component in this pattern, and all "don't care" terms are replaced by 0.

Algorithm 3 [20]   (Regular Boolean Algorithm).

Step 1. Retrieve the component subdivisions table and input t (the maximum number of simultaneous failures)
Step 2. Choose a subdivision and call the routines to derive the test results and the associated tabulated expression.
Step 3. Search for patterns which contain more than t 1's, and delete the impossible patterns.
Step 4. If this subdivision is the first one, then GOTO Step 2, otherwise,
Step 5. Call the routine to compute the product of the associated tabulated expression and the previous one.
Step 6. Search for the impossible patterns and delete them.
Step 7. Repeat the above steps until the actual faulty components are determined.

Since the regular Boolean algorithm often requires a great number of steps to accelerate the speed of convergence, two additional algorithms are presented [20]: namely, the Boolean exact algorithm and the Boolean Heuristic algorithm. The former is used for the single fault case, whereas the latter is employed for the multiple faults.

PARALLEL PROCESSING FOR ANALOG FAULT DIAGNOSIS

The computer-aided testing (CAT) problem is inherently a large scale systems problem; it is essential to exploit whatever computational power is available to reduce the computational requirements for both on-line and off-line test processes. In particular, digital CAT algorithms often use some degree of parallel processing in their implementation. Therefore, the degree to which an analog CAT algorithm can be implemented in parallel becomes a significant factor in determining its viability.

Due to the iterative nature of the self-testing algorithm, it requires many simulation steps to validate the final decision in order to locate the faults. This deficiency can, however, be alleviated by implementing parallel processing in the self-testing algorithm. In fact, it is possible to simulate several pseudocircuits simultaneously and to implement the test algorithm in parallel.

Parallel Algorithm

Consider the circuit of Fig 6–1. As shown in Table 6–1, the table consists of all allowable subdivisions that are generated in accordance with the self-test theory.

The implementation of Algorithm 1 is described as follows. After the subdivision table is generated, a weight, the number of components in Group 2 having unknown status, is initially assigned to each subdivision. In our implementation, a weight of the number of components in Group 2 is initially assigned to each subdivision simply because all components have unknown status at the very beginning. As shown in column 6 of Table 6–4, a weight of 4 is assigned to subdivisions #1–#24, but a weight of 3 is assigned to subdivisions #25–#34 because the components #5 and #6 represent the two ports of a single component, transistor Q1.

Suppose that component #1 (C1) is faulty, and the single fault case is considered. Among the possible subdivisions, the subdivision #1 with a maximum weight of 4 is first selected and simulated.

Subdivision Number	Group 1 Component Numbers				Test Results			
1	1	2	3	9	1	0	0	0

According to the discussion in Table 6–4, the simulation shows that the components #2, #3, and #9 are good, but the status of component #1 is unknown. In other words, after completing this simulation, the status of components #1, #4, #5 (#6), #7, #8, #10, and #11 are still unknown. In the subsequent steps, the weight of each subdivision is reassigned according to the number of components having unknown status, and a maximum weight subdivision is selected and simulated in the next step. The detailed selection process is

Table 6-4   Allowable Subdivisions with the Assigned Weight

Subdivision Number	Group 1 Components				Weights (Algorithm 1)							(Algorithm 4)		
					0	1	2	3	4	5	6	0	1	2
1	1	2	3	9	4	0	0	0	0	0	0	4	0	0
2	1	2	3	11	4	2	1	1	0	0	0	4	1	0
3	1	2	7	9	4	2	1	1	1	1	1	4	1	0
4	1	2	7	11	4	3	1	1	1	1	1	4	2	0
5	1	2	8	9	4	2	2	0	0	0	0	4	2	1
6	1	2	8	11	4	3	2	1	1	1	1	4	2	1
7	1	3	4	9	4	2	1	1	1	1	1	4	1	0
8	1	3	4	11	4	3	1	1	1	1	1	4	2	0
9	1	4	7	9	4	3	1	1	1	1	1	4	2	0
10	1	4	7	11	4	4	0	0	0	0	0	4	3	0
11	1	4	8	9	4	3	2	1	1	1	1	4	2	1
12	1	4	8	11	4	4	2	1	1	1	1	4	2	1
13	2	3	9	10	4	1	1	1	1	1	0	4	1	0
14	2	3	10	11	4	2	1	1	1	1	1	4	2	0
15	2	7	9	10	4	2	1	1	1	1	1	4	2	0
16	2	7	10	11	4	3	1	1	1	1	1	4	3	0
17	2	8	9	10	4	2	2	1	1	1	1	4	2	1
18	2	8	10	11	4	3	2	1	1	1	1	4	3	1
19	3	4	9	10	4	2	1	1	1	1	1	4	2	0
20	3	4	10	11	4	3	1	1	1	1	1	4	3	0
21	4	7	9	10	4	3	1	1	1	1	1	4	3	0
22	4	7	10	11	4	4	1	1	1	1	1	4	4	0
23	4	8	9	10	4	3	2	1	1	1	1	4	3	1
24	4	8	10	11	4	4	2	1	1	1	1	4	4	1
25	2	3	5	6	3	1	1	1	1	0	0	4	2	2
26	2	5	6	7	3	2	1	1	1	1	1	4	3	2
27	2	5	6	8	3	2	2	1	1	1	1	4	3	3
28	2	5	6	9	3	1	1	1	1	1	1	4	2	2
29	2	5	6	11	3	2	1	1	1	1	1	4	3	2
30	3	4	5	6	3	2	1	1	1	1	1	4	3	2
31	4	5	6	7	3	3	1	1	1	1	1	4	4	2
32	4	5	6	8	3	3	2	1	1	1	1	4	4	3
33	4	5	6	9	3	2	1	3	1	1	1	4	3	2
34	4	5	6	11	3	3	1	1	1	1	1	4	4	2

listed in Table 6–5, and the following simulation steps are executed sequentially.

Subdivision Number	Group 1 Component Numbers				Test Results			
1	1	2	3	9	1	0	0	0
10	1	4	7	11	1	0	0	0
5	1	2	8	9	1	0	0	0
2	1	2	3	11	1	0	0	0
25	2	3	5	6	0	1	1	1
13	2	3	9	10	0	1	1	1

The faulty component is #1 (C1)

From the simulation results of the first four steps, we know that the components #2, #3, #4, #7, #8, #9, and #11 are definitely good, and component #1 is possibly faulty. The following two steps show that components #5 (#6) and #10 are also good. In other words, the simulation results illustrate that all components except #1 are good. Consequently, the component #1 is found to be faulty. Otherwise, it contradicts the test results shown in the first four steps.

Using Algorithm 1 for every possible single fault, the simulation results are summarized in Table 6–5.

In fact, the on-line computational time and cost of a test algorithm are proportional to the number of simulation steps required to locate the faulty component. It is unrealistic, however, for a test algorithm to require an average of 5.1 simulation steps to locate a single faulty component in an 11-component circuit. Before describing the modification of this sequential-type decision algorithm, the following definitions are first considered [29–33].

Table 6–5 Simulation Results

Simulated Faulty Component		Required Simulation Steps	Detected Faulty Component(s)
1	(C1)	6	C1
2	(R1)	5	R1
3	(R2)	6	R2
4	(RC)	4	RC
5,6	(Q1)	4	Q1
7	(RE)	5	RE
8	(CE)	5	RE, CE
9	(C2)	6	C2
10	(RL)	5	RL
11	(R3)	5	R3

A *subdivision space* is defined as a collection of all possible component subdivisions generated from a circuit or system based on the self-test algorithm. A *subdivision basis* is a minimum subset of the subdivision space that contains all components. In other words, every component must appear at least once in Group 2 of a subdivision in the subdivision basis. Moreover, in a subdivision basis, we are guaranteed that there exists at least one subdivision which contains all good components in the Tester Group of a subdivision for single fault case. As a result, this subdivision will provide a reliable test for locating the faulty component. The generation of a subdivision basis is illustrated in Algorithm 4.

Algorithm 4 [29] (Generation of Subdivision Basis).

    *   Let S_i, $i = 1, 2, \ldots, s$, be all component subdivisions,
            BASE be the number of subdivisions in the subdivision basis, and
            C be the set of all components, i.e., $C = \{C_1, C_2, \ldots, C_n\}$
  1. DO $i = 1$ TO s
      BEGIN
            Subdivision # i is selected;
            $C = C - \{C_i$ in subdivision # $i\}$;
            COUNT = 1;
  2.   WEIGHT = number of components in both the set C and a subdivision;
            Select a subdivision that has the maximum weight, say #*k;*
            $C = C - \{C_k$ in subdivision #*k*$\}$;
            COUNT = COUNT + 1;
            IF COUNT > BASE, THEN
            BEGIN
              IF $C = \emptyset$ THEN
              BEGIN
                BASE = COUNT;
                Record the selected subdivisions;
              END
              ELSE
                GO TO Step 2.
            END
      END

According to the stepwise illustration of the weight assignment for the circuit described in Table 6-5, a subdivision basis consisting of three seed subdivisions, is generated as follows:

Subdivision Number	Group 2 Component Numbers			
1	1	2	3	9
22	4	7	10	11
27	2	5	6	8

In practice, the number of seed subdivisions is approximately $[n/m]$, where n and m are the numbers of the circuit components and the selected test points, respectively. In fact, the ratio n/m represents a natural measure of the possible trade-offs between test points and computational requirements. The on-line test process time may be decreased if the number of test points is increased. However, since the number of possible test points is limited due to geometrical effects [9] and fault diagnosability [12], our emphasis is then turned to how to reduce the on-line computational requirements for a given set of test points.

Suppose component #1 (C1) is faulty; the simulation results associated with these seed subdivisions are

Subdivision Number	Group 2 Component Numbers				Test Results			
1	1	2	3	9	1	0	0	0
22	4	7	10	11	0	1	0	1
27	2	5	6	8	0	1	1	1

According to the discussion in Table 6-4, we can easily locate the faulty component #1 (C1) by using these three simulation steps.

In the single fault case, if the simulation results can identify that there is only one component having unknown status, the component is then identified as faulty. However, due to the nature of component coupling, a good component in the Group 2 may be misjudged as faulty due to a faulty component contained in the Group 1. (This component is referred to as the *equivalent faulty component*.) The equivalent faulty components are, indeed, often encountered in our implementation. Therefore, it is necessary to apply more simulation steps to distinguish the equivalent faulty components from the actual one.

Suppose component #4 (RC) is faulty; three seed subdivisions are simulated as follows:

Subdivision Number	Group 2 Component Numbers				Test Results			
1	1	2	3	9	0	0	1	0
22	4	7	10	11	1	0	0	0
27	2	5	6	8	0	1	1	1

The simulation results identify the components #1, #2, #5 (#6), #7, #8, #9, #10, and #11 as good, but the components #3 and #4 are unknown. If subdivision #7 is further selected and simulated,

Subdivision Number	Group 2 Component Numbers				Test Results			
7	1	3	4	9	0	0	1	0

the equivalent faulty component #3 is then distinguished from the actual faulty component #4.

On the other hand, however, due to the topological structure of a given circuit or system, the subdivision space may not always contain all possible combinations of components. In many cases, it may not have a subdivision that can distinguish the equivalent faulty component(s) from the actual one. Consequently, an *ambiguity set* that consists of both equivalent and actual faulty components, results.

Suppose component #8 (CE) is faulty and the simulation results associated with the seed subdivisions are

Subdivision Number	Group 2 Component Numbers				Test Results			
1	1	2	3	9	1	0	1	0
22	4	7	10	11	0	1	0	0
27	2	5	6	8	0	0	0	1

We conclude that the components #1, #2, #3, #4, #5 (#6), #9, #10, and #11 are good, but components #7 and #8 are unknown. Unfortunately, there exists no subdivision that can distinguish between them. Thus, an ambiguity set consisting of the components #7 and #8 results.

Based on the above discussion, a modification of Algorithm 1 is given in Algorithm 5 and the number of steps required for each possible single fault is listed in Table 6–6. The number of simulation steps required for the same circuit has been reduced from an average of 5.1 steps to 3.4 steps. However, the on-line computation required for 3.4 simulation steps are still high for this 11-components circuit. A further improvement on both on-line test process time and cost is still needed.

Algorithm 5 [29]   (Modified Exact Algorithm).

* Let the subdivision basis $B = \{B_1, B_2, . . , B_r\}$, $Z = \emptyset$.
1. DO $i = 1$ TO r (r: the number of subdivisions in the basis)
   BEGIN
   Simulate the test results with each B_i.

IF Z_i is the only element with "1" in B_i, THEN $Z = Z \cup \{Z_i\}$.
END

2. IF the number of components in the set Z is 1, THEN STOP
    ELSE (Eliminate the equivalent faulty components)
    BEGIN
        DO $i = 1$ TO s (s: the size of the subdivision space)
        BEGIN
            WEIGHT: = number of components in both Z and S_i.
        END
        COUNT = 0.
        REPEAT
            Select and simulate the maximum WEIGHTed subdivision.
            COUNT = COUNT + 1
            Eliminate the equivalent faulty components from the set Z
            Reduce the WEIGHT of each subdivision.
        UNTIL the maximum WEIGHT is 1.
    END

3. IF $|Z| \neq 1$, THEN Z is defined as the ambiguity set.

Parallel Processing

Unlike the original exact algorithm that determines the next selected subdivision in terms of the previous simulation results, in the modified exact algorithm the determination of the next subdivision is based on the simulation of the seed subdivisions which can be simulated independently. In other words, the seed subdivisions can be simulated by using different processors. Therefore, a parallel implementation is possible.

Let S be the subdivision space and B be the subdivision basis, the numbers s and r are respectively denoted as the cardinalities of S and B. Suppose that

Table 6-6 Simulation Results

Simulated Faulty Component	Required Simulation Steps	Detected Faulty Component(s)
1 (C1)	3	C1
2 (R1)	3	R1
3 (R2)	5	R2
4 (RC)	4	RC
5,6 (Q1)	4	Q1
7 (RE)	3	RE
8 (CE)	3	RE, CE
9 (C2)	3	C2
10 (RL)	3	RL
11 (R3)	3	R3

r processors are available, namely, P_1, P_2, . . . , P_r. A parallel algorithm, Algorithm 6, is presented.

Algorithm 6 [29]   (Parallel Algorithm).

   *   Load the necessary data to each processor.
   1.   Central processor sends the test data to each processor.
   2.   Perform the simulation at each processor and then transmit the test outcomes back to the central processor.
   3.   (Central processor makes decision for next iteration)
       IF the number of components with unknown status is 1, THEN STOP.
   4.   IF no subdivision contains two or more components with unknown status, THEN STOP. (These components form the ambiguity set) ELSE
   5. $i = 0$
       REPEAT
           $i = i + 1$
           select the maximum weighted subdivision, and send the index of this subdivision to the ith processor.
           UNTIL ($i = r$ OR no subdivision with two or more of unknown components)
   6.   GOTO Step 2.

Suppose component #1 is faulty, and three processors are used to simulate the test results. The simulation results associated with the seed subdivisions in the first step of the process are

Processor	Subdivision Number	Group 2 Component Numbers				Test Results			
P_1	1	1	2	3	9	1	0	0	0
P_2	22	4	7	10	11	0	1	0	1
P_3	27	2	5	6	8	0	1	1	1

The faulty component is #1 (C1).

Similar to Tables 6–6 and 6–7, the performance of the parallel algorithm for each possible single component failure is shown in Table 6–7. The average number of simulation steps for the same circuit has been reduced to 1.3.

With the increased availability of microprocessors, the concept of the distributed test systems have been proposed. In order to demonstrate the potential applicability of the proposed parallel test algorithm, a parallel test system architecture is illustrated in Fig. 6–7.

The central processor (Microprocessor, or minicomputer/microcomputer) acts the role of test data management and decision making. The UUT (unit

Table 6-7   Simulation Results

Simulated Faulty Component		Required Simulation Steps	Detected Faulty Component(s)
1	(C1)	1	C1
2	(R1)	1	R1
3	(R2)	2	R2
4	(RC)	2	RC
5,6	(Q1)	2	Q1
7	(RE)	1	RE
8	(CE)	1	RE, CE
9	(C2)	1	C2
10	(RL)	1	RL
11	(R3)	1	R3

under test) test program and the generated UUT data are initially loaded into the central processor, and then the central processor distributes the above UUT data to each satellite processor (or microcomputer). The simulation program resides in each satellite processor.

Since the proposed self-test algorithm requires only a single test vector measurement, the measured responses (at various test points) and the test inputs (applied to the system) are then stored in a database of the central processor. The fault location process is started.

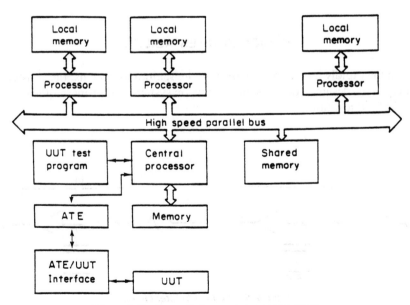

Figure 6-7   *A parallel processing test system.*

The central processor provides both the measured data and the index of the subdivision to be simulated to each satellite processor via a high speed parallel bus. The simulation results will be sent to the central processor for fault location after the satellite processors complete the simulations. If higher fault coverage is required, then the central processor will determine the next set of subdivisions to be simulated and send them to the appropriate satellite processors. The process will be repeated until the fault coverage is reached.

Although the proposed parallel test system has not yet been physically implemented on a parallel processor, a simulation program has been developed to demonstrate it via a multiple task facilities of the VMS operating system on a VAX 11/780.

To obtain an experimental estimate of the performance of the proposed parallel test algorithm for the single fault case, various linear and nonlinear circuits have been simulated.

Example 4.   Consider the cascade filter with 2, 4, 10, 20, or 40 stages [19], shown in Fig. 6–8. Suppose that four satellite processors are used, the simulation results are listed in Table 6–8. It shows that only one simulation step is required for each case.

Example 5. Consider the two nonlinear circuits shown in Fig. 6–5 and 6–9 [10,21]: a power supply (with seven components) and an astable multivibrator (with 11 components). The test results are shown in Table 6–9.

DESIGN FOR TESTABILITY

With the rapidly increasing complexity of circuits and systems, the ability to adequately design a diagnosable circuit or system is a prime requisite for rapid fault location.

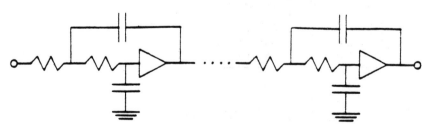

Figure 6–8   *A cascade filter circuit.*

Table 6–8 Simulation Results

Number of stages		2	4	4	4	10	10	20	20	40	40
Number of components		10	20	20	20	50	50	100	100	200	200
Number of test points		4	8	6	5	20	15	40	30	80	60
Number of inaccessive nodes		0	0	4	6	0	10	0	20	0	40
Fault coverage (%)		100	100	80	70	100	80	100	80	100	80
Size of the basis		4	4	4	4	4	4	4	4	4	4
Average of steps		1	1	1	1	1	1	1	1	1	1
	1	8	18	14	12	48	38	98	78	198	158
	2	2	2	2	2	2	2	2	2	2	2
Size of the	4			4							
ambiguity set	6				6						
	10						10				
	20								20		
	40										40

Given the fact that future electronic systems will rely heavily on CAD tools to reduce design costs, increase design accuracy, and reduce development times, it is clearly important that testability factors be integrated into these CAD tools. Testability as it now stands in the industry is a 'bottom-up'' process [30]. Virtually all the known techniques need a detailed circuit design before testability can be measured. However, design is a "top-down" process. The design engineer is given requirements for design, creates a design approach, analyzes it for performance, and finally involves a structural design that can be analyzed for testability. For testability to become an effective part of the CAD process the testability process will need to become more of

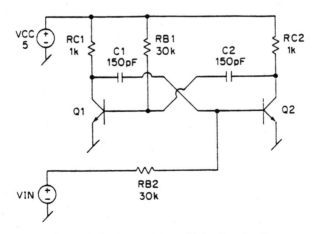

Figure 6–9 *An astable multivibrator circuit.*

Table 6–9   Simulation Results

Number of components	7	11
Number of test points	3	4
Number of inaccessive nodes	0	0
Fault coverage (%)	100	100
Size of the basis	3	4
Average of steps	1*	1**
Ambiguity set 1	4	10
2	3	1

*Three satellite processors are used.
**Four satellite processors are used.

a top-down approach instead of a bottom-up technique [31]. Therefore, if one can define a condition for the testability which depends only on the topological structure of the designed circuit, not on the component values, then design for testability can be established before analyzing the circuit performance.

Pseudocircuit Generation

In a linear circuit, at each step of the test algorithm, the required pseudo-circuit is formed via Eqs. (6-6), (6-12), and (6-13). The crucial assumption of this pseudocircuit approach is that $[L^2_{21}]^{-L}$ exists. This implies that the Group 1/Group 2 partition must be chosen so that $[L^2_{21}]^{-L}$ exists.

Consider the pseudo nominal tableau equations. In the linear case, they are simply a stacking of equations (6-6) and (6-8)–(6-10):

$$\begin{bmatrix} -I & 0 & Z^1 & 0 \\ L^{21}_{11} & -I & 0 & L^{22}_{11} \\ L^{11}_{11} & 0 & -I & L^{12}_{11} \\ L^1_{21} & 0 & 0 & L^2_{21} \end{bmatrix} \begin{bmatrix} b^1 \\ a^2 \\ a^1 \\ b^2 \end{bmatrix} = \begin{bmatrix} 0 \\ -L^2_{12}u \\ L^1_{12}u \\ y - L_{22}u \end{bmatrix} \tag{6-32}$$

where

$$T = \begin{bmatrix} -I & 0 & Z^1 & 0 \\ L^{21}_{11} & -I & 0 & L^{22}_{11} \\ L^{11}_{11} & 0 & -I & L^{12}_{11} \\ L^1_{21} & 0 & 0 & L^2_{21} \end{bmatrix}$$

is known as the tableau matrix [22].

Theorem 1 [32]. The tableau matrix T is left invertible if and only if the matrix

$$Q = \begin{bmatrix} -I + L_{11}^{11}Z^1 & L_{11}^{12} \\ L_{21}^1 Z^1 & L_{21}^2 \end{bmatrix}$$

is left invertible.

Note that if L_{21}^2 is left invertible, consider the matrix

$$Q^* = (-I + L_{11}^{11}Z^1) - L_{11}^{12}(L_{21}^2)^{-L}L_{21}^1 Z^1$$

$$= -I + [L_{11}^{11} - L_{11}^{12}(L_{21}^2)^{-L}L_{21}^1] z^1$$

$$= -I + K_{11}Z^1 \quad [\text{by eq.}(6-14)]$$

Since the matrix K_{11} is a connection structure, the matrix $(I - K_{11}Z^1)$ is invertible [22], and Q^* is left invertible. Therefore, the left invertibility of L_{21}^2 is a sufficient but not necessary condition [32].

Remark 1. The tableau matrix T is generically left invertible if and only if the matrix Q' is left invertible, where

$$Q' = \begin{bmatrix} -I + L_{11}^{11} & L_{11}^{12} \\ L_{21}^1 & L_{21}^2 \end{bmatrix} \tag{6-33}$$

Remark 2. In the linear case, the pseudocircuit exists with respect to a subdivision if and only if Q' is left invertible.

The salient feature of this condition is that Q' is a constant matrix and depends only upon the connection matrices $L_{11}^{11}, L_{11}^{12}, L_{21}^1$, and L_{21}^2, but not upon the component equations. Obviously, this condition depends only upon the connection structure of a given circuit. Moreover, for this reason the development for linear circuits can be immediately extended to nonlinear circuits.

Similarly, the tableau matrix T' for nonlinear circuits is given as follows:

$$T' = \begin{bmatrix} -I & 0 & [\frac{\partial g^1}{\partial x^1}]P + \frac{\partial g^1}{\partial a^1} & 0 \\ L_{11}^{21} & -I & 0 & L_{11}^{22} \\ L_{11}^{11} & 0 & -I & L_{11}^{12} \\ L_{21}^1 & 0 & 0 & L_{21}^2 \end{bmatrix}$$

where

$$P = \left\{ d_0 I - \frac{\partial f^1}{\partial x^1} \right\}^{-1} \left[\frac{\partial f^1}{\partial a^1} \right]$$

Remark 3.   The tableau matrix T' is generically left invertible, if and only if the matrix Q' is left invertible.

Remark 4.   In the nonlinear case, the pseudocircuit exists with respect to a subdivision if and only if Q' is left invertible.

The above development is summarized in the following theorem,

Theorem 2 (The Necessary and Sufficient Condition). The pseudocircuit exists with respect to a particular allowable subdivision if and only if the matrix T or T' is left invertible. The matrix T or T' is generically left invertible if and only if the matrix Q' is left invertible.

Design of a Testable Circuit

We start with a definition of diagnosability.

Definition 1 [25].   A system is t-diagnosable if, given the results of all allowable tests, one can uniquely identify all faulty units provided that the number of faulty units does not exceed t.

Lemma 1.   A system is t-diagnosable under the exact algorithm if and only if every $2t$-tuple of components appears in at least one Group 2.

Definition 2 [13].   Let B be an $m \times n$ matrix, $n \geq m$. The global column-rank of B is said to be t if every combination of t columns of B is linearly independent, and some combination of $(t + 1)$ columns of B is linearly dependent.

Defintion 3.   Given a set of m test points and the connection matrix

$$L = \begin{bmatrix} L_{11} \\ L_{21} \end{bmatrix}$$

a corresponding matrix of a given combination of t components is defined as a matrix Q', (33), whose Group 2 contains these t components.

Defintion 4.   The Q'-rank of L is said to be t, $t \leq m$, if, for every combination of t components, there exists at least one corresponding matrix Q' with full column rank, and for some combination of $(t + 1)$ components, there is no corresponding matrix with full column rank.

Theorem 3 [32]. A designed circuit is t-diagnosable if and only if the Q'-rank of the connection matrix L is at least $t + 1$.

Theorem 3 provides a criterion to determine the dignosability of a circuit under design. However, in addition to the diagnosability of the designed circuit, the problems that arise are (1) how many test points are required and (2) how to select the test points.

To determine the number of test points required, the following aspects may be considered: First, a geometric "rule of thumb" was proposed [9,18], in which the circuit complexity is proportional to the area of a printed circuit board (if not a power thereof), while the number of accessible test points is proportional to the edge length of the board; therefore, the number of test points should grow with the square root of the circuit complexity (or less).

Secondly, as discussed in the previous section, the number of components which may be tested at any step depends on the number of test points available, while the number of steps required (approximately n/m) is determined by the number of testee components. Since the on-line computational requirement is proportional to the number of simulation steps, more test points may reduce the number of steps and thus decrease the computational requirements.

Finally, for a t-diagnosable circuit design, by Theorem 3, the number of test points, m, must be greater than, or equal to, $t + 1$.

From the above considerations, the first and third define upper and lower bounds on the number of test points required, while the second provides the trade-offs between the number of test points and the on-line computational requirements.

In order to precisely identify faulty components, the remaining task is to select the test points for a diagnosable circuit design. In our application, two steps are employed to automatically generate the test points: selection and compaction [32].

Rule 1: If components are connected in parallel and they are all in either tree edges or cotree edges, then the test points at some component outputs are selected such that the corresponding columns of L are not identical. Here

$$ L = \begin{bmatrix} L_{11} \\ L_{21} \end{bmatrix} $$

Rule 2: Test points are selected so that the number of nonzero entries of each column of L is not less than $t + 1$ for a t-diagnosable circuit design.

If the test points are selected by following the Selection Rules 1 and 2, then they are called the *dominant test points.*

Rule 3: If the number of distinct dominate test points is less than m, then the remaining test points can be selected arbitrarily.

Finally, the compaction step is considered after the selection step has been performed. Of course, if the number of distinct dominant test points is not greater than m, the desired number of test points, then it is not necessary to perform the compaction step; otherwise, the test points are compacted such that the number of test points is reduced to m. To compact the selected test points, one may select an appropriate test point whose coefficients cover that of the dominant test points and hopefully cover as many of the test points selected by Selection Rule 2 as possible. Of course, during the compaction procedure, the Selection Rules 1 and 2 are checked recursively.

Evidently, the previous development for single-port components can be extended to the case of multiple-port components. Let

$$
L = \begin{bmatrix} L_{11} \\ L_{21} \end{bmatrix} = \begin{bmatrix} M_{11} & M_{12} & \cdot & \cdot & \cdot & M_{1r} \\ M_{21} & M_{22} & \cdot & \cdot & \cdot & M_{2r} \\ \cdot & \cdot & \cdot & \cdot & \cdot & \cdot \\ M_{s1} & M_{s2} & \cdot & \cdot & \cdot & M_{sr} \end{bmatrix}
$$

where the block matrices M_{ij}'s contain the columns and rows of the corresponding components. Let w_i be the number of columns in the submatrix $M_{1i}, i = 1,2, \ldots, r$; then $\sum_{i=1}^{r} w_i = n$, where $w_i = r$ for the r-port components.

The definition of Q'-rank may be generalized to the block matrix M_{ij} for the multiple-port case. Under the definition of the generalized Q'-rank, it is easy to verify that Theorem 3 is still valid for the multiple-port components. For a t-diagnosable circuit design, the number of test points required is defined as the summation of $w_i, i = 1,2, \ldots, t + 1$, which are the $(t + 1)$'s highest number of the component ports in the circuit. Obviously, in the case of single-port components ($w_i = 1$), the summation is equal to $t + 1$.

REFERENCES

[1] R. Saeks, and S. R. Liberty, *Rational Fault Analysis,* Marcel Dekker, New York, 1977.

[2] P. Duhamal, and J. C. Rault, "Automatic Test Generation Techniques for Analog Circuits and Systems: A Review," *IEEE Trans. Circuits Syst.,* Vol. CAS-26, pp. 411–440, July 1979.

[3] W. A. Plice, "Automatic Generation of Fault Isolation Test for Analog Circuit Boards: A Survey," presented at ATE EAST '78, Boston, Sep. 1978, pp. 26–28.

[4] J. W. Bandler, and A. E. Salama, "Fault Diagnosis of Analog Circuits," *IEEE Proc.,* pp. 1279–1325, Aug. 1985.

[5] R.-W. Liu, *Analog Fault Diagnosis,* IEEE Press, New York, 1987.

[6] R.-W. Liu, and R. Saeks (Eds.), Report on the ONR Workshop on Analog Fault Diagnosis, University of Notre Dame, Notre Dame IN, May 1981.

[7] W. A. Plice, "A Survey of Analog Fault Diagnosis," presented at the workshop on Analog Fault Diagnosis, University of Notre Dame, Notre Dame, IN, May 1981.

[8] R. Saeks, "A Self-Testing Algorithm for Analog Fault Diagnosis," presented at the workshop on Analog Fault Diagnosis, University of Notre Dame, Notre Dame, IN, May 1981.

[9] R. Saeks, "Criteria for Analog Fault Diagnosis," in *Nonlinear Fault Analysis,* Technical Report, Texas Tech University, Lubbock, pp. 19–28.

[10] R. Saeks, S. P. Singh, and R.-W. Liu, "Fault Isolation via Component Simulation," *IEEE Trans. Circuit Theory,* Vol. CT-19, pp. 634–640, Nov. 1972.

[11] N. Sen, and R. Saeks, "A Measure of Testability and Its Application to Test Point Selection—theory," *Proc. 20th Midwest Symp. on Circuits and Systems,* Lubbock, TX, Aug. 1977.

[12] Z. F. Huang, C.-S. Lin, and R.-W. Liu, "Node-Fault Diagnosis and a Design of Testability," *IEEE Trans. Circuits Syst.,* Vol. CAS-30, pp. 257–265, May 1983.

[13] C. S. Lin, Z. F., Huang, and R.-W. Liu, "Fault Diagnosis of Linear Analog Networks: A Theory and Its Application," *Proc. IEEE Int. Symp. Circuits Syst.,* pp. 1090–1093, May 1983.

[14] R. M. Biernacki, and J. W. Bandler, "Multiple-Fault Location of Analog Circuits," *IEEE Trans. Circuits Syst.,* Vol. CAS-28, pp. 361–366, May 1981.

[15] T. N. Trick, W. Mayeda, and A. A. Sakla, "Calculation of Parameter Value for Fault Detection in Analog Circuits," *1980 IEEE Int. Symp. on Circuits and Syst., IEEE,* New York, pp. 1057–1077.

[16] L. Rapisarda, and R. DeCarlo, "Analog Multifrequency Fault Diagnosis," *IEEE Trans. Circuits Syst.,* Vol. CAS-30, No. 4, pp. 223–234, Apr. 1983.

[17] E. Flecha, and R. DeCarlo, "The Nonlinear Analog Fault Diagnosis Scheme of Wu, Nakajima, Wey, and Saeks in the Tableau Context," *IEEE Trans. Circuits Syst.,* Vol. CAS-31, pp. 828–830, Sept. 1984.

[18] R. Saeks, and R.-W. Liu, "Fault Diagnosis in Electronic Circuits," in *Nonlinear Fault Analysis,* Texas Tech University, Lubbock, pp. 3–7.

[19] C.-C. Wu, K. Nakajima, C.-L. Wey, and R. Saeks, "Analog Fault Analysis with Failure Bounds," *IEEE Trans. Circuits Syst.,* Vol. CAS 29, No. 5, pp. 277–284, May 1982.

[20] C.-L. Wey, and R. Saeks, "On the Implementation of an Analog ATPG: The Linear Case," *IEEE Trans. Instrumentation Measurement,* Vol. IM-34, pp. 277–284, 1985.

[21] C.-L. Wey, and R. Saeks, "On the Implementation of an Analog ATPG: The Nonlinear Case," *IEEE Trans. Instrumentation Measurement,* Vol. IM-37, No. 2, pp. 252–258, Jun. 1988.

[22] R. A. DeCarlo, and R. Saeks, *Interconnection Dynamical Systems*, Marcel Dekker, New York, 1981.

[23] L. W. Nagel, *SPICE2: A Computer Program to Simulate Semiconductor Circuit*, University of California, Berkeley, 1976.

[24] C. L. Wey, *AATPG: Analog Automatic Test Program Generation. User Manual*, Technical Report, Texas Tech University, Lubbock, 1983.

[25] F. P. Preparata, G. Metze, and R. T. Chien, "On the Connection Assignment Problem of Diagnosable Systems," *IEEE Trans. Electronic Comput.*, Vol. EC-16, pp. 448–454, 1967.

[26] T. Amin, unpublished notes, Bell Laboratories, 1980.

[27] L. S. Hakimi, "Fault Analysis in Digital Systems—A Graph Theoretic Approach," in *Rational Fault Analysis*, R. Saeks and S. R. Liberty, Eds., Marcel Dekker, New York, 1977, pp. 1–12.

[28] R.-W. Liu, unpublished notes, University of Notre Dame, Notre Dame, IN, 1980.

[29] C. L. Wey, "Parallel Processing for Analog Fault Diagnosis," International Journal of Circuit Theory and Applications. Vol. 16, No. 3. pp. 303–316, July 1988, Wiley, NY.

[30] M. A. Breurer (Ed.), *Digital System Design Automation: Languages, Simulation & Database*, Computer Sciences Press, Potomac, MD, 1975.

[31] T. L. Fennell, and T. A. Nicolino, "Computer Aided Testability," *Proc. IEEE Annual Reliability and Maintainability Symp.*, pp. 6–10, 1984.

[32] C. L. Wey "Design of Testability for Analog Fault Diagnosis," *Int. J. Circuit Theory Appl.*, Vol. 15, No. 2, pp. 123–142, Apr. 1987, Wiley, NY.

[33] C. L. Wey, "A Decision Process for Analog System Fault Diagnosis," *IEEE Trans. Circuits Syst.*, Vol. CAS-34, No. 1, pp. 107–109, Jan. 19

7

An Artificial Intelligence Approach to Analog Systems Diagnosis

FRANK PIPITONE,
KENNETH DEJONG,
and
WILLIAM SPEARS

This paper describes some general diagnostic reasoning techniques which exploit recent advances in the field of artificial intelligence. They are applicable to a variety of human-engineered systems, including hydraulic, mechanical, and optical ones, but the primary focus has been on electronic systems. These techniques were developed over a period of several years of research in this area at the Naval Research Laboratory. One of the products of this research is a fully implemented diagnostic reasoning system called FIS which embodies these techniques and is in use at a variety of government and industrial laboratories.

The FIS system itself is described in considerable detail in other publications [1,2]. The intent of this chapter is to present the methods in a way that they can be adapted and used by others.

The Need For Artificial Intelligence-Based Diagnostic Systems

The maintenance of electronic equipment has drawn increasing attention during the past decade as a potential artificial intelligence application, particularly in the military. This has been motivated by the increasing complexity of military electronic systems and the resulting high maintenance costs as well as the scarcity of highly trained technicians.

The Navy has been particularly interested in and supportive of the development of fault isolation expert systems which can improve the quality of their maintenance and trouble-shooting activities. As an example, Navy technicians on aircraft carriers may be responsible for troubleshooting several hundred different (sub)systems for which they have had varying amounts of training (frequently little or none). To compensate, the Navy has invested and continues to invest heavily in automatic test equipment (ATE) to aid or replace these technicians. The quality of the "test programs" which drive these ATE stations varies dramatically in spite of a uniformly high cost to acquire them.

For the past few years, we have had the opportunity to explore the use of AI and expert system technology in this setting. We feel that we have now evolved a set of methods which directly addresses the issues discussed above and have shown the effectiveness of these methods by implementing a diagnostic system (FIS) which embodies these techniques.

A Statement of the Diagnosis Problem

Since there are many different kinds of diagnosis problems, it is important to understand more precisely the diagnostic reasoning problem addressed in this chapter. We will do so by describing what questions are to be answered by the diagnostic reasoning system, and what kinds of knowledge about the unit under test (UUT) are assumed to be available to support the diagnostic process.

The questions to be answered by the diagnostic system are intuitively quite simple. We want the system to be able to recommend at any point the next *best* test to make on the UUT from a set of predefined available tests, and we want it to estimate the probability that a given replaceable component (or Boolean combination of components) is faulty, given some test results. These are usually done cyclically, as shown in Fig. 7–1.

Deciding what kind of knowledge about a UUT must be available and how it should be represented in machine-readable form for effective diagnosis is a more difficult problem. In the field of artificial intelligence this is known in general terms as *the knowledge representation problem.* Closely related to this is *the knowledge acquisition problem:* Having chosen a representation, how easy/difficult is it to get the required knowledge about a particular problem into this format? In many artificial intelligence applications, knowledge acquisition is a crucial consideration because it can involve a high cost in terms of time and money. This is also true of fault diagnosis. In order to create a computer program which can troubleshoot a piece of equipment with useful accuracy and efficiency, one must invest a considerable amount of effort in knowledge acquisition. Therefore, we wish to represent the UUT with the minimal amount of knowledge that still allows effective diagnostic reasoning.

Let us briefly consider some different approaches to diagnosis in light of the relative ease or difficulty of the knowledge acquisition required to sup-

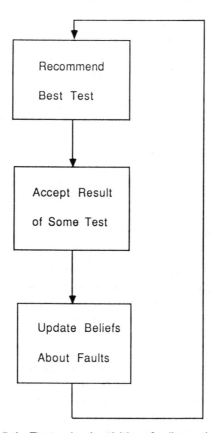

Figure 7-1   *The top level activities of a diagnosis system.*

port them. First, consider the approach of directly writing a test decision tree. This corresponds to the conventional practice of writing programs to control ATE gear in which the burden of diagnostic reasoning lies primarily on the human. What he enters into the computer is essentially a decision tree which is to control the ATE autonomously or with minimal human interaction. Although converting such a decision tree into computer code is usually not very labor-intensive, considerable time and effort is usually involved in producing the decision tree itself, because the human needs to think through a large number of diagnostic situations. This decision tree approach therefore has high knowledge acquisition cost. It also has the disadvantages of limited fault coverage, inflexibility, lack of explanation capability, and susceptibility to human error and suboptimal decisions.

At another extreme is the approach of entering into the computer a detailed circuit-level model of the UUT sufficient to simulate its behavior. This approach holds out the possibility of low knowledge acquisition cost since

CAD/CAM data could be used to provide the information in computer readable form, and only the important aspects of behavior (performance specifications) would need to be largely human specified. The difficulty with this approach lies in our inability to use such a low level description of a UUT efficiently for diagnosis. Even simple circuit-level simulations can take hours of computer time, although this may improve in the future with advances in computing hardware and simulation methods.

As a consequence, a primary focus of our research has been to develop a knowledge representation scheme which is both easy to acquire and useful (in a practical sense) for developing efficient diagnostic systems. We have achieved that goal by exploiting from the artificial intelligence community emerging ideas about knowledge representation.

Related Work in AI

Some notable recent work has been directed at some of the same problems we address here. For example, DeKleer and Williams [3] give a clear analysis of the problems of computing fault hypothesis probabilities, test result probabilities, and the use of entropy for test recommendation. However, this approach requires a strong UUT model; one must be able to predict module output values from module input values. It is often impractical to provide such a model for analog systems, although digital systems lend themselves well to this approach. Also, computational efficiency is not addressed. For the results to be used widely in applications, one needs fast probability and entropy algorithms and module simulations. Genesereth [4] and Davis [5] have done considerable work in the area of diagnosis based on structural and functional UUT descriptions, but focus on digital systems. Other recent work [6], based on Bayesian belief networks [7] provides a powerful mathematical approach to treating the joint statistics of component faults and signal abnormalities.

Summary of Our Approach

When looking at AI technology, it is tempting to leap to the conclusion that one could significantly improve this sort of troubleshooting activity with reasonably straightforward applications of current expert system technology. However, there are several aspects to the problem which raise significant technical issues. First, with several hundred different systems to maintain, it seems infeasible to think in terms of independently developed expert systems for each one. Rather one thinks in terms of a more general fault isolation shell providing a common knowledge acquisition/representation scheme for use with all subsystems. However, even with this level of generality, there are still several hundred knowledge bases to be built, debugged, and maintained in a context in which there can be considerable overlap and/or similarity in the content of many of the knowledge bases. These observations strongly suggest the development of a sophisticated knowledge acquisition system which can be used to facilitate the construction of a new knowledge base for a specific system in a variety of ways including reusing and/or adapting existing knowledge modules.

Compounding the problem of applying current expert system technology is the fact that, for many of the subsystems being maintained, there is little human expertise in the traditional sense of finding someone who is good at fixing a particular subsystem and capturing his/her knowledge in a set of associative rules. This is particularly true for newly developed systems for which empirical experience is absent. Rather, technicians depend heavily on the structural and functional descriptions contained in the technical manuals of the many subsystems they attempt to maintain. This suggests that simple rule-based architectures are not likely to be sufficient for the task at hand, and that a model-based approach may be appropriate.

At the same time, it is clear (as discussed earlier) that detailed quantitative models are in general too inefficient for effective diagnosis. As a consequence, we have adopted an intermediate approach of providing to the diagnostic system a simplified model of the qualitative behavior of the replaceable modules and the structure (connectivity) of the UUT which is both easy to acquire and can be efficiently used for diagnosis. We refer to these models as *qualitative causal models.*

By using this form of knowledge representation, we have been able to develop an effective diagnostic system with the following notable features:

a. The ability to do accurate diagnosis using a qualitative behavior model of a complex analog/digital UUT without simulation
b. The possibility of efficient UUT knowledge acquisition
c. An efficient probabilistic reasoning method specialized for device troubleshooting based on Bayesian principles
d. A natural treatment of multiple faults
e. An efficient method for computing the entropy of a complex system for use in best test selection.

The core set of techniques which provide these features is described in more detail in the following sections. The techniques range from very general ones, such as the algorithms for computing the probability and the entropy of an arbitrary Boolean expression, to highly domain-specific ones, such as the heuristic methods for certifying modules after passed tests.

QUALITATIVE CAUSAL MODELS

As previously mentioned, a central element of our approach to diagnosis is the capturing of the important aspects of the behavior of a UUT for diagnostic purposes in a qualitative causal model. A qualitative causal model of a UUT consists of: (1) a causal description of the set of replaceable modules (determined by the level to which fault isolation is to occur), (2) a description of the connectivity (structure) of the replaceable modules, and (3) a set of possible tests from which diagnostic sequences can be constructed. In addition, the model can contain (if available) estimates of *a priori* failure rates as well as the costs of making tests and replacing modules.

The diagnostic power comes from the requirement that the description of each replaceable module must include a set of *local causal rules* describing its behavior. The diagnostic system then uses both the structural (connectivity) information as well as the sets of local causal rules to determine the set of possible global causes (ambiguity set) of any failed test. This information is used in conjunction with *a priori* fault probabilities (which are assumed to be uniform if not readily available) by an efficient Bayesian algorithm to estimate posterior probabilities of module faults and test outcomes. These are used along with test cost data and module replacement costs (both of which are assumed to be uniform if unavailable) to make next best test or replacement recommendations. Two strategies are described for computing the next best test; one based on specialized heuristics and one based on information theoretic entropy. The latter uses an efficient new algorithm for computing the Shannon entropy of a complex system. An important advantage of our approach to diagnosis is that no single-fault assumptions need to be made.

Local Causal Rules

The heart of the UUT description is a network of local qualitative causal rules relating measurable (at least in principle) parameters among various terminals of each module. These are intended to describe the behavior of each module in its context. Thus where loading and other effects of Kirchoff's laws affect behavior, these are assumed taken into account. We are not restricted to unidirectional modules with fixed I/O voltage behavior. There are two types of rules, *through rules* containing information about the correct behavior of UUT modules and *module rules* containing information about fault modes of modules, as discussed below. The forms of the two types are as follows:

Through Rule.   Given *precondition, parameter1 abnormality1* at *terminal1* can cause *parameter2 abnormality2* at *terminal2*.

Module Rule.   Faulty *modulename* can cause *parameter abnormality* at *terminal*.

Here a precondition is a predicate on the state of the UUT inputs (or input history). Preconditions are optional and are used primarily to model devices such as multiplexers and devices with enable inputs in which a causal path is present or absent, depending on some signal conditions. Although we have experimented with elaborate precondition schemes involving estimating probabilities of control signal values, we have found it quite adequate to simply include in the description of each test the states of all the preconditions. Then they can be looked up for the current test. An *abnormality* is a qualitative value such as *high* or *low*. For example, a through rule is: *"Given that power-supply-3 is in the "on" state, DC voltage high at t3 can cause frequency low at t4."* This might describe the way a voltage-controlled oscillator propagates a voltage error, given that its power supply voltage is in spec. In the case of a module with two inputs both affecting the same output parameter, such as a summing junction, a problem can arise. Suppose two of the rules are *"input1 DC high can cause output DC high"* and *"input2 DC high can cause output DC high."* Then if *"output DC high"* is suspected, both inputs are to be suspected high. However, one might be very high and the other slightly low, and the latter would be missed. However, if such a case occurs, the system will find a fault leading to the high input, and the ensuing repair may even cure the slightly low input. Otherwise, a second diagnostic pass can search for it. Each causal rule is associated with the module immediately connected to the terminals appearing in the rule.

Through rules represent the correct behavior of a module in context in the form of qualitative relationships among quantities at its terminals. *Module rules* represent limited knowledge about how a given module can fail. Note that even if we had no such fault model knowledge available, we could allow the system to include all conceivable module rules by default and still have a viable diagnosis system. That is, we could assume that any abnormality at a terminal could have been caused by the failure of any directly connected module. This would lead to somewhat larger ambiguity sets (suspect sets) than with a more minimal set of module rules, but most of the diagnostic power of this kind of model comes from through rules, since it is largely by chaining them that we determine what portion of the UUT affects a given measurement. When in doubt about the inclusion of any rule, we must include it, or else we risk missing some faults.

The Need for Predefined Tests

It is necessary to predefine a set of tests for a diagnostic system because no matter how complete a model it uses of the structure and input/output behavior of a UUT, it cannot know the intended use of the UUT. For example, in a radar receiver, a diagnostic system must know for what frequencies it must operate correctly, and what tested parameters must be correct to within what tolerance.

Our notion of a test is a specified *terminal* to be used as a test point, an electrical (or other) *parameter* to be measured there, and a set of *abnormali-*

ties such as {bad} or {hi, lo} with associated numerical ranges. A range for "ok" is also required. Note that the triple (*terminal parameter abnormality*) is of the same form as the right-hand side (effect) of a causal rule. In fact each such triple occurring in a test must occur in the right-hand side of at least one rule. Also, the states of all rule preconditions, if any, must be given for each test, as discussed in the previous subsection. Finally, each test should have a prescribed *stimulus setup* state. This is simply a unique symbol for each distinct state of the input stimuli of the UUT used in the tests. It is useful in determining the relevance of a passed test to a suspect module (see Passed Tests and Certification Strategies in the next section).

Ambiguity Sets

Central to our approach is the notion of an *ambiguity set.* One ambiguity set is associated with each abnormal result of each defined test, and is defined to be the set of all modules which can fail so as to cause that failed test result. If one can obtain such sets, then one can determine what combinations of good and bad modules are possible after more than one test has failed. In Boolean terms, each ambiguity set is a disjunction of propositions that the included modules are faulty, and two or more ambiguity sets represent a conjunction of such disjunctions. For example, the ambiguity sets {1,2} and {1,4} represent the fact that at least one of modules 1 and 2 is faulty and at least one of the modules 1 and 4 is faulty. In Boolean terms, $(x_1 \vee x_2)$ & $(x_1 \vee x_4) = 1$, where x_i is the proposition that module i is faulty. Note that ambiguity sets alone do not allow the representation of an arbitrary Boolean function. For example, they cannot represent the exclusive or of two modules; but we believe that our forms cover the majority of cases occurring in diagnostic applications, and the separability of the ambiguity sets is convenient for *undoing* a test already made.

In diagnostic applications, we will find it useful to precompute the ambiguity set for each failed outcome of each test. Also, for each module occurring in an ambiguity set it is useful to precompute *immediate effects*. These are simply the signal abnormalities at terminals of the module which both lead causally to the failed test result and which occur as the right-hand side of a rule whose left-hand side is the module. *Immediate effects* are useful as a simple approximation of failure modes (see Passed Tests and Certification Strategies in the next section).

The general probabilistic techniques of the next two sections can be applied no matter how the ambiguity sets are obtained, but if the causal model of the previous subsections are used, then they can be found by following the network of local causal rules upstream from each failed test result until all modules causally upstream are found. If ambiguity sets are directly produced by humans, they constitute global symptom/cause association rules.

Figure 7–2 illustrates the diagnostic power of our simple causal rule

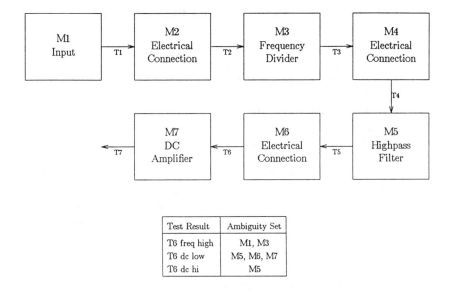

Test Result	Ambiguity Set
T6 freq high	M1, M3
T6 dc low	M5, M6, M7
T6 dc hi	M5

Rules Fired in Propagation of above Test Results

Cause	Effect	Comments
T5 freq high	T6 freq high	
T4 freq high	T5 freq high	
T3 freq high	T4 freq high	
T2 freq high	T3 freq high	
M3	T3 freq high	M3 not dividing
T1 freq high	T2 freq high	
M1	T1 freq high	M1 has high frequency
T5 dc low	T6 dc low	
M6	T6 dc low	M6 open, M7 pulls low
M7	T6 dc low	M7 input grounded
M5	T6 dc low	M5 output has offset
M5	T6 dc high	M5 output has offset
T5 dc high	T6 dc high	

Figure 7–2 *Simple examples of the propagation of a test result.*

model. Three failed tests at the same test point are shown, all with different
ambiguity sets. The ambiguity sets can be verified by visually chaining from
effect to cause through the given list of causal rules, starting at a test result
and ending at set suspect modules. Earlier model based diagnostic systems
[8,9] are not as specific because they represent only the topology of the UUT.
Such systems suspect all upstream modules from any failed test.

THE TREATMENT OF FAULT PROBABILITIES

This section describes an analysis of the joint statistics of UUT faults. A UUT is regarded as having 2^n fault states, since the proposition x_i that module i of the n modules is faulty can be true or false. The probability of an arbitrary fault hypothesis, represented as a Boolean function of the x_i, is developed in stages. First we consider a UUT selected from the entire population of a given UUT type, then a UUT from the population actually undergoing diagnosis, and finally a UUT for which various combinations of passed and failed tests have been made.

In problem domains for which models relating structure and behavior are incomplete and uncertain, such as medical diagnosis, it is often impossible to do probabilistic reasoning in a precise manner, since the relevant joint statistics are unavailable. Therefore, approximate methods have been found useful such as those in MYCIN [10] and PROSPECTOR [11] and the Dempster–Shafer [12] formalism. However, in the domain of diagnosis of human-engineered systems constructed from discrete modules, it is possible to use more precise probabilistic methods exploiting the known causal and statistical relationships of this domain. For example, the information gleaned from a failed test can often be described as an ambiguity set, a set within which at least one faulty module must lie. Also it is often an acceptable approximation to assume that the replaceable modules fail independently of one another with their own *a priori* probabilities.

A Priori Probability Model

We make the assumption that over the entire population of a UUT type the individual module fault propositions x_i are statistically independent of each other with *a priori* probabilities a_i, so that $a_i a_j$ is the *a priori* probability of $x_i \& x_j$, for example. We are thus ignoring the case of one component failing first and stressing a second component so that it fails also. This will cause some error in probability calculations, which will affect primarily the selection of tests, and therefore the cost (time, money, etc.) of diagnosis rather than its accuracy. Barring this coupling, we can view double faults as independent events the second of which occurred by chance in the time between the occurrence of the first and the time of testing.

A diagnostic system does not see the population described above, however. We assume that it sees a population which differs in that a certain number of good UUTs are omitted, so that one is more likely to perform diagnosis on UUTs that have malfunctioned. Specifically, suppose we know empirically that P_0 is the probability that a UUT about to undergo diagnosis is faulty. Now let us refer to the two module UUT example of Fig. 7–3, in which area represents probability. Each of the 2^n rectangles represents the probability of one of the fault states (each module good or faulty) of the

UUT. The crosshatched area of the upper left represents the good UUTs which are preferentially omitted in the population undergoing diagnosis, so that the remaining area in the "all modules good" rectangle divided by the entire remaining area is $1 - P_0$, the probability that the UUT is good at the start of diagnosis. This analysis extends to arbitrary dimensionality (number of modules) n, but it is not amendable to graphical description.

At the start of diagnosis, the probability that module i is faulty is

$$p_i = \frac{P_0 \, a_i}{1 - \prod_{j=1}^{n} \bar{a}_j}$$

This is simply the probability P_0 that there is a fault times the fraction of the "faulty area" covered by module i.

Calculating Fault Probabilities after Passed Tests

We now consider how to update the overall UUT fault probability and the module fault probabilities if one or more tests have been made and passed, and none have failed. We make the simplifying assumption that the information gleaned from passed tests can be represented by a single number c_i for each module i. This is called the *certification factor* and is initially 1.0. It approaches zero as successive passed tests are made. It represents the factor by which the relative *a priori* fault probability a_i of module i is reduced by the passing of tests. The manner in which we compute c_i needs careful consideration and is discussed in a later subsection. Thus in Fig. 7–3 the a_i become $a'_i = c_i \, a_i$ after at least one test passes.

The effect of this on the current probability P_{UUT} that the UUT is faulty is given by the following equation. It simply reflects a renormalization of the probabilities of the 2^n rectangles of Fig. 7–3 after removing the area between the "all good" rectangle and the dotted lines. Then P_{UUT} is the sum of the probabilities of all areas other than the "all good" area.

$$P_{UUT} = 1 - \frac{1}{1 + \dfrac{P_0(1 - \prod_i c_i \, \bar{a}_i}{(1 - P_0)(1 - \prod_i \bar{a}_i)}}$$

In a similar vein, each module fault probability p_i becomes the sum of the probabilities of the 2^{n-1} rectangles for which that module is faulty, after the renormalization mentioned above:

$$p_i = \frac{P_0 c_i \, a_i}{(1 - P_0)(1 - \prod_j \bar{a}_j) = P_0(1 - \prod_j c_j \, \bar{a}_j)}$$

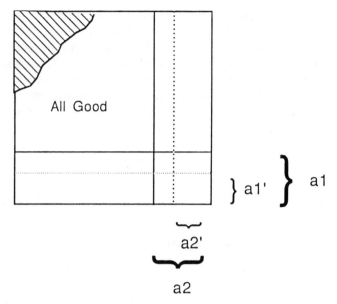

Figure 7–3 *Probability analysis before any test fails: a two-module graphical representation.*

Calculating Fault Probabilities after Failed Tests

For clarity, we first describe the processing of failed test results only. Then we will treat the case of some failed and some passed tests. As described above, each failed test gives rise to an ambiguity set containing all modules that could have caused that abnormal measurement. The set of these ambiguity sets corresponds to a Boolean conjunctive normal form expression in the module fault propositions x_i; at least one member of the first ambiguity set is faulty and at least one member of the second ambiguity set is faulty, etc. Let T denote this expression and H denote an arbitrary Boolean function of the x_i and their complements, describing a fault hypothesis whose current probability is desired. A fault hypothesis is defined here as a Boolean combination of assertions that individual modules are good or faulty. For example, x_1 & $\bar{x}_2$ & x_3 is the hypothesis that modules 1 and 3 are bad and module 2 is good, without regard for the other modules.

From elementary probability theory the current probability of H is given by

$$P(H|T) = \frac{P(H\&T)}{P(T)} \tag{7-1}$$

where $P(B)$ is defined for an arbitrary Boolean function B as the *a priori* probability of the proposition B, i.e., the *a priori* probability that the fault state of the UUT is consistent with B. $P(B)$ is expressible as

$$P(B) \; = \; \sum_{B \,=\, 1} A_i$$

where

$$A_i \; \equiv \; \prod_k f_1(a_k)$$

and

$$
\begin{aligned}
f_i(a_k) \; &\equiv \; a_k, \text{ if the } k^{th} \text{ bit of the binary representation of } i \; = \; 1 \\
&\equiv \; \bar{a}_k, \text{ if the } k^{th} \text{ bit of the binary representation of } i \; = \; 0
\end{aligned}
$$

where $\bar{a}_k$ denotes $1 - a_k$. The complexity of computing $P(B)$ with the explicit summation is $O(2^n)$. Therefore, we introduce a more efficient algorithm for this computation.

Our algorithm computes $P(B)$ for an arbitrary Boolean function of the literals x_i, although B must be given in conjunctive normal form. The strategy is to manipulate B so that all terms of conjunctions are statistically independent (involve no common x_i) and all terms of disjunctions are nonoverlapping (mutually exclusive). We then can replace the x_i with the corresponding *a priori* component failure probabilities a_i and the three Boolean operations with arithmetic operations using the following three laws from probability theory:

A. If $P(X) = p$, then $P(\bar{X}) = 1\text{-}p$.
B. If $P(X) = p$ and $P(Y) = q$, then $P(X \vee Y) = p + q$ iff $X \& Y = 0$.
C. If $P(X) = p$, $P(Y) = q$, and X and Y are statistically independent, then $P(X \& Y) = p \times q$.

We perform the Boolean manipulation with the following algorithm. We assume that B is presented to the algorithm in conjunctive normal form. Complexity will be discussed in terms of the number a of conjuncts at the top level of B and the number n of literals occurring. Note that in the diagnosis application a is the number of ambiguity sets (one per failed test) and n is the number of modules. An example follows the algorithm for clarity.

Boolean Manipulation Algorithm.

1. Perform Boolean absorption to remove all redundant conjuncts.
2. Apply DeMorgan's law to B so that it is in complemented disjunctive normal form.

3. Order the disjuncts by length (number of conjuncts x_i or $\bar{x}_i$) longest leftmost.
4. Correct the disjuncts for overlap with others, from left to right, by ANDing certain terms onto each (to be elaborated later). The entire conjunctive expression thus appended to each disjunct will be called a correction expression. Terminate the algorithm if the conjuncts in this correction expression are all literals.
5. To each correction expression, apply this algorithm recursively, starting at step 1.

Steps 1 and 4 of the above Boolean manipulation algorithm need additional explanation. In step 1 we remove all redundant conjuncts as follows. For each conjunct, compare it with each conjunct to its right. Whenever a pair is encountered such that all terms of one are present in the other, delete the larger conjunct. For example, $(X \vee Y)\&(X \vee Y \vee Z) = X \vee Y$. The complexity of step 1 is $O(a^2 n)$, assuming that the literals were presorted within each conjunct.

Step 4 (the overlap correction) of the Boolean manipulation algorithm proceeds by:

4a. Working from left to right, take the next disjunct D_N.
4b. For each disjunct D to the right of D_N, perform step 4c.
4c. Note whether any literal x_i occurs complemented in D and uncomplemented in D_N, or vice-versa. If so, terminate step 4c; this pair is already mutually exclusive. Otherwise compute D^-, defined as what remains of D after removing from it those conjuncts (x_i or $\bar{x}_i$) present in D_N and append (AND) the complement of D^- (expressed as a disjunction, using DeMorgan's law) onto D_N. Step 4 has complexity $O(a^2 n)$, again assuming that the literals were presorted within each conjunct.

A worst case complexity of the above algorithm is $O(a^a n)$. This follows from the fact that the complexity of the first recursion is $(a^2 n)$ (from steps 2 and 4) and each additional recursion (step 5) introduces an extra factor of a via step 4. The number of recursions is bounded by a, since step 4 produces a correction expression with at least one less top level term than its input expression at each recursion. There may exist a smaller upper bound than $O(a^a n)$. In practice, most functions B yield few if any recursions, so that the typical complexity is closer to $a^2 n$. Also, in the diagnosis application, n may be large ($\sim$100 modules) but a, the number of failed tests, is typically less than 10.

Example. The following is an example of the application of the above algorithm. In keeping with our diagnostic topic, suppose that three tests have failed and our current ambiguity sets are $\{2,3,4\}$, $\{4,5,6\}$, and $\{6,7\}$. Let us compute the probability of the hypothesis x_7 that module 7 is faulty. The ambiguity sets overlap interestingly (at least two faults are present) and make a good illustration. We define the shorthand notation $\overline{P}(B) \equiv 1 - P(B)$ and x_i is denoted by i. Then the numerator of Eq. (7-1) becomes $P(H\&T) = P[2v3v4)\&(4v5v6)\&(5v7)\&7]$. Note that laws A, B, and C cannot be applied at this point to compute the numerical value of $P(H\&T)$. In particular, the four conjuncts are not all statistically independent of one another, since they contain some common literals. Therefore, we will apply the Boolean manipulation algorithm:

$$
\begin{aligned}
H\&T \quad &= (2v3v4)\&(4v5v6)\&(6v7)\&7 \\
&= (2v3v4)\&(4v5v6)\&7; \text{ Step 1 (Boolean absorption)} \\
&= \overline{(\overline{2}\&\overline{3}\&\overline{4})v(\overline{4}\&\overline{5}\&\overline{6})v\overline{7}}; \text{ Step 2 (DeMorgan's law)} \\
&= \overline{\overline{2}\&\overline{3}\&\overline{4}\&(5v6)\&7)v(\overline{4}\&\overline{5}\&\overline{6}\&7)v\overline{7}}; \text{ Step 4 (disjunction overlap removal)}
\end{aligned}
$$

(5v6)\&7 becomes $\overline{(\overline{5}\&\overline{6})v\overline{7}}$; Steps 5 and 2, recursively (DeMorgan's law)

$$
= \overline{(\overline{5}\&\overline{6}\&7)v\overline{7}}; \text{ Step 4 (disjunction overlap removal)}
$$

Finally,

$$
H\&T = \overline{\overline{(\overline{2}\&\overline{3}\&\overline{4}\&\overline{(\overline{5}\&\overline{6}\&7)v\overline{7}})v7}v(\overline{4}\&\overline{5}\&\overline{6}\&7)v\overline{7}}.
$$

Now we can apply laws A, B, and C to all negations, conjunctions, and disjunctions, respectively,

$$
P(H\&T) = 1 - \overline{P}(2)\overline{P}(3)\overline{P}(4)(\overline{(\overline{P}(5)\overline{P}(6)P(7) + \overline{P}(7))} - \overline{P}(4)\overline{P}(5)\overline{P}(6)P(7) - \overline{P}(7)
$$

The $P(i)$ are simply the a_i. The numerator of Eq. (7-1) can be treated similarly.

The above method can be used to compute the current fault probabilities of the individual modules after each test. It can also be invoked by the user to compute the probability of any fault hypothesis, even one including some fault states inconsistent with T.

Now we will treat the case of having at least one passed test in addition to the failed test(s). As described in the previous and following subsection, for each module i we compute a certification factor c_i which represents the evidence from passed tests. Thus module i is regarded as certified by the amount c_i and the *a priori* failure rate a_i is simply replaced with $c_i a_i$ in the probability calculations above.

Passed Tests and Certification Strategies

Now we will focus on how to compute the certification factors c_i used in the previous subsections. Since we assume the unavailability of failure mode statistics here, we take a somewhat heuristic approach. We will motivate our discussion of certification with the example of Fig. 7–4, in which a diagnosis system currently suspects that at least one of two modules amp1 and amp2 contains a fault. In particular, an RMS amplitude test fails at T3, leading us to suspect a gain problem in the upper of two amplifier channels in both modules. Then it might be able to determine which module is likely to be faulty by making a test dependent on amp1 but not on amp2. Then if the test fails, amp1 is faulty, and if the test passes, amp1 is less suspect than it was, and amp2 more suspect. If a human interpreted that passed test, he would think about what failure mode of amp1 tested ok. If it were the same failure mode that made amp1 initially suspect, amp1 would be exonerated (reduction of c_i to nearly zero). If the passed test depended on a completely independent failure mode of amp1, then amp1 would be only slightly certified (small reduction of c_i).

The desiderata for the c_i are as follows:

1. Each c_i should be 1.0 initially and never be less than zero.
2. Each passed test fed by module i should reduce c_i.
3. The different ways a module can fail are often not mutually exclusive. This successive passed tests fed by module i should have progressively less effect on c_i, all other factors being equal.
4. If a module is currently suspected of being faulty because one or more test depending on it failed, then, it should be certified more strongly by some passed tests than by others. In particular, a passed test dependent on *immediate effects* (an approximation of failure modes; see Ambiguity Sets) which are currently suspect should yield a larger reduction of c_i than other passed tests depending on module i.
5. A passed test satisfying 4 above, which also was made under the same UUT stimulus conditions, should yield an even larger reduction of c_i.

In earlier versions of the implemented FIS system we tried a simple linear scheme. For example, if a module has 10 *module rules* and four of the rules have right-hand sides on the causal path to some test that passed, then the certification factor for the module is $c_i = 1 - 4/10 = 0.6$. Thus the *a priori* fault probability of the module would be multiplied by 0.6 before being used

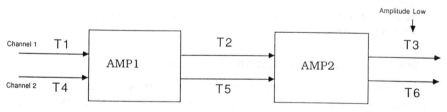

Figure 7–4   *The difficulty of interpreting passed tests.*

in the probability calculations of the previous subsection. However, this violates the above desiderata except 1.

One way to satisfy the desiderata while still avoiding requiring joint statistics data for the failure modes of a module is the following scheme. Keep track of how many of the tests that depend on each *immediate effect* of the given module have been made and passed. Then take the sum s of these and compute e^{-ks} as the certification factor for the module, with the constant k chosen empirically to optimize performance. This addresses desiderata 1, 2, and 3. Now if the module in question is contained in any ambiguity set, i.e., if it feeds any failed test, then $e^{-ks-k_a s_a}$ is taken as the certification factor, where s_a is the number of passed tests that depend on those particular *immediate effects* of the module that are responsible for that module being in an ambiguity set. That is, for each passed test we note for each module on which the test depends how many of the abnormalities it can immediately cause (at its terminals) lie on the causal path to the *failed* (e.g., low or high) outcomes of the *passed* test. The causal connections between the various *immediate effects* and the test outcomes can be found by direct lookup of precompiled *ambiguity sets* of tests (see Ambiguity Sets). The constant k_a is chosen empirically to optimize performance. This satisfies desideratum 4. Finally, to cover 5, one could extend the above exponential expression to $e^{-ks-k_a s_a-k_s s_s}$, where s_s is the number of passed tests that depend on those particular *immediate effects* of the module that are responsible for that module being in an ambiguity set *and* which share the same setup as a failed test implicating such an immediate effect. Many other strategies are possible for the approximate certification of modules in the absence of failure mode joint statistics. The above ones may suggest other ideas.

BEST TEST STRATEGIES

We define the *optimal* best test strategy as the one which minimizes the average total cost of the tests required to achieve some specified degree of certainty about which modules in the UUT are faulty and which ones are not. Optimality is an unrealistic goal in most applications, but there are various ways to achieve adequate suboptimal performance. In succeeding sections we will cast the best test problem in terms of game trees and then argue for the direct evaluation of the available tests without tree search. Two practical forms of evaluation are described; heuristic strategies which lend themselves to automated explanation, and a more rigorous information theoretic approach. For the latter we introduce an algorithm for computing the entropy of a set of statistically independent propositions constrained by an arbitrary Boolean function.

Testing and Game Trees

The problem of finding the *best* test to make next in diagnostic reasoning is analogous to that of playing a game against an opponent who responds randomly. The test result is the opponent's move and the test selection is our move. The object of our side is to minimize the total cost of finding the fault(s). We could think of the opponent as confounding our efforts by giving test results which sometimes further our goal and sometimes don't.

One method that is optimal in the above sense is the miniaverage algorithm. Figure 7–5 shows an example of a *game tree* corresponding to a diagnostic problem. The strategy is to propagate the total test costs given at the terminal nodes back to the root node. This is done by recursively computing the *backed-up* cost of a node from the costs of its offspring. There are two cases. The backed-up cost of a test node is the weighted average of the backed-up costs of the offspring result nodes, where the weights are the probabilities of the results. The backed-up cost of a result node is the minimum of the backed-up costs of its offspring test nodes. When the propaga-

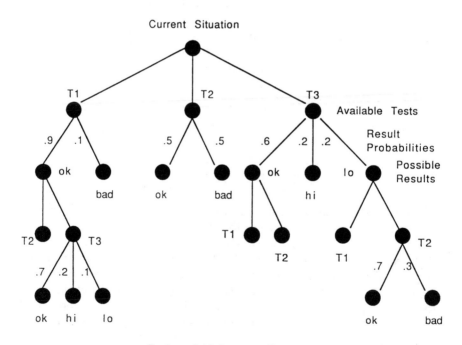

Portion of Miniaverage Tree

Figure 7–5 *Miniaverage methods: optimal but costly.*

tion reaches the root node, a result node, the minimizing test node is noted. This node corresponds to the best test.

Although this is an optimal solution, it is infeasible for large problems. This branching factor at the result nodes is then large since the number of available tests is typically large. The tree size is roughly this branching factor raised to the power d, the average depth of the tree, and d increases with the problem size.

This problem can be mitigated by using the gamma miniaverage algorithm [8,13]. This method performs the miniaverage calculation more efficiently by computing the backed-up costs in an order which allows considerable pruning of the tree. Also, it [8] reduces the depth of the tree by starting the propagation not at the terminal nodes of the tree, but at some fixed depth, and estimating the backed-up costs at these nodes with evaluation functions.

We regard a depth of 1 to be the most practical choice, since the number of available tests is often several hundred. Then the miniaverage method degenerates to simply iterating once over the list of available tests. For each, a weighted average is taken of the evaluation function applied to the UUT states resulting from the several possible test results, where the weights are the estimated test result probabilities. The minimum valued test is then recommended.

Information Gain versus Cost

It is difficult to find an evaluation function which directly computes an estimate of the *backed-up cost* of a UUT state without performing the tree search. However, instead of trying to pick a test leading to a minimum expected remaining cost of testing, one can pick a test which *maximizes* the ratio of the expected information gain for that test to its cost (a predefined test cost). This expected information gain is a weighted average of the reduction in the Shannon entropy of the UUT over the several possible test results, where the weights are the estimated test result probabilities. The reasoning here is that since the entropy of the UUT is a measure of how much information is required to know its failure state exactly (each module good or bad) and the entropy monotonically decreases at each test, there is no risk of retrogressing from our goal of certainty. Therefore, it is reasonable to seek maximal progress in one step.

Estimates of the probabilities of test results are needed for use in the best test calculations. The probability of an abnormal (such as high or low) result can be rapidly estimated by looking up the ambiguity set for that result and noting the associated *immediate effects* of each module. Then an estimate is made of the fraction f_i of the current probability P_i that module i is faulty that is causally related to those immediate effects, using the certification information for module i. The estimated test result probability is $1 - \prod_i (1 - f_i P_i)$. More simply put, we estimate the amount of the probability mass of various possible faults that causally lies upstream of the hypothesized test result.

Heuristic Strategies

The information theoretic approach described in the previous subsection has the advantage of theoretical rigor, but despite the efficient entropy algorithm elaborated later in the next subsection it still can be too slow for real time applications. This is because one has to process the results of many hypothetical tests to obtain the UUT states whose entropy is to be computed. Therefore, we have experimented with a more heuristic approach. This approach has the advantages of speed and transparency. That is, it allows the development of explanation software. This is of great practical importance for technician's aide and training aide applications. It has the disadvantage that it is difficult to prove anything about its performance.

First we will discuss the case in which no test has failed yet. In this case the objective is to find a test which fails quickly (i.e., at low cost) if there is any fault. If there is not any fault, then it doesn't matter in what order the tests are done; we simply exhaust a given list of tests and declare the UUT not faulty. A reasonable heuristic is then to select a test which maximizes the estimated probability of test failure divided by the test cost. One simple and efficient way to estimate test result probabilities is given in the previous subsection.

Next we will discuss the case in which at least one test has failed so far. In this case the objective is to isolate the fault(s) at minimal cost. One of the most useful heuristics is that tests dependent on some, but not all of a *suspect set* (defined below) of modules are powerful. If such a test fails, the suspect set tends to becomes smaller, essentially by a process of intersection. If it passes, it tends to become smaller by a process of elimination; the certification process reduces the c_i values of the modules on which the test depends. A *suspect set* can be defined in various ways; for example, as a set of modules of whose current fault probabilities satisfy some criterion, or, better, as a nonnull intersection of some or all of the ambiguity sets of failed tests. Further refining this heuristic, tests are better which not only depend on a subset of the suspect set, but which depend on suspect *immediate effects*. Better still are tests which share the same *stimulus setup* with failed tests depending on suspect *immediate effects*. The latter two are directed toward achieving strong certification if the test passes. Note the relevance of Passed Tests and Certification Strategies. Finally, tests which have low cost are to be preferred to tests of otherwise equal merit but with higher cost. Many variants of these ideas are possible; empirical experience should be used as a guide in specific applications.

Fast Entropy Algorithm

The UUT entropy discussed above can be expressed as follows:

$$H(T) = - \sum_{i=1}^{2^n} p_i \log p_i, \quad \text{where } \log \equiv \log_2 \tag{7-2}$$

Here p_i is the current probability of the ith complete fault hypothesis (all modules hypothesized good or bad) and n is the number of modules in the UUT. Expression (7-2) is not in a suitable form for efficient computation because its complexity increases exponentially with the number n of modules. For only 20 modules, $2^{20} = 1,048,576$ terms would need to be computed. Therefore, we compute this quantity more efficiently by the drastic automatic simplification of (7-2) after manipulating the Boolean function T representing the failed test results to date using the algorithm in Calculating Fault Probabilities after Failed Tests. This procedure introduces no approximations but greatly improves running time. It is also generally applicable to the problem of efficiently computing the entropy of a set of statistically independent propositions constrained by an arbitrary Boolean function.

We assume that the description of the state probabilities p_i is that provided by the Boolean algorithm of Calculating Fault Probabilities after Failed Tests. That is, the Boolean function B describing the *feasible states* is represented in a form such that a negation appears at the top level, with a disjunction below that and a conjunction below that. Each conjunct of such a conjunction is either a literal (complemented or uncomplemented) or an expression of the form described in the preceding sentence, recursively. Finally, all disjunctions are of mutually exclusive terms and all conjunctions are of statistically independent terms (no common literals).

The strategy will be to decompose $H(B)$ from the top down using several mathematical identities about entropy expressions, until it is explicitly computable in terms of arithmetic and transcendental functions of the *a priori* probabilities a_i of the Boolean literals. Thus, our efficient entropy algorithm is in the same spirit as the efficient probability algorithm of Calculating Fault Probabilities after Failed Tests, although the details are different. Gallager [14] provides a good background for the remainder of this subsection.

Definitions.

$$A_i \equiv \prod_k f_i(a_k) \text{ where}$$

$f_i(a_k) \equiv a_k$, if the k th bit of the binary representation of $i = 0$.

$\equiv a_k$, if the k th bit of the binary representation of $i = 1$.

where $\bar{a}_k$ denotes $1 - a_k$. Thus the A_i are the 2^n state probabilities with no Boolean constraint.

$A_{Si} \equiv \prod\limits_{k \in s} f_i(a_k)$, as above, except only a subspace of size 2^l is covered, where l is the size of the given subset S of literals.

$H(B) \equiv - \sum\limits_{B=1} cA_i \log cA_i$, where $1/c = \sum\limits_{B=1} A_i$. This is just the Shannon entropy of the probabilities A_i normalized to unity over those states i for which $B = 1$.

$H_n(B) \equiv - \sum\limits_{B=1} A_i \log A_i$. This *nonnormalized entropy* is not a true entropy, since the A_i are not normalized to unity over the states i for which $B = 1$.

$H_s(B) \equiv \sum\limits_{B=1} cA_{Si} \log cA_{Si}$. This is the entropy over the subspace s spanned by those variables occurring in B. S in A_{Si} is the set of those variables.

$H_S \equiv \sum\limits_{i=1}^{2^l} A_{Si} \log A_{Si}$, where S is a given subset of l Boolean literals of the n Boolean literals occurring in the complete problem. Note that H_S can be computed in $O(l)$ steps by using the identity *unconstrained independent literals* below.

Entropy Identities Needed.

Negation: $H_n(\bar{B}) = H_n(l) - H_n(B)$.

Normalization: $H(B) = cH_n(B) - \log c$, where $1/c = \sum\limits_{B=1} A_i = P(B)$.

Independent conjunction: $H_s(B\&C) = H_s(B) + H_s(C)$, if B and C contain no common literals, and are thus statistically independent.

Nonoverlapping disjunction: $H_n(B \lor C) = H_n(B) + H_n(C)$, if B and C are mutually exclusive.

Unconstrained independent literals: $H_S = - \sum\limits_{i \in S}(a_i \log a_i + \bar{a}_i \log \bar{a}_i)$.

Algorithm.   The following is a statement of the efficient entropy algorithm:

1. Express $H(B)$ in terms of $H_n(B)$ using *normalization*.
2. Express $H_n(B)$ in terms of $H_n(\bar{B})$ using *negation*.
3. Express $H_n(\bar{B})$ as a sum of terms of the form $H_n(D)$, where D denotes each disjunct of $\bar{B}$.
4. Express each $H_n(D)$ in terms of $H(D)$ using *normalization*.
5. Express each $H(D)$ as $H_s(D) + H_S$, where S is the set of Boolean literals not occurring in D but occurring in the complete problem.
6. Express each $H_s(D)$ as a sum of the $H_s(C)$ over the various conjuncts C of D, using *independent conjunction*.
7. For each literal C, set $H_s(C) = 0$.
8. For each nonliteral C, apply the whole algorithm recursively to $H_s(C)$, since it has the form of B.
9. Expand any H_S terms produced by Step 5, using *unconstrained independent literals*.

Example. Suppose we wish to compute the entropy $H(\bar{1}\&\bar{2}\&3\vee\bar{3})$ of the set of 16 states of the four propositions x_1, x_2, x_3, x_4 with a priori probabilities a_1, a_2, a_3, a_4, respectively, constrained by the Boolean relation $\bar{x}_1\& \bar{x}_2\& \bar{x}_3\vee\bar{x}_3 = 1$. (Note the shorthand; i for x_i, and $\bar{a} \equiv 1 - a$ for *numerical* expressions a only.)

Step 1:

$$H\,\overline{(\bar{1}\&\bar{2}\&3\vee\bar{3})} = cH_n\,\overline{(\bar{1}\&\bar{2}\&3\vee\bar{3})} - \log c$$

where

$$1/c = P\,\overline{(\bar{1}\&\bar{2}\&3\vee\bar{3})} = 1 - \bar{a}_1\bar{a}_2 a_3 - \bar{a}_3$$

Step 2:

$$H_n\,\overline{(\bar{1}\&\bar{2}\&3\vee\bar{3})} = H_n(1) - H_n\,(\bar{1}\&\bar{2}\&3\vee\bar{3})$$

Step 3:

$$H_n\,(\bar{1}\&\bar{2}\&3\vee\bar{3}) = H_n\,(\bar{1}\&\bar{2}\&3) + H_n\,(\bar{3})$$

Step 4:

$$H_n(\bar{1}\&\bar{2}\&3) = \frac{H(\bar{1}\&\bar{2}\&3)\ + \log\ c'}{c'}$$

where $1/c' = P\,(\bar{1}\&\bar{2}\&3) = \bar{a}_1\bar{a}_2 a_3$, and

$$H_n(\bar{3}) = \frac{H(\bar{3}) + \log 1/c''}{c''}$$

where $1/c'' = P\,(\bar{3}) = \bar{a}_3$.

Step 5:

$$H\,(\bar{1}\&\bar{2}\&3) = H_S\,(\bar{1}\&\bar{2}\&3) + H_{\{4\}} \text{ and } H(\bar{3}) = H_S(\bar{3}) + H_{\{1,2,4\}}$$

Step 6:

$$H\,(\bar{1}\&\bar{2}\&3) = H_S\,(\bar{1}) + H_S(\bar{2}) + H_S(3)\,H_{\{4\}}$$

Steps 7 and 9:

$$H(\bar{1}\&\bar{2}\&3) = H_{\{4\}} = -[a_4 \log a_4 + \bar{a}_4 \log \bar{a}_4], \text{ and}$$

$$H(\bar{3}) = H_{\{1,2,4\}} = -\,[a_1 \log a_1 + a_1 \log a_1 + a_2 \log a_2 + \bar{a}_2 \log \bar{a}_2 \\ + a_4 \log a_4 + \bar{a}_4 \log \bar{a}_4]$$

Now, given the a_i values, one can substitute backwards through the above equations to obtain $H(\overline{1\&2\&3v3})$. For example, if $a_1 = a_2 = a_3 = a_4 = 0.5$, we obtain $H(\overline{1\&2\&3v3}) = 1 + \log 3$. We can readily verify this special case by noting that this problem has six states of equal nonzero probability 1/6. Thus its entropy is $6(1/6 \log(6)) = \log(6) = 1 + \log 3$.

The complexity of the entropy algorithm is closely related to the complexity of the probability algorithm of Calculating Fault Probabilities after Failed Tests, since they both use the same Boolean manipulation algorithm as their first stage. Although the probability algorithm introduces no significant complexity beyond that of the Boolean algorithm, the entropy algorithm does so in step 9. Every disjunct encountered in the output of the Boolean algorithm invokes an application of *unconstrained independent literals,* which requires only $2l$ operations, where l is the number of literals occurring in the problem but not in the disjunct. Therefore, if there are d disjuncts, $O(dl_{max})$ computation is introduced beyond the Boolean computation, where l_{max} is the maximum l over all the disjuncts. Since l_{max} is bounded by the total number n of literals, this complexity becomes $O(dn)$. But $d = O(a^a)$, the number of terms generated in step 4 of the Boolean algorithm in Calculating Fault Probabilities after Failed Tests. Therefore, the total complexity added by the numerical part of the entropy algorithm is $O(a^a n)$, the same as that of the Boolean algorithm. Thus a total worst case complexity of the entire entropy algorithm is $O(a^a n)$, although, as mentioned in Calculating Fault Probabilities after Failed Tests, the typical case is far better than this, often approximately $a^2 n$.

FIS: AN IMPLEMENTED DIAGNOSTIC SYSTEM

As we have mentioned earlier, these ideas have been incorporated into a working diagnostic system which we have named FIS (for fault isolation system). In this section we will give a brief overview of FIS from a user's point of view.

The major components of FIS, as well as its two principal users, are illustrated in Fig. 7–6. We will describe the components chronologically as they are used. First, the knowledge engineer, whose principal expertise is a detailed understanding of the type of equipment to be diagnosed, describes the UUT to the computer. He does this at a computer terminal via the knowledge acquisition interface (KAI), producing the UUT description, which is then stored in a file. A principal concern in the design of the KAI is to maximize the ease with which a user with a good electronics background but little familiarity with computer science can generate a description of the UUT which will yield acceptable diagnostic performance in FIS. This description contains such information as *a priori* rates of failure of the replaceable modules, costs (primarily in time) of setup and test operations, connectivity and qual-

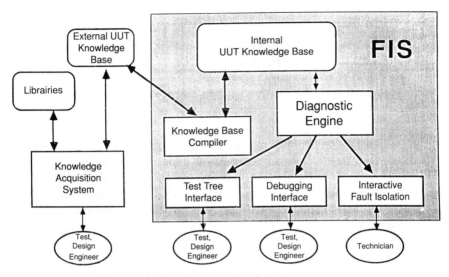

Figure 7–6   *A global view of the implemented FIS system.*

itative functional descriptions, a set of allowed tests, and a graphics description for displaying a block diagram of the UUT.

The Electronics Library is primarily intended to store partial or complete qualitative functional descriptions of modules which occur frequently in the UUTs being described. The Electronics Library is to be referred to whenever possible while using the Knowledge Acquisition Interface to enhance speed. The resulting approximate module descriptions can then be edited using the KAI. Also, the KAI can be used to add, delete, or modify items in the library. After its completion, the UUT description is processed by the knowledge compiler. This produces a file containing the compiled UUT knowledge.

The purpose of the Knowledge Compiler is simply to transform knowledge from a form suitable for editing to a form suitable for efficient diagnostic computation. The Knowledge Compiler is run after the UUT Description is completely finished, and stores the Compiled UUT Description in a file.

Once we have compiled UUT descriptions available, the diagnostic reasoning subsystem can be invoked to perform a variety of diagnostic tasks. The diagnostic reasoning subsystem uses a compiled UUT description to dynamically construct and maintain a belief model about what is properly and improperly functioning as test results become known. This belief model in turn is used to find the best test to make next or recommend the replacement of some module of the UUT.

We currently provide two user interfaces to the diagnostic subsystem. The first is a "mixed initiative" interface intended to be used by a technician as an aide during a diagnostic troubleshooting session. In this mode, FIS is capable of :

1. Updating the current beliefs about the UUT based on a technician's entry of test results
2. Responding to a technician's query regarding the probability of a fault hypothesis, the merit of a test, the UUT description, or the belief state of FIS
3. Making suggestions/recommendations about the next best action to take (further tests or replacements).

The second mode of use is to use the diagnostic subsystem to produce a traditional test tree by invoking the next best action generator, following its advice (hypothetically), and recursively invoking the next best action generator for each of the possible outcomes of the previously recommended action. In this way, large, complex test trees are generated automatically with no human intervention.

We have discussed, but have not currently implemented, several other possible user interfaces including a tutorial interface for use in teaching troubleshooting, and a testability interface for evaluating proposed systems early in the design phase.

CURRENT APPLICATIONS OF FIS

We have been testing and refining FIS on real analog UUT's to assess its performance and practicality and to provide ideas for improvements. We have been modeling a radar receiver/exciter subsystem with the goal of generating test trees (called diagnostic and functional flowcharts) which are comparable in quality to those written by test programmers. As a second application, we have been applying FIS to a Navy sonar system as a technician's aide.

In the radar application, the goal is to demonstrate that FIS can relieve the human test programmer of part of the labor of producing a *test program set* (TPS), which is a program that controls ATE gear in the automatic execution of a test tree. It is the automatic test tree generation capability of FIS that is used here. The part of the human effort that is relieved is the sequencing of the possible tests and the determination of when some module(s) warrant replacement and which ones. In exchange for this, FIS places a modest knowledge acquisition burden on the user, primarily in the form of causal rules and test cost information. Other parts of this task that we leave under human control are the choice of test equipment and the determination of what constitutes a sufficient set of tests to certify that the UUT is performing correctly and to do fault isolation. Figure 7–7 shows a hardcopy version of the more detailed CRT color graphics display of the radar unit. This is useful during the development of the UUT description, when the technician's aide mode is

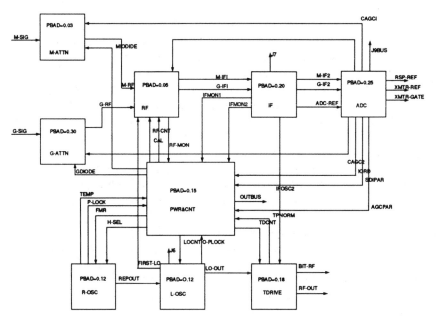

Figure 7–7 *A hardcopy approximation of the color FIS UUT display.*

invoked to interactively test the diagnostic performance before test trees are generated.

This application has suggested some refinements in FIS to make it practical for TPS applications. By making some improvements of the speed and accuracy of the best test computation and implementing a more intelligent handling of passed tests, FIS now generates fault isolation trees which are as good or better than existing ones generated manually.

The second application involves the use of FIS as a maintenance advisor to a technician. It will be installed in a rugged portable computer and will direct or assist a technician in the troubleshooting of a complex, primarily analog sonar subsystem consisting of 105 replaceable modules, using manual test equipment. The primary functions will be the recommendation of a next best test and the reporting of FIS' beliefs after a test is made.

In addition to these activities in which we are directly involved, we have also initiated a technology transfer program in which we provide current versions of FIS to approximately 25 sites in other government labs and private industry. Our goal is to make people aware of the potential of AI-based diagnostic systems like FIS, and to receive feedback from this community concerning their perceptions of the usefulness of FIS.

CONCLUSIONS

The goal of this research effort has been to exploit ideas from the area of AI in order to build effective diagnostic systems. We have achieved this goal by developing a knowledge representation technique called *qualitative causal modeling* which has the property that sufficient behavioral knowledge of a UUT can be captured without high knowledge acquisition costs to allow for generation of efficient diagnostic sequences. This representation technique is complemented by a set of efficient algorithms for computing fault probabilities, recommending tests, and making module replacements.

This approach has made it possible to provide two features which are not part of most current diagnostic systems: (1) no single fault assumptions, and (2) the ability to dynamically decide (during fault isolation) what the next best test should be.

In addition, this research has introduced efficient new algorithms for two general problems: (1) computing the probability that a given conjunctive normal form Boolean expression is true, given statistically independent literals, and (2) computing the Shannon entropy of such a set of literals, given that such a Boolean function is true. These were motivated by the goal of avoiding computational bottlenecks everywhere in the FIS system when scaling up to large systems. This has been achieved.

Our current efforts are primarily focused on making minor improvements to FIS based on user feedback. However, we have targeted FIS as an opportunity to exploit some of the recent advances in machine learning. It is clear that any UUT model needs to be continually refined as failure rates change, systems age, etc. Our goal is to use machine learning techniques to automate this refinement without the need for significant human intervention.

REFERENCES

[1] F. Pipitone, "The FIS Electronics Troubleshooting System," *IEEE Comput. Mag.* pp. 68–76, Jul. 1986.

[2] F. J. Pipitone, K. De Jong, W. M. Spears, and M. P. Marrone, "The FIS Electronics Troubleshooting Project," in *Expert System Applications to Telecommunications,* J. Liebowitz, Ed., Wiley, New York, 1988.

[3] J. DeKleer, and B. C. Williams, "Diagnosing Multiple Faults," in *Artificial Intelligence,* North-Holland, Amsterdam, 1987.

[4] M. R. Genesereth, "Diagnosis Using Hierarchical Design Models," *Proc. National Conference on Artificial Intelligence,* Pittsburgh, PA, 1982, pp. 278–283.

[5] R. Davis, H. Schrobe, W. Hamscher, K. Wieckert, M. Shirley, and S. Polit, "Diagnosis Based on Description of Structure and Function," *Proc. National Conference on Artificial Intelligence,* Pittsburgh, PA, 1982, pp. 137–142.

[6] H. Geffner, and J. Pearl, "Distributed Diagnosis of Systems with Multiple

Faults," Technical Report R-66 CSD-8600, UCLA Computer Science Department, Los Angeles, CA, 1986.

[7] J. Pearl, "Distributed Revision of Belief Commitment in Multi-Hypotheses Interpretation," *Proc. 2nd AAAI Workshop on Uncertainty in Artificial Intelligence,* Philadelphia, PA, Aug. 1986, pp. 201–209.

[8] R. R. Cantone, F. J. Pipitone, W. B. Lander, and M. P. Marrone, "Model-Based Probabilistic Reasoning for Electronics Troubleshooting," *Proc. Eighth International Joint Conference on Artificial Intelligence,* Karlsruhe, West Germany, 1983, pp. 207–211.

[9] W. R. Simpson, and H. S. Balaban, "The ARINC Research System Testability and Maintenance Program (STAMP)," *Proc. 1982 IEEE Autotestcon Conference,* Dayton, OH, 1982.

[10] E. H. Shortliffe, *Computer-Based Medical Consultations: MYCIN,* Elsevier, New York, 1976.

[11] R. O. Duda, P. E. Hart, K. Konolige, and R. Reboh, *A Computer-Based Consultant for Mineral Exploration,* Artificial Intelligence Center, SRI International, Menlo Park, CA, 1979.

[12] G. Shafer, *A Mathematical Theory of Evidence,* Princeton University Press, Princeton, NJ, 1976.

[13] James R. Slagle, Richard C. T. Lee, "Applications of Game Tree Searching Techniques to Sequential Pattern Recognition," *Commun. ACM,* Vol. 14, No. 2, pp. 103–110, Feb. 1971.

[14] R. G. Gallager, *Information Theory and Reliable Communication,* Wiley, New York, 1968.

8

Automatic Testing for Control Systems Conformance

DENIS R. TOWILL

HISTORICAL DEVELOPMENT OF ATE

The history of automatic test equipment (ATE) to some extent parallels the use of computers in machine tool control, both with regard to hardware and software characteristics. This is shown in the following list in which the history of ATE is expressed in generations defined by specific hardware and software characteristics [1]. This chapter is especially concerned with the use of ATE for control systems checkout prior to fault location, that is, conformance testing against a specification related to mission success.

ATE Generation	Characteristics
First	Fixed Sequence
	Tape Controlled
Second	Digital computer as test manager
	Analogue distributed data processing and instrumentation
Third	Reduction in usage of dedicated analogue instrumentation
	Use of digital computer for data processing
Fourth	Combination of the sampled data approach of third generation with distributed digital computation
Fifth	Closed loop simulation of mission scenario to optimize checkout
	Artificial intelligence diagnostic aids

The machine tool industry was an early user of ATE. Figure 8–1 shows a second generation ATE. It is a milling machine checkout system based around the digital version of the Fourier response analyzer (FRA), which, because of noise rejection capabilities, is an ideal device to include in custom-built ATE [2]. Ever since those early days the digital FRA has remained at the heart of one particular family of commercial ATE which now includes the outputting of an SUT transfer function model as one of the available software options [3].

In testing nonlinear systems, the FRA noise rejection characteristics take on a special significance, since the higher harmonics can be readily estimated and put to good use in checkout and fault diagnosis. The instrument is then known in the United States as a multiharmonic Fourier filter (MHFF). It is an advantage of fourth generation ATE that, for a given response, the test designer can exploit the power of the computer to yield various "signatures" of the SUT. Mathematical manipulation permits moving from time to frequency domain representation at will.

ATE is concerned with the ability of an individual SUT to perform the task for which it is intended, i.e., in American terms to achieve mission success. In the event of the SUT being declared "sick," then diagnosis down to the appropriate component/line replaceable unit (LRU) is required. A typical specification, in this case in the condition monitoring mode, is that the ATE should detect all faults, and have a 90% success rate in correct diagnosis to LRU level [4].

However, especially with the higher generations of ATE, it is becoming

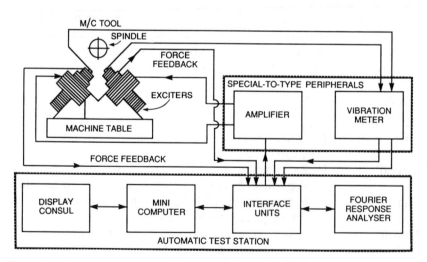

Figure 8–1   *Second-generation ATE developed for milling machine testing. (From D. R. Towill, "Automatic Testing of Control Systems—Past, Present and Future." IERE Diamond Jubilee, Vol. 57, No. 2, 1987).*

increasingly possible (and desirable) to view ATE as an integral part of the quality assurance function. The purpose here is to keep component vendor, manufacturing process, assembly process, and field trials under constant surveillance so that the quality level of the product family may be maximized [5].

Hence, as shown in Fig. 8–2, we are applying a "systems approach" to quality assurance. It is therefore necessary to provide appropriate quality management software for trend detection, data simplification, and assessing the information content of individual measurements and grouped measurements. A comprehensive program suite is available at Cardiff for the purpose [5]. By assessing the information content in this way, superfluous factory tests may be eliminated in the early stages of the manufacturing process, thus accelerating progress up the learning curve.

The measurements acquired for quality assurance purposes can be static and/or dynamic. They may be used to establish transfer function families for the SUT, and to check how the transfer function changes with SUT aging. An extension of this approach has recently been proposed [6]. United States Naval electronics system maintenance support has traditionally been fractionated between a number of communities (testing, training, human engineering, documentation, etc.) To reduce costs and mean repair times, a united systems design approach to maintenance has been proposed. This will integrate ATE, BITE, test design, and the quality assurance system into a common database.

TRANSFER FUNCTION TESTING

The present author views transfer function testing as any method whereby a signature which adequately describes SUT dynamic response is obtained. In addition to the transfer function model, such a signature might be the SUT step response, the gain/phase plot of frequency response, or any equivalent description. For a linear system, all such signatures essentially contain the same information, although the reliance which can be placed on the signature depends on the method of test.

Transfer function testing is not restricted to linear systems, although care must be taken in designing tests for a nonlinear SUT and in the consequent interpretation of the results. It is widely used for the following tasks:

- Mathematical modeling of SUT prototypes
- SUT design certification
- Vendor verification of individual SUT
- User acceptance of individual SUT
- Routine periodic checkout
- Fault diagnosis of "sick" SUT

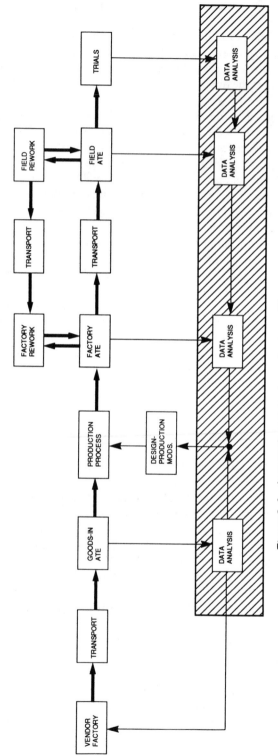

Figure 8–2 Automatic test equipment as a quality assurance tool.

- Control system "fine tuning"
- Performance matching for selective assembly
- Trend analysis for SUT preventive maintenance
- Trend analysis for SUT manufacturing process feedback

The prime reason for using transfer function testing is that one single test signature such as step response or frequency response can give the system user sufficient confidence that a complex SUT with hundreds, if not thousands, of components is in a state of operational readiness [7].

RETURN SIGNAL PROCESSING

For transfer function testing of control systems within an ATE, we may make decisions on the basis of any of the following information [1]:

1. Injection of step/ramp/impulse stimulus plus direct observation on SUT response.
2. Range of discrete frequencies injected sequentially, plus estimation of gain/phase characteristics.
3. Swept frequency response and display.
4. Injection of broad-band PNS signals and estimation of impulse response.
5. Injection of broad-band PNS signals and "direct" estimation of frequency response.
6. Injection of broad-band PNS or related signals and estimation of frequency response via FFT.

Using the ATE computational power for signal generation, return signal processing, data transformation, and curve fit modeling, shown in Fig. 8–3, gives the user a wide range of options. The "best" test method depends on the degree of nonlinearity of the SUT; the signal-to-noise ratio; uncertainty of environment; spread of response due to nonfaulty parameters; and particular SUT characteristics to be highlighted. For example, PNS properties and return signal processing can be deliberately selected to filter out secondary resonances which do not significantly affect system rise times.

TUNING OF LARGE ELECTROMECHANICAL SERVOSYSTEMS

The return signal processing capability of fifth generation ATE may also be used for tuning large electromechanical servosystems. These have traditionally been tuned manually during refit [8]. Adjustments are thus made on the

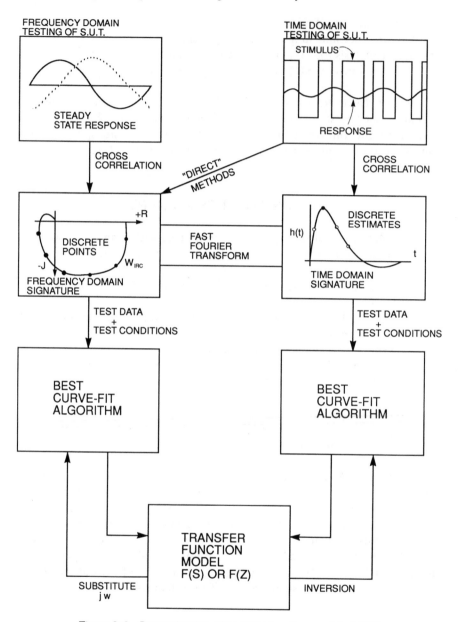

Figure 8–3 *Determination of transfer function model of SUT.*

basis of observations of the SUT error response to a very low frequency sinewave which simulates ship motion. Parameter settings are subsequently verified by extensive (and expensive) sea trials. In practice, it has been found that the "after refit" variability in performance measured among a family of

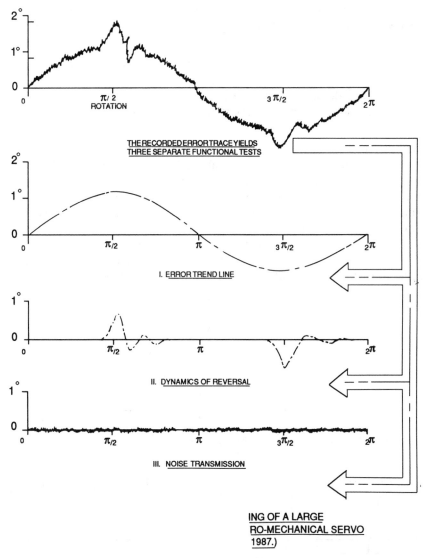

Figure 8–4 *Functional testing of a large shipborne electromechanical servo system. (From D. R. Towill, "Automatic Testing of Control Systems—Past, Present and Future," IERE Diamond Jubilee, Vol. 57, No. 2, 1987).*

SUTs is quite wide. It is therefore natural to consider ATE as a tuning aid, especially as a considerable amount of "expert" option can be gleaned from accessing the present vast stock of manual test records.

A typical functional testing result is given in Fig. 8–4. Discussions with "expert" artificers suggests that efficient tuning is achieved by noting the following three characteristics:

a. Error sinusoidal trend line, and in particular the peak error.
b. The nonlinear dynamics of reversal effect with regard to both magnitude and duration of the transient.
c. Noise transmission, and in particular the residual MSE.

With the SUT tuning parameters presently available to the artificer, there is a trade-off observable between the above three characteristics. Thus, increasing the loop gain reduces the peak error, but increases the residual MSE and possibly worsens the nonlinear dynamics as well. As an aid to efficient tuning it is therefore helpful to decompose the SUT return signal into the three constituent parts.

The resulting computer based tuning aid is shown in block diagram form in Fig. 8–5. A number of different filters have been developed at Cardiff in order to provide a "menu" of techniques with which to estimate the trend,

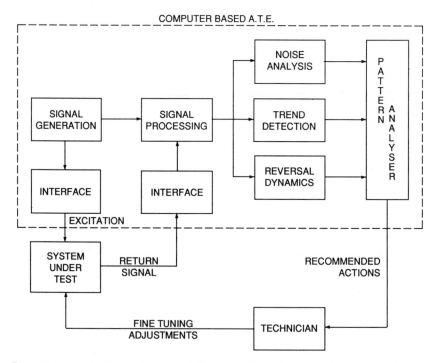

Figure 8–5 *Exploiting an ATE to provide fine tuning information for a large ship-borne electromechanical servo system.*

noise, and nonlinear dynamic components prior to entry into the pattern analyzer for comparison with known good profiles. Least squares, exponential smoother/corrector, and Kalman filters are all available for this purpose [9].

Subsequent to return signal filtering and pattern recognition, the recommended tuning adjustments can then be displayed for the artificer's consideration. Action then proceeds in an iterative manner until he is satisfied that a "good" system results. This use of ATE has the advantage of building on existing "expert" knowledge obtained historically from testing a particular SUT. For a particular class of system, a range of "fingerprints" can be stored in the ATE after every refit and used within the pattern analyzer to minimize the time taken for the "fine tuning" exercise.

THE SUT TEST SIGNATURE

The ATE will generate a measurement vector which will be a test signature or "fingerprint" for that particular SUT. This measurement signature will be of the form:

$$Y = \begin{bmatrix} y_1 & y_2 & y_3 & y_4 & \cdots & y_N \end{bmatrix}^T \tag{8-1}$$

and may be compared to DC values, step response at specific time delays, frequency response gain/phase characteristics, etc. They may refer to measurements made at one SUT access point, or may be obtained from a range of access points. Where the measurement vector is to be additionally used for diagnosis, there is a definite trade-off between the number of access points and the number of discrete frequency response gain/phase measurements needed to obtain a desired level of fault location [10].

It should also be noted that the measurement vector may be printed out in several ways. The elements may be: *differenced,* i.e., subtracted from nominal values; *scaled,* i.e., divided by nominal values so that all elements are non-dimensionalized; and/or *normalized* by dividing each element by a factor relating (for example, the Euclidean norm) to the magnitude of that particular vector. This latter step is found to be particularly useful in the subsequent fault diagnosis of "sick" SUTs, via both the "voting" and "nearest neighbor rule" techniques for pattern recognition.

To recognize the different nature of the various signals which make up the measurement vector, Eq. (8-1) may be partitioned to take the following form:

$$Y = \begin{bmatrix} \bar{y}_a & | & \bar{y}_b & | & \bar{y}_c & | & \bar{y}_d & | & etc. \end{bmatrix}^T \tag{8-2}$$

where $\bar{y}_a$ now represents a reduced vector of like physical measurements.

This grouping can subsequently be used to describe the dimensional commonality between signals, or the information content across signals.

TRANSFER FUNCTION MODELS OF CONTROL SYSTEMS

A linear SUT (or quasilinear SUT) may be reasonably described in the operational mode by a transfer function of the form:

$$F(s) = \left[\frac{\sum\limits_{i=0}^{i=v} b_i\, s^i}{\sum\limits_{i=0}^{i=n} a_i\, s^i} \right] \tag{8-3}$$

where s is the Laplace operator. If the test method determines the transfer function coefficients as output, then for a linear SUT the behaviour will be known for any input. For mildly nonlinear systems, a *set* of such transfer functions will be required to provide an adequate description of the SUT. Go/no go limits may be placed directly on the transfer function coefficients. However, as the SUT becomes more complex, tolerancing the coefficients becomes more involved. Either go/no go surfaces must be established, or tolerances set independently for each coefficient which are tighter than otherwise need be the case; thus at the margin unnecessarily failing "healthy" systems.

An interesting benefit of using the transfer function approach is that similarity between physically different SUTs may be readily identified. One particularly powerful technique which enables such comparison is the coefficient plane model [11]. For example, a family of complex high order tracking systems may be approximated by the type II coefficient plane model defined by

$$F(s) = \left[\frac{1 + c(s/\omega_0)}{1 + c(s/\omega_0) + b(s/\omega_0)^2 + (s/\omega_0)^3} \right] \tag{8-4}$$

where b and c are the coefficient plane parameters which determine dynamic response ω_0 is a scaling frequency which determines the speed of response of a given coefficient plane model. Furthermore, as shown in Table 8–1, for well-designed systems, the b and c values will lie in a very restricted part of the coefficient plane.

The coefficient plane modeling method is so powerful that if a tracker type SUT is tested and found to lie outside the "preferred" range of b and c, doubts are cast either on the adequacy of the SUT for the intended purpose,

Table 8-1   Coefficient Plane Type II Models Adequately Describing the Performance of High-Order Hardware Systems

	Hardware System		Coefficient Plane Model		
Description	Number of system zeros (q)	Number of system poles (n)	b	c	ω_0 (rad/sc)
Aircraft autoland system	1	6	1.80	1.89	0.18
Aircraft tracker	2	6	2.30	2.31	2.30
Satellite tracker	1	5	2.85	2.86	6.30
Gun control servo	4	10	2.17	1.98	10.70
Electrohydraulic drive	1	8	3.10	2.50	47.00

Source: D.R. Towill, *Coefficient Plane Models for Control System Analysis and Design,* Research Studies Press/Wiley, Chichester, U.K., 1981.

or alternatively on the modeling technique adopted. An additional advantage of using the coefficient plane model of the SUT is that general rules may be developed for modeling algorithms and checkout frequencies. For example, using sensitivity function analysis [12], it may be established that realistic test frequencies are $\omega_0/2$, ω_0, and $2\omega_0$. The SUT test signature then becomes

$$Y = \left[|F(\omega_0/2)|; \underline{/F(\omega_0/2)}; |F(\omega_0)|; \underline{/F(\omega_0)}; |F(2\omega_0)|; \underline{/F(2\omega_0)} \right] \quad (8\text{-}5)$$

in which each term relates to the input–output transfer function Eq. (8-5). Many simulations and associated field tests verify that this vector is perfectly adequate for checkout testing to validate satisfactory dynamic behavior of the SUT.

Under some circumstances, in order to obtain good correlation between simple dynamic tests and mission success rates, it is sometimes necessary to augment the above measurement vector. In our experience, direct measurement of system low frequency error greatly increases confidence in tracking system tests for large electromechanical systems. Extra data may also be needed for constraints on secondary resonances, noise cut-off rates, etc.

THE "FUZZY" NATURE OF CONTROL SYSTEM BEHAVIOR

By the nature of analogue systems, even if the prototype SUT exactly meets the design specification, there is no reason to suppose:

a. The prototype system will retain an identical response throughout its working life.

b. Subsequently manufactured SUTs will match the response of the prototype (they may, conceivably, be better, and may continuously improve in quality as the product line settles down).

The first factor is due to drift and aging, the second is because individual components have finite production tolerances. On average, these latter variations will balance out, but the second factor will result in natural spread around the average response. This envelope denotes the "fuzzy" nature of analogue SUT response in which a surprisingly loose acceptable "grey" performance region exists between the average response and an unacceptable response of a "sick" or "failed" system. Together with commonality encountered in poor test signal-to-noise ratios, such fuzziness substantially accounts for the difficulty in fault diagnosis of a "sick" analogue system.

The fuzzy envelope can be set by predicting the effect on the dynamic response of individual component tolerances and/or by feeding back results from a design stage simulation of system operational performance with various parameters perturbed to determine their effect on mission success [13]. An SUT whose performance lies within the resulting fuzzy envelope of Fig. 8–6, is defined as "healthy," i.e., will reasonably perform the mission, whereas an SUT with performance which lies outside the envelope is defined as "sick."

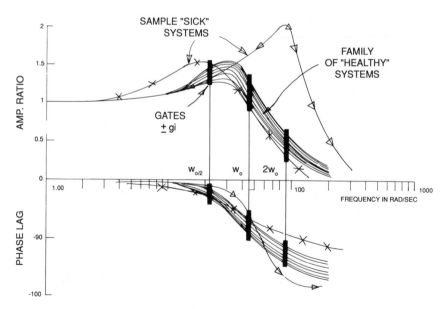

Figure 8–6 *Frequency domain checkout vector for high-confidence level in dynamic response conformance.*

The purpose of ATE checkout is to reliably classify the particular SUT as "sick" or "healthy." If the test is too stringent, an excessive number of "healthy" SUTs will be wrongly classified "sick"; if the test is too slack, too many "sick" SUTs will be wrongly classified as "healthy." In the first case the rework inventory will be excessive, whereas in the second case the mission success rate will decrease.

CHECKOUT BASED ON QUADRATIC PERFORMANCE CRITERIA

For checkout, we wish to select those data test features in Eq. (8-1) which give a high guarantee of rejecting "sick" systems. Broadly speaking, for checkout we are seeking a few features which are sensitive to changes in any parameter. The fault diagnosis problem, on the other hand, requires us to select features which discriminate between parameters.

With some judicious selection of test features, it is not difficult to make sure that each potentially "sick" system fails at more than one data point. The number of measurements denoting an SUT failure, averaged over the complete simulation, can then be used as a measure of effectiveness of the sampling scheme. Suitable algorithms are available for optimizing the best checkout features for a given method of test [14]. Basically, the algorithms seek to establish those test features sensitive to as many parameters as possible, at the same time seeing that all parameter variations are observable with the final vector selected.

ATE also permits us to form composite performance indices for checkout of an individual SUT. For example, if we sample the frequency response of N data points and then square the deviations, the performance index, written in the normalized form, becomes

$$PI = \sum_{i=1}^{i=N} \left\{ \frac{\Delta y_i}{\bar{g}_i} \right\}^2 \qquad (8\text{-}6)$$

where Δy_i is the response deviation at delay time t_i and g_i is the gate width applicable at the time delay. Such an index is intuitively appealing in control systems with their inherent "fuzzy" nature since large deviations indicating a "sick" system are weighted heavily. On the other hand, one single deviation just outside a gate would not necessarily classify the system as "sick" as the SUT would still perform reasonably well, but obviously not optimally.

A logical extension of this approach made possible by ATE developments is to insert a software model in parallel with the SUT, and subjected to the same stimulus. The outputs of model and SUT are then compared, and a judgment made via a deviation index which can be of the same form as Eq. (8-6). Any time varying stimulus, including normal operating signals, can be used. In the latter case the ATE will be used in an on-line condition monitoring mode, for example, in unmanned machining on flexible manufacturing systems (FMS) [15]. For preventive maintenance and scrap avoidance, additional software will be added to predict ahead to the time when the machine will be performing outside of tolerances. The machine will then be stopped at a convenient moment for remedial action via substitution of the appropriate line replaceable unit (LRU).

"CLOSED LOOP" TESTING

The added computing power of the fifth generation ATE plus the greatly increased reliability of digital devices has recently permitted the effective implementation of "CLOSED LOOP" testing. In this instance, "CLOSED LOOP" refers to the ATE simulating the mission on which the SUT is to be employed, and then estimating "real life" performance.

This idea dates back in the United Kingdom to at least 1970, when an aircraft blind landing autopilot was treated in closed loop mode [16]. An analogue computer was used to simulate the aircraft dynamics and space kinematics. Autopilot performance was assessed by measuring estimated aircraft vertical velocity and pitch rate at touchdown. Unfortunately, this test was rendered ineffective due to frequent malfunctions of the analogue computer. It therefore never came into regular airline service as was originally intended.

More recently, routine closed loop testing by simulation of the aerodynamics and kinematics has been proposed for guided missiles. Miss distance is the performance criterion used [17]. The relevant ATE is shown in Fig. 8–7, and is now operational at the U.S. Navy Weapons Quality Engineering Centre (WQEC). It is used in both closed-loop and open-loop modes. In the top-down approach closed-loop performance is related to subsystem parameters [and hence can be used to refine transfer function tests such as that illustrated in Eqs. (8-2) and (8-6).] A bottom-up approach is then implemented to relate the transfer function tests to components quality. This dual evaluation methodology has considerable cost-savings benefits realized via:

a. Acceleration of the system development and deployment process.
b. More efficient usage of the missile stockpile.
c. Elimination of unnecessary repairs and refurbishment.

Transfer function testing is still, of course, necessary as part of this ATE for a number of purposes such as fault diagnosis of "sick" SUTs and will be retained for minimizing rework problems. Also, the WQEC is not designed for rapid checkout of an SUT immediately prior to operational use. For such a confidence check a simple go/no go check is still preferred [18].

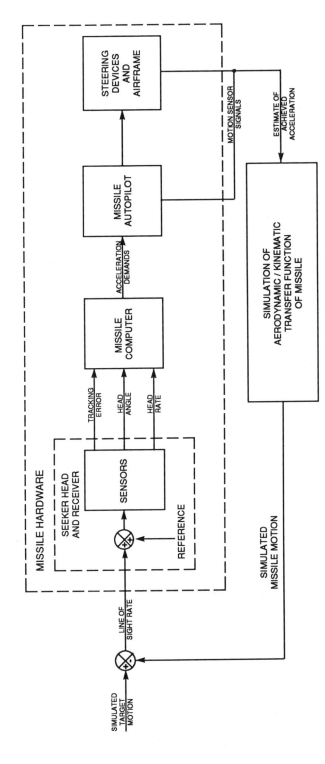

Figure 8-7 Use of ATE for "closed-loop" missile testing leading to checkout based on estimated miss distance for chosen mission. (After R. N. Schowengerdt and W. P. Koch, "Closed Loop Testing Best for Missiles," Microwave Syst. News, Vol. 11, Part 3, 1981).

CONCLUSIONS

Effective checkout must precede diagnosis. We have seen how ATE has evolved to the stage where fifth generation ATE is well placed to make judgments on system conformance, especially via "closed-loop" testing. However, for many nonmilitary applications, such sophistication is not cost effective. It is then necessary to build "insight" into the selection of appropriate procedures and associated "optimum" level of test automation. In particular, ATE built around the digital FRA is capable of making valuable contributions to test productivity and total quality assurance.

REFERENCES

[1] D.R. Towill, "Automatic Testing of Control Systems—Past, Present and Future," *IERE Diamond Jubilee,* Vol. 57, No. 2, pp. 67–80, 1987.

[2] R. Brown, "Calculator-Controlled Testing of Rate Gyroscopes," *Proc. Autotestcon '76,* 1976, pp. 81–86.

[3] P.J. Lawrence and G.J. Rogers, "Sequential Transfer-Function Synthesis From Measured Data," *Proc. IEEE,* Vol. 126. No. 1, pp. 104–106, 1979.

[4] L.H. Wedig, "Diagnostics and Productivity," *Proc. 25th IEEE Machine Tools Industry Conference,* Cincinnati, 1981, pp. 4–6.

[5] D.R. Towill and J.H. Williams, "The Automatic Test Station as a Quality Assurance Tool," *Proc. Autotestcon '78,* San Diego, 1978, pp. 257–261.

[6] G.W. Neuman and M. Battaglia, *Proc. AGARD-CD-361,* Brussels, 1984, pp. 25.1–25.6.

[7] P. Blenkinsop, "Automated Testing of Mechanical Products," *Automation (GB),* Vol. 20, No. 1, pp. 10–14, 1984.

[8] H.V. Harley and D.R. Towill, Automation of Large Electro-Mechanical System Testing," *IERE Conference Proceedings No. 30,* 1975, pp. 169–184.

[9] C. Cresswell, D.R. Towill and J.H. Williams, "Statistical Analysis of a Signal for Fault Location," in *Advances in Control,* Reidel, Dordrecht, 1980, pp. 388–398.

[10] M.A. Sarram, J.H. Williams, D.R. Towill and K.C. Varghese, "Optimisation of Access Points for ATE and Fault Location in Large Analogue Circuits and Systems," *Radio Electron. Eng.* Vol. 51, No. 9, pp. 435–446, 1981.

[11] D.R. Towill, *Coefficient Plane Models for Control Systems Analysis and Design,* Research Studies Press/Wiley, Chichester, U.K., 1981.

[12] D.R. Towill, "Analogue Model Identification of System Dynamic Error Transfer Functions," *Proc. 3rd IFAC Symposium,* The Hague, 1973, pp. 267–270.

[13] D.R. Towill and P.A. Payne, "Frequency Domain Approach to Automatic Testing of Control Systems," *Radio Electron. Eng.* Vol. 41, pp. 51–60, 1971.

[14] C. Morgan and D.R. Towill, "Frequency Domain Checkout of Aerospace Systems via Sensitivity Analysis," *Proc. IXth International Symposium on Technical Diagnostics* (IMEKO), London, 1981, pp. 1–11.47.

[15] A. Davies and C.G. Harris, "Automatic Fault Location—An Essential Requirement for Advanced Manufacturing Systems," *Maintenance Manage. Int.,* Vol. 4, pp. 109–116, 1984.

[16] J.D. Lamb, A.R. Pankhurst, and D.R. Towill, "Correlation Techniques Applied to the Dynamic Testing of Aircraft Autoland Systems," *Proc. 7th International Aerospace Symposium,* Cranfield, U.K., 1971, pp. 23.1–23.7.

[17] R.N. Schowengerdt and W.P. Koch, "Closed Loop Testing Best for Missiles," *Microwave Systems News,* Vol. 11, Pt. 3., pp. 100–113, 1981.

[18] D.R. Towill, "Dynamic Testing of Control Systems," *Radio Electron. Eng.,* Vol. 47, No. 4, pp. 505–521, 1977.

9

Testing of Analog Integrated Circuits

V. VISVANATHAN

The broad aim of an integrated circuit (IC) designer working on a specific product is to provide certain functionality at minimum cost. In practice this translates into many specific goals. Some of these goals, as, for example, the optimization of certain performance measures or the minimization of chip area, are well supported by computer tools for simulation and layout. Others, such as the design of manufacturable circuits, i.e., circuits whose performance is insensitive to the unavoidable fluctuations in the manufacturing process, are supported to some extent—and increasingly so in recent years— by computational methods and computer aids (see [1] for a good review). In all these instances, the state-of-the-art of computer tools is more advanced for digital design than for analog design. This is primarily due to the fact that digital circuits are more structured than analog circuits. In the digital world, the main problem that has to be addressed is one of managing the scale and the size of the design, while in the analog world the issues are often complex and competing, and of a detailed electrical nature.

Two aspects of the design process in which this disparity is particularly acute are test-program generation and design for testability. In digital design, methodologies such as built-in self test [2] can be used right from the early stages of the design process to address the issue of testability of the integrated circuit. In addition, fault simulation [3,4] (though computationally intensive) is often used to assess the effectiveness of a set of test vectors in detecting faults that might occur during manufacture. The combination of these techniques results in a design methodology where testing is an issue that is addressed early in the design. Thus, a complete design not only has the mask specifications for manufacture but also a set of test vectors that can uncover most faults in a resonable amount of testing time after manufacture.

In contrast, the analog design process is much less structured. No formal design-for-testability methodology exists, and fault simulation is rarely used to develop a set of tests that minimize testing costs. Although this is due to the complexity and relative intractability of the problem, it is nevertheless one that needs to be addressed. There have been many cases, in various companies, where an analog chip has had to go back for costly redesign due to the inordinate cost of the testing required to verify the goodness of the chip.

In this chapter, we aim to achieve two goals. First, we will describe the critical aspects of the analog testing problem and highlight the difficulties and challenges that confront the development of a general solution. Wherever appropriate, we will make a comparison with the corresponding issues in digital testing. Having established this background, we will describe some recent works that attempt to use a theoretical basis to develop testing strategies that minimize costs. We do not intend to provide a clear set of tried and proven techniques for test engineers since an established methodology does not exist at this time. Rather, the aim is to provide a glimpse of some attempts towards systematic solution. The hope is that this might interest and challenge researchers to tackle this difficult and important problem.

TESTING VS. DIAGNOSIS

The topic that we address in this chapter, should strictly speaking, be referred to as production testing—which is but one aspect of the various testing and diagnosis issues that arise in the design and manufacture of analog integrated circuits. When the first prototypes of an IC are built, complex and time-consuming diagnosis techniques are often used, if (as usual) the circuit does not behave as anticipated. Further, even when the design is deemed to be manufacturable, circuit diagnosis is often needed during the early phase of manufacture, in order to make modifications to the circuit with a view towards enhancing yield. However, for circuits that are produced in volume, as the manufacturing process stabilizes, the focus shifts from diagnosis to production testing.

In production testing, measurements are made solely to be able to decide whether an IC is good or not. For brevity, we will refer to this process simply as testing. Interestingly, IC testing can be viewed as a special case of the circuit diagnosis problem. In diagnosis, the aim is to be able to distinguish each fault from every other possible fault and the fault-free state. In contrast, in testing, it is only necessary to distinguish the good circuit from all faulty ones. In other words, testing is a diagnosis problem with the simplification that only the good circuit needs to be diagnosed.

In the volume production of mature ICs, the focus of the diagnosis effort is on the process line. This is due to two reasons. First, in most cases, it is either impossible or too expensive to repair individual ICs that fail testing. Second, for well-designed circuits, when the yield of a manufacturing line drops, it is typically due to a process fault that has eluded the process monitoring system. At this stage, it is imperative that the fault be speedily diagnosed. Often, this requires detailed analysis of measurements made on the ICs [5], and the techniques used are not unlike those used for circuit diagnosis. However, it is the process that is diagnosed, not the circuit.

To reiterate, the primary aim of production testing is to distinguish good ICs from bad ones. This selection is typically made at two stages of the manufacturing process: before and after packaging. The former stage is called wafer probe and the latter, final test. As the name suggests, wafer probe involves probing the individual ICs while they are still part of the wafer. Only those that pass testing at this stage are diced and assembled in their package. The reason for this two-step procedure is that packaging and final testing are more expensive than all other manufacturing steps [6]; therefore, only those ICs that have a high probability of passing the final test are packaged. However, packaging can also introduce faults; hence final testing is necessarily complete. As a consequence, the complete set of tests need not be applied during the wafer probe. The testing techniques that we will be discussing in this chapter exploit this fact. In order to achieve the goal of reducing overall manufacturing and testing costs, they may occasionally fail good circuits or pass faulty ones during wafer probe.

DIGITAL VS. ANALOG TESTING

A major reason why analog testing is more difficult than digital testing is that, although the latter is *fault-model*-driven, the former is *specification*-driven. In this section, we will explain these terms and their impact on testing methodology.

In the digital case, testing techniques are based on a fault model. The simplest of these is the single stuck-at 0 or 1 model. In this model, it is assumed that all failure mechanisms manifest themselves as a single node stuck at logic 0 or 1. Given such a model, one can use simulation to assess the fault coverage of a set of test vectors (inputs) [3,4]. Given a set of test vectors, if the simulated output (signature) of a fault is different from that of the good circuit, then this set of test vectors can detect the fault. Thus, simulation before manufacture can be used to determine a set of test vectors for post-manufacture testing. Similar analyses can be done to determine the testability of a design. If, for example, a very long set of vectors is required for adequate

fault coverage, it may be prudent to redesign the circuit before it is committed to manufacture. The field of digital testing is a rich one and it is not our
intention here to attempt to survey it. Nor do we wish to suggest that digital
testing is a closed field in which there are no open questions or major challenges.
However, in order to highlight the difference between the current state-of-the-
art of analog and digital testing, we wish to emphasize two points:

1. Every second of testing time (quite literally) adds to the cost of each
    unit being manufactured. Thus, in designs that are to be produced in
    volume, it is economical to use compute-intensive simulation-based
    techniques to determine a set of test vectors that provide adequate fault
    coverage while minimizing testing time.
2. Such a simulation-based methodology is made possible in the digital
    case because an adequate fault model exists.

In contrast, a generally accepted fault model does not exist for analog circuits. As a result, analog testing is usually specification-driven. Such an approach in its simplest form consists of testing the circuit for all its
specifications both during wafer-probe and final test. Consider for example
an operational amplifier with the following specifications:

DC gain $\geq$ 80 db
$f_T \geq$ 20 MHz
Total harmonic distortion at 4 kHz $\leq$ 0.002%
Total harmonic distortion at 1 MHz $\leq$ 0.1%
Settling time $\leq$ 200 ns
Power dissipation $\leq$ 3 mW

In a straightforward approach, the circuit is tested during wafer-probe to see
if it meets all of these specifications and only those that pass are packaged
and subject to final test.

In practice, certain simplifications are made during wafer-probe. Specification testing is preceded by simple parametric tests based on DC voltage and
current measurements that can detect obviously faulty chips. Also, high frequency measurements are avoided since probe capacitances make such measurements either erroneous or impossible. The above discussion suggests that
wafer-probe tests can and should be manipulated in order to minimize the
cost of the product. In [6], Maly and Pizlo provide an approach to wafer-
probe test specification that is based on statistical optimization techniques.
We shall describe their work in the following two sections.

We conclude this section with a discussion on how specifications are ar-
rived at. Given a set of specifications for a circuit, a basic question is: Are
these specifications necessary and sufficient? The sufficiency question arises
because a specified behavior is required of an analog circuit for a whole

range of input signals—for example, a frequency range—but it can be tested at only a finite subset of it. Returning to our simple op amp example, the following questions might be asked:

1. Is it sufficient to measure total harmonic distortion at 4 kHz and 1 MHz?
2. Is the settling time in response to a step input an adequate indicator of the circuit's performance in response to any transient signal that may appear at its input?
3. Will the circuit perform correctly when subject to unavoidable power supply and temperature variations in the field?

Conversely, one might argue that not all the specifications are necessary. This is an important issue since complex measurements require expensive data acquisition systems and also add to the total testing time.

Little work has been done to help answer these questions in a formal way even for subclasses of analog circuits. The answers are usually circuit and application dependent and are based on the insight and experience of the designer. Typically, specifications are negotiated between the IC designer and the designer of the system of which the IC is a part, or are dictated by the market place. For these reasons, the approaches that we shall discuss in the remainder of this chapter assume that the set of final tests is given and cannot be modified. However, these techniques exploit to their advantage the flexibility that is allowed in wafer-probe test specification.

SPECIFICATION-BASED TESTING

In [6], Maly and Pizlo provide a solution to the test tolerance assignment problem. In this section we shall formulate the problem and show that it is a subproblem of the more general problem of optimal specification-based testing. In the following section, we describe its solution. To this end, let $X^w \in \mathbf{R}^m$ (the space of real m-tuples) denote the values of m measurements made during wafer-probe, and $X^f \in \mathbf{R}^n$ denote the values of n measurements made during final test. Let L^w and U^w denote the lower and upper bounds for wafer-probe testing. In other words, a chip with measurements X^w is said to pass wafer-probe, if

$$L^w \leq X^w \leq U^w \qquad (9\text{-}1)$$

where the inequalities operate component-wise. Similarly, L^f and U^f denote the bounds for final testing. Note that a component of X^f may represent the same test measurement as a component of X^w. Also, some of the entries in L^f may be $-\infty$ while some of those in U^f may be ∞; i.e., some of the final specifications may be one-sided bounds.

For simplicity, in the rest of this section we shall sometimes refer to wafer-probe testing as Selection 1 and to final test as Selection 2. Let N denote the total number of chips manufactured, of which N_{P1} and N_{P2} denote respectively, the number of chips that pass Selection 1 and Selection 2. Then, Y_1 and Y_2, the yields of Selection 1 and Selection 2, respectively, are

$$Y_1 = N_{P1} / N \tag{9-2a}$$

$$Y_2 = N_{P2} / N_{P1} \tag{9-2b}$$

Let V_C denote the value of one packaged chip and C_P the manufacturing cost computed per chip for all fabrication steps except packaging and final testing. Let the cost of packaging and final testing for one chip be denoted by C_A. The total value added by manufacturing N chips is

$$V_T = NY_1Y_2V_C - NC_P - NY_1C_A$$

$$= N\left[Y_1\left(Y_2V_C - C_A\right) - C_P\right] \tag{9-3}$$

The test tolerance assignment (TTA) problem can now be stated as: Choose values L^w_{opt} and U^w_{opt} that solve

$$\max\nolimits_{L^w, U^w} V_T \tag{9-4}$$

Note the following features of the problem formulation:

1. No fault model is assumed.
2. The variables in the optimization do not include L^f and U^f, i.e., the bounds for final testing can not be changed.
3. No indication is given as to how the wafer-probe tests are selected. Since C_P includes the cost of applying wafer-probe tests, V_T will change if these tests are changed. Hence the problem being solved here is not the general specification-based testing problem, in which both the set of wafer-probe tests and the corresponding values of L^w_{opt} and U^w_{opt} would be selected to maximize the total value added. Rather, a more specific TTA problem is being addressed, where optimal values for L^w and U^w corresponding to a predetermined set of wafer-probe tests are sought.

The tests made in selection 1 are usually different from those made in Selection 2. Typically, Selection 1 would include simple parametric tests based on DC measurements and exclude any high-frequency tests that may be required in Selection 2. Nevertheless, the choices made for L^w and U^w impact upon Y_2 and hence V_T. This is because X^w and X^f fluctuate due to common process disturbances and are therefore correlated [5,7]. Thus, by using appropriate vectors L^w and U^w, a preselection of ICs can be performed by rejecting those that are likely to fail final test. To summarize:

1. If the tolerances $[L^w, U^w]$ are too tight, many chips that would have passed Selection 2 will fail Selection 1.
2. If the tolerances $[L^w, U^w]$ are too relaxed, many chips that pass Selection 1 will be packaged and then rejected in Selection 2.

In either case the total value added (V_T) would decrease. Hence the need for selecting L^w and U^w optimally.

SOLUTION OF THE TEST TOLERANCE ASSIGNMENT PROBLEM

The TTA problem (9-4) is an optimization problem in which the objective function V_T is not known explicitly in terms of the variables L^w and U^w. Therefore, before we attempt an optimization we must be able to estimate the function, that is, given a choice for L^w and U^w, we should be able to determine a sufficiently good approximation (denoted by V^*_T) to the corresponding value of V_T. This function-estimation problem is complicated by the fact that the quantity being estimated is statistical in nature. As a further consequence, the solution to the TTA problem determined using this estimate is meaningful only in a statistical sense; i.e., the payoff will be seen in a real process only when sufficiently many circuits are manufactured.

Broadly, there are two approaches to statistical estimation: design of experiments and statistical simulation. Design of experiments is a fairly mature discipline in the field of statistics. However, its application to computer-aided design and testing of integrated circuits is in its infancy. We will therefore provide a brief overview of the approach as it applies to the problem of estimating V_T. The reader is referred to [8] for a more thorough and general exposition.

The basic idea in design of experiments is to use various choices for the tolerance window $[L^w, U^w]$ and record the yields Y_1 and Y_2 corresponding to each choice. V_T is then easily calculated using (9-3). Based on this information, a multidimensional polynomial V^*_T is constructed. Usually, the quadratic function

$$V^*_T = \alpha + a^t z + z^t \mathbf{A}\, z \qquad (9\text{-}5)$$

the vector $z \in \mathbf{R}^k$, $k = 2m$, denotes the concatenation of L^w and U^w suffices, provided that the right values are chosen for the coefficients α, a, and $\mathbf{A}$. Note that $\alpha \in \mathbf{R}$, $a \in \mathbf{R}^k$, and $\mathbf{A} \in \mathbf{R}^{k \times k}$ is a symmetric matrix. The superscript t denotes transpose.

The construction procedure is as follows. First, for each component of the vector z, a low, nominal and high value are determined based on the knowledge of the process and design engineers. This results in 3^k possible choices for z. Running an experiment for each one of these combinations—called a full factorial experiment—is prohibitively expensive. However, since α, a, and $\mathbf{A}$ contain only $k^2/2 + 3k/2 + 1$ coefficients, some of which may be known *a priori* to be zero, a small subset of a full factorial experiment will be sufficient, provided that the *right* subset is used. The key contribution of design-of-experiments techniques is the methodology to determine which experiments give the best information for constructing a V^*_T that is a good approximation of V_T. After a set of experiments have been conducted and the corresponding values of V^*_T determined, the coefficients of (9-5) are easily determined through standard regression analysis techniques [8]. The solution to the TTA problem, $z_{\text{opt}} = [L^w_{\text{opt}}, U^w_{\text{opt}}]$, is

$$z_{\text{opt}} = -\mathbf{A}^{-1}a \qquad (9\text{-}6)$$

The value of z_{opt} calculated using (9-6) may fall outside the range of the values of z used in the experiments. Since this is equivalent to using extrapolation (which is often unreliable) to determine V^*_T, z_{opt} may be a poor approximation to the solution of (9-4). The reader is referred to [6] for details on how this situation is handled, additional refinements to the technique, and an example of its application.

In the procedure described above, in order to determine the V_T corresponding to a choice of z (an experiment), one needs to manufacture sufficiently many ICs and test them with this choice of test tolerances, so that the corresponding measured yield is statistically significant. Since the experimental test tolerances can be far from the optimal settings, this constitutes a definite, albeit ultimately worthwhile, learning cost. One could, in principle, reduce this cost by using some advanced statistical techniques whereby yields can be accurately estimated from small samples. These approaches are, however, unattractive since they involve making significant perturbations to the process line. A more promising and far less invasive approach is in the use of simulation.

The main idea in a simulation-based approach is to have a suite of simulators, which when properly calibrated and linked together, accurately mimic the various stages of the process line. The reader is referred to [1] for a broad overview of the application of IC process simulation to various aspects of circuit design, manufacture, and testing. The paper by Maly, Strojwas, and Director [9] concentrates on yield prediction—which is the aspect of manufacturing-based simulation that is relevant to the TTA problem—and provides a detailed and thorough exposition.

Since yield prediction requires simulating the aggregate behavior of the manufacturing line, these simulators are necessarily statistical in nature [7].

Further, unlike simulators that are used to understand the behavior of IC processes and devices at a detailed physical level [10], statistical simulators are used to predict the behavior of an existing process line. As a result, they use to their advantage various statistical model-building techniques to accurately predict input-output behavior with far fewer computations than a physical simulator. Because of this computational efficiency, Monte Carlo simulation and hence yield prediction is possible.

The above discussion should not be construed to mean that no information about the physical behavior of manufacturing processes is incorporated into statistical simulators. Indeed, especially in the context of yield prediction, it is important that models of the failure mechanisms in IC manufacturing be included in these simulators. However, these physics-based approaches are judiciously mixed with statistics-based techniques, resulting in simulators that are both computationally efficient and accurate for their application domain.

It is easy to see that if such a simulation system is available and has been tuned to mimic the manufacturing line of interest, the TTA problem can be solved entirely on a computer. The experiments are designed as before, and the manufacture and testing of a large number of ICs is simulated and the yields corresponding to each choice of wafer-probe test tolerances is obtained. Next, regression analysis is applied as described previously, the quadratic function (9-5) is determined and the optimal test tolerances derived from (9-6).

The simulation-based approach has a number of addition advantages. Various combinations of wafer-probe tests can be tried, and for each one a more exhaustive set of test tolerances can be experimented with than if one were working directly on the real process line. Most importantly, this work can be done hand-in-hand with circuit design, thereby reducing the possibility of an unpleasant and costly surprise after the design has been committed to manufacture. The principal challenges in making such an approach practically viable are in the modeling area. Special attention should be paid to the development of accurate and computationally efficient techniques that can be used to predict the effect of local defects (those that affect a very small region of an IC) on electrical behavior.

CONSIDERATIONS FOR FAULT-MODEL-BASED TESTING

In the previous section, we described one approach to effective wafer-probe testing based on optimal test tolerance assignment and concluded with a discussion on how its impact on the product realization process could be further enhanced through the use of statistical simulation. The availability of a fault model opens other avenues to the realization of the goal of easing the testing bottleneck. We therefore devote the remainder of this chapter to the fault-model-based testing. We discuss background issues in this section and continue in the next one by describing an approach to fault-model-based wafer-probe testing.

A fault model captures the likely failures that can occur in manufacturing as modifications to the circuit description used for simulation. These modifications can in general fall into one of two types: structural faults or parametric faults. Changes to the topology of the circuit are structural faults, whereas variations in device model parameters are parametric faults. The effect of these faults is that they cause circuit failures, which can be classified as hard failures or soft failures. When the value of a performance measure lies marginally outside the specification range, then the failure is referred to as being soft, while a large error in a performance measure or qualitatively incorrect circuit performance (for example, instability) is a hard failure.

Structural faults usually cause only hard failures, whereas parametric faults can cause both hard and soft failures. These faults are themselves caused by what is called process disturbances [5,7], i.e., perturbations to the manufacturing process. These disturbances can be classified as local or global. Local disturbances, which include spot defects and oxide pinholes, affect a small region of an IC. On the other hand, global disturbances affect all the devices on a chip and often an entire wafer or even a complete lot. These disturbances are caused by fluctuations in the manufacturing process that result in large, unacceptable variations in quantities like substrate concentration or surface mobility.

As even this brief description suggests, the chain of cause and effect relationships from process disturbances to circuit faults is a complex one which must be understood and modeled if a viable fault model is to be developed for analog testing. The reader is referred to [5] , [9], and [11] for details on a fairly sophisticated attempt to solve this problem. Here we will take a more simplistic approach.

We begin by observing that prior to wafer-probe testing, there are a number of inspection and selection steps in which entire wafers are discarded if parameters that have a global effect (like resistivity or oxide thickness) have values outside a prescribed range. Hence, one can (if somewhat simplistically) assume that the wafers that arrive at the wafer-probe testing station have not been affected by acute global disturbances that manifest themselves as hard failures caused by "large" parametric faults. Within this line of argument, the circuits that are tested at wafer-probe fall into one of two categories:

1. Those with hard failures due to structural faults caused by local disturbances.
2. Those with soft failures.

Since in practice it is often necessary to determine the value of each performance measure—which is done in final test—to screen out all soft failures, our focus here is on the development and use of a fault model to efficiently detect the former category of failures during wafer-probe testing. Of course, it is advantageous if the resulting wafer-probe tests also screen out most soft failures without failing too many good circuits. We shall briefly touch upon this issue in the final section.

To reiterate, our aim in the remainder of this section is to describe fault models that can be used to determine the structural faults that are likely to occur in an IC. In the following section, we will describe a technique developed by Milor and Visvanathan [12], whereby inexpensive DC tests are used during wafer-probe to detect circuits with structural faults.

As described previously, structural faults are typically caused by local disturbances which are also known as spot or point defects. These defects can be classified into one of three categories: silicon substrate inhomogeneities, local surface contaminations, and photolithography related point defects [13]. Complete and accurate physical modeling of these defects is difficult. Hence, Shen, Maly and Ferguson [11] have developed a statistical approach based on data obtained from actual measurements. Further, the effect of these disturbances on a circuit is dependent on design rules and more specifically on the circuit layout. Therefore, the approach described in [11] combines process and layout information to determine a rank ordered list of structural faults that are likely to occur in a given circuit.

This approach—though possibly necessary for analog circuits—is complicated. Hence, Milor and Visvanathan [12,14] use a considerably simpler fault model based on work reported in [15] and [16] to evaluate the applicability of their approach. The model used for CMOS circuits assumes that multiple faults are very unlikely. Further, it is assumed that the likely single faults are one of the following four types: gate-drain short, gate-source short, drain open, and source open. Additionally, no probabilities are associated with each fault, i.e., it is implicitly assumed that the gate-drain short of one mosfet is as likely as, say, the drain contact of some other mosfet being open. Not withstanding its simplicity, this model serves the useful purpose of demonstrating the viability of the approach to be described in the next section. The development of a fault model that can accurately predict the effect of process disturbances on a circuit, without requiring complicated line measurements or compute-intensive analysis, is an important area that needs investigation.

AN APPROACH TO FAULT-MODEL-BASED TESTING

Using the simple fault model just described, we can, for a given circuit, describe each fault as a modified (faulty) circuit which is structurally slightly different from the described (good) circuit. Then, the outputs (signature) corresponding to a set of test inputs can be determined through simulation for the good circuit and for each faulty circuit. If the signature of each fault is distinguishable from that of the good circuit, then, clearly, this set of tests is sufficient for detecting all faults in the fault list. Note that the criterion for a good set of tests is that it should be able to detect all faults on a fault list and need bear no resemblance to the specification tests used after packaging. Further, such a set of tests and the associated test procedure can be developed prior to manufacture.

Two aspects of analog testing makes fault signature calculation a nontrivial problem. First, even for (active) linear circuits, the testing problem is necessarily nonlinear. For example, if a resistor is open-circuited, it will completely change the bias point of some of the transistors in the circuit. Therefore, the fault cannot be modeled as a low-rank modification of the small-signal characteristics of the good circuit. Second, variations in process-related parameters result in variations in the circuit output. For example, the DC output voltage would typically vary if there are variations in the oxide thickness. Since even for a well-controlled process there is a certain amount of variation in certain process-related parameters, the signature of even the good circuit is not a single point in the space of output measurements but rather a probability density function in that space.

Since structural faults distort the DC behavior of a circuit significantly, and since DC testing is inexpensive, in this section we describe an approach to wafer-probe testing that is based on DC test measurements. We first describe a technique for efficiently finding meaningful approximations to the signatures of both the good and faulty circuits. Next, a simple procedure for determining the ambiguity set, i.e., the set of faults which are indistinguishable from the good circuit, is described. Following this, a greedy heuristic algorithm for selecting additional test points, in order to reduce the size of the ambiguity set, is given. The combination of these algorithms results in a promising approach to fault-model-based wafer-probe testing and test point selection; its viability is demonstrated with an example.

Let the allowed process variations be described as variations in n statistically independent parameters, $\beta_1-\beta_n$. Given the probability density functions associated with each of the β_i's, we define a process tolerance box C in n-space with probability $p < 1$—the value of p is chosen to be close to 1—as follows [17]:
We split the probability p equally among the n parameters, i.e.,

$$p_i = p^{1/n}$$

Then, if $\overline{\beta}_i$ is the nominal value of the ith parameter, we determine $\Delta\beta_i$, which solves

$$P(\beta_i - \Delta\beta_i \le \beta_i \le \overline{\beta}_i + \Delta\beta_i) = p_i$$

where $P(S)$ denotes the probability of S. Since the $\beta_i's$ are statistically independent, the hyper-rectangle C resulting from the Cartesian product of these intervals has an associated probability p, i.e., if $\beta \equiv [\beta_1, \cdots, \beta_n]^t$, then

$$P\,(\beta \in C) = p \qquad (9\text{-}7)$$

Now suppose that the circuit has m test outputs. Then, for a given set of values for the DC inputs, the nominal values of the DC output measurements for the good circuit is denoted by

$$\bar{y} = F\,(\bar{\beta}) \qquad (9\text{-}8)$$

and can be evaluated via a DC operation point analysis. Now consider the region

$$R = F(C)$$

and let y denote an arbitrary test measurement at the outputs. Then, for the good circuit, due to (9-7),

$$P(\,y \in R) = p$$

We call the region R the good signature—a physically meaningful definition if p is close to 1—and will describe an efficient algorithm to find a good approximation to it. Since the process tolerance box is a small region around the nominal parameter values $\bar{\beta}$, we linearize F around this point and approximate R by

$$\hat{R} = \bar{y} + AC \qquad (9\text{-}9)$$

where the origin in β-space has been moved to $\bar{\beta}$, and

$$A \;=\; \frac{\partial F}{\partial \beta}\,(\bar{\beta})$$

is the sensitivity matrix.

Similar to the good signature, there is a fault signature associated with each fault k, $k = 1, \cdots, K$, given by

$$R^k = F^k\,(C)$$

where F^k represents the circuit equations describing the modified circuit associated with the kth (structural) fault. As with the good signature, R^k can be approximated by

$$\hat{R}^k = \bar{y}^k + A^k C \qquad\qquad (9\text{-}10)$$

where $\bar{y}^k$ and A^k are the nominal response and sensitivity matrix, respectively, for the kth faulty circuit. Then, given that p is close to 1 and that the linearization of the good and faulty circuits (with respect to process parameter variations) is a valid approximation, we can, with a high degree of confidence, say that

$$\textit{If } \hat{R} \cap \hat{R}^i = \emptyset \text{ for all } i = 1, \cdots, K$$

Then an IC is good if and only if the test measurement $y \in \hat{R}$

If, for a particular fault k,

$$\hat{R} \cap \hat{R}^k \neq \emptyset \qquad\qquad (9\text{-}11)$$

Then we say that the fault k belongs to the ambiguity set (called Ω).

We will now briefly describe the algorithms for signature calculation and test point selection. The reader is referred to [12], [14], [18] for further details. Note from (9-9) and (9-10) that calculating the good and faulty signatures amounts to finding the image of a hypercube under a linear transformation. The linear transformation and the nominal response can be determined from DC operating point and sensitivity analyses of the good and faulty circuits. The hypercube C is transformed by the sensitivity matrix into a centrosymmetric polytope which can be determined efficiently using computational geometry techniques. The algorithm works as follows. Consider the transformation

$$Y = AC$$

where each column of A is a vector in $\mathbf{R}^3$ and C is a hypercube in $\mathbf{R}^n$ centered at the origin with vertices at ± 1. Clearly, Y is the convex hull of the images of the vertices of C; however, it is impractical to determine Y by determining the image of each of the 2^n vertices of C. Instead, one can directly determine all the boundary planes of Y. Every pair of linearly independent columns of A defines a plane and there can be a maximum of $n(n-1)/2$ of them, this being the case when each pair of columns defines a unique plane. For each of these planes P_i, we flip the columns of A not on the plane onto one side of it and add them up to get a point p_i. The planes passing through p_i and $-p_i$ and parallel to P_i, are boundary planes of Y. Further, there are no other boundary planes than the ones just described. When there are m (more than three) test measurements, the intuitive explanation is essentially the same, except, of course, that the planes P_i described above generalize to $(m-1)$—dimensional hyperplanes. Each one of these boundary hyperplanes is defined by

$(m-1)$ columns of A and can be determined by solving an $m \times m$ system of linear equations.

For a given set of test points, the ambiguity group Ω can be determined by testing the condition (9-11). If Ω is sufficiently small, then the fault coverage is deemed to be adequate and the wafer-probe tester can be programmed to check if the test measurements lie within $\hat{R}$. If Ω is large, additional tests are required. The heuristic suggested in [12,14] is to pick the test (from a set of candidates) for which the nominal response of the faulty circuits in Ω deviate the most from that of the good circuit. Having picked this test, the new good and faulty signatures (for the elements of Ω) are computed, and those faults that are now detectable are removed from Ω. This iterative process is continued until there is sufficient fault coverage.

We conclude this section with an example from [14]. The circuit studied was a CMOS opamp with 22 circuit nodes, two primary outputs, and 114 structural faults. Process variations were captured as normal distributions in 13 MOS model parameters. It was determined that 81% of the faults were detectable from DC measurements at the primary outputs, 99% of the faults with five test points, whereas seven test points were needed for 100% fault coverage. Clearly, a high percentage of structural faults can be detected with very few test points. It also appears that it may be best to settle for less than 100% fault coverage with DC tests since the savings obtained by avoiding packaging and final testing for a few faulty circuits will not offset the cost (in terms of chip area) of introducing additional probe points.

ACKNOWLEDGMENTS

The author is grateful to P. Sadayappan for constant encouragement and feedback, without which this chapter would not have been completed. He would also like to thank H. Khorramabadi for carefully reviewing the manuscript and providing helpful comments.

REFERENCES

[1] S. W. Director, "Manufacturing-Based Simulation: An Overview," *IEEE Circuits Devices Mag.*, Vol. 3, No. 5, pp. 3–9, Sep. 1987.

[2] E. J. McCluskey (Guest Ed.), *IEEE Trans. Comput. Aided Des.*, Special Issue on Testable and Maintainable Design, Vol. CAD-7, No. 1, Jan. 1988.

[3] R. E. Bryant and M. D. Schustor, "Fault Simulation of MOS Digital Circuits," *VLSI Des.* Vol. 4, No. 6, pp. 24–30, Oct. 1983.

[4] C-Y. Lo, H. N. Nham, and A. K. Bose, "Algorithms for an Advanced Fault Simulation System in MOTIS," *IEEE Trans. Comput. Aided Des.*, Vol. CAD-6, No. 2, pp. 232–240, Mar. 1987.

[5] A. J. Strojwas and S. W. Director, "A Pattern Recognition Based Method for IC

Failure Analysis," *IEEE Trans. Comput. Aided Des.,* Vol. CAD-4, No. 1, pp. 76–92, Jan. 1985.

[6] W. Maly and Z. Pizlo, "Tolerance Assignment for IC Selection Tests," *IEEE Trans. Comput. Aided Des.,* Vol. CAD-4, No. 2, pp. 156–162, Apr. 1985.

[7] S. R. Nassif, A. J. Strojwas, and S. W. Director, "FABRICS II: A Statistically Based IC Fabrication Process Simulator," *IEEE Trans. Comput. Aided Des.,* Vol. CAD-3, No. 1, pp. 20–46, Jan. 1984.

[8] G. E. P. Box, W. G. Hunter, and J. S. Hunter, *Statistics for Experimenters: An Introduction to Design, Data Analysis and Model Building,* Wiley, New York, 1978.

[9] W. Maly, A. J. Strojwas, and S. W. Director, "VLSI Yield Prediction and Estimation: A Unified Framework," *IEEE Trans. Comput. Aided Des.,* Vol. CAD-5, No. 1, pp. 114–130, Jan. 1986.

[10] W. L. Engl (Ed.), *Process and Device Modeling,* Elsevier, New York, 1986.

[11] J. P. Shen, W. Maly, and F. J. Ferguson, "Inductive Fault Analysis of MOS Integrated Circuits," *IEEE Des. Test,* Vol. 12, No. 6, pp. 13–26, Dec. 1985.

[12] L. Milor and V. Visvanathan, "Detection of Catastrophic Faults in Analog Integrated Circuits," *IEEE Trans. Comput. Aided Des.,* to appear; also, Memorandum No. UCB/ERL M88/3, University of California, Berkeley, and Technical Memorandum *52173-871228-01TM,* AT&T Bell Laboratories.

[13] K. W. Ravi, *Imperfections and Impurities in Semiconductor Silicon,* Wiley, New York, 1981.

[14] L. Milor and V. Visvanathan, "Efficient Go/No-Go Testing of Analog Circuits," *Proc. IEEE Int. Symp. Circuits Syst.,* IEEE, NY, pp. 414–417, 1987.

[15] P. Banerjee and J. A. Abraham, "Fault Characterization of VLSI MOS Circuits," *Proc. IEEE Int. Conf. Circuits and Computers,* IEEE, NY, pp. 564–568, 1982.

[16] J. Galiay, Y. Crouzet, and M. Vergniault, "Physical Versus Logical Fault Models in MOS LSI Circuits: Impact on Their Testability," *IEEE Trans. Comput.,* Vol. C-29, No. 6, pp. 527–531, Jun. 1980.

[17] V. Visvanathan. "Variational Analysis of Integrated Circuits," *Proc. IEEE Int. Conf. Comput. Aided Des.,* IEEE, N.Y., pp. 228–231, 1986.

[18] V. Visvanathan and L. Milor, "An Efficient Algorithm to Determine the Image of a Parallelepiped Under a Linear Transformation," *Proc. ACM Symp. on Computational Geometry,* Assoc. for Computing Machinery, NY, pp. 207–215, 1986.

10

A Unified Theory on Test Generation for Analog/Digital Systems

LANG TONG
and
RUEY-WEN LIU

Fault testing is a crucially important issue in the development of VLSI circuits. Although fault testing problems have been studied extensively for digital systems, especially in the context of classical faults in logic circuits, most of the work deals exclusively with the problem of finding an efficient algorithm for generating test. Very little effort has been devoted to revealing the underline fundamental structure of testing problem. As a result, the techniques and theories developed in digital system testing have not been successfully extended to more general cases. On the other hand, the demand is mounting for techniques and theories of fault testing not only for digital systems, but also for analog/digital hybrid systems. Therefore, a unified theory for fault testing is needed.

Complexity is a fundamental issue to the fault testing, digital, and analog. A large system comprises many subsystems and each subsystem may have a set of faults under test. We want to design a test signal so that if any one of the faults occurs, the output of the test signals will indicate a fault. Since there may be thousands of possible faults for each subsystem and there may be hundreds of subsystems in each system, the test signal to be designed has to cover a gigantic number of faults. Furthermore, each fault may interact with others in many different ways through the interconnections of subsystems; this will make the test signal design problem very difficult indeed.

In the fault testing community, the most successful case is the testing of classical stuck-at-fault in logic circuits. In this case, the issue of complexity has been resolved to a large extent. A close observation of the reasons that make the testing of classical faults successful shows that its test generation uses two important properties:

Property I.   The test signal for a subsystem to cover its entire fault set can be derived from the test signals of individual faults in the fault-set.

Property II.   The test signal for an interconnected system can be derived from test signals of its subsystems.

With these two properties, the complexity of generating a test signal to cover all possible faults of an interconnected system is completely "decoupled" to many simple problems of designing test signals for a single fault of an individual subsystem.

A closer examination reveals that the two properties cited above are characteristics of the system and the faults under test. They are not characteristics of the method employed for the generation of the test. Hence, one may ask a fundamental question: Are there other systems which share the same two properties, and what kind of systems are they if they exist? If so, the generation of testing signals of these systems can then also be done in the decoupled way similar to that for the classical faults of digital systems. The purpose of this paper is to give a complete answer to the above question.

Since the above question is general in nature, we have to approach this problem in a general system theoretical setting. In the first section, abstract definitions of systems, faults, test, etc. are first presented, and then it is shown that if both the original system and the faulty system are causal and time-invariant, then Property I will be satisfied. Note that this condition does not require the system to be memoryless. The question regarding Property II is completely answered in the second and third sections. Three case studies are then presented in the fourth section. The first case shows that the general theory is consistent with the case of the classical stuck-at-fault in digital systems. The nonclassical faults for memoryless logic circuits is considered next. Some new results with regard to the length of testing sequence are obtained and application to the test generation of iterative logic array (ILA) is presented. Finally, an example of a digital/analog hybrid system is given for illustration.

NOTATION AND BASIC CONCEPTS

The main function of this section is to provide a conceptual and notational framework in terms of which the techniques and theories of fault testing of general systems can be presented in a clear and concise fashion.

Let the system be described completely by the input–output state equation [1]:

$$y = A(s,u), \quad s \in \Sigma \tag{10-1}$$

where u and y are the input and output of the system, respectively. Σ is the state space while s is the state of the system. Input u and output y are defined on the same finite time interval. This system can be analog, digital, or analog/digital hybrid.

Definition 1 (Observable Fault).   Let $\mathcal{F}$ be the set of possible (physical) faults. For each $f \in \mathcal{F}$, let system $\mathcal{A}$ be changed to a fault system $\mathcal{A}_f$ described by $A_f(\cdot\,;\cdot)$ and Σ_f. $\mathcal{A}$ is said to have an *observable fault* f if there exists an input u such that

$$\exists\, s \in \Sigma, \quad A_f(s_f, u) \neq A(s,u) \quad \text{for all } s_f \in \Sigma_f \tag{10-2}$$

or

$$\exists\, s_f \in \Sigma_f, \quad A_f(s_f, u) \neq A(s,u) \quad \text{for all } s \in \Sigma \tag{10-3}$$

Remarks.

1. The list of faults are usually physical faults. They are derived from fault modeling, fault analysis, and/or fault collapsing.
2. In the literature, the conventional definition for the sequential circuit assumes that the state spaces of $\mathcal{A}$ and $\mathcal{A}_f$ are the same, i.e., $\Sigma_f = \Sigma$, and the initial conditions are unaltered by faults. In this case, the above equations can be reduced to the simpler form:

$$\exists\, s \in \Sigma, \quad A_f(s,u) \neq A(s,u) \quad \text{for some } u$$

Definition 2 (Test).   An input u defined on a finite time interval is a *test for fault* $f \in \mathcal{F}$ if

$$A_f(s_f, u) \neq A(s,u) \quad \text{for all } s \in \Sigma \text{ and all } s_f \in \Sigma_f \tag{10-4}$$

An input u is a test for $\mathcal{F}$ if u is a test for every f in $\mathcal{F}$.

Remark.   There is a crucial difference between these two definitions. When $\mathcal{A}$ has observable fault, it is necessary that an erroneous output can always be generated by some input signal u. On the other hand, in order for an input signal u to be a test, it is necessary that any output generated by u is erroneous, regardless of the initial condition.

The purpose of test generation is to find a test for a given fault set $\mathscr{F}$, which requires it to be a test for *all* f in $\mathscr{F}$. This would be a complex problem if $\mathscr{F}$ is large. The following two theorems provide a general condition so that this complex problem can be "decoupled" into many simpler problems.

Theorem 1. Let $\mathscr{A}$ and $\mathscr{A}_f$ be causal and time-invariant [2]. If u is a test for a fault $f \in \mathscr{F}$, then $u' \cdot u$ and $u \cdot u'$ are also tests for f, where u' is any input defined on a finite interval. Here $u \cdot v$ denotes the signal obtained by concatenate v after u.

Proof. Let us first prove that $u' \cdot u$ is also a test. We need to show that

$$A_f(s_f, u' \cdot u) \neq A(s, u' \cdot u) \quad \text{for all } s \in \Sigma \text{ and } s_f \in \Sigma_f \qquad (10\text{-}5)$$

Since $\mathscr{A}$ and $\mathscr{A}_f$ are causal and time-invariant, they satisfy a separation property of state, i.e.,

$$A_f(s_f, u' \cdot u) = A_f(s_f, u') \cdot A_f(s_{f'}, u) \qquad (10\text{-}6)$$

and

$$A(s, u' \cdot u) = A(s, u') \cdot A(s', u) \qquad (10\text{-}7)$$

where $s_{f'} \in \Sigma_f$ is the state transferred from s_f by u' in the fault system $\mathscr{A}_f$ and $s' \in \Sigma$ is the state transferred from s by u' in the normal system $\mathscr{A}$. Since u is a test, we have

$$A_f(s_{f'}, u) \neq A(s', u) \qquad (10\text{-}8)$$

Hence (10-5) is evident and $u' \cdot u$ is a test. Similarly, we can also prove the case of $u \cdot u'$. Theorem 1 is then proved.

A general condition for Property I is given in the next theorem.

Theorem 2. Let $\mathscr{A}$ and $\mathscr{A}_f$ be causal and time-invariant. If u is a test for fault f and u' for fault f', then $u \cdot u'$ is a test for $\{ f, f' \}$.

Proof. By Theorem 1, $u \cdot u'$ is a test for both f and f'.

This is good news. Since almost all systems under testing are causal and time-invariant, Property I is valid for almost all systems, including nonlinear systems and systems with memory. Property I implies that if $\mathscr{F}$ is finite, then the test of the entire set $\mathscr{F}$ can be derived by finding the test of individual fault f, one at a time. This is a significant reduction of complexity. This approach has been extensively used by the community of testing for memory-less logic circuits. This fact can now be extended to more general systems.

TESTABILITY OF INTERCONNECTED SYSTEMS

An interconnected system consists of many components. Both intercon-nected system and its components can be modeled by (10-1). Hence all the conclusions in the previous section can be applied to both components and interconnected systems. The important question, as far as test generation is concerned, is whether a test of a fault in an interconnected system can be generated from the set of tests of the components in which the fault occurs. In this section, we shall give positive answers for two special cases: feedforward components and memoryless components. As a consequence, the complexity of test generation can be greatly reduced because the test of the interconnected system is generated by tracing the test (known) of the components and its erroneous output to the primary input and output of the interconnected system. In fact, this is the basic principle on which the cele-brated D-algorithm is based. We shall extend this principle beyond logic cir-cuits.

We need only to consider the case that there is only one component at fault. This is due to the fact, from Theorem 2, that we can find a test for all components by finding the test for each component in the system and then concatenating them together. The model of a fault component in an inter-connected system is shown in Fig. 10–1, where A is the particular component at fault and A' represents the rest of the system which is not at fault. Con-sider a particular fault $f \in \mathcal{F}$ in $\mathcal{A}$; we have

$$\mathcal{A}: \quad v = A(s,u), \quad s \in \Sigma \qquad (10\text{-}9a)$$

$$\mathcal{A}_f: \quad v = A_f(s_f,u), \quad s_f \in \Sigma_f \qquad (10\text{-}9b)$$

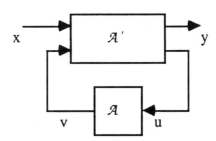

Figure 10–1 *Interconnected system with component $\mathcal{A}$ having fault.*

Let $\mathscr{A}'$ be completely described by an input–output state equation as follows:

$$\mathscr{A}': \ y = g(\sigma; \ x, v) \tag{10-10a}$$

$$u = h(\sigma; x, v), \ \ \sigma \in \Delta \tag{10-10b}$$

With the above system description, the following theorem is a direct consequence of the definition of test.

Theorem 3.   An input x is a test for a fault f in component $\mathscr{A}$ if and only if for every $\sigma \in \Delta$, $s \in \Sigma$, and $s_f \in \Sigma_f$, we have

$$g\big(\sigma; x, \ A(s, u)\big) \neq g\big(\sigma; x, \ A_f(s_f, u_f)\big) \tag{10-11}$$

where u and u_f satisfy

$$u = h\big(\sigma; x, \ A(s, u)\big) \tag{10-12a}$$

$$u_f = h\big(\sigma; x, \ A_f(s_f, u_f)\big) \tag{10-12b}$$

Although Theorem 3 is primitive in its form, it does show the complexity of the test generation of an interconnected system. Theoretically, a test can be generated by searching through those x satisfying (10-12a) and (10-12b), while checking the output of the system according to (10-11). The shortcoming of the above theorem, however, is that it shows no relation between x, u, and u_f. In other words, the relation between the tests of the interconnected system and tests of the component as fault are not revealed in Theorem 3. In the following, we shall discuss several special cases in which this relation can be expressed explicitly.

Case I. $\mathscr{A}$ is a feedforward component.

In this case, $\mathscr{A}'$ is characterized by the following system equations:

$$\mathscr{A}': \ y = g(\sigma; x, v) \tag{10-13a}$$

$$u = h(\sigma; x), \ \sigma \in \Delta \tag{10-13b}$$

We then have the following:

Corollary 4.   Let the interconnected system under test be described by (10-

9) and (10-13). Then, input x is a test for fault f in a feedforward component A if and only if for every $\sigma \in \Delta$, $s \in \Sigma$, and $s_f \in \Sigma_f$, we have

$$g(\sigma; x, A(s,u)) \neq g(\sigma; x, A_f(s_f,u)) \qquad (10\text{-}14)$$

where $u = h(\sigma;x)$. $\qquad\qquad$ (10-15)

As it can be seen from (10-13b) that $u = u_f$, i.e. the input to $\mathscr{A}$ and $\mathscr{A}_f$, initiated by a test signal x are the same. This is due to the fact that $\mathscr{A}$ is a feedforward component of the system and the erroneous output of this component is not fed back to $\mathscr{A}$. This allows us to take advantage of the concept of test set given below:

Definition 3 (Test Set). A *test set* $T_f(A)$ for a fault in a component $\mathscr{A}$ is the set of all tests for the fault, i.e., $T_f(A) = \{u \mid A_f(s_f,u) \neq A(s,u)$ for all $s \in \Sigma$ and all $s_f \in \Sigma_f\}$

Note that the test set $T_f(A)$ depends *only* on the component A, and hence can be generated independently from the system configuration. Now the relation between the test for the interconnected system and test for the component (test set) is shown in the following theorem.

Theorem 5. Let the interconnected system under test be described by (10-9a), (10-9b) and (10-13a), (10-13b). If an input x is a test for the interconnected system, then for any $\sigma \in \Delta$, $u = h(\sigma;x)$ is a member of $T_f(A)$.

Proof. Equation (10-14) implies that

$$A_f(s_f,u) \neq A(s,u) \quad \text{for all } s \in \Sigma \text{ and all } s_f \in \Sigma_f$$

Hence u is a test for $\mathscr{A}$ and $u \in T_f(A)$. $\qquad\qquad\square$

Theorem 5 implies that, for a fault to be testable, it has to be testable at the component level. In other words, the necessary condition for an interconnected system to be testable is that its components are testable. This theorem also suggests a simpler way of generating tests. Instead of searching for an input x in the input domain of the interconnected system, the search can now be restricted to the input domain of the component, particularly in $T_f(A)$, which is usually much smaller set. Notice that such strategy is successful only if the test set $T_f(A)$ is finite.

Case II. $\mathscr{A}$ and $\mathscr{A}_f$ are memoryless.

If A and A_f are memoryless, Eqs. (10-9a) and (10-9b) become

$$\mathscr{A}:\ v = A(u) \qquad\qquad (10\text{-}16a)$$

$$\mathscr{A}_f:\ v = A_f(u) \qquad\qquad (10\text{-}16b)$$

Similar to Case I, it will be shown that the testability of the component is necessary for a fault to be testable at system level. More importantly, tests for the interconnected system can be generated from the tests for the component at fault.

Theorem 6. Let the interconnected system be defined by (10-10) and (10-16). An input x is a test for a fault f in a component A if and only if for every $\sigma \in \Delta$, we have

$$g\big(\sigma;\ x,\ A(u)\big) \neq g\big(\sigma;\ x,\ A_f(u_f)\big) \qquad\qquad (10\text{-}17)$$

where u and u_f satisfy

$$u = h\big(\sigma;\ x,\ A(u)\big) \qquad\qquad (10\text{-}18a)$$

$$u_f = h\big(\sigma;\ x,\ A_f(u_f)\big) \qquad\qquad (10\text{-}18b)$$

and $u,\ u_f \in T_f(A) = \{u \mid A(u) \neq A(u)\}$.

Proof. Equations (10-17) and (10-18) follow directly from (10-11) and (10-12) via (10-16). Finally, we need to show that

$$A(u) \neq A_f(u)$$

and

$$A(u_f) \neq A_f(u_f)$$

If either one of the above is false, then (x, u, v, y) will satisfy both the normal system described by (10-10) and (10-16a), and the faulty system described by (10-10) and (10-16b), i.e., x is not a test. Hence u and u_f are in $T_f(A)$. $\qquad\square$

Note that in Theorems 5 and 6, the feedforward condition as well as the memoryless condition are applied only to the component under test. The rest of the system can indeed have feedback and memory. These two theorems also imply that their validity will be nontrivial if the component under test is part of feedback of the system, or it has memory. The validity of Theorems

5 and 6 can no longer be taken for granted as it is in the case of classical faults of digital systems.

Theorems 5 and 6 provided the foundation under which the test for the interconnected system can be generated from the test sets of individual components.

REACHABILITY, OBSERVABILITY, AND TESTABILITY

In this section, it is assumed that the set of tests for a fault f in some component is known. We shall examine if the test of the interconnected system for f can be derived *without* knowing the internal structure of the component and the behavior of the fault. This is practically important especially in a large scale interconnected system where the internal information of a component may not be available.

As we have shown in the last section, the tests of the interconnected system, in some cases, can be derived via searching through a certain restricted set, i.e., test set $T_f(A)$. Here, we investigate two properties of an interconnected system which is independent of the fault and their relation with testability. The two properties referred to here are *reachability* and *observability*. The concept of reachability is concerned with the question of whether certain signal can be sent to a particular component of the system from the primary input of the system. On the other hand, the concept of observability is concerned with the question of whether an output change of a component can be observed at the primary output of the system. These two properties are well known and used for the generation of tests for classical faults in digital systems. Together, these two properties determine the testability of the interconnected system. We shall extend the results to the general case.

Case I. $\mathscr{A}$ is a feedforward component.

Again, the system description follows (10-13a) and (10-13b). Define the reachable set $X_r(\cdot,\cdot)$ and observable set $X_o(\cdot,\cdot)$ as follows:

$$X_r(u,\ \sigma) = \{x \mid u = h(\sigma;\ x)\} \tag{10-19a}$$

$$X_o(u,\ \sigma) = \{x \mid g(\sigma;\ x,\ A(s,u)) \neq g(\sigma;\ x,\ A_f(s_f,u))\ \text{for all}\ s \in \Sigma,\ s_f \in \Sigma_f\} \tag{10-19b}$$

Define

$$X(u,\sigma) = X_r(u,\ \sigma) \cap X_o(u,\ \sigma) \tag{10-20}$$

Theorem 7.   Let $T_f(A)$ be the test set of fault f in a component A. Then, fault f is testable if and only if

$$T_f = \cap_{\sigma \in \Delta} \{ \cup_{u \in T_f(A)} X(u, \sigma) \} \neq \emptyset$$

Furthermore, any t in T_f is a test for f.

Proof. From the definitions, $X(u, \sigma)$ is the set of primary inputs so that when the state of $\mathscr{A}'$ is at σ, the input to the faulty component is u, and, at the same time, the erroneous output of the faulty component is observable. It follows from Theorem 5 that $\{ \cup_{u \in T_f(A)} X(u, \sigma) \}$ is the set of tests for the fault f when the state of $\mathscr{A}'$ is at σ. Taking into consideration all possible states of $\mathscr{A}'$, we can conclude that every element of T_f is a test for f.   □

Remark.   This theorem shows that the testability of a fault in feedforward component depends on the reachability of the test signal and observability of the erroneous output of the faulty component. Also, the tests of the interconnected system can be generated by first forming the union of reachable and observable set for each state $\sigma \in \Delta$ and then taking the intersection among all states $\sigma \in \Delta$. As we shall discuss in the next section, this theorem presents the principle idea behind the well known D-algorithm.

Case II. $\mathscr{A}$ and $\mathscr{A}_f$ are memoryless.

In this case, the description of $\mathscr{A}$ and $\mathscr{A}_f$ are given in (10-16a) and (10-16b). As was in the previous case, we define the reachable set and observable set as follows:

$$X_r(u, u_f, \sigma) = \{ x \mid u = h(\sigma; x, A(u)), u_f = h(\sigma; x, A_f(u_f)) \} \quad (10\text{-}21a)$$

$$X_o(u, u_f, \sigma) = \{ x \mid g(\sigma; x, A(u)) \neq g(\sigma; x, A_f(u_f)) \} \quad (10\text{-}21b)$$

Define

$$X(u, u_f, \sigma) = X_r(u, u_f, \sigma) \cap X_o(u, u_f, \sigma) \quad (10\text{-}22)$$

we obtain the following theorem:

Theorem 8.   Let $T_f(A)$ be the test set of a fault f in component $\mathscr{A}$. Denote

$$T^* = \{ (u, u_f) \mid A_f(u_f) \neq A(u); u, u_f \in T_f(A) \} \quad (10\text{-}23)$$

Then, the fault f is testable if and only if

$$T_f = \cap_{\sigma \in \Delta} \{ \cup_{(u,u_f) \in T^*} X(u, u_f, \sigma) \} \neq \emptyset$$

Furthermore, any t in T_f is a test for f.

Proof. The proof is similar to that of Theorem 7 and hence omitted. ☐

Remark. As we can see from this theorem, the test generation for feedback system is much more difficult even in the case of memoryless fault. Nevertheless, the testability at the component level is still necessary in order for the interconnected system to be testable. Again, the test can still be generated by searching through a restricted set characterized by the reachable set and the observable set.

Case III. General case.

For the general case, the reachable set and the observable set can be defined as follows:

$$X_r(u, u_f, \sigma, s, s_f) = \{x \mid u = h(\sigma; x, A(s, u)), u_f = h(\sigma; x, A_f(s_f, u_f)) \} \quad \text{(10-24a)}$$

$$X_o(u, u_f, \sigma, s, s_f) = \{x \mid g(\sigma; x, A(s, u)) \neq g(\sigma; x, A_f(s_f, u_f)) \} \quad \text{(10-24b)}$$

Define

$$X(u, u_f, \sigma, s, s_f) = X_r(u, u_f, \sigma, s, s_f) \cap X_o(u, u_f, \sigma, s, s_f) \quad \text{(10-25)}$$

Theorem 9. Fault f is testable if and only if

$$T_f = \cap_{\sigma \in \Delta,\, s \in \Sigma,\, s_f \in \Sigma_f} \{ \cup_{(u, u_f) \in T^*(s, s_f)} X(u, u_f, \sigma, s, s_f) \} \neq \emptyset \quad \text{(10-26)}$$

where

$$T^*(s, s) = \{ (u, u_f) \mid A(s, u) \neq A_f(s_f, u_f) \} \quad \text{(10-27)}$$

Furthermore, any t in T_f is a test for f.

Proof. The proof is similar to that of Theorem 6 and hence omitted. ☐

Remark. In general case, the testability of the interconnected system does not necessarily imply the testability of its components. It is rather surprising that a fault f which is testable at the system level may not be testable at the component level. Furthermore, even if the test set of a component under test can be found, it will not make the test generation at system level any easier.

In summary, the validity of Theorems 7 and 8 cannot be taken for granted. When they are true, a test at the interconnected system level can be derived from a test at the component level. This involves basically three steps: *First at component level, we need to obtain the test set $T_f(A)$, which depends only on the component and the fault under test. Then, we need to construct the reachable set X_r and observable set X_o, which are independent of the component and the fault under test. Finally at system level, tests for the fault are obtained by searching through the reachable set X_r and observable set X_o.*

TEST GENERATION FOR INTERCONNECTED SYSTEMS: CASE STUDIES

In this section, we give some examples to demonstrate how the techniques discussed in the last section can be applied in the test generation. First, we shall show that the theories developed are consistent with the well-known results, particularly for the case of stuck-at-fault in digital systems. Then, a class of nonclassical faults will be studied. Finally, an example of test generation for hybrid system with digital fault is presented.

Classical Faults for Memoryless Logic Circuits

This is the class of problems well-studied and well-understood. The system is memoryless logic circuits without feedback. The classical faults such as stuck-at-fault are also memoryless faults. From (10-16a) and (10-16b), the system description can be simplified as follows:

$$\mathscr{A}: v = A(u) \tag{10-28a}$$

$$\mathscr{A}_f: v = A_f(u) \tag{10-28b}$$

The rest of the system

$$\mathscr{A}': y = g(x, v) \tag{10-29a}$$

$$u = h(x) \tag{10-29b}$$

This case which is memoryless system with the faulty component in the feedforward path is the simplest case under our general system model. Let T be the set of all tests for the fault f at component $\mathscr{A}$. The reachable and observable set can then be constructed and conditions in Theorem 5 tested. In fact, this kind of exhaustive method will be successful for any system in which $\mathscr{A}$, $\mathscr{A}'$, and $\mathscr{A}_f$ are memoryless and T is finite. Observe also that, because of Theorem 5, there is no need to exhaust all signals u, but on those in T. When A_f is represented by a truth table, only the part concerning $u \in T$ is needed for the purpose of test generation. This essentially is the basic idea of the celebrated D-algorithm by Roth [3]. The D-algorithm is the first completely satisfactory solution of test generation for stuck-at-fault. The most prominent feature of the algorithm is that it guarantees to find a test if such test exists. The D-algorithm basically has the following steps:

1. Select fault site and generate *primitive D-cubes of failure.* In this step, the set T of all tests of the fault considered (primitive D-cubes of failure) is first generated.
2. Generate *primitive D-cubes* for normal logical functions. Primitive D-cubes is the logic function of fault-free part of the circuit.
3. Choose a member in *primitive D-cubes of failure.*
4. Using the calculus of D-cubes, propagate the output fault signals (consist of D's and D'''s) to the primary output line. This step is called error propagation. If this step fails, go to step 6.
5. Using the calculus of D-cubes, propagate the input signals to the primary input line. This step is called consistency justification. If a test is found, stop. If this step fails, go to step 6.
6. Choose another member in *primitive D-cubes of failure.* Go to step 3. If all members of *primitive D-cubes of failure* have been tried yet no test is found, the fault is not testable.

It is easy to realize that the D-algorithm actually solved the testing equation by exhaustive method. Although it is time-consuming for a large system, it guarantees a solution.

Nonclassical Faults for Memoryless Logic Circuits

In 1978, Wadsack [4] defined a nonclassical fault in MOS logic circuits. He found that certain stuck open fault will create memory for the faulty component and it can be modeled by a two-state finite-state machine. Hence, we have the case that both $\mathscr{A}$ and $\mathscr{A}'$ are memoryless, but $\mathscr{A}_f$ has memory. Hence, the equation for testing becomes

$$\mathscr{A}: \quad v = A(u) \tag{10-30a}$$

$$\mathscr{A}_f: \quad v = A_f(s, u), s_f \in \Sigma_f \tag{10-30b}$$

In the case of stuck-open fault at gate level, Σ_f consists of only two elements.

From Theorem 5, even though the faulty component now has memory, the exhaustive method can still be applied, if the set $T_f(A)$ of all tests is finite. In the case of stuck open faults of the MOS circuit, Reddy et al. [5] have shown that a test sequence with length of 2 is needed, and hence $T_f(A)$ is finite. Agrawal [6] provided an algorithm to generate $T_f(A)$ for the MOS gate, and then used the D-algorithm to generate a test for the entire MOS circuit. In general, the fact that $T_f(A)$ is finite set may be less obvious. From Theorem 1, it is easy to see that $T_f(A)$ is actually always *infinite* in general. However, when the fault can be modeled as a finite state machine, there is a possibility of finding a finite subset of $T_f(A)$ so that a test can be derived from this finite set. We first introduce the concept of *fundamental test set* (FTS).

Definition 4 (Reduced Test).   Let $u = (t_1, t_2, \ldots, t_k)$ be a test. Then $u' = (\tau_1, \tau_2, \ldots, \tau_{k'})$ is called a *reduced test* of u if

1. u' is a test.
2. $k' < k$.
3. $\tau_j \in \{t_i\}$, $1 \le i \le k$, $1 \le j \le k'$.

Remark.   As far as test generation is concerned, u and u' are equivalent in the sense that if u can be used to generate test for the entire system, so can u'. Notice that the u' is not necessarily a subsequence of u. The order of τ_i's may be different from that of t_i's.

Definition 5 (Fundamental Test Set).   The *fundamental testing set* (FTS) $\mathbb{T}$ is the set of tests which cannot be further reduced.

Clearly, the fundamental testing set of fault $\mathscr{F}$ depends on the structure of a particular finite state machine. Since the structure of the finite state machine is usually unknown to us, we need to find the properties that belong to all such finite state machines. In fact, the estimation of the length of testing sequence will be our primary interest. The following theorem gives the least upper bound on the length of testing input sequence. The proof is a constructive one. Not only does it show the correctness of the theorem, but it also reveals the basic structure of the fault modeling problem. In addition, it gives a method of finding FTS, although it may not be practical due to the fact that the structure of the finite state machine created by fault is usually unknown.

Theorem 10.   The length of any irreducible testing sequence of finite state machine fault model with N states is bounded by N^0, where

$$N^0 = N(N+1)/2 \qquad (10\text{-}31)$$

Furthermore, there exists a finite state fault model such that the length of any testing sequence is at least N^0.

Proof. The following lemma will be useful for the proof of the theorem.

Lemma 11. Let the set S of the states be partitioned into two nonempty parts U and V. If an input sequence T transfers $\mathscr{A}_f$ from a state s in U to a state s' in V, then there exists a subsequence T' of T transfers $\mathscr{A}_f$ from a state s'' in U to s', and

$$\text{length of } T' \leq \text{number of states in } V$$

The states s and s'' may or may not be the same.

Proof. (1) The bound on the length of testing sequence: Let $T = (t_1, t_2, \ldots, t_k)$ be the sequence that transfers $\mathscr{A}_f$ from a state s in U to a state s' in V and $(s_0 = s, s_1, s_2, \ldots, s_k = s')$ be the state sequence associated with the input sequence T. Let s_j be the last state in U in the state sequence. Hence, the state subsequence $(s_j = s'', s_{j+1}, \ldots, s_k = s')$ can be realized by the input subsequence $T' = (t_j, t_{j+1}, \ldots, t_k)$. Without loss of generality, we may assume that there is no loop in the state transition from s'' to s', i.e., $s_n \neq s_m$ for all s_n, s_m in the state subsequence, since all the loops can be removed by removing simultaneously the corresponding input subsequences in T'. Note that, in the state subsequence, all states but s'' are in V. Therefore, T' is the subsequence of T which transfers $\mathscr{A}_f$ from a state s'' in U to a state s' in V and

$$\text{length of } T' \leq \text{number of states in } V$$

Proof (Theorem 10). Let T be a test, and let

$$\Sigma_f(T) = \{ s \in \Sigma_f \mid A_f(s, t^*) \neq A(t^*) \text{ for some } t^* \in T\}$$

i.e., the set of detectable states of T. Since any fault state is detectable by T, $\Sigma_f(T)$ is nonempty. We construct a test $T' = I_0 \cdot I_1 \cdots \cdot I_J$ as a concatenation of input sequence $I_0, I_1, \ldots, I_J$ as follows:
Since the fault state can be anywhere in Σ_f, to begin with, let

$$U_0 = \Sigma_f$$

Choose

$$I_0 = t_0 \in T$$

such that $A_f(s_0, t_0) \neq A(t_0)$ for some $s_0 \in \Sigma_f$. Such t_0 exists because $\Sigma_f(T)$ is not empty. Clearly, I_0 is a subsequence of T and the fault state will be detected by I_0 if $\mathcal{A}_f$ is at s_0.

Now let

$$U_1 = \{ X(s, I_0) \mid s \in U_0 - \{s_0\} \}$$

where $X(s, I_0)$ is the new state transferred from s by the input sequence I_0. After I_0 is applied, the fault state is either detected by I_0 or it is in U_1.

Let

$$W_1 := U_1 \cap \Sigma_f(T)$$

if $W_1 \neq \emptyset$. Choose

$$I_1 = t_1 \in T$$

where t_1 is such that $A_f(s_1, t_1) \neq A(t_1)$ for some s in W_1. Note that s_1 and s_0 are not necessarily distinct.

Otherwise, if $W_1 = \emptyset$, then $\Sigma_f(T)$ must be a subset of V_1 which is the complement of U_1. Then, a subsequence of T will transfer some fault state s in U_1 to some state s_1 in Σ_f, and hence $s_1 \in V_1$. In addition, there will be a $t_1 \in T$ such that

$$A_f(s_1, t_1) \neq A(t_1)$$

By Lemma 3, there exists a subsequence T_1 (of T) that transfers $\mathcal{A}_f$ from some state s' in U_1 to s_1 in $\Sigma_f(T)$. Now let

$$I_1 = T_1 \cdot t_1$$

Clearly, I_1 is a subsequence of T, and by Lemma 11, length of $I_1 \leq 1 +$ number of states in V_1. Further note that the above inequality holds no matter whether W_1 is empty or not. After the sequence $I_0 \cdot I_1$ is applied, the fault state is either detected or in U_2 defined as follows:

$$U_2 = \{ X(s, I_1) \mid s \in U_1 - \{s_1\} \}$$

If $U_2 = \emptyset$, then $I = I_0 \cdot I_1$ is a test. Otherwise, define W_2 the same way as we did for W_1, i.e., the intersection of U_2 and $\Sigma_f(T)$. Similarly, choose

$$\begin{aligned} I_2 &= t_2 \in T, \quad \text{if } W_2 \neq \emptyset \\ &= T_2 \cdot t_2, \quad \text{if } W_2 = \emptyset \end{aligned}$$

where t_2 and T_2 are similarly defined as t_1 and T_1. In either case,

$$\text{length of } I_2 \leq 1 + \text{number of states in } V_2$$

where V_2 is the complement of U_2. This process is repeated until U_{J+1} is empty.

Let

$$T' = I_1 \cdot I_2 \cdot \cdots \cdot I_j$$

Clearly, T' is a test. Since each I_i in I is a subsequence of T, (ii) in the theorem is justified. It remains to show that $T' \in \mathbb{T}_L$. Let u_k be the number of states in U_k and v_k the length of I_k.

Then, at each step

$$u_k \leq u_{k-1} - 1 \tag{10-32}$$

$$v_k \leq 1 + (N - u_k) \tag{10-33}$$

Let L be the total length of I. Then we have

$$\mathit{L} = v_0 + v_1 + \cdots + v_J$$

From (10-33)

$$\mathit{L} \leq (1) + (1 + N - u_1) + (1 + N - u_2) + \cdots + (1 + N - u_J)$$

$$\leq J + 1 + NJ - (u_1 + u_2 + \cdots + u_J)$$

From (10-32)

$$\mathit{L} \leq J + 1 + NJ - J(J+1)/2 = f(J), \text{ where } J \leq N - 1$$

Since $f(J)$ is a monotone increasing function when $J < N$,

$$\mathit{L} \leq f(J) \leq f(N-1) \leq (N-1) + 1 + N(N-1) - (N-1)N/2$$

$$\leq N(N+1)/2$$

(2) The finite state machine fault which needs test of length $N(N+1)/2$:

Let $S = \{s_0, s_1, s_2, \ldots, s_{N-1}\}$ denote the set of states created by $\mathcal{F}$. Let $t_1, t_2, \ldots t_{N-1}$ be the input vectors that has the following properties:

$$X(s_i, t_i) = s_{i-1}$$

$$X(s_{i-1}, t_i) = s_i$$

$$X(s_j, t_i) = s_j \quad \text{for all } j, \ 0 \le j \le N-1, \text{ and } j \ne i$$

For all other input vectors t

$$X(s_i, t) = s_i, \text{ for all } 1 \le i \le N$$

Let t^* be the only input vector such that

$$A_f(s_0, t^*) \ne A(t^*), \quad \text{for } t^* \ne t_i, \ i = 1, 2, \ldots, N-1$$

It is not difficult to verify that, to test this fault, a sequence of $N(N+1)/2$ inputs are needed. $\qquad\qquad\qquad\qquad\qquad\qquad\qquad\qquad\qquad$ ☐

The bound obtained from Theorem 10 is under a very general assumption. In a practical situation, we can take advantage of the physical constraints of digital circuit to lower the bound. We shall make a practical assumption. In essence, we assume that the faulty function is stable. This implies the following:

Assumption A: $X(s_i, t) = s_j$ implies:

i. $X(s_j, t) = s_j$.
ii. $X(s_k, t) \ne s_i$ for all k.

Under this assumption, any testing vector will transfer the finite state machine from a state to another state or stay unchanged. The situation of the limit cycle is ruled out.

Theorem 12. Under Assumption A, the length of any irreducible testing sequence is bounded by M^0, where

$$M^0 = (N^2 + 4N - 4)/4 \qquad\qquad\qquad\qquad (10\text{-}34)$$

Proof. The prove is in the same spirit as the one given in Theorem 10 and hence is omitted here.

Remark. It is commonly accepted, without theoretical proof, that for a single stuck-open fault, we only need the test of length 2. This is the special case of the above theorem, with $N = 2$.

Definition 6 (Fault Relation).   The *fault relation* $F_{\mathscr{F}}(L)$ of physical failure $\mathscr{F}$ in $\mathscr{A}_f$ is defined as the set of all erroneous input output pairs initiated by the input sequences from FTS:

$$F_{\mathscr{F}}(L) = \{(T, O_s) \mid T \in \mathbb{T}_L, \, O_s = A_f(s, T) \text{ for some } s \in S\} \quad (10\text{-}35)$$

The above definition may look complicated at first; actually it is based on a very simple idea used by Roth more than 20 years ago: To model the fault as a set of erroneous input–output pairs. One of the building blocks in the calculus invented by Roth [3] is the definition of the D-cube of failure. The definition given here is a natural extension of the D-cube of failure to a more general setting so that faults other than stuck-at-fault can be dealt with in the same fashion.

After FTS is proved as the nucleus of all input sequences that make the faulty function exhibit its erroneous behavior, it is straightforward to complete our fault modeling by modeling the fault as a set of all erroneous input–output pairs, where the input sequences are taken from FTS. For the nonclassical fault such as stuck-open fault, the fault cannot be tested by a single testing input. Instead, a sequence of inputs have to be employed. To extend the D-algorithm for the nonclassical faults, the primitive D-cubes must be replaced by fault relation $F_{\mathscr{F}}(L)$ given in Definition 6. From Theorem 7, it is not hard to see why this is necessary and sufficient. After this is done, the rest of the steps in the D-algorithm can be used directly. We highlight the *extended D-algorithm* in the following:

1.   Select fault site and generate *fault relation*.
2.   Generate *primitive D-cubes* for normal logical blocks.
3.   Choose one member in the *fault relation*.
4.   For each erroneous output in the output sequence, replace the erroneous signal at each output bit by D or D' (use the same convention used in the D-algorithm) and propagate the fault signals (consisting of D and D') to the primary output line. Note that this has to be done for every wrong output in the output sequence. For those outputs that produce no error, do nothing. D-calculus is used in all the propagations. If this step fails, go to 6.
5.   For each input in the input sequence, back-propagate the input signals to the primary input line. Again, the D-calculus is used. If a test is found, stop. If this step fails, go to step 6.
6.   Choose another member in *fault relation*. Go to step 3. If all members in *fault relation* have been used yet no test is found, the test is not testable.

It is easy to realize that the extension proposed here is nothing more than applying D-algorithm to each individual input and output among the input output sequence. However, the theoretical foundation of this extension lies on the development of *fault relation* and the necessary and sufficient condition of testability. There are two important advantages in above extension. First, the extension ensures the test being derived if the fault is testable, which is one of our original motivations. Secondly, the structure of the *d*-algorithm is preserved. This means only a very small part of the software needs to be modified. Obviously, the extension also inherits the weaknesses of the *D*-algorithm, i.e., the computation complexity.

We now illustrate the extended *D*-algorithm by following example: Let us consider a 4-bit adder which consists of four identical cells as shown in Fig. 10–2. Lines 1, 3, 4, 7, 8, 11, 12, 15, and 16 are primary input lines. Line 1 is the carry-in input and lines 3, 4, 7, 8, 11, 12, 15, and 16 are inputs. Line 17, which is the carry-out, is the primary output line. For demonstration purposes, assume the summation outputs are not available. The fault can only be observed at primary output line 17. Figure 10–3 shows the circuit structure of one cell. Let an open fault happen at P. This fault changes the combinatorial cell to a sequential cell. The output depends on the initial state (voltage) at C'. Define s_0, s_1 to be the states when initially C'' is at 0, 1 respectively. In this case s_1 is the only state at which the erroneous output can be observed. Assume Cell I and only the Cell I has the fault. It is not hard to see that any input with length 1 is not a test. Therefore, $\mathbb{T}_L$ will consist of only those tests with length 2. There are total four tests $(T_1–T_4)$ found. The fault relation for the cell is easily defined in Table 10–1.

Inputs	T_1	T_2	T_3	T_4
A	11	01	01	01

The singular cover and the propagation *D*-cube are shown in Table 10–2. Assume the fault happens at the first cell; we now apply the *D*-algorithm on the first test in $\mathbb{T}_L$, $T_L = (t_1 t_2)$, where $t_1 = [1\ 0\ 0]$ and $t_2 = [1\ 1\ 0]$. The elements in t_1 and t_2 represent the input at A, B, C. Since when t_1 is applied, the output will be correct no matter which state the cell is at, only the back-tracking

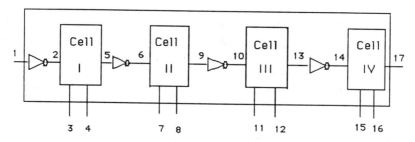

Figure 10–2   *A 4-bit adder.*

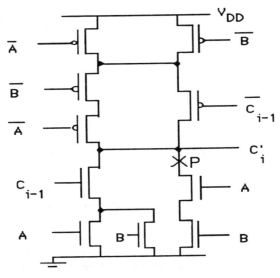

Figure 10–3 *The cell circuit.*

procedure will be performed, as is shown in Table 10–3. After t_1 has been applied, the state of the cell is at s_0 and t_2 is the input that will exhibit the fault at output. The corresponding D-cube of failure is formed to be $(0\ 1\ 1\ D)$. The propagation of D is listed in Table 10–4. Finally, from Tables 10–3 and 10–4, the test is found $T = (I_1\ I_2)$, where

$$I_1 = (1\ \ 0\ 0\ x\ x\ x\ x\ x\ x)$$
$$I_2 = (1\ 1\ 1\ 1\ 0\ 1\ 0\ 1\ 0)$$

In this example, the extended D-algorithm successfully derives the test from the member we chose in $F_{\mathscr{F}}(L)$. Otherwise, another member in $F_{\mathscr{F}}(L)$ should be selected to construct the primitive D-cube of failure. If none of the four members results in a test, the circuit is simply not testable.

We now apply our theoretical studies in the previous two sections to a special yet very important case, iterative logic array (ILA). Figure 10–4 shows a one-dimensional ILA. All the cells in the ILA have the same logic function and implementation. ILA which can be tested by a constant number of tests is called C-testable. It is important that ILA has C-testability because the test can be found regardless of the length of the size of ILA. There is

Table 10–1 Fault Relation

B	01	01	11	01
C_{i-1}	00	10	00	00
Output C_i (no fault/fault)	10/11	10/11	10/11	10/11

Table 10–2   Singular Cover and Propagation D-Cube

A	B	C_{i-1}	C_i	A	B	C_{i-1}	C_i
0	0	x	1	D	0	1	D'
x	0	0	1	0	D	1	D'
0	x	0	1	1	D	0	D'
1	1	x	0	1	0	D	D'
1	x	1	0	D	1	0	D'
x	1	1	0	0	1	D	D'
	Singular cover				Propagate D-cube		

much in the literature on this problem [7–9]. The existing algorithms are based on the assumption that the fault will not create memory in the cell. This certainly is not the case when such a fault as the stuck-open fault is concerned. From Theorem 6, we know that a fault in a cell is testable if and only if one of the tests in the fundamental testing set can be reached from the primary input line and the resulting fault output can be propagated to the primary output line. Clearly, as far as testability is concerned, this result applies to the ILA system if we treat the cell as the subfunction of ILA. Although the necessary and sufficient condition for ILA to be C-testable for memory fault still needs to be found, it is not hard to give a sufficient condition for ILA C-testable for the stuck-open fault which creates one memory.

We consider the similar problem to the previous example (n-bit ripple carry adder) except the length of the adder may be arbitrarily long. Figure 10–5 shows the ILA structure. The cell circuit is shown in Fig. 10–6 with an inverter connected to the carry output. To demonstrate the problem, we assume that the summation output for each bit is not available. Only the carry-out output at the leftmost end in Fig. 10–5 can be observed. The similar open fault in a cell is shown in Fig. 10–6. The fault relation for this case is defined in Table 10-5. We start with arbitrary test in Table 10–1, say T_2. The following initializing input I_0 is first applied, where I_0 is defined as follows:

$$I_0: \quad \begin{array}{ccccccccc} C_0 & A_1 & B_1 & A_2 & B_2 & A_2 & B_3 & \cdots & A_n & B_n \\ 1 & 0 & 0 & 1 & 1 & 0 & 0 & \cdots & 1 & 1 \end{array}$$

The initialization signal propagation is shown in Fig. 10–7. After I_0 is ap-

Table 10–3   Backtracking Procedure for t_1

Line #	1	2	3	4	5	6	7	8	9	10	11	12	13	14	15	16	17
				0	0	x	1										
		1	0														
				1	0	0	x	1	x	x			x	x			x	x

Table 10-4   the Propagation of D-Cube for t_2

Line #	1	2	3	4	5	6	7	8	9	10	11	12	13	14	15	16	17
		0	1	1	D												
					D	D'											
						D'	1	0	D								
									D	D'							
										D'	1	0	D				
													D	D'			
														D'	*1*	0	D'
	1	0															
	1	0	1	1	D	D'	1	0	D	D'	1	0	D	D'	1	0	D'

plied, the $(2k-1)$th cell is properly initialized, where $1 \leq k \leq n/2$. Then the test input I_1 is applied.

$$I_1: \begin{array}{ccccccccccc} C_0 & A_1 & B_1 & A_2 & B_2 & A_2 & B_3 & \cdots & A_n & B_n \\ 1 & 1 & 0 & 1 & 0 & 1 & 0 & & 1 & 0 \end{array}$$

From Fig. 10–8, when I_1 is applied, the fault happens in the $(2k-1)$th cell will be observed from the carry-out output. To detect the fault in rest of cell, ILA needs to be reinitialized by I_3.

$$I_3: \begin{array}{ccccccccccc} C_0 & A_1 & B_1 & A_2 & B_2 & A_2 & B_3 & \cdots & A_n & B_n \\ 1 & 1 & 1 & 0 & 0 & 1 & 1 & & 0 & 0 \end{array}$$

Finally, I_2 is applied again. The test for this fault is found as

$$I = I_1 \cdot I_2 \cdot I_3 \cdot I_2$$

It should be noticed that C-testability is achieved. Although not every ILA is

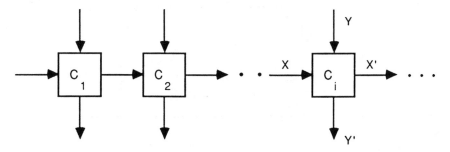

Figure 10–4   *One-dimensional ILA.*

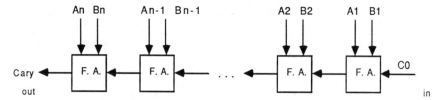

Figure 10-5 *The ILA structure of adder.*

C-testable, if there is no test that can be found from $F_{\mathscr{F}}(L)$ such that the ILA is C-testable, the ILA is not C-testable.

In conclusion, we summarize our results for the fault modeling at the logic function level. The fault can be modeled as a relation between a set of tests whose length is bounded by B1 or B2 (FTS) and their corresponding erroneous output sequence. In contrast with the traditional fault modeling, our approach does not depend on the specific information of physical failure, whether it is a line stuck-at-fault or it is a transistor stuck-open fault, whether there is a single fault or there are multiple faults. The only information of the fault we used is the number of states created by a fault or by a number of faults. Secondly, the model derived here contains a complete information of the fault. No other information is needed to derive the test at system level. Obtaining the

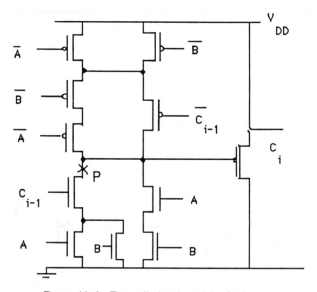

Figure 10-6 *The cell circuit and the fault.*

Table 10–5 Fault Relation of the Cell

Inputs	T_1	T_2	T_3	T_4
A	11	01	01	01
B	00	00	10	00
C_{i-1}	01	11	01	01
Output Ci (no fault/fault)	01/00	01/00	01/00	01/00

fundamental testing set of a fault for the particular function can be done by either exhausting the input sequences satisfying the length bound or using the internal circuit structure to find all the tests that satisfy the length bound. The latter approach is much more attractive in a practical situation as we can see in the last example. On the other hand, the exhaustive method is more like a theoretical possibility than a practical method and should only be used when there is absolutely no information of the circuit implementation of the function.

Testing of Hybrid System: An Example

In the following, we demonstrate the test generation problem via a practical example. We use the example studied by Liu et al. [10] in the context of fault diagnosis. The circuit under test is a switching voltage regulator given in Fig. 10-9. The circuit has following properties: It (1) is nonlinear, (2) is an analog/digital hybrid, and (3) has feedback.

The circuit has four components C1, C2, C3, C4. We follow the same notation used in [7]:

Notation: $v^+(v^-)$ denotes a voltage significantly greater (less) than zero.
v^0 denotes the voltage close to 0.
i^+, i^-, i^0 denote current similarly defined.
$\uparrow (\downarrow)$ denotes an increase (decrease) in voltage or current.

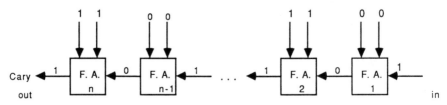

Figure 10–7 *The propagation of initialization input.*

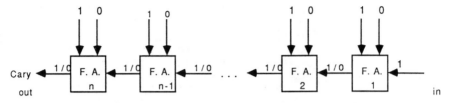

Figure 10–8 *The propagation of testing signal and error signal (normal/fault).*

Component function:

C1:   Input $| \; v_0 < v_r \; | \; v_0 > v_r$

Output $| \; v_1^0 \; | \; v_1^+$

C2:   Input $| \; v_1^0 \; | \; v_1^+$

Output $| \; v_2^+ \; | \; v_2^0$

C3:   Input v_c | Input v_2 | Output i_3

$v_c^0 \; | \; v_2^+ \; | \; \uparrow$
$\quad | \; v_2^0 \; | \; \downarrow$

$v_c^+ \; | \; * \; | \; ?$

Note: * represents any input; ? represents unspecified output.

C4:   Input i_3 | Output v_0

$\uparrow$ | $\uparrow$
$\downarrow$ | $\downarrow$

Although C1, C2, C3, and C4 are analog in nature, functionally, they perform more like a digital system. The above system can be further simplified by introducing the following equivalent input/output description for each function block:

C1: $f_1(v_0, v_r) = 1, \quad v_0 > v_0$
$\qquad\qquad\quad = 0, \quad$ otherwise
C2: $f_2(v_1) = 1, \quad v_1 = 0$
$\qquad\qquad = 0, \quad$ otherwise
C3: $f_3(v_2) = v_2$
C4: $f_4(i) = i$

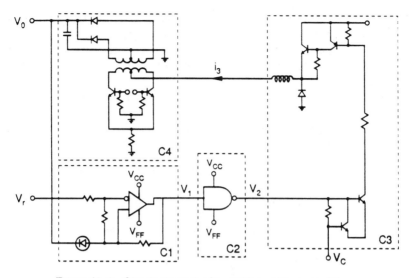

Figure 10–9 *Circuit diagram of switching voltage regulator.*

With the above equations, the system is a memoryless system with feedback. In this example, the stuck open fault f of C2 is to be considered. Figure 10–10 shows the internal CMOS realization. Assume that there is a broken line at P. Due to the effect of stray capacitance, there is one memory element introduced. The faulty component C2 can be described as follows:

$$C2': \quad v_2 = f'_2(s_f, v_1) = s_f(1 - v_1) \quad s_f \in \{0,1\} \tag{10-36}$$

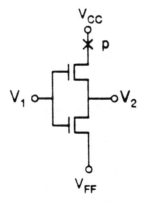

Figure 10–10 *Open fault p in block C2.*

where s_f is the state determined by the voltage across the stray capacitance. Realizing that this problem does not belong to Case I and Case II, only Theorem 9 for the general case is applicable. In this example, there is only one state variable (introduced by fault). Therefore, we have

$$T^*(s_f = 0) = \{ (v_1, v'_1) \mid f_2(v_1) \neq f'_2(s_f = 0, v_1) \} \qquad (10\text{-}37)$$

$$= \{(w \cdot 0 \cdot y, z) = w, y, z; \text{ arbitrary binary sequence including empty string} \}$$

$$T^*(s_f = 1) = \{ (v_1, v'_1) = f_2(v_1) \neq f'_2(s_f = 1, v_1) \}$$

$$= \{(0,1), (1,0), (00,01), (00,10), (00,11), (01,10), (01,11)$$

$$(10,00), (10,01), (10,10), (11,00), (11,01), (000,010), \ldots \}$$

Choose any one in $T^*(s_f = 0) \cap T^*(s_f = 1)$, say $(10,10)$, we have

$$(01) \in X_r(01,01, s_f = 0) \cap X_0(01,01, s_f = 0) \cap X_r(01,01, s_f = 1) \cap X_0(01,01, s_f = 1)$$

where

$$X_r(v_1, v'_1, s_f) = \{x \mid v_1 = f_1(f_4 \circ f_3 \circ f_2(v_1,) x), v'_1 = f_1(f_4 \circ f_3 \circ f_2 (v'_1), x) \} \quad (10\text{-}38a)$$

$$X_0(v_1, v'_1, s_f) = \{x \mid f_4 \circ f_3 \circ f_2(v_1), x) \neq f_4 \circ f_3 \circ f_2(v'_1), x) \} \qquad (10\text{-}38b)$$

With Theorem 9, (01) is a test for the stuck-open fault. Taking the inverse map we made, the test and the erroneous output along with the normal output is as follows:

Test	Output: Fault	Fault Free
$v_r: v_r^+ \bullet v_r^-$	$v_0^0 \bullet v_0^0$	$\uparrow$
$v_c: v_c^0 \bullet v_c^0$		

REFERENCES

[1] L. A. Zadeh and C.A. Desoer, *Linear System Theory,* McGraw-Hill, New York, 1963.

[2] R. Saeks, *Resolution Space, Operators and Systems,* Springer-Verlag, New York, 1973.

[3] J. P. Roth, "Diagnosis of Automata Failures: A Calculus and a Method," *IBM J. Res. Dev.,* Vol. 10, pp. 278–291, Jul. 1966.

[4] R. L. Wadsack, "Fault Modeling and Logic Simulators and CMOS and MOS Integrated Circuits," *Bell Syst. Tech. J.,* Vol. 57, pp. 1449–1473, May-Jun. 1978.

[5] S. M. Reddy, M. K. Reddy, and V. D. Agrawal, "Robust tests for stuck-open faults in CMOS combinational logic circuits," Proc. *IEEE14th Int. Conf. Fault-Tolerant Comput.,* Kissimmee, FL, Jun. 1984, pp. 44–49.

[6] P. Agrawal, "Test Generation at Switch Level," *Proc. IEEE Int. Conf. Computer-Aided Design,* Santa Clara, CA, IEEE, New York, 1984, pp. 128–130.

[7] W. H. Kautz, "Testing for Faults in Cellular Logic Arrays," *Proc. 8th Annu. Symp. Switching Automat. Theory,* 1967, pp. 161–174.

[8] A. D. Friedman, "Easily Testable Iterative Systems," *IEEE Trans. Comput.,* Vol. C-22, pp. 1061–1064, 1973.

[9] R. Parthasarathy and Sudhakar M. Reddy, " A Testable Design of Iterative Logic Arrays," *IEEE Trans. Comput.,* Vol. C-30, No. 11, pp. 833–841, Nov. 1981.

[10] R. Liu et al., "Petri Net Application to Functional Fault Diagnosis," *Proc. IEEE ISCAS,* San Jose, CA, IEEE, New York, 1986, pp. 1323–1326.

Index